PUBLIC OPINION, POLITICS
AND SOCIETY IN
CONTEMPORARY IRELAND

PUBLIC OPINION, POLITICS AND SOCIETY IN CONTEMPORARY IRELAND

PAT LYONS

IRISH ACADEMIC PRESS
DUBLIN • PORTLAND, OR

First published in 2008 by
IRISH ACADEMIC PRESS
44, Northumberland Road
Dublin 4
Ireland

Suite 300
920 NE 58th Avenue
Portland, Oregon 97213-3786

© 2008 Pat Lyons

www.iap.ie

British Library Cataloguing in Publication Data
A catalogue entry is available on request

ISBN 978 0 7165 2941 5 (cloth)
ISBN 978 0 7165 2942 2 (paper)

Library of Congress Cataloging-in-Publication Data
An entry can be found on request

All rights reserved. Without limiting the rights under copyright reserved alone, no part of this publication may be reproduced, stored in or introduced into a retrieval system, or transmitted, in any form or by any means (electronic, mechanical, photocopying, recording or otherwise), without the prior written permission of both the copyright owner and the above publisher of this book.

Typeset in 11/13pt Sabon by FiSH Books, Enfield, Middx.
Printed by Biddles Ltd., King's Lynn, Norfolk

*Dedicated to the memory of
Pauline (Nolan) Lyons*

Contents

List of Figures	ix
List of Abbreviations	xii
List of Tables	xiii
Acknowledgements	xv
Introduction	1
1 Public Opinion Data and Opinion Poll Design	22
2 Public Opinion Measurement and Questionnaire Design	39
3 The Electoral Record of Irish Opinion Polls	66
4 Satisfaction with the Government, the Taoiseach and Party Leaders	91
5 Public Opinion towards the Liberal Agenda	118
6 Public Opinion in the Republic of Ireland towards the Northern Ireland Question	150
7 Economic Opinion in Ireland and Left–Right Orientation	173
8 Irish Public Opinion towards the European Union	204
Conclusion	232
References	246

Appendix 1
Notes for Table 3: Confidence, Trust or Perceived Leadership Attributed to Irish Public Institutions and Media, 1981–2003   262

Appendix 2
Taxation and Spending Questions used in Table 15   263

Appendix 3
Public Opinion among the Irish Public on Certain Liberal
Agenda Issues   268

Appendix 4
Opinion Poll Data on the Maastricht Treaty Referendum.   271

(1) Voting Intentions in the Maastricht Treaty Referendum
Before and after the Danish 'No' vote on 2 June 1992   271

(2) Comparison of Specific Survey Responses before and
after the Danish 'No' Vote on 2 June 1992   272

(3) Eurobarometer Questions used to Construct
an EU sentiment measure   272

(4) List of Eurobarometer Questions used to Construct an
EU Interest/Awareness Measure   276

(5) Some Technical Details of the Construction of the
EU Sentiment and Interest/Awareness Measures   277

Index   281

List of Figures

1. Typology of the Form and Function that Opinion Poll Results Provide with Regard to Examining the Nature of Public Opinion — 7
2. Public Opinion towards Legalising Divorce in the Republic of Ireland during the 1995 Referendum Campaign — 9
3. Comparison of Hard and Easy Facets of Public Opinion Support for a United Ireland in the Republic of Ireland, 1968–2003 — 16
4. Number of Polls Undertaken in the Republic of Ireland Annually, 1969–2005 — 25
5. Number of Survey Questions Asked by General Issue Domain, 1974–98 — 26
6. Example of a Question Ordering Effect: First Preference Vote Intentions for Fianna Fáil in MRBI surveys, 1987–92 — 57
7. Investigation of a 'Question Format Effect' for the Vote Intention items used by IMS, Lansdowne and MRBI through Comparison of the Levels of 'Don't Know' in Polls between 1992 and 1997 — 70
8. Absolute Error in Final Poll Predictions of Main Party Support in Nine General Elections, 1977–2002 — 78
9. Evolution of Uncertainty concerning Party Support during the General Election Cycle, 1969–2002 — 85
10. Decline in Level of Voter Uncertainty concerning Party Support during the General Election Cycle, 1969–2002 — 86
11. Evolution of Party Support through the General Election Cycle and Comparison with Actual Election Results, 1977–2002 — 87

12	Boxplots of Satisfaction with the Performance of Irish Governments, 1973–2005	100
13	Boxplots of Satisfaction with the Performance of Successive Taoisigh, 1978–2005	101
14	Boxplots of Satisfaction with the Performance of Irish Party Leaders, 1976–2005	103
15	Comparison of Mean Support for the Three Main Party Leaders in the Republic of Ireland, 1978–2002	105
16	Comparison of Voting Intentions for Parties in Government with Government and Taoiseach Satisfaction Ratings, 1977–2005	107
17	Comparison of Vote Intentions for Government with Government and Taoiseach Satisfaction Ratings during the Inter-Election Cycle, 1969–2002	109
18	Granger Causal Relationships between Vote Intentions for Government parties, and Satisfaction Ratings for the Government and Taoiseach, 1978–2005	112
19	Popular Support for a Constitutional Referendum on Abortion in the Republic of Ireland, 1982–2002	128
20	Comparison of Hard and Easy Facets of Public Opinion towards Legalising Divorce in the Republic of Ireland, 1970–95	129
21	Comparison of Hard and Easy Facets of Public Opinion towards Legalising Abortion in the Republic of Ireland, 1981–2002	131
22	Change in Position within the Irish Public on certain Liberal Agenda Issues	134
23	Percentage in Six Birth Cohorts who felt that Abortion, Divorce or Homosexuality were 'Never Justified' in the Republic of Ireland in 1981, 1991 and 1999	139
24	Public Opinion towards Proposals to make Changes to Articles 2 and 3 of the Irish Constitution, 1974–99	159
25	Comparison of Hard and Easy Facets of Public Opinion Support for a United Ireland in the Republic of Ireland, 1968–2003	161
26	Public Opinion towards Proposals for the Withdrawal of British Troops from Northern Ireland, 1970–2002	165
27	Public Opinion among Different Age Cohorts towards Proposals to Make Changes to Articles 2 and 3 of the Irish Constitution, 1974–99	168

28 Comparison of Left–Right Self-Placement and Opinions Associated with Left–Right Ideology in Ireland, 2001–2002 179
29 Evolution of Net Change in Left–Right Self-Placement in Ireland, 1973–2004 184
30 Comparison of Left–Right Self-Placement Scales Implemented in Eurobarometer and European Values Surveys in 1981, 1990 and 1999 186
31 Left–Right Positions of the Main Parties and Public in Ireland on the basis of Public Perceptions, 1976–2004 193
32 Perceptual and Preferential Agreement on Parties and the Public's Left–Right Positions in Ireland, 1976–2004 195
33 Popular Support for European Integration in Ireland, 1978–2005 214
34 Net Support for European Integration in Ireland in Comparison to the EU Average, 1973–2004 (per cent) 215
35 Public Sentiment and Interest towards the European Integration Project in Ireland, 1973–2002 219
36 A Two Dimensional Representation of Popular Sentiment in Ireland towards the EU and the Process of Integration, 1973–2002 221

List of Abbreviations

AAPOR	American Association for Public Opinion Research
ASES	ASia Europe Survey
CFSP	Common Foreign and Security Policy
CSO	Central Statistics Office
DED	District Electoral Division
EB	Eurobarometer
EMU	Economic and Monetary Union
ESOMAR	European Society for Opinion and Marketing Research
ESRI	Economic and Social Research Institute
ESS	European Social Survey
EU	European Union
EVS	European Values Surveys
IMS	Irish Marketing Services
INES	Irish National Election Survey
IOPA	Irish Opinion Polls Archive
ISPAS	Irish Social and Political Attitudes Survey
ISSP	International Social Survey Programme
JNRR	Joint National Readership Research
Lansdowne	Lansdowne Market Research
MRBI	Market Research Bureau of Ireland
PLAC	Pro-Life Amendment Campaign
PSU	Primary Sampling Unit
QNHS	Quarterly National Household Survey
RAS	Receive-Accept-Sample (model of survey response, Zaller 1992)
RTÉ	Radio Telefís Éireann (Irish state television)

List of Tables

1 Cross-Tabulation of Attitudes towards the Availability of Abortion in Ireland and Vote Intention in the Abortion Referendum of November 1992   46
2 Comparison of Attitudes towards the Availability of Abortion in Ireland and Vote Intention in a Future Abortion Referendum, Winter 2001/2   48
3 Confidence, Trust or Perceived Leadership attributed to Irish Public Institutions and Media, 1981–2003   59
4 Response Option Effects in Attitudes towards the Future of Northern Ireland in the Winter of 1988 and Spring of 1989   62
5 Accuracy of Twenty Final National Opinion Poll Predictions of First-Preference Support for the Main Parties in Nine General Elections 1977–2002   79
6 Correlations between Mean Poll Estimates and Actual Election Results For Fianna Fáil, Fine Gael and the Labour Party, 1977–2002   81
7 Correlations between Mean Inter-Election Poll Estimates during the Electoral Cycle for Fianna Fáil, Fine Gael and the Labour Party (including 'Don't Knows'), 1977–2002   83
8 Public Support for the View that Abortion is 'Never Justified' in the Republic of Ireland, 1981–99   141
9 Estimation of the Effects of Generational Replacement on Public Opinion towards the View that Abortion is 'Never Justified', 1981–91   142
10 Comparison of the Effects of Generational Replacement and Intracohort Change on Public Opinion towards Four Liberal Agenda Issues in Ireland, 1981–99   144
11 Results of Agreement Measure Estimations using the Davis and Sinnott (1978) and INES (2002) Survey Results to Estimate Self and Party Placements on Preferences for a United Ireland   156

12 Summary of Public Opinion in the Republic of Ireland
   towards Ending Partition, 1970–2001   163
13 Principal Component Analysis of the Major Value
   Dimensions in Irish Society, October–December 2000   182
14 Regression Analysis of Net Change in Left–Right
   Self-Placement on the Eurobarometer Ten-Point Scale
   in the Republic of Ireland, 1977–2004   192
15 Opinions towards Taxation and Spending in the
   Republic of Ireland, 1976–2003   198
16 Regression Analysis of the Influence of Key Economic
   Indicators and Interest in the EU on Sentiment toward
   European Integration in the Republic of Ireland,
   1973–2000   226

Acknowledgements

The research for this book has been completed with the aid of funding from a variety of sources. I was the recipient of a Government of Ireland Ph.D. scholarship from 1998 to 2000. During the period 1999 to 2002 I benefited from membership of an EU-funded Training and Mobility for Researchers (TMR) network examining 'Participation and Representation in Europe'. Between 2000 and 2003, I was a Research Fellow at the Geary Institute, University College Dublin through my participation in an EU Commission-sponsored Fifth Framework project entitled 'Democratic Participation and Political Communication in Systems of Multi-level Governance' (HPSE-CT-1999-00029). From 2003 to 2005, I was a member of a Research Training Network (RTN) funded by the EU Commission examining the 'Dynamics and Obstacles of European Governance' (HPRN-CT-2002-00233). During this latter period, I was kindly hosted by the Department of West European Studies, Charles University, Prague, Czech Republic.

I would like also to take this opportunity to express my thanks to those who have contributed numerous suggestions and advice during the research and writing of this volume. A special thanks is due to Professors Michael Marsh and Michael Gallagher, and Kenneth Benoit, all at Trinity College Dublin; Professor John Curtice, University of Strathclyde; and Professor Richard Sinnott, Dr Fiachra Kennedy and Elva Hannan at University College Dublin. I would also like to express appreciation to my colleagues at Charles University and the Institute of Sociology within the Czech Academy of Sciences. I am especially grateful to Frank Cass and Lisa Hyde of Irish Academic Press for their enthusiasm and support in the process of publishing this book. On a personal note, I would like to thank my family for all their help and support.

Introduction

> The polls can make a useful contribution to social science if they are treated rigorously and with certain precautions.
> Pierre Bourdieu (1979: 124)

A key argument in many articles and books is that the citizens of twenty-first-century Ireland think differently about the society within which they live, the economy within which they work, and the political system within which they participate and are represented, than was the case in the 1970s. In short, what is being argued is that 'public opinion' in Ireland has undergone a fundamental change for a host of social, economic and political reasons.[1]

Surprising as it might seem, much of the evidence put forward to support this thesis of great societal change is based on indirect measures. Many examinations of Irish society are historically based with an emphasis on the actions of key political actors or the adoption of groundbreaking pieces of legislation. While reference is often made to 'public opinion' and how important it is in understanding the status quo and sources of change in Irish society, there has been to date no comprehensive attempt to evaluate the nature of public opinion in Ireland and how it has changed over time. In contrast to all other forms of evidence on public preferences, with the possible exception of election results, public opinion polls are the only means by which citizens are directly asked to express their views on a regular basis.

Consequently, until public opinion is brought more directly into investigations of societal change in Ireland, existing research must be seen as lacking a fundamental component. In order to bring this missing piece of the puzzle to its rightful place in discussions of sources of stability and change within Irish society it is necessary to fill an important gap. At present we do not have a comprehensive picture of public opinion in Ireland although there are over 200 opinion poll reports available in the public domain for consultation.[2] This set of polls not only represents Irish citizens' opinions on public affairs, but is also a primary source that is unrivalled because of its frequency (at least four to eight polls per year).

To a startling degree answers to questions such as 'what do Irish people believe in with regard to politics, the economy, the liberal agenda, Northern Ireland and the European Union', are scattered across a wide range of publications. In this book I will endeavour to demonstrate what the voices represented in opinion poll reports tell us about public opinion.

While opinion polls undoubtedly have their limitations, and are by no means the only method of studying public opinion, they are unique in giving citizens a direct voice. Moreover, opinion polls do so in a manner where the usual barriers to public representation, such as economic disadvantage or peripheral geographical location, are compensated for in the polling process. In essence, one could argue, 'sample surveys provide the closest approximation to an unbiased representation of the public because participation in a survey requires no resources and because surveys eliminate the selection bias inherent in the fact that participants in politics are self-selected' (Verba 1996: 1). In short, this book aims to bring citizens to centre stage, rather than treating them as 'bit players' in the larger social, political and economic dramas that have shaped Ireland since 1970.

If one considers for a moment the opinion poll data available one discovers a curious puzzle. Across a number of areas, trends in expressed opinions on the same issue elicited very different levels of response from those interviewed. It seems that with regard to topics such as Northern Ireland and abortion the Irish public did not have single opinions, but had different views relating to various facets of these issues. Such dissimilar trends, while intrinsically important, have key implications for how we evaluate public opinion poll data and if these data should be taken at face value.

As a precursor to our examination of Irish public opinion it is necessary to construct solid foundations and create an inventory of what public opinion poll data are available for investigation. While a more detailed overview is provided in Chapter 1, here I will introduce the main sources of data and their key characteristics so as to illustrate why Irish public opinion poll data merit a more detailed investigation than that provided in previous research work. From the outset it is important to be aware that not all opinion polls are the same, and that the opinion poll evidence may be broadly divided into two strands.

Media-Commissioned Public Opinion Polls

The primary sources of data used in this book are public opinion poll results that have been published in the Republic of Ireland since 1970. Three commercial marketing companies have undertaken this work: Irish Marketing Services (IMS), Lansdowne Market Research and the Market Research Bureau of Ireland (MRBI). The results of these polls have been published predominantly in the *Irish Independent*, *Sunday Independent* and *The Irish Times* and occasionally on Irish state television (RTÉ).[3] These opinion poll results exist in the form of reports of aggregated statistics where the opinions expressed by individual respondents have been summed up on the basis of socio-demographic and partisan categories.

Between 1970 and 1998, IMS, Lansdowne and MRBI asked about 3,600 survey questions in the Republic of Ireland in more than 220 polls.[4] All of these data are available at the *aggregate level*. While all opinion poll results are based on individual responses, it is the aggregated opinions of groups that are of primary interest to pollsters and the media who commission them, as they represent the potential answers of many other citizens. In this respect, poll reports are based on a fundamentally important assumption: 'Opinions cluster by groups... [e.g. sex, age, marital status, class, region, urban–rural, partisanship]... consciously or unconsciously people tend to identify with such groups... and to draw their opinions from these identifications' (Lane and Sears 1964: 2).

Academic Surveys of Public Opinion

Fortunately, media-commissioned polls constitute only one strand in the opinion poll evidence available for examination. In addition, there have been a series of academic surveys, many of which are cross-national in nature, thereby providing us with the opportunity to do comparative research and tell a much richer story. Moreover, a number of these academic surveys have been undertaken at more than one point in time, thus facilitating some measure of change in attitudes, beliefs and values. In contrast to media-commissioned polls that have been implemented by commercial marketing companies, the surveying unit of the Economic and Social Research Institute (ESRI) has for the most part undertaken academic surveys.

The most important academic surveys relating to public opinion undertaken in Ireland since the 1980s are the European Values Surveys (EVS) carried out in 1981, 1990 and 1999 and various modules of the International Social Survey Programme (ISSP) that have examined a variety of themes such as 'role of government' since 1985. More recently there have been the Irish Social and Political Attitudes Survey (ISPAS) undertaken during the winter of 2001/2, the Irish National Election Studies (INES) of 2002 and 2007, and the two waves of the European Social Survey (ESS) during the 2002 to 2005 period.

However, the greatest opinion polling project in the European Union is Eurobarometer, a Commission-sponsored biannual series of surveys undertaken in all member states since 1970. This is the best source of public opinion towards the EU and process of integration. Fortunately, Eurobarometer (EB) contains other questions on a wide variety of topics relating to policy preferences, general values such as left–right orientation and satisfaction with democracy. While Eurobarometer is not strictly speaking an academic surveying programme, it has been widely used by scholars in their work aimed at developing a better understanding of public support for European integration (see Niedermayer and Sinnott 1995; Marks and Steenbergen 2004).

All of these academic surveys have a number of features in common. First, academic survey questionnaires are generally longer than those of media-commissioned polls and they often use standardised question formats allowing strict comparison across time and between countries. Second, apart from Eurobarometer polls, academic surveys take place infrequently; for example, the EVS series of surveys are carried out once a decade. This means that they are not suited to charting change as it occurs. This is where media-commissioned polls have a distinct advantage. Third, the opinion data from academic surveys are available at the *individual level* in electronic data files for the purpose of statistical analysis. For this reason, academic surveys facilitate more detailed investigations than is possible with the aggregated poll reports available from IMS, MRBI and Lansdowne.[5]

Comparison of Media-Commissioned Polls and Academic Surveys

One can readily see from these brief descriptions of the main forms of opinion polling undertaken in Ireland that not all mass surveys are the same. The IMS, Lansdowne and MRBI polls are characterised by their strong contemporary focus where the goal is to take the pulse of public opinion with fewer than two dozen questions. Their scope is focused on the 'dynamic' nature of Irish politics, investigating who is currently popular and some reasons as to why this is the case (for example, unpopular government budgets, political scandals and so on). This feature is both their greatest strength and weakness.

The media-commissioned polls' strength comes from the fact that they provide the most proximate public opinion evidence to contemporary events, while their weakness is that the number of questions that have been asked consistently in all media-commissioned polls is small. This means that we have quite a lot of information on changing levels of party support and measures of the prevailing political mood as indicated by ratings of satisfaction with government, the Taoiseach and party leaders. Unfortunately, the polling evidence on policy preferences is much less extensive. This is because many of the policy questions asked examined current events such as proposed hospital closures. This is where the use of academic surveys has definite advantages because of their more extensive questionnaires and adoption of standardised question formats in successive surveys across time and within different countries.

In short, commercial and academic polls are complementary rather than rivals. They have different goals and are essentially designed to ask different kinds of questions and hence provide different types of answers. Commercial polls published in the media are constructed with the specific purpose of measuring opinion change on a small number of key indicators and mirroring such change as frequently and as accurately as possible. Consequently, IMS, Lansdowne and MRBI polls chart what aspects of public opinion have changed. In contrast, relatively infrequent academic surveys are interested in understanding, in as much detail as possible, what is the nature of opinion stability and why it exhibits particular patterns. This broad division of opinion polls leads us to a more detailed discussion of what opinion poll data can tell us about public opinion.

Conceptualising the Relationship between the Form and Function of Different Types of Opinion Polls

We have just seen that the 'form' or type of opinion poll (that is, media-commissioned or academic) tells us important things about how much we can learn about public opinion from opinion polls. By comparing and contrasting the advantages and disadvantages of different types of opinion polls we immediately begin to see the link between the form of polls and their function in answering 'what' and 'why' questions. In other words, all opinion polls measure what opinion is and also give some measure of why opinion is one thing and not another. Commercial polls published in the media aspire to be 'snapshots' and to give the most comprehensive picture of *what* public opinion is at many points in time. The key function here is to provide a 'mirror' of public opinion in society.

In contrast, academic surveys with the facility of asking many questions look more deeply into *why* public opinion has a specific configuration and in this respect these surveys try to illuminate like a 'lamp' meaningful patterns among opinions. To clarify this line of reasoning more clearly one could say that the key functions of public opinion poll results can be summarised in the metaphor of 'the mirror and the lamp'.

From one perspective, opinion poll results try to describe the world as it really is, by representing social reality as accurately and as neutrally as is possible. This represents a vision prevalent in the media and among pollsters, that published opinion poll results should reflect like a mirror what is happening in the world. In essence, pollsters, like newspapers, envisage themselves as embarking on a (Humean) search for 'the facts' that are presented to the public, who are then free to make their own interpretation.

Alternatively, the goal of those wishing to measure public opinion is to highlight and analyse the attitudes that are prevalent within society but are nonetheless not well understood. Here there is the underlying theme of a Platonic search for an essence of what lies behind the façade of daily life. Opinion poll results enlighten society by bringing to public notice what was once hidden from view. Quite

Number of questions in a poll

	High	Low
High (Frequency of polling)	[1] Polls act as *strong mirrors and lamps*. Opinion poll results facilitate individual or subgroup based analyses across time.	[2] Polls with a handful of core questions operate primarily as *mirrors* of public opinion. Analysis is limited to subgroups.
Low (Frequency of polling)	[4] Polls act mainly as a *lamp* and are typically academic in nature. These polls facilitate individual or subgroup analyses, but are less useful in examining trends.	[3] Isolated polls give limited information that is context specific. Such polls act as *weak mirrors and lamps* on public opinion.

Figure 1 *Typology of the Form and Function that Opinion Poll Results Provide with Regard to Examining the Nature of Public Opinion*

Note: A 'high' frequency of polling refers to survey series that have at least four polls per year. A 'high' number of poll questions refers to questionnaires with more than twenty items. The number of questions in a survey gives a measure of the information content of a poll where interpretation of the survey results can be undertaken with information generated within the poll itself. For example, if a poll only asked vote intention questions such data provides, at best, a mirror of the electorate's intent. However, interpretation as to why the electorate has a particular preference ordering would have to come from information outside the poll, such as recent economic news, media coverage of political developments, previous election results, etc.

often this is primarily an academic goal, but one where mass survey results and subsequent analyses are sometimes publicised in the media. Figure 1 illustrates in a simple typology our expectations of what we might be able to learn about public opinion from opinion polls.

The four cells of this typology show the information potential of opinion polls in terms of questionnaire size and frequency of polling. The main message stemming from this typology is that the form and function of polls arise from the goals underpinning their original design. This figure shows that polls that act either as mirrors or lamps on society are best seen as ideal types. All polls perform to some degree both of these descriptive and analytical functions.

As media-commissioned polls form the vast bulk of opinion polling undertaken in Ireland and reflect most closely on all elections and national developments that have occurred since 1970, these polls will be the primary source of data used in this book. Academic surveys will play a supporting role as many of these projects have been analysed elsewhere. In the next section a practical demonstration of the mirror and lamp functions of opinion polls will be given.

Opinion Polls as Mirrors and Lamps on Public Opinion

In the previous sections I have outlined how media-commissioned opinion polls used to measure public opinion are a unique and under-utilised resource within Irish social science. If Irish public opinion is to be given 'centre stage' and extensive use is to be made of media-commissioned polls, a key consideration is: how much can such polls tell us about Irish public opinion? Here, the example of the 1995 divorce referendum will be used to illustrate the mirror and lamp functions of opinion polls. This referendum campaign was remarkable for three reasons.

First, the final result was the closest recorded in all Irish referendums. Second, during the campaign the rules of the game were changed with the Supreme Court's 'McKenna judgment', where the government was forbidden to spend public money to secure a 'yes' vote. Third, in a High Court case challenging the legality of the referendum, opinion poll evidence proved to be crucial and reveals the most important official example of mass surveys being used to understand *what* were the vote intentions of citizens during the campaign and *why* voters voted as they did. In short, the High Court case examined through the use of expert witnesses the mirror and lamp functions of Irish opinion polls to answer the important question: did the Government's advertising campaign materially affect the outcome?

Polls as mirrors of public opinion

Jack Jones (2001: 212–3) emphasised in light of his expert testimony during the High Court case following the 1995 divorce referendum that the term 'opinion poll' was restricted to two situations: (a) the provision of basic poll figures for publication with 'limited factual commentary' by a staff journalist, and (b) publication of poll results with 'objective and factual' interpretive analysis by the polling company.[6]

From this perspective, opinion poll results are seen to be political measurements that reflect like a mirror the state of opinion. The most typical example is the use of vote intention questions during election campaigns. If the polls act as accurate mirrors and reflect what public sentiment is towards a party, they should be able to predict the election result (within the limits of sampling error).[7]

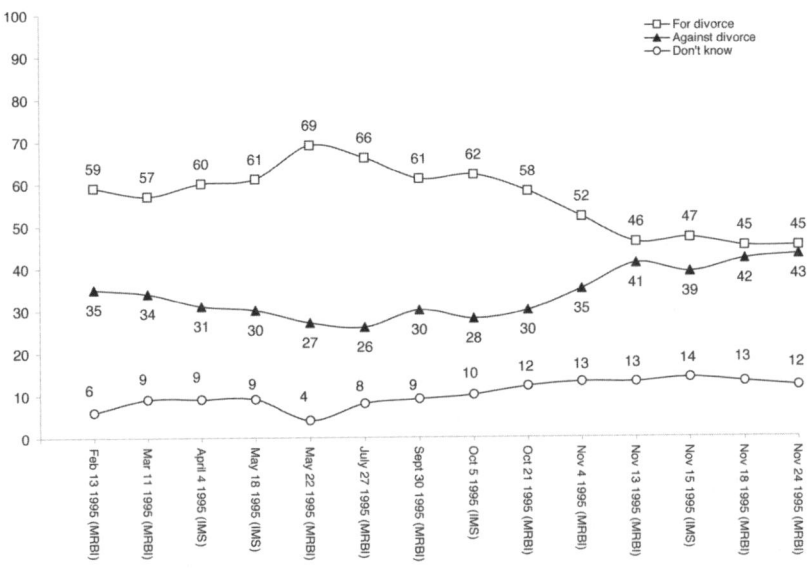

Figure 2 *Public Opinion towards Legalising Divorce in the Republic of Ireland during the 1995 Referendum Campaign (per cent)*

Note: This figure presents all known poll questions inquiring about vote intention in the 1995 divorce referendum. In the early polls, prior to 30 September, the public knew neither the exact wording nor the timing of the referendum.

Examples of poll questions used to construct this time series:

If you were asked to vote on a law to permit divorce in Ireland, would you vote in favour of or against such a law? (a) Would vote in favour, (b) would vote against, (c) don't know. IMS/CMC/sos/mc/J.2S191, 4 November 1992, Independent Newspapers, question 1.

The referendum will be held next Friday to remove the ban on divorce from the Constitution. If the referendum was held today would you vote yes to remove the ban and allow for divorce or vote no to keep the ban on divorce? (a) Would vote in favour, (b) would vote against, (c) don't know. MRBI/4331/95, 18 November 1995, *Irish Times*, question 5.

The opinion poll data shown in Figure 2 demonstrate public support for reform during the second divorce referendum campaign. This campaign could be said to have started in early 1995, when it became public knowledge that a referendum would be held before the end of the year. Figure 2 reveals that the countdown to the referendum had three distinct phases: (a) increase in support for divorce between February and May, (b) decline in support for divorce between May and 4 November, and (c) stabilisation in support for divorce from 13 November to polling day. Within the media much ink was spilt in trying to explain a 22 per cent change in support in the 'yes' and 'no' camps, as the polls were seen to mirror public opinion in a factual and objective manner. This belief was underscored by the fact that the final poll predictions of the 'yes' and 'no' votes were very accurate, being within one percentage point of the actual result.

Polls as lamps on public opinion

In the High Court case following the divorce referendum of 1995, the Anti-Divorce Action Group contended that the Irish government's spending of public funds (half a million pounds) on an advertising campaign had 'materially affected the outcome'. The difference between the 'yes' and 'no' votes in the referendum was 9,114 votes out of 1.6 million (0.6 per cent) implying that a swing of as few as 5,000 votes could have changed the result from a 'yes' to a 'no'. The core question in the High Court case was whether it was possible to demonstrate that the Government's advertising campaign influenced the outcome. Consequently, the case depended on being able to show *why* the Irish public voted by a tiny margin to support legalising divorce in Ireland, and parcel out the independent effects of various factors such as the Government's advertising campaign. The MRBI opinion poll evidence could not definitively answer this very specific legal question. This was primarily because no poll questions were asked to track this aspect of the campaign (Jones 2001: 196).

During the final month before the referendum MRBI measured not only vote intentions, but also *why* respondents were 'for' or 'against' legalising divorce. This polling data highlighted two key patterns. First, there was a dramatic change (22 percent) in vote intentions. Second, the reasons given for intending to vote 'yes' or 'no' remained largely consistent. The MRBI series of referendum polls illuminates why the public supported or opposed the proposed divorce legalisation. For the 'yes' voters the key reason given seems to have been freedom to start a new life. In contrast, 'no' voters were mainly concerned about preserving the integrity of the family and following Catholic Church doctrine. However, this evidence also puts us on our guard. Some key features of opinion change during the three weeks between these polls were not captured in these results. Although there was a large change (a 12 per cent decline in the 'yes' vote and an 11 per cent increase in the 'no' vote, between 21 October and 13 November) in voting intentions, this was not reflected in equally large changes in the reasons given by 'no' voters – other than a 7 per cent increase in the 'other comments' category.[8]

In this section I have demonstrated how polls reflect what public opinion is, and how polls can illuminate why public opinion exhibits a certain pattern. We have also seen that opinion poll results do have inherent limitations and that the data do not speak for themselves. These themes will be developed in more detail in Chapter 2. For now, we will turn to what previous research has been undertaken using public opinion poll data in Ireland.

Previous Work on the Analysis of Public Opinion in Ireland

The literature on Irish 'public opinion' in its most general sense is rather scant. In fact, there has been no academic book-length examination of public opinion. There are numerous articles and book chapters using opinion poll data where public opinion is treated as a causal factor helping to explain, for example, an election result. Public opinion is rarely treated as the focus for study. However, such a generalisation obscures important differences in the portrait of Irish public opinion painted by the two different types of opinion polling.

Media-commissioned poll literature on public opinion

The only book that has addressed Irish public opinion as its central theme is Jack Jones's *In Your Opinion* (2001). This partly autobiographical work examines the history and evolution of political opinion polling in Ireland since 1970. The main focus of his book is polls undertaken by MRBI for *The Irish Times* between 1982 and 2001. Consequently, this is primarily a professional pollster's account of the opinion polling process and illustrates the accuracy of

MRBI polls in mirroring election results. The weakness of the book is that the data examined are restricted to MRBI polls and there is little consideration of how to critically evaluate published poll results. Moreover, interpretation of the polling data is restricted to specific events, and there is little overall sense as to how public opinion has evolved and changed over time.

Beyond this single book, opinion poll data is most often used where public opinion is treated as an explanatory factor for change in society. A good example is Chrystel Hug's (1999) treatment of *The Politics of Sexual Morality in Ireland*. This is a sociological and legal history of 'liberal agenda' issues in contemporary Ireland. At various points in this book, most often relating to referendums on divorce and abortion, public opinion poll results are introduced to help explain public sentiment toward proposed legislation and voting behaviour. Beyond treating the poll results as a mirror of contemporary public opinion, little further use is made of the polling data. The focus is on change in legislation rather than public opinion.

Use of opinion data in Ireland has been very strongly linked with electoral politics. Following all general elections since 1977 there have been analyses of 'how Ireland voted' using opinion poll data (see Penniman 1978; Penniman and Farrell 1987; Laver, Mair and Sinnott 1987; Gallagher and Laver 1993; Marsh and Mitchell 1999; Gallagher, Marsh and Mitchell 2003). Individual chapters in each of these edited works range from aggregate-level mirror-like profiles of the electorate to detailed individual level analyses of the socio-demographic and attitudinal factors associated with vote choice. Richard Sinnott's *Irish Voters Decide* (1995a) is the most definitive work dealing with voting behaviour in Ireland in all elections since 1918. This book combines official election results, census data and public opinion poll findings to examine voter turnout, vote choice, party and candidate support and the nature and extent of issue voting. Here opinion polls are used to examine why voters voted in the manner that they did. However, again the focus is squarely on explanations of electoral behaviour where public opinion is used to help explain patterns of stability and change.

Academic survey literature on public opinion

There have been a number of books and articles that have examined Irish public opinion, mainly using the European Values Survey (EVS) and the International Social Survey Programme (ISSP) mass survey results.[9] The three waves of EVS facilitate an examination of change in Irish beliefs and values between 1981 and 1999. The key goal of works such as Fogarty, Ryan and Lee (1984), Whelan (1994) and Fahey, Hayes and Sinnott (2005) has been to reflect like a mirror contemporary values on a wide range of topics such as religion and morality; work; politics and partisanship; identity; Northern Ireland; left–right values and confidence in political institutions. In addition, using mainly subgroup, cross-national and cross-time comparisons, there have been detailed investigations that have illuminated (in a lamp-like manner) which specific groups hold particular values, why this might be the case, and whether public opinion in particular domains has been stable or represents a significant deviation from international patterns or a break with the past.

While EVS has been used to examine the different value systems of various subgroups, Michael Mac Gréil has undertaken the only book-length work on how different subgroups see each other and the attitudinal and socio-demographic basis for such perceptions. Using the same survey questions asked first in 1972–3 and later in 1988–9 Mac Gréil (1980, 1996) used a specific social-psychological perspective to examine why the Irish public have various types of prejudices, and how these have evolved. A key feature of this work, which is typical of other research in this field, has been the use of survey data first and foremost to cast a mirror on Irish society and then through attitudinal and subgroup analyses to illuminate why specific attitudinal patterns are observed.[10]

In fact, most analyses of academic surveys are aggregate level, that is, they involve comparisons and contrasts between subgroups. Despite the fact that individual-level datasets are used in conducting these analyses, relatively little individual-level model building is presented in published work.[11] Consequently, the methods used to illuminate the underlying features of Irish public opinion are often more restricted than the limits imposed by the survey data itself.

A Key Puzzle within Irish Public Opinion

There is little doubt that Ireland has undergone considerable change since public opinion polling began in 1970. With fundamental institutional reforms it is assumed that citizens' attitudes and values adjusted accordingly. And there is much evidence to suggest that there have been great changes in Irish values over the last four decades.

- In 1970 there was strong support for a united Ireland in the Republic where the effects of the 'Troubles' dominated the news. Yet by 1998 the Irish public seemed to sacrifice a core political goal for the sake of peace within Northern Ireland. Was this change accompanied by an equally dramatic evolution in nationalist values, and if so, when did this happen?
- In 1970 discussion of liberal agenda issues such as abortion, contraception, divorce, and homosexuality were almost taboo subjects. Nevertheless, by the late 1970s support for new legislation in most of these areas led to great public debates. The series of referendums on abortion and divorce highlight remarkable changes in opinion, but also the persistence of traditional conservative values.
- In 1970 the Irish economy was predominantly agricultural and oriented towards serving the British market, where emigration was an ever-present strategy for relieving the problems associated with a labour surplus. By the late 1990s, Ireland had a labour shortage and was trying to cope with the effects of immigration. The pessimistic outlook of the past seemed to be replaced by a self-assured confidence in the future and the ability of the Irish economy and workforce to be successful at an international level.
- In 1970 a key goal of the Irish government was accession to the European Economic Community. For much of the Irish public the Common Market was largely unknown and it was only through a strong government-led campaign that the accession referendum was successful. During the 1980s and 1990s popular support for integration in Ireland was often the highest in the whole European Union. And yet, despite the substantial level of financial transfers to Ireland from the EU, the Irish electorate rejected the Government's attempts to ratify the Nice Treaty in 2001.

While at one level there would seem to have been significant opinion change in each of these four issue domains, the opinion poll data suggest a rather puzzling picture. If we take the Northern Ireland question, for example, one can see from Figure 3 that although the Irish electorate voted in the Belfast/Good Friday Agreement referendum of May 1998 to amend constitutional claims toward creating a united Ireland, public opinion on this issue has changed little since 1968.

In fact, Figure 3 illustrates two distinct sets of opinions towards Northern Ireland. The top line in Figure 3 shows public opinion on the 'easy' question of whether Irish citizens would like to see a united Ireland. Here we see that there has always been strong support for the principle of having a united Ireland and that these sentiments have not changed over time, as one might have expected with the peace process. In contrast, the bottom line represents responses to 'hard' questions where the goal of a united Ireland has been compared with other desirable objectives, such as creating peace.

The key pattern in Figure 3 is that there are persistent differences in levels of opinion between considerations of desirable goals (easy facet) and the means to achieve such goals (hard facet). The two distinct trends represented in this figure demonstrate that consideration of different facets of the same issue leads the public to give consistently different response profiles. Moreover, the pattern represented in Figure 3 reveals that public opinion towards Northern Ireland is marked by considerable stability. This is an important finding as it indicates that, despite important political changes with the peace process, public attitudes in the Republic have remained constant. Similar dual trends to those revealed in Figure 3 can be shown for public opinion towards the liberal agenda, the economy and the European Union.

This highlights an important question: why is public opinion on different facets of the same issue so different? One would expect that opinions relating to an issue, especially salient ones such as Northern Ireland, would be represented by a single overarching perspective. Figure 3 suggests that this is not the case. Respondents often do not have single opinions on public issues, but hold a number of opinions related to different facets of questions of public concern such as abortion, Northern Ireland, the EU, and so on. This fact has two important implications. First, great care must be taken in the interpretation of poll results as they do not refer to a single opinion, they cannot be taken at face value. Second, interpretation of poll results can only be built upon an understanding of how respondents answer poll questions during interviews.

As we will see in Chapter 2, the puzzle highlighted in Figure 3 arises in part because different types of questions on the same issue lead respondents to take different considerations into account. Thus, as students of public opinion, we need to be careful in trying to understand what opinion polls measure. Failure to do so will lead us to mix up what are in reality different questions, resulting in conclusions that are grounded in methodological artefacts rather than in real opinion change.

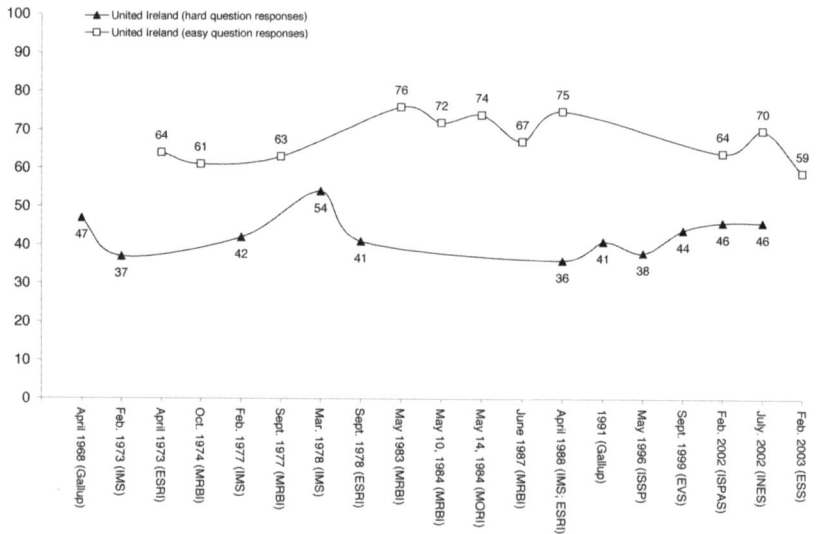

Figure 3 *Comparison of Hard and Easy Facets of Public Opinion Support for a United Ireland in the Republic of Ireland, 1968–2003 (per cent)*

Note: The top line refers to poll questions that simply asked respondents their personal preferences for a united Ireland. The bottom line is based on responses to questions where the future status of Northern Ireland was discussed with reference to a variety of political solutions, of which a united Ireland was just one choice. Given the differences in question format, these 'easy' and 'hard' questions are represented as different time series.

Example of a hard question:

Which of the following options, in your opinion, would best help to bring peace to Northern Ireland? (a) Full integration with Britain, (b) a return to majority rule, (c) power sharing between the Unionist and Nationalist Community (with constitutional guarantees to protect the minority), (d) an independent Ulster, (e) a federal Ireland or (f) a united Ireland. IMS: PMacN/mb.J.11345, Independent Newspapers, April 8–10 1988, question 20.

Example of an easy question:

Personal reaction to a United Ireland today... (a) very much in favour, (b) somewhat in favour, (c) not really in favour or (d) very much against? MRBI, Report for *Magill* magazine, 1 (1), October 1977, p 13; Rose, McAllister & Mair (1978: 35); Survey undertaken in September 1977.

Roadmap of the Book

In this book I will aim to demonstrate how public opinion polls can be used to inform our knowledge of public opinion in the Republic of Ireland. This research represents an important advance on previous work for two reasons. First, the focus is squarely on public opinion and not on how public opinion helps to explain some other phenomenon. Second, this book will examine all of the public opinion poll data available in the public domain. No previous work has attempted such a task. In addressing this core issue of what opinion polls tell us about public opinion this research will investigate four main questions:

- What is public opinion in Ireland on a variety of issues?
- How does one interpret opinion poll results – should they be taken at face value?
- How does public opinion change over time and what factors help explain opinion stability and change?
- Why does public opinion exhibit certain patterns?

The 'what' question evaluates the 'mirror function' of opinion polls and provides information about the nature of public opinion. As I have noted in the last section, understanding what opinion poll questions tell us may not be a straightforward matter. The 'how' and 'why' questions assess the degree to which opinion polls can perform the 'lamp function' and facilitate understanding the foundations of Irish public opinion.

Given the task at hand, this book will have four main organising principles or integrating components within all chapters. The data component forms the foundation for this research and determines the substantive themes that can be investigated. The methodological component alerts us to the limitations inherent in the data available and the type of inferences that may be drawn from analysis. The substantive component reflects the core content of the polls. This component reveals the nature of public opinion in specific issue areas, and whether the survey data reflect policy-making or electoral concerns. The final theoretical component relates to the meaning that may be inferred from using opinion polls to investigate public opinion, and will be dealt with in the conclusions to separate chapters and most directly in the final chapter. Let me now briefly outline the content of this book.

Chapter 1 will provide an overview and inventory of all the opinion polls commissioned and published by the Irish media (*The Irish Times*, Independent Newspapers and RTÉ). This chapter outlines the substantive content of opinion poll questions asked and describes general features of the poll data available for analysis, and represents the main data component section of the book. In addition, this chapter will critically describe the sampling design and methodology used in Irish polls.

In Chapter 2 the core methodological component of the book is introduced. Here key features of the questionnaire design used in Irish opinion polls are described and critically evaluated. Furthermore, this chapter will outline a model of how respondents answer questions, as this has a direct bearing on how opinion polls and public opinion itself is conceptualised. This chapter shows that the mirror and lamp functions of opinion polls are susceptible to certain types of bias. The presence of such bias presents serious problems in the interpretation of opinion polls and lessons we might learn about public opinion.

Chapter 3 introduces the theme of poll accuracy and precision and builds on the previous two chapters by examining a central question asked in all media-commissioned opinion polls: vote intention in the next general election. By comparing poll predictions and actual election results we have the only definitive test of how well opinion polls mirror public opinion. In this chapter we see that poll estimation of vote intentions illustrates many of the methodological difficulties in effectively measuring public opinion. Moreover, many of the technical problems associated with election prediction are associated with the theoretical conceptualisation of the function of opinion polls. Is their main function to accurately mirror public (that is, electoral) behaviour, or is it to aid understanding by illuminating key facets of public opinion?

In Chapter 4 the focus, while remaining on politics, shifts away from voting to consideration of how the general 'political mood' evolves over time. As the media are in both the information and the entertainment business they commission poll questions that emphasise the 'horse race' nature of political competition in order to generate newsworthy headlines. While vote intention questions are often interpreted in this manner, the media also try to assess the political mood of the electorate using a variety of satisfaction ratings. Examination of these ratings brings together important substantive, methodological and theoretical considerations. In this chapter, use will be made of a special statistical (time series) technique to analyse the interrelationship between satisfaction ratings and vote intentions for incumbent government parties.

Chapter 5 initiates the substantive part of this book. In this chapter I begin by examining public opinion towards the two key 'liberal agenda' issues of abortion and divorce. There are relatively few poll data on the other liberal agenda issues such as contraception and homosexuality, primarily because legislation in these areas did not involve referendums. Here I approach a key theme within opinion polling – the different response patterns to 'hard' and 'easy' questions. The existence of such patterns allows us, through a process of comparison and subgroup analysis, to evaluate both the descriptive and the analytical potential of opinion polls as a means of studying public opinion.

Chapter 6 examines Irish public opinion towards the Northern Ireland question. Most of the poll questions relating to this topic deal with political initiatives towards creating peace. In this chapter I will look at trends in opinion on four topics – support for Articles 2 and 3 of the Irish Constitution, public aspirations for a united Ireland, attitudes towards the border and withdrawal of the British Army from Northern Ireland. The findings of previous research are tested with more extensive data and I illustrate the importance of distinguishing between 'hard' and 'easy' questions. As in Chapter 5, I will look at what the mirror and lamp functions of opinion polls tell us about Irish citizens' attitudes towards the Northern Ireland question.

The final two substantive chapters are alike in that both use Eurobarometer data and address directly the question of opinion change. I start this process in Chapter 7, where an examination is made of what left–right means in Ireland by comparing opinion poll data from a variety of sources. Just as in Chapters 5 and 6, the methodological and theoretical components of opinion poll research play an important role in understanding what left–right poll questions might mean to the Irish public. Again we see that identification of questions as being 'easy' or 'hard' provides important insights into how opinion polls reflect what public opinion is and illuminate why it exhibits particular patterns.

In Chapter 8, Irish public opinion towards the European Union and the integration project is examined in terms of polls relating to the five referendums held on this issue between 1972 and 2002. Here some important methodological concerns arise where I try to assess levels of public support for integration and reasons for such support using IMS and MRBI poll results. As much of these poll data are linked to specific time points, i.e. 'referendums', I will use Eurobarometer poll data to investigate the long-term evolution of Irish opinion towards integration. This chapter will show how Eurobarometer poll data may be used to reflect public opinion and investigate whether popular sentiment towards the EU is changing, and some possible reasons as to why.

The concluding chapter will pull together the evidence presented in Chapters 1 to 8 and evaluate what opinion polls tell us about public opinion in Ireland, how public opinion has changed in Ireland over the last three decades and the utility of using a 'mirror' and 'lamp' conceptualisation of mass survey data. Such an evaluation will be placed within the context of the data, methodological, substantive and theoretical considerations outlined in each of the chapters. In addition, I will summarise the evidence assembled regarding the what, how and why questions within Irish public opinion and the answers that are given to us in the polling data. Some remarks will also be made on the key puzzle identified within Irish public opinion and fruitful lines of inquiry for future research.

Notes

1 There is an extensive literature on various facets of societal change in Ireland since 1970. The following references provide a recent snapshot of the main themes: Schmitt (1998: 210–22); Inglis (1998b: 249–59); Hug (1999: 4); Finnegan and McCarron (2000: 239–40, 271–8); Cassidy (2002b: 40–4); Coakley (2005a: 39–60); Fahey, Hayes and Sinnott (2005: 218–33).
2 Much of this information is available in the Irish Opinion Polls Archive (IOPA). IOPA was created by Professor Michael Marsh, Department of Political Science, Trinity College Dublin. The archive or database may be searched over the internet and is located at www.tcd.ie/Political_Science/IOPA/.
3 IMS and MRBI were founded in the early 1960s and remained independent domestic companies until the late 1990s, when IMS became part of the international conglomerate Millward Brown and MRBI joined Taylor Nelson, Sofres (TNS). For the sake of consistency the original company names will be used throughout the text. The *Irish Independent* and *The Irish Times* are the two main broadsheet daily newspapers, while the *Sunday Independent* is the most popular Sunday paper. Lansdowne Market Research was founded in 1979. Many of the polls conducted by IMS have been produced in cooperation with Lansdowne, hence the use of the term 'IMS/Lansdowne' in this book.
4 Other polling companies within Ireland such as Behaviour and Attitudes Ltd., Bluebird, Red C and agencies based in the UK such as Gallup, MORI and ICM have undertaken opinion polls on political issues for a number of other Irish newspapers such as *Ireland on Sunday*, the *Sunday Tribune* and the *Star* (Irish edition). Where appropriate, reference will be made to these polls, but the main focus will be on polls produced by IMS, Lansdowne

and MRBI. These three companies have undertaken the vast majority of polls published in the Republic of Ireland.
5 IMS, MRBI and Lansdowne have provided a few individual-level data files to researchers, mainly in the context of elections. It is only recently that the individual-level files used to create the aggregate-level reports have been made available for analysis following publication. For more details, see the Irish Social Science Data Archive (ISSDA) website www.ucd.ie/~issda>.
6 In the *Irish Times*/MRBI series, Jack Jones as Chairman of MRBI regularly wrote such 'formal' commentaries as a 'service for *Irish Times* readers' (Jones 2001: 213).
7 This is a question that will be examined in some detail in Chapter 3.
8 In fact, there is a strong case to be made here that only a panel design (i.e. the same people interviewed on two or more occasions) could have provided reliable data on the impact of the campaign.
9 Research on ISPAS and INES also strongly relates to theme of public opinion in Ireland. See Garry, Hardiman and Payne (2006) and Marsh, Sinnott, Garry and Kennedy (2007).
10 See Nic Ghiolla Phadraig (1976); Fogarty, Ryan and Lee (1984); Breslin and Weafer (1985); Whelan (1994); Cassidy (2002a); Fahey, Hayes and Sinnott (2005).
11 This may arise for two reasons. First, the theory being tested is not an individual-level one. Second, individual-level models of survey data require a certain technical sophistication on the part of readers. For the sake of public accessibility such individual-level statistical analyses are often not presented.

Chapter 1

Public Opinion Data and Opinion Poll Design

> Essentially, there are three main elements in an opinion poll: the content; the sample of persons to be interviewed; and the interpretation of the findings.
>
> Jack Jones (2001:19)

The question of whether opinion polls can act as a mirror or lamp on public opinion is fundamentally influenced by the nature of the opinion poll data and the design of opinion polls. Any assessment of what IMS, Lansdowne and MRBI opinion polls tell us about Irish public opinion must start with an examination of the types of questions asked and the technical criteria used to implement questionnaires to a national sample of the Irish population. In this sense, what opinion polls tell us about 'public opinion' can be divided into two distinct questions: (a) What types of questions or 'opinions' are investigated in opinion polls? (b) Which members of the 'public' are interviewed? Consequently, the twin goals of this chapter are to outline the types of opinion poll questions that have been asked in Ireland since 1970 and to describe the sampling design used by IMS, Lansdowne and MRBI.

The work undertaken in this chapter provides the necessary foundations for the investigations undertaken in Chapter 2, which will look at questionnaire design in the Irish context and outline an influential theory of how respondents answer survey questions. In Chapter 3 there will be an examination of the electoral record of Irish opinion polls where the ability of commercial surveys to efficiently select national samples and implement appropriate questionnaire designs is put to the test. The focus in Chapters 1, 2 and 3 is thus on providing a framework for assessing the ability of Irish opinion polls to mirror public opinion. These three chapters provide the necessary background to our analysis of what citizens think on a range of substantive issues that are examined in Chapters 5 to 8. These substantive chapters have a common theme in the sense that the goal is to see *what* polls tell us about public opinion, but also *why* poll results exhibit certain patterns.

This chapter will start by briefly summarising the opinion poll data available for examination in the Republic of Ireland. This will be followed by an inventory of the opinion polls where all survey questions have been coded on the basis of content. The discussion will then move to consideration of the sampling design and methodology used in IMS, Lansdowne and MRBI polls, and this is followed by some remarks on the reporting of polls in the media. In the concluding section some brief comments will be made concerning the question of how well Irish opinion polls reflect public opinion.

Opinion Poll Data Available in the Republic Of Ireland

The data used in this book are taken from opinion polls undertaken by Irish Marketing Services (IMS), Lansdowne Market Research and the Market Research Bureau of Ireland (MRBI). The origins of opinion polling in the Republic of Ireland can be traced back to the early 1960s. However, it was only in the 1970s that the current form of political opinion polling for the main national daily and Sunday newspapers began. Between 1970 and 2005 these three market research companies undertook more than 340 public opinion polls.

In addition, political parties and governments have commissioned private opinion polls. MRBI undertook 24 such polls between 1973 and 1982. This figure grew to 100 between 1983 and 2001 (Jones 2001: 295). However, political opinion polling constitutes only a small, albeit salient, portion of the total work done each year by market research companies in Ireland. In the early 1980s, for example, MRBI undertook on average 80 commercial polls annually while political opinion polling for *The Irish Times* typically involved five surveys a year. Thus political opinion polling probably accounts for less than 10 per cent of all annual market surveying projects (note Jones 2001: 292). This is not to deny that there have been other marketing companies who have undertaken public opinion polls that have been published in the media. However, these other polls have been much less extensive in nature.

What makes the IMS, Lansdowne and MRBI polls unique in the Republic of Ireland is their orientation towards contemporary public affairs and the very public way in which their results have been disseminated. For the media, political elites and public these polls are one of the few systematic indications of public sentiments towards political actors and public policy. For academics and election pundits, media-commissioned polls were for many years the only source of empirical data on political preferences beyond election results.[1]

Profile of the Content of Irish Opinion Polls

Within the Republic of Ireland most opinion polling has been undertaken by IMS/Lansdowne (59 per cent) and MRBI (39 per cent), with the remaining 2 per cent consists of isolated polls undertaken by smaller Irish market research companies, or contracts given to British companies such as ICM or MORI. Figure 4 illustrates that opinion polling in Ireland effectively started on a consistent basis in 1977. In fact, it was the success of the polls during this general election campaign to correctly predict the election result, in contrast to the efforts of the pundits, that resulted in the emergence of media commissioned polling in Ireland (Meagher 1980; Jones 2001: 15–18, 291).

There is, unsurprisingly, a definite cycle to polling each year where most surveys are undertaken during May and June and later during October and November.[2] These months match the times generally chosen by Irish governments for holding elections and referendums. An examination of the annual count of questions asked by IMS/Lansdowne and MRBI in the domain of general elections and party politics (the largest category of survey items) shows a strong relationship between the number of questions asked and whether the year in question had a general election. In Figure 4 we can see that the general elections of 1981, 1982 (February and November), 1997 and 2002 stand out particularly clearly, while the Dáil contests of 1987, 1989 and 1992 appear to have involved less media-commissioned polling. Such evidence demonstrates the primary interests of the media who commission IMS, Lansdowne and MRBI to undertake polls on their behalf.[3]

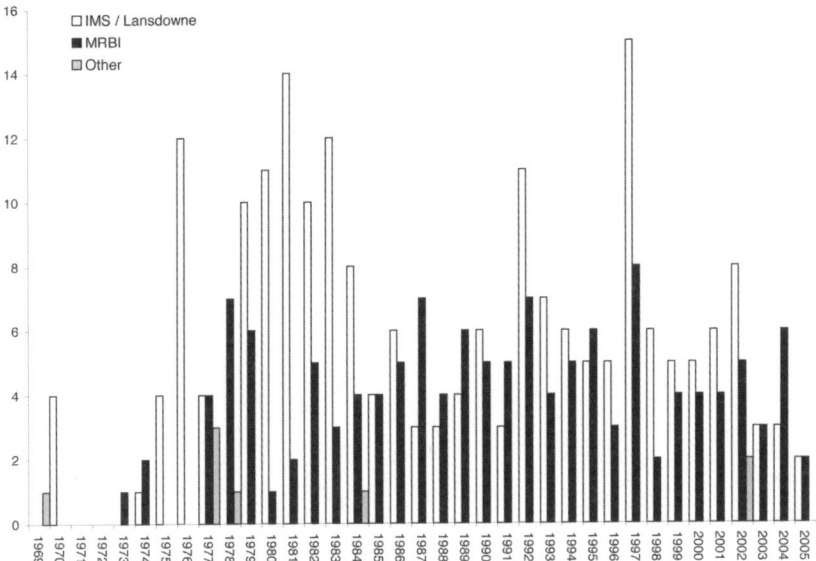

Figure 4: *Number of Polls Undertaken in the Republic of Ireland Annually, 1969–2005 (count)*

Note: The majority of polls in this figure refer to newspaper-commissioned polls. This annual estimation of polls is a conservative figure as not all polls have been archived. Also the estimation for IMS is influenced by the availability of omnibus data (i.e. monthly market research surveys with some political questions).

Turning to the substantive content of Irish opinion polls undertaken between 1970 and 1998 one can see from Figure 5 that almost two-thirds of all questions asked related to general elections and party politics. These items dealt primarily with vote intentions, reasons for vote choice, government satisfaction, and party leader ratings. The second largest group of questions relates mainly to key public issues such as divorce and abortion that were subject to a series of seven referendums. In addition, this category contains questions relating to perceptions of important institutions in Irish society and attitudes towards crime, corruption, the legal system and key policy areas such as education.

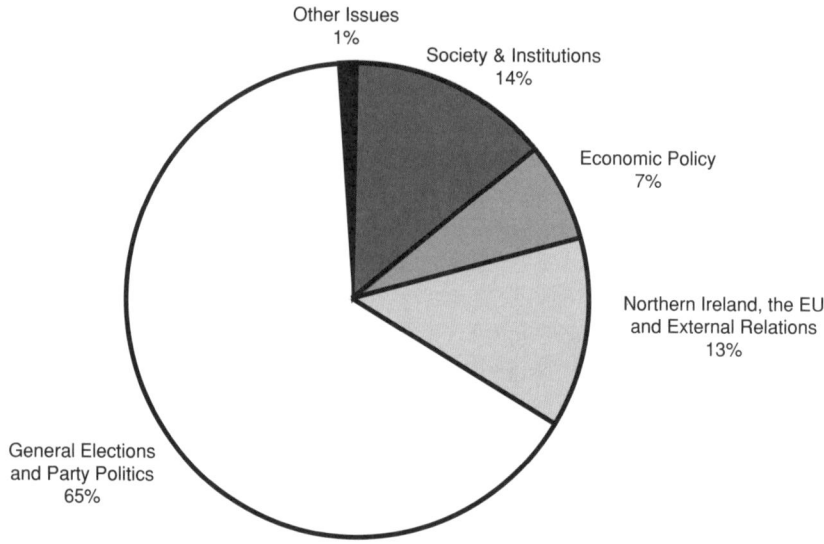

Figure 5: *Number of Survey Questions Asked by General Issue Domain, 1974–98 (per cent)*

Note: within this book this categorisation of poll questions has been modified. For example, questions on Northern Ireland and the EU are dealt with in separate chapters, as are items relating to vote intention and satisfaction with government and party leaders.

The third and almost equally large category relates to poll questions asked on Northern Ireland and relations with Britain, the EU and associated referendums and Ireland's policy of neutrality. It is interesting to see that despite the huge economic changes that occurred during this era, when Ireland went from 'bust to boom', economic issues have accounted for a relatively small number of questions – in fact about one in fourteen of the total number of items asked.

Another important feature of the poll data is the fact that the two main surveying companies have developed 'spheres of expertise', perhaps reflecting the priorities of their clients. IMS/Lansdowne have asked more questions on issues relating to national politics, Northern Ireland, the EU and so on. In contrast, MRBI has asked more questions relating to society and the economy. Having examined the content and nature of Irish opinion poll data, we will now turn our attention to the sampling design and methodology used by Irish polling companies during face-to-face interviewing.

Sampling Design and Methodology

Within all opinion polls there is always the key question of whether the poll is representative of the target population. This involves consideration of sampling design and related issues of survey non-response, survey weighting, design effects and mode of interviewing. Each of these topics will now be examined in terms of Irish opinion polling practice.

Sampling design

Each public opinion poll is designed to select a sample that is representative of the total electorate. The sampling procedure is based on the most recent decennial Central Statistics Office (CSO) census data. In the last two decades such census information has been updated with 'mid-term' data (1986, 1996) and more recently with Quarterly National Household Survey (QNHS) data. To create a representative sample of adult respondents (aged 18 years or more), all Irish marketing companies use a multi-stage probability quota sample of clusters of households located within a 'District Electoral Division' (DED) or ward.[4]

The sampling process takes place in three stages. In the first stage, approximately ten Primary Sampling Units (PSU) are used as a sampling frame for choosing one hundred sampling points at random. All sampling points are based on the DED, ward or groups of these. These are the smallest administrative units for which the CSO can generate aggregated data. PSUs and sampling points are selected by the method of probability proportional to size, where areas of larger population have a greater chance of being selected. In the second stage, one household is chosen at random from the current electoral register within each of the selected 100 sampling points. Finally, in the third stage, interviewers go to the selected households and select a respondent (typically aged 18 years or more) to be interviewed.

Having completed the first interview the interviewer proceeds from the initial household address. A 'random walk algorithm' determines which subsequent households are chosen to conduct further interviews. This random walk procedure is designed to ensure that all households within a sampling point have an equal probability of being selected. Within each sampling point the random walk is repeated nine times following the initial interview. Overall the team of interviewers will administer a questionnaire to around 1,000 respondents across the entire country.[5]

Interviewers have a control sheet detailing the demographic, class and occupational profile required by the polling agency to have a nationally representative sample. Respondents are selected using quotas where those interviewed are chosen to reflect important characteristics of the electorate, that is sex, age, marital status, occupation/class and area of residence.[6] Interviewers continue through their random walk until they fill their quotas.

To summarise, Irish pollsters when undertaking face-to-face interviewing for media commissioned surveys implement what is technically referred to as a 'multistage stratified cluster based quota sample.' In the next two sub-sections I will briefly examine two aspects of this sampling methodology and their impact on poll quality.

Use of quota samples

For historical reasons there is mistrust among public opinion researchers of the quota sampling procedure used by Irish pollsters. Companies such as Gallup in the United States used a similar non-probabilistic form of quota sampling until 1948 for political polling and election prediction. In the 1948 presidential election, while all the main survey companies had representative samples, their final polls predicted the wrong election result.[7] This historical example highlights three considerations that have direct application to Irish opinion polling.

First, having nationally representative samples is not enough to ensure valid and reliable polls – how individual respondents are chosen within the framework of quotas is also fundamentally important. One of the reasons why the final 1948 presidential polls were seen to be wrong related to the use of quota sampling. Interviewers were free to choose the individuals to be interviewed within the specified criteria, for example five males, five females, two aged 18–24 years, and so on. This interviewer freedom resulted in *selection bias* where easily accessible and approachable potential respondents were targeted for interviewing. While the explicit random walk instructions attenuates this effect by taking choice out of the hands of interviewers, the practice of allowing household (and hence respondent) replacement makes potential selection bias a non-trivial consideration, as will be seen a little later.

A second, equally important consideration is a key assumption made with quota sampling. Quota samples are valid only if the quotas closely reflect political preferences. More specifically age, sex, education, occupation and regional variables must constitute some meaningful division on the basis of political attitudes and behaviour, otherwise the poll results will also be biased (Scheaffer, Mendenhall and Ott 1990: 29–33). Within societies that undergo rapid social and economic change the relationship between quota variables and political preferences may change over time. This may be a legitimate concern in the case of Ireland, which has experienced considerable social and economic change since 1970.

Third, doubts have been cast on the assumption that 'random walks' are strictly speaking random, implying that such techniques do not result in non-probability samples (Lyberg 2000). This deviation from true probability sampling is exacerbated by two factors. First, the practice of allowing samples where respondents can be replaced if they are not available during the short timeframe of the surveying period will inflate the sampling error (McElroy and Marsh 2003: 160). Second, surveys that do not use simple random sampling will have design effects that have higher levels of sampling error. In practice, both of these factors imply that the sampling error of ±3 per cent quoted in published polls is not strictly speaking correct. More will be said on both of these points in later sections and in Chapter 3.

Survey non-response

Even if survey companies ensure that their samples are representative of the national population, there is still the important question of non-response. Non-response can make opinion polls that are otherwise representative misleading if respondents who refuse to answer, or cannot be contacted, have some systematic features – effectively leading to selection bias in the final sample (Groves and Couper 1998; Loosveldt 1995; Stoop et al. 2000). In other words, the people who agree to be interviewed might well have distinctly different attitudes from those who refuse to participate. Typically, the expectation is that such non-respondents are less interested in politics, and have lower levels of education and less knowledge of politics and current affairs.[8]

Currently, the level of non-response varies considerably from country to country (typically ranging between 40 and 80 per cent), and is universally declining.[9] Traugott and Lavrakas (2000: 124) advise that response rates below 75 per cent should cause concern. Pollsters can compensate for high non-response rates, which are often a practical consequence of trying to do a national survey over a very short period of time where there is little scope for multiple contact attempts, by weighting the data.[10] Often it is not clear if the impact of weighting will have the desired effects. More generally, surveys that have low response rates or allow respondent replacement may effectively become polls of those interested in politics and not a true sample of the entire population. Ironically for election prediction it is the politically interested population that is of most importance, as these are the people who will go to the polls and determine who will win the election. For this reason, relatively low response rates may in fact aid election prediction.

The response rate to an IMS poll in September 1976 was quite high, with four in five respondents selected being interviewed. However, this rate appears to have fallen in more recent times. For example, an ISSP survey in 1988 recorded a 78 per cent response rate, while a similar survey undertaken a decade later had a 60 per cent rate. In general, commercial Irish public opinion poll reports do not give information on non-response rates. Moreover, it is not clear what strategies Irish polling companies adopt, if any, to counter the loss of respondents other than using respondent replacement.[11] This simple rule, as noted earlier, was employed in quota sampling by Gallup and others in the US prior to 1948, but is now generally seen to be a risky sampling strategy.

The reason is that respondent replacement introduces *systematic sampling bias* into a survey, as there is an overrepresentation of the cooperative and accessible segment of the population. This bias stems in part from interviewers not being as persistent as they might be in attempting to gain a response from the original household address (Elliot 1993). The systematic bias caused by respondent substitution is judged to be sufficiently serious that many surveying projects such as the European Social Survey (ESS) prohibit use of this strategy.

In Irish opinion polls the effects of respondent substitution are essentially unknown as there are no published studies of its impact.

This stems in part from a lack of sufficient information about the interviewing and surveying process. As a result, it is difficult to make definitive inferences about the likely effects of respondent substitution. In fact, respondent substitution may be an important contributing factor in explaining the systematic error in pre-election and exit poll estimations of party support. This is a topic that will be studied in greater detail in Chapter 3.

More generally, the orthodox view that low response rates automatically introduce bias into surveys is no longer accepted as being always true (see Hansen and Hurvitz 1946; Curtin, Presser and Singer 2000; Keeter et al. 2000; McCarty 2003). In summarising the available evidence, Martin (2004) made four key points with regard to non-response bias:

(1) Response rates are not a measure of the quality of a survey. Other factors such as the quality of questions used, length of interview, saliency of the survey topic(s) can be equally if not more important in assessing the quality of a survey.
(2) There is no minimum response rate below which a survey is no longer representative or valid. Non-response bias occurs when the factors related to participation in a survey are strongly correlated with the variables being examined. Therefore, non-response bias is not necessarily low when survey response rates are high or vice versa. Unfortunately there is relatively little guidance on which survey topics are most susceptible to non-response bias, and how these change over time and context (Teitler, Reichman and Sprachman 2003).
(3) Response rates do matter because they reduce the validity of making inferences from a sample to a population, lead to underestimates of standard errors and can be a strong source of bias for some variables where it is currently not possible to identify which variables suffer most from this bias (Groves and Couper 1998).
(4) A solid record of prediction in elections does not imply that survey companies can afford to ignore non-response rates. For example, non-response bias and sample bias can offset one another and give the impression that all is fine, however, with changed circumstances these two forms of bias can become a compounded source of error (Keeter et al. 2000).

These four points highlight the importance of understanding the survey response mechanism in order to be able to ascertain the impact that high or low non-response rates can have on opinion poll estimates of public attitudes. As will be seen in Chapter 3, one key feature of contemporary polling in Ireland are 'shy' Fine Gael respondents. Why this group has a higher non-response (or misreporting) rate is not known.

Survey weighting

One last concern related to a survey's representativeness is what to do if the demographic proportions of a poll do not match those of a census. The most common post-surveying method of dealing with this problem, as I noted earlier, is to weight the data, that is assign to each respondent a numerical value greater or less than one (for example, 0.62 or 1.27) so as to yield an aggregate level value that matches the census proportions exactly.

The weighting of survey data can be a complex process. For IMS in the 1970s the procedure took place in two stages. First, there was a weighting for the different response rates among the primary sampling units. Second, a series of weights were used on three key demographic variables: sex, age and region. It is typical in media polls for women to be over-represented and for the young to be under-represented. As noted above, weighting can also be used to adjust for non-response rates.

For quota surveys such as those undertaken by MRBI a weighting procedure is unnecessary if interviewers fill their quotas as stipulated in their instructions, as these instructions ensure that the one thousand people interviewed will match exactly the proportions found in the census. However, almost all Irish opinion polls are based on households, and households vary in size. Therefore the polling data should be weighted to adjust for the unequal size of households, while maintaining the actual number of respondents to reflect the unequal probability of selection. This weighting adjustment is rarely implemented in commercial polls.

Survey design effects

Multistage stratified cluster-based quota sampling is one method of producing national surveys in a cost effective manner with interviewing taking place over one or two days. As noted earlier, respondents are chosen typically from 100 sampling points. These sampling points are effectively 'clusters' of respondents. Statistically speaking selecting an additional respondent from the same sampling point adds less new information than would a completely independent selection. For this reason Irish polls do not have the same variance as a true random sample, meaning that *effective sample size* is reduced (Levy and Lemeshow 1999).[12]

Effective sample size is the actual sample size divided by the *design effect*. The design effect is a factor that reflects the precision of a poll estimate based on the difference between the sample design actually used and a simple random sample. Design effects vary not only across survey companies (sometimes known more generally as *house effects*), but also across questions within the same survey due to *intraclass correlation*.[13] For example, respondents who live near to each other (that is, within the zone covered by a sampling point) are likely to have the same socio-economic characteristics and similar political preferences.[14] In general, design effects increase when the number of sampling points is relatively low and when intraclass correlation is high. In Ireland, the number of sampling points used by pollsters has increased over time (from 50 in the 1970s, to 75 in the early 1990s, to 100 since 1997), implying that the accuracy of recent survey estimates is likely to have improved.

It should be noted that the sampling errors quoted by Irish polling agencies in their reports refer to simple random samples rather than cluster samples.[15] Simple random samples of about 1,000 respondents have an 'accuracy level' of ±3 per cent at the 95 per cent confidence interval level.[16] By taking design effects into consideration a more appropriate estimate for a multistage stratified cluster-based quota sample would be ±4 per cent; that is, the sampling error from a simple random sample multiplied by the square root of two as a reasonable approximation of the design effect of clustering (Levy and Lemeshow 1999).

Survey mode effects

The method used for interviewing respondents or 'mode' of interviewing can take place in a variety of formats, ranging from postal or internet questionnaires where there is indirect contact to direct contact with telephone or in-home interviews. All of the poll results examined in this book were derived from face-to-face interviews.

Face-to-face interviews achieve higher response and completion rates than other modes of interviewing such as telephone, postal or internet. This makes such surveys more representative. However, face-to-face interviewing is more expensive, thereby introducing opportunity costs of frequency of polling, number of questions asked and so on.

In addition, this mode of interviewing suffers most from *social desirability effects*, where respondents do not always give honest answers to questions that are of a sensitive or socially embarrassing nature. Also, face-to-face interviews tend to be more strongly affected by *recency effects*, where information encountered lately has a greater impact on respondents' answers than earlier information (Holbrook, Green and Krosnick 2003).

It is worth keeping in mind that ICM's telephone polls in the 2002 general election and the second Nice Treaty referendum were much more accurate in predicting electoral support than contemporary face-to-face surveys (Lyons 2003: 9–10, 15–16). Such evidence indicates that, in Ireland, survey mode may have non-trivial effects. The success of ICM in 2002 suggests that the widespread use of telephone and internet polling in Ireland is increasingly likely as response rates decline and face-to-face surveying costs increase.[17]

Media Reporting of Opinion Poll Results

The surveying company generally decides the design and structure of opinion polls published in Irish newspapers. However, it is the newspaper that decides the content of the questions (Jones 2001: 19). When the results are reported in the newspaper, not only are the sampling procedures outlined along with the date of interviewing, but readers also see the exact wording of each question along with response options. This is in line with the European Society for Opinion and Marketing Research (ESOMAR) guidelines for the publication of poll results.

It is very rare to find information provided in newspaper articles (or the more extensive survey reports on which they are based) about survey non-response. In this respect, there is an unknown and unreported limitation in the representativeness of the survey being reported. This is characteristic of media-based polling at the international level. One of the main reasons for this situation is that media organisations rarely ask for such information. Because of the tight deadlines for media commissioned polls; polling companies themselves will often not have this information to hand. Perhaps for this practical reason, professional polling organisations such as the American Association for Public Opinion Research (AAPOR) and ESOMAR have no set policy on the publication of this information.

Opinion polling agencies make an important distinction between 'political opinion polls' and 'political surveys'. Political opinion polls are typically supplied to the media. Most often the basic poll results are published with 'limited factual commentary' written by a staff journalist. Within the *Irish Times*/MRBI poll series, Jack Jones and successive chairmen of MRBI have regularly written professional interpretations of the poll results outlining inferences that may be legitimately derived from what respondents had said in a poll interview. In contrast, political surveys are confidential strategic research projects undertaken for political parties or the Government (Jones 2001: 212–3). One can differentiate between political opinion polls and political surveys on the basis of two criteria. The former are geared towards demonstrating *what* public opinion is on an issue. In contrast, the latter are designed to reveal not only what public opinion is, but also *why* it exhibits a particular pattern. The purpose here is both to inform and to outline 'remedial action' to achieve a desired goal such as winning an election. Consequently, the reporting of political opinion polls in the print media is primarily conceptualised as a service to both the newspaper and to readers, where polls are presented as neutral mirrors of public opinion. This fits with the journalistic ethic of unbiased reporting and presentation of the facts.

An important aspect of the reporting of poll results is a statement of the sampling error, or what is also known as the 'margin of error' in the United States, or 'accuracy level' in Ireland. Typically, IMS/Lansdowne and MRBI make a statement such as the following 'the accuracy level [of this poll] is estimated to be approximately plus or minus 3%'. There is generally no other information given to the public in newspaper articles as to how poll results should be interpreted with regard to the 'accuracy level'. Therefore, it is quite likely that relatively few of those who read poll results in Irish newspapers have a good understanding of what the 'accuracy level' warning actually means in practice. For the record, the correct interpretation of the margin of error is that if 'repeated samples of one thousand people were taken approximately 95% of the time the sample proportions would lie within 3 percentage points of the true population proportion' (Thornton and Thornton 2004: 131; Traugott and Lavrakas 2000: 59–60, 160).

Conclusion

At the start of this chapter it was argued that what public opinion polls tell us about 'public opinion' may be reduced to two questions: first, what types of 'opinion' are investigated in opinion polls? And second, what members of the 'public' are interviewed?

With regard to the first question, we have found in examining the profile of Irish opinion polls that IMS/Lansdowne have asked the largest number of questions and that these two polling agencies have implemented most survey items on politics, Northern Ireland, the EU and external affairs. In contrast, MRBI has asked most questions on society and institutions and the economy. This comparison implies that IMS and MRBI offer somewhat different mirrors on Irish society and illuminate different aspects of public opinion.

Turning to our second question, the evidence presented shows that opinion polling is not simply a matter of going out and asking the public a series of questions, recording the answers given and tabulating the results. Opinion polls as measuring instruments depend fundamentally on appropriate sampling procedures and on questionnaire design – a topic that will be addressed in the next chapter. The sampling methodology used within Irish opinion polls is one that is consonant with the professional code of practice espoused by ESOMAR. There has been some discussion of the sampling methodology used by Irish pollsters following problems associated with election predictions in the 1997 and 2002 general elections. While some remarks will be made later on this issue in Chapter 3, this book will assume that the polling data examined derives from representative national samples.

More generally, the manner in which opinion poll results are presented in the media demonstrates that the poll reports used throughout this book were primarily constructed to be mirrors of public opinion. However, because of space constraints within the daily media agenda much of the richness of polls and their potential to illuminate many more details of Irish public opinion is rarely utilised. One of the goals of this book is to assess and exploit this potential. Before pursuing this objective there is still an important task to accomplish, and that is to critically evaluate the questionnaire design used in Irish opinion polls. While this chapter has shown how opinion polls reflect the views of the Irish public through the use of sampling procedures, this is of course no guarantee that the responses derived from a representative sample match in any meaningful way what the public is thinking. In Chapter 2 our focus will switch to what happens during an opinion poll interview and what this tells us about the ability of opinion polls to measure public opinion.

Notes

1 Many of these polls are available from the Irish Opinion Polls Archive (IOPA) located at www.tcd.ie/Political_Science/cgi/. This archive contains 217 polls (i.e. 134 IMS and 83 MRBI polls) reporting the results of interviews undertaken between 1970 and 1998. Within this book data (mainly related to vote intention and satisfaction ratings) an additional 125 polls have also been consulted from scattered sources.
2 The most influential study of seasonality in surveying by Vigderhous (1981: 257) found that completion rates were highest in January to March, while April, June, July, August and December had lower rates. Later research by Steeh et al. (2001) and Losch et al. (2002) has found that seasonality does not seriously affect survey data collection, and most likely plays a relatively minor role in dealing with increased non-response rates.
3 In general, pollsters work exclusively with a single (media) newspaper company. Initially, IMS/Lansdowne worked with *The Irish Times* and MRBI with Independent Newspapers. However, in October 1982 IMS and MRBI 'switched' clients and this is the pattern that persists to this day.
4 Stratified random sampling assumes that measurements within the strata, being homogenous with differing stratum means, have a smaller variance than if simple random sampling was used for the whole population with the same sample size.
5 In order to ensure that each interview is a standard one, all interviewers are given training and specific instructions regarding particular questionnaires. Quality control checks are also used where in the case of IMS interviewer supervisors re-contact 20% of the respondents interviewed to ensure they have been contacted and to elicit any problems with the interview from the respondent's perspective. In 2004–5, IMS had a team of 350 field interviewers, while MRBI had somewhat fewer field staff (120).
6 These demographic data on which the quotas are based on estimates derived from the Quarterly National Household Survey (QNHS) undertaken by the CSO on national samples of about 39,000. The data for occupation that is used to construct a measure of social class is derived from the Joint National Readership Research (JNRR) biannual surveys undertaken by Lansdowne Market Research. Irish polls' definition of social class is unique to the marketing industry.
7 A similar event took place in Britain during the 1992 general election, where most pollsters using 'tried and tested' quota sampling procedures predicted incorrectly that Labour would win the election. Thereafter, quota sampling was abandoned by most polling companies, with the notable exception of MORI.
8 In examining the American National Election Surveys (ANES) and General Social Surveys (GSS), Brehm (1993) found that these academic surveys tend to over-represent the elderly, African–Americans, women, the poor and the less well-educated.
9 For details see Steeh (1981), Bradburn (1992: 392), Smith (1995, 2005), Steeh et al. (2001) and de Leeuw and de Heer (2002).
10 Research by Holbrook, Krosnick and Pfent (2007) comparing news media surveys and

federal government-sponsored surveys found that the lower response rates in media based surveys did not lead to significantly less accurate representative polls.

11 The Irish National Election Study (INES) of 2002 used a raffle system where respondents had the opportunity through participation in the hour-long survey to win a number of cash prizes (€500, €1,000, etc.).

12 For constituency polls this becomes an even greater problem because the clustering effect increases within smaller geographical areas (see McElroy and Marsh 2003).

13 Intraclass correlation is the likelihood that two respondents in the sample cluster have the same value for a given variable, relative to two respondents chosen completely at random from the entire population. With geographically determined sampling points (or clusters) intraclass correlation tends to be low on demographic variables but higher for socio-economic and attitudinal variables (Kalton 1977).

14 For evidence of clustering effects within the Irish context, see Fahey and Williams (2000: 234); McElroy and Marsh (2003: 171).

15 An example illustrates the importance of design effect. With a national three-strata cluster sample of 5,546 households with 20 sampling points, poll estimates have a confidence interval (CI) of +/– 13.2%. For 60 sampling points the CI falls to +/– 7.2% while with a simple random sample the CI is +/– 4.2%. See www.cpc.unc.edu/projects/rlms/project/eval_sample.html.

16 This means that with repeated sampling there is only a one-in-twenty chance that the survey estimate is more than plus or minus 3 per cent away from the true population mean value.

17 In 2004, an Irish polling company, Red C, produced three national telephone polls for the *Sunday Post*, illustrating increasing use of telephone polls which are said to be more accurate, faster and more cost effective. For an interesting explanation and justification of telephone polling from the managing director of REDC, see Colwell (2004: 12).

Chapter 2

Public Opinion Measurement and Questionnaire Design

> Despite their importance for understanding and evaluating surveys, the study of the survey response process is in its infancy, having only begun in earnest in the 1980s.
>
> Tourangeau, Rips and Rasinski (2000: 2)

For opinion polls to be a mirror on society or a lamp that illuminates facets of public preferences, there must be an object to reflect or illuminate. A fundamental, and rarely discussed, assumption behind opinion polling is that opinions can be measured.[1] However, for something to be measured it must exist. The building blocks of public opinion research are typically denoted as opinions, attitudes, beliefs and values.[2] In an ideal world respondents would always tell the truth as they see it and opinion poll questions would in a transparent and neutral scientific manner validly and reliably measure respondent's opinions. In short this (ideal) model of the opinion polling process contends that what opinion polls measure may be equated with public opinion (note Converse 1987: S14).

Consequently, in opinion poll reports it would be a simple matter of presenting results in a tabular or graphical format. Moreover, charting opinion movements over time would be a straightforward process of comparing questions on the same issue and charting the evolution in response patterns. In Chapter 1 the importance of ensuring that an opinion poll has an accurate representative sample of the population was stressed. However, this is a necessary though insufficient condition for measuring public opinion.

In this chapter, I will focus on the interviewing process and questionnaire design and demonstrate how both of these considerations determine the quality of an opinion poll. This chapter also forms a bridge between Chapters 1 and 3 in revealing how accurate sampling of respondents is no guarantee of polling accuracy or precision. A central theme examined in this chapter is that respondents may not have real opinions on an issue and may simply make up an answer on the spot.

Moreover, even if respondents have real informed opinions they can only respond to the question asked. Consequently, if the question is 'faulty' (for example, if it is open to more than one interpretation) the resulting opinion poll data will also be faulty or biased. In addition, opinion poll questions differ in a qualitative sense, where some questions are 'hard', requiring lots of information and consideration, and some are 'easy' as they stem from standing predispositions.

Many of the insights outlined in this chapter are theoretical and methodological in nature, but nonetheless have fundamental implications for our assessment of what opinion polls can tell us about public opinion. As we shall see, many of the ideas outlined in this chapter will surface again, most especially in the substantive Chapters five to eight. This chapter will start by outlining two theoretical models of survey response, which it is argued provides an invaluable insight into the nature of opinion poll data. The second section will provide an example of the response process and reveal the complex nature of opinion measurement. The following section, which forms the heart of this chapter, will examine questionnaire design and implementation issues using six different criteria. In the final section there will be some concluding comments.

Two Influential Theories of Survey Response

In Chapter 1, I noted that pollsters and many consumers of poll reports typically see opinion polls as 'mirrors' of public opinion. For simplicity, I will denote this perspective as the *Mirror Theory of Opinion Polling*. Such a perspective is based on the view that when a respondent answers an opinion poll question they simply recall a 'ready-made' answer. On this basis poll questions are true measurements in that they measure opinions on topics on which respondents have opinions. One important implication from such a theory of how respondents answer poll questions is that all citizens (that is, potential poll respondents) have constructed answers in advance to any questions a pollster might wish to ask.

The Mirror Theory of Opinion Polling and subsequent revisions

This Mirror Theory of Opinion Polling was seen from the 1930s to have two main problems. First, small changes in the wording or response options in poll questions may influence how interviewees respond (Schuman and Presser 1981). Second, if the same people are asked the same poll questions on two successive occasions, for example in a panel survey, there is often considerable inconsistency in the answers given (Converse 1964, 1970). These two phenomena, known as 'response effects' and 'response instability' respectively, led to two modifications of the basic Mirror Theory of Opinion Polling.

The first modification, called the *Non-Attitude Model*, argued that the Mirror Theory of Opinion Polling worked only for a subsection of the public who had real opinions. For this group opinions were measured in an opinion poll like a mirror without error. The remaining group effectively answer poll questions in an idiosyncratic manner whose overall response pattern gives the appearance of random answering. At an individual level, treating the public as being 'all the same' leads to a distorted picture of public opinion. In essence the relationship between public opinion and poll results was seen for those with real opinions to be:

$$\text{Public opinion} = \text{Opinion poll measurement} \qquad (1)$$

For those without real opinions, the argument in defence of polling, was that opinion polls could not be expected to measure accurately something that did not exist (although respondents felt compelled in interview situations to provide some sort of response other than 'don't know').

The second revision of the Mirror Theory of Opinion Polling, called the *Measurement Error Model*, contended that all poll estimates of public opinion included an irreducible amount of 'measurement error' inherent in all poll questions.[3] In effect, the error in polls was not caused by the public who kindly and patiently answered the questions posed in survey interviews, but by the questions themselves due to faulty design (Achen 1975). The basic logic of the Measurement Error Model may be represented by equation 2:

$$\text{Public opinion} = \text{Opinion poll measurement} + \text{Error} \qquad (2)$$

As the error term was seen to be essentially random (technically the error for each individual is independent and normally distributed), public opinion poll estimates are assumed to deviate from true public opinion by a random amount where, theoretically speaking, estimates would be either too high or too low on roughly half of the occasions on which the poll question was used (assuming that it was not a perfectly-designed question that produced no error).

Despite these modifications resting on very different assumptions, the Non-Attitude and Measurement Error Models still none the less support the basic intuition lying behind the Mirror Theory of Opinion Polling. However, research during the 1980s showed that some of the key implications of both of these modifications of the Mirror Theory of Opinion Polling did not fit with the polling results being analysed. For example, let us focus on the problem of response inconsistency. Research has demonstrated that the Non-Attitudes Model prediction that response instability depends on the salience of an issue is not always the case. Furthermore, the Measurement Error Model's contention that response instability should be independent of respondent characteristics was also found to be incorrect. The respondent's level of knowledge can be an important factor (Feldman 1989; Zaller 1990, 1992).

The Belief-Sampling Model of survey response

Such evidence prompted a move away from the Mirror Theory of Opinion Polling where citizens are seen implausibly to have 'real opinions' on all subjects on which a pollster might conceivably ask questions (Wilson and Hodges 1992). One of the most influential new theories of opinion poll response is the *Belief-Sampling Model*.[4] Here, citizens are no longer seen as 'filing cabinets' from which pollsters pull information. All respondents do not answer opinion poll questions in the same way. This is not simply because some citizens are more informed than others, but stems primarily from different processes by which information is used as a basis for providing an answer.

This perspective has two important implications that differentiate it from the Mirror Theory of Opinion Polling (and its two variants). First, citizens do not answer poll questions by recalling 'pre-cooked' opinions. Instead opinions are conceived to be 'distributions of considerations' – that is, a set of information that may be used to answer a particular question. Second, the information set used to answer a poll question is not fixed and will vary systematically across differing interview situations. In effect, the Belief-Sampling Model of public opinion may be represented as:

$$\text{Public opinion} = \text{Opinion poll measurement} + \text{Bias} + \text{Error} \quad (3)$$

According to the model of survey response given in equation 3, different kinds of poll interview situations will *bias* the type and content of information used by a respondent to answer a question (Zaller 1992; Feldman 1995; Tourangeau, Rips and Rasinski 2000: 178–9). As a result, opinion polls can never act as true mirrors of public opinion because poll responses are inherently unstable, as they are based on a sample of relevant information and considerations. In addition, the design of 'better questions' will not remove this variability in responses. Different situations bias the sampling of considerations used to answer poll questions, leading to response effects and opinion instability. Zaller (1992: 35) argues that in this respect opinion polls are best thought of as measuring 'opinion statements' rather than 'public opinion.'

If the Belief-Sampling Model is a more realistic explanation of the response process than the Mirror Theory of Opinion Polling, are we to conclude that the public has very few fixed opinions on any matter and that opinion polls cannot effectively mirror something that is inherently fuzzy? One important insight in providing an answer to this question is to understand that what we think opinion polls can tell us about public opinion depends fundamentally on how one conceptualises public opinion. Over 50 years of polling has revealed one simple truth: very few citizens have fixed opinions or high levels of knowledge on public affairs.[5]

In short, as Lippmann (1922) cogently argued in a pre-polling era, the democratic state where the public have stable and reasoned views on a wide range of public issues does not exist. Moving away from this naive and constricted view of public opinion fundamentally changes our conceptualisation of opinion polls and how one views citizens. What the Belief-Sampling Model highlights are unrivalled opportunities for using opinion polls to illuminate the nature of public opinion itself through a deeper understanding of how citizens provide answers to poll questions.

Implications of the Belief-Sampling Model for understanding poll questions

The key point here is that factors that were once thought of as 'problems' within opinion polls now appear to be central features of public opinion. If public opinions are not fixed, one may argue that different kinds of opinion poll questions can simulate the responses likely in different kinds of public debates (see Kinder and Sanders 1990). I briefly discussed in the introductory chapter, with regard to a key puzzle in Irish public opinion, the idea of *hard* and *easy* facets of an issue with the example of attitudes toward Northern Ireland (see Figure 3). I will demonstrate in a number of later chapters how hard and easy poll questions reflecting different facets of an issue elicit very different response patterns (Carmines and Stimson 1980).

In essence, different kinds of questions lead to *framing effects*, where the types of questions asked and the topics discussed do not tell the public what to think but do influence what the public think about. By comparing responses to different types of questions we have the opportunity to examine not only how opinions are created, but also the effectiveness of opinion polls. In summary, the existence and importance of hard and easy facets of a single issue – and hence hard and easy poll questions referring to these two facets – suggest that the Belief-Sampling Model is a more realistic theory of how respondents answer survey questions.

So far I have outlined two of the most influential theories of survey response, namely the Mirror Theory of Opinion Polling and the Belief-Sampling Model, and the merits of the latter conceptualisation for studying public opinion. I will now attempt to demonstrate some of the practical advantages of using the Belief-Sampling Model as a means of evaluating opinion poll responses in the Irish context. Here, use will be made of opinion poll data on the abortion issue. The abortion issue is a useful case study because it seems reasonable to think that few people are likely to give 'top of the head' answers to poll questions on this emotive issue. For this reason, it represents a difficult test for the Belief-Sampling Model.

Belief-Sampling Model and the Abortion Issue

One of the most salient and divisive issues within public opinion in Ireland is abortion. This issue has been the subject of five referendums (in 1983, three separate proposals in 1992, and most recently in 2002) and a considerable amount of opinion polling. Moreover, the responses given to opinion poll questions provide one of the few sources of information on why respondents supported amending the Constitution in 1983 so as to give a mother and her unborn child equal rights. The anti-abortion proponents of this amendment believed it would prohibit any abortion legislation being introduced in the Republic of Ireland by the legislature or judiciary, as had occurred in Britain (1967) and the USA (1973) respectively.[6]

At first sight the abortion issue would seem to be a straightforward one, as most citizens would be expected to have some opinion on this controversial issue. However, referendum campaigns have shown that making amendments to the Constitution is a complex matter as sometimes it is not clear how these amendments will be interpreted by the Courts. For example, in 1992 the Irish Supreme Court in the X case stated that abortion is legal in Ireland for specific health-related reasons, and this is the current legal situation. However, for many the Irish electorate's support of a constitutional amendment giving equal rights to the life of a pregnant mother and her unborn child in 1983 amounted to a legal ban on abortion. This was the view taken by the Attorney-General and the High Court in the X case. However, the Supreme Court subsequently ruled that the Irish electorate in 1983 did not vote for a complete ban on abortion.[7]

During the 1992 referendum on abortion, voters were asked to make abortion illegal in Ireland except where abortion was necessary to 'save the life, as distinct from the health of the mother'. While this distinction between the 'life' and 'health' of the mother might seem like legal casuistry it ensued from the fact that the X case allowed abortion in Ireland on the grounds of threatened suicide by the mother. For many pro-life (conservative) groups this amounted to a liberal abortion regime, as they argued that the grounds of suicide effectively made abortion available to anyone who sought it.

MRBI found 'considerable confusion' among the Irish electorate during the abortion referendum campaign of late 1992 (Jones 2001: 135–6). A quarter of those interviewed admitted to being confused; a further third expressed opinions towards the availability of abortion that did not match with their vote intentions in the referendum. In fact, as Table 1 shows, fewer than half of those interviewed (44 per cent) had what could be called consistent opinions.

Jones (2001: 137) interpreted such results in his expert commentary in *The Irish Times* as evidence of an 'information deficit' among

Table 1 *Cross-Tabulation of Attitudes towards the Availability of Abortion in Ireland and Vote Intention in the Abortion Referendum of November 1992, (per cent)*

		Attitude to the availability of abortion in Ireland					
Vote intention in the 1992 abortion referendum on the 'substantive' issue		Should be available to everybody	Available on threat to physical life of the mother	Available on threat to physical life and suicide	Never in any circumstances	No opinion	Total
	Will vote 'yes': favour limited abortion	10[C]	21[B]	11[C]	5[C]	1[A]	48
	Will vote 'no': retain 1983 ban on abortion	6[B]	6[C]	6[C]	11[B]	1[A]	30
	Don't know/ no opinion	3[A]	6[A]	4[A]	4[A]	5[A]	22
	Total	19	33	21	20	7	100

Source: Jones (2001: 136-7, tables 9.3 and 9.4). Note letter superscripts refer to a categorisation of public opinion on the basis of a cross-tabulation of the answers to these two poll questions:

[A] Segment of public opinion that had no fixed opinion (24 per cent)
[B] Segment of public opinion whose vote intentions were consistent with their attitudes toward abortion (44 per cent)
[C] Segment of public opinion whose attitude toward abortion was mismatched with the vote intention in the referendum (32 per cent)

Which of the phrases on this card comes nearest to your own opinions about the availability of abortion in Ireland?

ROTATE OPTIONS: (a) Should be available for anyone who wants it; (b) Should be available if a threat to the life of the mother; (c) Should be available if a threat to the life of the mother including suicide; (d) Never in any circumstances. MRBI/4090/92, 9 November 1992, *The Irish Times*, question 14.

The wording on the Ballot Paper on the Right to Life/Abortion issue will be – SHOW CARD – It shall be unlawful to terminate the life of an unborn unless such termination is necessary to save the life, as distinct from the health, of the mother where there is an illness or disorder of the mother giving rise to a real and substantial risk to her life, not being a risk of self-destruction. Will you vote 'yes' to put the amendment in the Constitution, or 'no' not to put it in? MRBI/4090/92, 9 November 1992, *Irish Times*, question 15.

the electorate. In short, he argued that opinion inconsistency was greatest among those who were unable to express their 'true opinions' because they did not fully understand the constitutional amendment. Such an interpretation fits in with the Mirror Theory of Opinion

Polling and the assumption that all members of the Irish public had an opinion about abortion, but could not match it coherently with vote intentions as political leaders had not explained the referendum proposal in an effective manner. Is this true? Do Irish citizens have strong opinions on abortion that are related to level of political knowledge? The Belief-Sampling Model would lead us to think that the situation is not that simple.

A similar referendum occurred again in March 2002, when voters were asked to remove suicide as grounds for abortion.[8] Fortunately, the Irish Social and Political Attitudes Survey (ISPAS) undertaken during the winter of 2001/2 investigated attitudes toward liberalisation of abortion in Ireland. The advantage of this survey is that it examined vote intentions on the relatively straightforward issue of 'strengthening the ban on abortion' or opposing such a move. In addition, ISPAS examined the acceptability, using a four-point scale, of four different scenarios when abortion might be allowed under law. These scenarios, briefly described in Table 2, ranged from a restricted to a less restrictive abortion regime. In March 2002, the Irish electorate voted in a referendum on scenario 1 and this proposal was rejected.

The primary merit of using the ISPAS survey is that it allows us to see whether vote intentions in an abortion referendum were consonant with attitudes toward abortion, and additionally whether such consonance was influenced by level of political information. The Mirror Theory of Opinion Polling would lead us to expect that vote intentions should match opinions towards abortion, with more liberal regimes being most unacceptable for those who supported a ban on abortion. Furthermore, those who are more informed should exhibit higher levels of consistency between their vote intentions and opinions. In contrast, the Belief-Sampling Model would argue that the link between opinions on abortion and vote intentions is not likely to be so simple because respondents, regardless of level of informedness, may not have single opinions on abortion. As a result, the four different scenarios outlined in ISPAS may not have been seen by respondents as representing a steady progression from conservative to liberal options.

As ISPAS was fielded before the referendum campaign, the opinions expressed would have reflected the predispositions or values of respondents rather than the short-term effects of a campaign. In addition, ISPAS has a measure of level of political knowledge, allowing us to examine whether this factor is important in explaining

Table 2 *Comparison of Attitudes toward the Availability of Abortion in Ireland and Vote Intention in a Future Abortion Referendum by Level of Political Information, Winter 2001/2 (per cent)*

Scenario 1: Abortion to save a woman's life *excluding the risk of suicide*				Scenario 2: Abortion to save a woman's life *including the risk of suicide*			
Low information	Acceptable	Unacceptable	Total	**Low information**	Acceptable	Unacceptable	Total
Favour abortion ban	24	18	42	Favour abortion ban	13	27	40
Against abortion ban	24	34	58	Against abortion ban	23	37	60
Total	48	52	100	Total	36	64	100
Phi=0.170, p=0.003				Phi= -0.045, p=0.429			
Medium information	Acceptable	Unacceptable	Total	**Medium information**	Acceptable	Unacceptable	Total
Favour abortion ban	30	23	53	Favour abortion ban	18	35	53
Against abortion ban	21	26	47	Against abortion ban	16	31	47
Total	51	49	100	Total	34	66	100
Phi=0.123, p=0.003				Phi= -0.001, p=0.981			
High information	Acceptable	Unacceptable	Total	**High information**	Acceptable	Unacceptable	Total
Favour abortion ban	39	19	58	Favour abortion ban	22	35	57
Against abortion ban	14	29	43	Against abortion ban	14	29	43
Total	53	48	100	Total	36	64	100
Phi=0.346, p<0.001				Phi=0.072, p=0.210			

Cont.

Scenario 3: Abortion to save a woman's life including the risk of suicide or pregnancy resulting from rape or incest				Scenario 4: Abortion to save a woman's life including the risk of suicide OR pregnancy resulting from rape or incest OR to protect the woman's physical or mental health			
Low information	Acceptable	Unacceptable	Total	Low information	Acceptable	Unacceptable	Total
Favour abortion ban	23	17	40	Favour abortion ban	25	16	41
Against abortion ban	47	13	60	Against abortion ban	44	15	59
Total	70	30	100	Total	69	31	100
Phi= -0.207, p=<0.001				Phi= -0.143, p=0.013			
Medium information	Acceptable	Unacceptable	Total	Medium information	Acceptable	Unacceptable	Total
Favour abortion ban	29	24	53	Favour abortion ban	28	25	53
Against abortion ban	33	24	47	Against abortion ban	35	12	47
Total	62	38	100	Total	63	37	100
Phi= -0.165, p=<0.001				Phi= -0.222, p=<0.001			
High information	Acceptable	Unacceptable	Total	High information	Acceptable	Unacceptable	Total
Favour abortion ban	26	31	57	Favour abortion ban	23	33	56
Against abortion ban	34	9	43	Against abortion ban	33	10	43
Total	60	40	100	Total	56	43	100
Phi= -0.337, p=<0.001				Phi= -0.349, p=<0.001			

Source: ISPAS, questions A17, F39 and Q15. Vote intention was a 7-point scale (1 = definitely vote in favour of strengthening the ban on abortion; 7=definitely vote against strengthening the ban on abortion) where points 1 and 2 were coded as 'favour abortion ban' and 6 and 7 were coded as 'against abortion ban'. Circumstances for an abortion were rated on a 4-point scale (1 = most acceptable; 4 = least acceptable) where points 1 and 2 were coded as 'acceptable' and 3 and 4 as 'unacceptable'. Level of information is based on the number of correct answers given in a simple political knowledge quiz where those interviewed were asked to identify five political leaders. Respondents who answered four or five correctly were coded as 'high information', two or three correctly 'medium information' and one or none correctly 'low information.'

Scenarios 1 to 4 represent a progression from limited abortion (as proposed by the Irish government in the March 2002 referendum) to progressively more liberal grounds for abortion. Phi is a measure of association for variables at the nominal level of measurement where –1 is a perfectly negative association, 0 indicates no association and +1 a perfectly positive association.

differences in opinion consistency within the Irish public. As noted earlier, pollsters such as Jack Jones (2001: 137) have argued that consistency between vote intentions in abortion referendums and preferred legal framework governing the provision of abortion were strongly conditioned by level of informedness.

Our expectation is that those who favoured strengthening the ban on abortion would have found the most limited circumstances for abortion the 'most acceptable'. Table 2 reveals that this is not true for those with the lowest level of political knowledge and is in fact only true for those with high information. However, the expectation that those against strengthening the ban on abortion would express increasing support for a more liberal abortion regime is also not true. The implication here is that many respondents only favoured abortion under limited circumstances. For those who supported an abortion ban, differences in the level of political knowledge were important as those with high levels of information found scenario 1 the least unacceptable (19 per cent) of all the scenarios outlined. For the low-information segment the most liberal abortion scenario (4) was not any more unacceptable than the least liberal scenario (1). Such invariance suggests that this group was against abortion regardless of the circumstances.

For each abortion regime scenario in Table 2, measures of association for each level of information have been calculated to see how well vote intentions in a future abortion referendum tallied with opinions towards abortion. Where vote intentions and expressed opinions are consonant the measure of association (Phi) should be positive and statistically significant ($p \leq 0.05$). This is the case for all levels of information in scenario 1. In contrast, if vote intentions and attitudes towards abortion are logically mismatched (for example, intend to vote for an abortion ban and yet express opinions that favour allowing abortion) the measure of association should be negative and statistically significant, as revealed in scenarios 3 and 4. Finally, if there is little association between vote intentions and opinions toward abortion the coefficient of association will not be statistically significant – a pattern evident for all levels of information in scenario 2 of Table 2.

For those against the abortion ban, scenarios 1 and 2 drew the highest levels of support among the low and highly informed implying, once again, that for many a liberal abortion law was not desired. Significantly, scenario 2 that relates directly to the Supreme Court judgment in the X case had a powerful impact on the opinions expressed for all information groups. It was the most unacceptable scenario for all information levels, although it was not the most liberal of circumstances proposed for abortion. Moreover, the measures of association (Phi) between vote intentions in an abortion referendum and opinions toward abortion for scenario 2 are the only ones to show no standard level of statistical significance.

All of this evidence demonstrates the framing effects of the issues raised in the X case and the 1992 abortion referendum. For scenario 2, respondents were drawing on very specific considerations that led those against abortion to find this option to be the most unacceptable. Such a stance appears at first sight to be illogical. However, this pattern does make sense within the Belief-Sampling Model, because the considerations relating to the X case and the legacy of the 1992 abortion referendum would have framed the abortion issue in a particular way for many (older) respondents.

The data presented in Table 2 also suggest that many less politically-informed citizens had not considered scenarios 3 and 4 as grounds for abortion. Consequently, the observed information effects were greatest in the response patterns revealed in scenario 1. Here the measures of association (Phi) are all positive, significant and increase in value with higher levels of political information. Furthermore, the negative coefficient of association for scenarios 3 and 4 for all information levels indicates that there is a mismatch between vote intention in a future abortion referendum and attitude towards abortion. However, the Belief-Sampling Model warns us to be mindful that scenarios 3 and 4 included the emotionally powerful terms of 'rape' and 'incest'. Not surprisingly, any discussion of abortion including these terms is likely to have involved different considerations from scenarios 1 and 2.[9] The differential data patterns and associations evident in Table 2 demonstrate that this is most likely the case.

The purpose of this section has been to illustrate poll response effects and the role that level of political knowledge and different considerations can play in the answers chosen by respondents. While the Non-Attitude Model (one variant of the mirror theory of opinion polling) contends that real opinions are more prevalent among the highly informed, I have demonstrated from a simple analysis shown in Table 2 that this is not the whole story. Even the most knowledgeable segments of public opinion do not always give coherent responses. Overall, this evidence fits most closely with the insights offered by the Belief-Sampling Model of survey response.

Belief-Sampling Model and Types of Opinion Poll Questions

The Belief-Sampling Model of survey response predicts that in different interview contexts respondents will interpret the questions asked by an interviewer differently. Reversing this logic, Kinder and Sanders (1990) have argued that different types of questions on the same issue can have similar effects on observed survey responses as those associated with contextual changes. This is because by asking a specific sort of question respondents are primed in line with the logic of the Belief-Sampling Model to use particular considerations in providing an answer.[10]

However, by changing the wording or format of a poll question on the same issue very different considerations may be used in formulating an answer. Consequently, one may say that different survey questions relating to a single issue illuminate different facets of this issue. Carmines and Stimson (1980) applied a similar type of logic in their study of issue voting when they put forward the idea that there are broadly two main types of issues – 'hard' and 'easy' issues.

Stemming from this work the intuition being developed here is that not all opinion poll questions on a *specific issue* are of the same type. Therefore, it is reasonable to expect that in a database of poll questions there will be subsets of survey items that measure different facets of public opinion on a specific topic such as abortion. Moreover, it is important to identify these facets and to construct separate poll trends in order to ensure valid inferences. Following the broad logic outlined by Carmines and Stimson, the argument presented in this book will assume that poll questions on a topic can be broadly divided into 'hard' and 'easy' ones. Such a strategy raises the problem of how it is possible to differentiate between hard and easy questions.

In this book poll questions that refer to a hard facet of an issue outline the means by which a specific policy will be implemented and require knowledge and careful thought to be answered. In contrast, questions that refer to easy facets of an issue relate either to policy goals or symbolic considerations that often have a long history and refer typically to unresolved conflicts. Undoubtedly, this categorisation of opinion polls as being either 'hard' or 'easy' is an over-simplification of reality. For this reason, it is better to think of survey items as exhibiting different degrees of 'hardness' rather than seeing them as being either ' hard' or 'easy'. Nevertheless, in order to provide a consistent basis for the use of the 'hard/easy question' concept it is appropriate at this point to provide a definition.

Definition of hard and easy poll questions

The theory developed by Carmines and Stimson (1980: 82) contends that differential responses to an issue question will be conditioned by a key variable. For issue voting this key variable was seen to be the level of political information possessed by a respondent. As we are dealing in this book primarily with different opinions on the *same issue*, the impact of respondent's level of political knowledge is not likely to be always important. Empirical analyses of the Northern Ireland, abortion and EU issues show this to be the case. Such a finding makes sense if one accepts that issues *in toto* are either important to the public, or they are not.

However, the insight of Carmines and Stimson's theory that opinion differences should be conditional on a key variable remains valid. In Chapters 5 and 7 the case will be made that the impact of age as a conditioning variable is fundamentally important in understanding public opinion relating to the liberal agenda and Northern Ireland respectively. In these chapters, the age variable will be used as an indicator of differential socialisation.

However, in elaborating a more precise definition of Carmines and Stimson's concept of hard and easy issues and to use these concepts to categorise opinion poll questions it is necessary to take account of four additional criteria that relate directly to the nature of the opinion poll questions asked. First and foremost consideration must be made of the *content* of the questions. Hard questions refer to the policies or means used to achieve a desired goal. Easy poll items refer to policy goals that have a long history or relate to widely supported symbolic considerations (Carmines and Stimson 1980: 80; Pollock, Lilie and Vittes 1993: 30–1).

Second, consideration of the *format* of the poll questions implemented is also crucial. Items that simply ask a respondent to agree or disagree with a single goal or policy are much easier to answer than items that involve the respondent making a choice between two or more desired policies to achieve a specific objective (see Chapter 6). Typical examples of hard questions include:

- Questions that ask about preferences for increased government spending in conjunction with possible consequences such as increased taxation (see Chapter 7)
- Survey items that force respondents to choose between two desirable goals such as protecting Irish independence or supporting efforts to unite fully with the EU (see Chapter 8)

Third, items in a poll that involve considering policy options also prompt respondents into considering the possible *consequences* of different courses of action. Typical examples in Ireland are responses to constitutional amendment questions asked in polls during referendum campaigns (see Chapter 5).

Finally, the *context* under which polling takes place is important because the considerations used by respondents to answer questions during referendum campaigns is likely to be different when an issue is not the subject of intense partisan and media debate. In effect, the timing of poll questions will influence the degree to which respondents will consider the consequences of expressing a specific opinion (see Chapter 5). Moreover, as the political context changes over time the considerations used by respondents to answer such trend questions will change as the meaning of the poll item evolves. This implies that poll items that were once easy questions can become hard ones, or vice versa. This process is best shown with an example. Desiring a united Ireland in 1970 at the start of the 'Troubles' was something quite different to expressing a preference for a united Ireland during the Belfast/Good Friday Agreement campaign in 1998 (see Chapter 6).

In summary, these four criteria – that is, poll question content, format, policy consequences, and context of polling – determine whether respondents are asked hard or easy questions. This definition of the hard and easy distinction in poll items provides a more precise operationalisation of Carmines and Stimson's (1980) key insight that survey questions that examine hard issues require much more mental effort for respondents to answer than easy ones remains intact. Here I also incorporate a central aspect of the Belief-Sampling Model of survey response, which is that the considerations used by respondents to answer poll questions vary systematically across contexts and over time. In the next section I will move beyond definitional issues and demonstrate how the theoretical considerations of the Belief-Sampling Model inform our understanding of the methodological problems of questionnaire design and implementation.

Questionnaire Design and Implementation

The Belief-Sampling Model of survey response conceptualises most respondents as having only a passing interest in politics and public affairs. Consequently, when relatively uninterested citizens are confronted in an interview situation with questions on issues that they only consider occasionally this has important consequences for how they are likely to react to specific types of questions. Lacking any firm opinions on an issue, respondents will use whatever information first comes to mind when answering many opinion poll items. This implies that questionnaire design and implementation is a crucial element in the opinion polling process.

Consequently, salient features within the construction of the questionnaire and the interview itself are likely to have important effects. In this section I will demonstrate that many of the well-known questionnaire design effects are not isolated phenomena, but can be profitably understood within the framework of the Belief-Sampling Model (note, Zaller 1992: 76–96; Tourangeau, Rips and Rasinski 2000: 178–95). In the following sub-sections I will demonstrate, using six examples, the importance of questionnaire design.

Question wording effects

A good example of a question wording effect occurred during 1978, when IMS and the ESRI asked questions about Northern Ireland. In particular both surveying agencies were interested in measuring attitudes in the Republic towards the communities in Northern Ireland and assessing the degree of perceived social distance. The logic behind both the IMS and ESRI survey items are the same, but the phrasing is different, as one can readily see:

> Here are some statements about people in the North. I would like to know if you agree or disagree with these statements. (a) People in the North, Protestant and Catholic have more in common with each other then they have with people in the South? (IMS: CMC/md/J.780/6, 9 March 1978, question 11a).

> Northern Ireland is a topic of interest and concern for many people. I would like to get your views on some aspects relating to the Northern problem. Would you agree or disagree with each of the following statements. Catholics in Northern Ireland have more in common with Northern Protestants than they have with Catholics in the Republic? (ESRI, July–September 1978, question 5; see Davis and Sinnott 1979).

These two surveys, undertaken within six months of each other, exhibit a 20 per centage point difference in support for the view that citizens living in Northern Ireland have more in common with each other, despite their denominational differences, than with citizens living in the Republic of Ireland. The more 'bland' IMS question format, which did not state anything about Northern Ireland being a 'concern for many people' or place undue emphasis on 'Catholics in Northern Ireland' and 'Northern Protestants', elicited a much lower level of perceived social distance than the ESRI survey item.[11]

Question bias effects

Many of the social welfare questions asked by pollsters both in Ireland and elsewhere ignore economic realities. Quite often these questions ask a respondent whether they would like to have more social services, but no account is given of the potential costs and benefits of the policies proposed. MRBI in October 1988 asked a typical social welfare question: 'Are you in favour or not of the Government spending more money to reduce the level of poverty in Ireland?' Unsurprisingly, 88 per cent of respondents were in favour of increased government spending.[12] However, when this question was followed with 'Would you still be in favour if it meant that better-off people would have to pay higher taxes?' there was a 22 percentage point drop in support for such a policy (see Table 14).

These 'increase government spending' types of questions are easy for surveying companies to write and convenient for respondents to answer. However, such questions take no account of economic realities. In fact, such polling data are of no use to policy-makers although such items are of course useful within the realm of political rhetoric. There is strong reason to believe that if respondents are given some idea of the downsides to these types of social spending proposals, support will be much less. More generally, almost all social welfare poll questions are biased as they equate increased government spending with social improvements. Respondents might feel that social provisions would be greater if government intervention were less. In short, pollsters rarely ask social welfare questions that are based on economic realities and coax respondents to give answers that are of dubious utility (see Wiebe 1953: 349; Yankelovich 1991: 24–7; Weissberg 2002).

Question ordering or priming effects

The most frequently asked question in Irish opinion polls is the vote intention item. Normally, this question is asked at the same point in an interview, most often close to the start. There is a good reason for this questionnaire design decision. It is well known in polling research that questions relating to partisanship are susceptible to the influence of answers to other questions relating to government performance and policy preferences. In January 1991, MRBI asked its vote intention question at the end of its survey interview rather than at the beginning, as is normally the case.

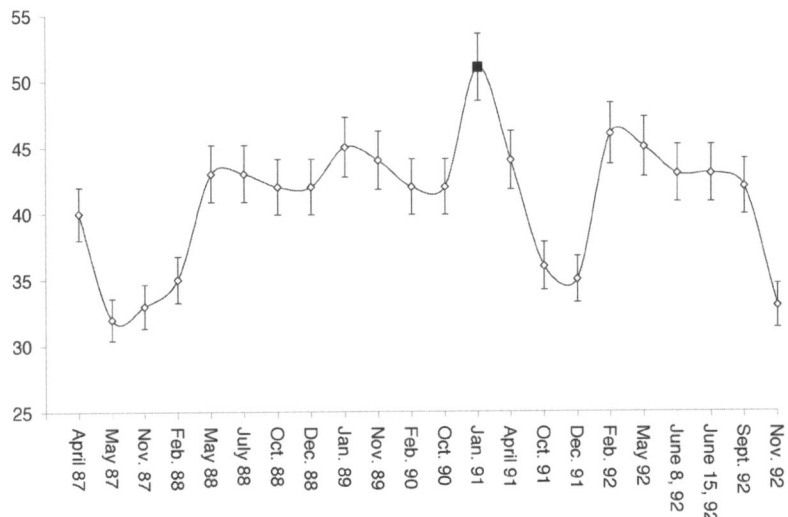

Figure 6 *Example of a Question Ordering Effect: First Preference Vote Intentions for Fianna Fáil in IMS/Lansdowne and MRBI Surveys, 1987–92 (per cent)*

Note: All MRBI surveys had total samples of 1,000 respondents. The sampling error for registered voters is ±3 per cent, at a 95 per cent confidence interval. Thus if 50 percent of Ireland's registered voters were found to be willing to give Fianna Fáil a first preference vote in the next general election, one would be 95 per cent sure that the true figure would be between 47 and 53 per cent (50±3) had all registered voters been interviewed in many polls, rather than just a single sample. Sampling error increases as the sample size decreases, so statements based on various population subgroups, such as separate figures reported for Fianna Fáil, Fine Gael or the Labour Party, are subject to more error than are statements based on the total sample. Typically Fianna Fáil (subgroup) support contains about 300–400 respondents. Such estimates would often have a sampling error of approximately 5 per cent, represented here as a confidence interval. The MRBI Fianna Fáil estimate for January 1991 is indicated by a larger black square.

The resultant estimates for Fianna Fáil were higher than the preceding (+9 points) and subsequent (+7 points) poll estimates respectively. In order to set this question in the proper context, all MRBI poll estimates of support for Fianna Fáil from early 1987 to late 1992 (that is, during the 25th and 26th Dáils) are shown in Figure 6. One can see from this figure that the MRBI estimate for January 1991 is rather high. It is beyond the upper bound of the 95 per cent confidence interval for contemporary polls. So while it is not possible to definitely say that this poll estimate is an outlier due to a question ordering effect, the evidence is none the less suggestive. Significantly, MRBI did not place the vote intention item as the last question in its survey again, indicating some internal concerns about question ordering effects.[13]

Ambiguous poll questions

Given the revelations from the various tribunals of inquiry since 1997 into political corruption in Ireland, IMS asked in late 2001 what voters thought of political parties more generally. The most salient point in these poll results is that Fianna Fáil scored highest on all the party attributes investigated by IMS. Significantly, 39 per cent of Fianna Fáil's own supporters thought that the party was the 'most politically corrupt'. What is most telling from these data is that Irish voters, especially supporters of the smaller parties, were willing to endorse positive attributes such as 'best at getting things done' to other parties and, more particularly, Fianna Fáil. For example, only half of all Fine Gael identifiers stated that Fine Gael was best in this respect, while over three-quarters of Fianna Fáil supporters stuck with their party. In fact, 17 per cent of Fine Gael voters believed that Fianna Fáil was best at getting things done.[14]

While these poll results are interesting, this 'party image' question is less than satisfactory because the item is ambiguous. Respondents could have expressed what they thought was the prevailing opinion on parties as depicted in the media. Alternatively, those interviewed may have expressed their own personal opinion. What this really tells us about party image in Ireland is difficult to say. More generally, the Belief-Sampling Model warns us that data that we suspect results from different considerations cannot be taken at face value. To do so is equivalent to mixing the results of two different poll questions, and thereafter proceeding to make inferences based on what are effectively heterogeneous data.

Table 3 Confidence, Trust or Perceived Leadership Attributed to Irish Public Institutions and Media, 1981–2003 (per cent)

Source	EVS			IMS						EB 47, 52 & 59			ASES	MRBI	Substantive change
Concept measured	Confidence			Confidence in leadership						Trust			Confidence	Trust	
Year	1981	1990	1999	Jul 92	Nov 96	Oct 98	Oct 00	Mar 02	Mar 03	1997	2002	2003	2000	Oct 02	
Institutions															
Religious/church institutions	78	72	58	38	31	28	32	28	19	58	38	31	–	–	Decline
Army/military	75	–	–	–	–	–	–	–	–	83	80	75	73	–	Decline
Education	67	73	63	–	–	–	–	–	–	–	–	–	–	–	Increase
Trade Unions	37	43	47	25	25	31	–	27	26	54	46	48	–	–	Increase
Police	86	86	86	–	–	–	50	–	–	78	71	64	–	–	Same
Parliament	52	50	33	–	–	–	–	–	–	38	45	35	35	34	Decline
Civil service (bureaucracy)	54	59	62	–	–	–	–	–	–	61	64	–	64	59	Same
Social welfare system	59	–	59	–	–	–	–	–	–	–	–	–	–	–	Same
European Union (EU)	71	60	–	–	–	–	–	–	–	57	52	50	–	53	Decline
United Nations (UN)	–	59	64	–	–	–	–	–	–	–	66	59	–	–	?
Health care	–	–	59	–	–	–	72	–	–	–	–	–	–	–	–
Justice/legal system	57	47	56	41	37	40	28	36	30	59	58	50	55	–	Decline
Political parties	–	–	20	–	–	17	10	–	–	20	24	20	27	26	Same
Commercial companies (large)	50	52	–	33	38	37	–	36	30	39	35	31	56	–	Decline
Government	–	–	–	22	21	20	–	26	16	39	43	32	34	34	Same
Political leaders	–	–	–	–	–	–	–	–	–	–	–	–	30	–	–
Media															
Press	43	36	35	37**	49**	49**	26	43**	44	37	45	52	51*	33	?
Radio	–	–	–	–	–	–	–	–	–	73	71	75	–	–	Increase
Television	–	–	–	–	–	–	–	–	–	69	67	75	–	44	Increase

See Appendix 1 for details of question wording. * Refers to 'the mass media' ** Journalists (newspapers and RTE)

Similar but incomparable poll questions

A persistent theme within the media has been that extensive reporting of corruption in public institutions has had an undermining effect on public confidence and trust. There has been consistent interest within the media and among academics in this issue. For this reason, there are survey datasets for Ireland on national and some international institutions for two decades, which facilitates observation of stability or change over time. Previous research has found that Ireland has similar levels of confidence in public institutions to other European countries and for many institutions 'the level of confidence expressed is somewhat greater than the European average' (Hardiman and Whelan 1994: 103).

Table 3 shows data on public confidence and trust from five different surveys that ask what at first sight seems to be the same question. However, they do so in ways that do not make them strictly comparable. The EVS and Asia Europe Survey (ASES) items are very similar in terms of question format and their focus is on *confidence*. Eurobarometer questions concentrate on the *level of trust* and use dichotomous response options, and this makes the marginal distributions somewhat different. In contrast, IMS is somewhat unique in focusing on the concept of providing *leadership*, while MRBI followed the example of Eurobarometer. Moreover, IMS and MRBI chose to focus on different institutions.

The key problem here is that the type of survey question helps determine the expressed level of public response because the concepts of 'confidence', 'level of trust' and 'providing leadership', while strongly related nonetheless yield different response patterns. There is also the problem here of question wording and response option differences. All of these measurement concerns undermine the *face validity* of these items – which survey item is most appropriate for examining specific research questions associated with theories of mass–elite linkage? From a public opinion perspective, these results highlight the need to be cautious about statements that argue public confidence in institutions is changing.

Response effects

In survey questions with a closed response format respondents are expected to choose the option that best fits their answer to the question asked. This assumption seems intuitively plausible, especially for salient issues. Unfortunately, polling experience indicates that the type and number of response options given can greatly influence a survey's estimates of public preferences.

Here I will look at two survey questions asked in 1988 on the preferred constitutional status for Northern Ireland. Both items had a similar wording in substantive terms, but had a different response option format (see bottom of Table 4 for details).

Within the IMS poll the most popular options for bringing peace to Northern Ireland were 'a united Ireland' (30 per cent), followed closely by 'power sharing between the Unionist and Nationalist communities with constitutional guarantees to protect the minority' (29 per cent) and, third, a federal Ireland (14 per cent). However, when comparison is made with the data from the ESRI survey we discover a surprising result – the power-sharing option that was supported by almost three in ten respondents in the IMS poll was much less popular in the ESRI survey. In fact, the ESRI research found that 19 per cent thought power-sharing was desirable, and this option for solving the problems in Northern Ireland was ranked fifth out of seven options given.

This rather dramatic dissimilarity in rankings appears to have resulted from differences in the response options implemented. Specifically, in the ESRI survey the power-sharing response option made no reference to 'constitutional guarantees to protect the minority.' Furthermore, the IMS survey item was simpler in that respondents just picked the option they liked most, while in the ESRI question, the respondent had to rate each option as being desirable, not desirable but acceptable, or undesirable. Which of these survey items was most representative of Irish public opinion is impossible to assess, but it does indicate that both sets of results need to be treated with some caution. In general, the logic of the Belief-Sampling Model warns us to be vigilant towards question formats that have the potential to prompt different considerations during survey interviews.

Within this section I have shown through six examples that there is evidence within Irish opinion poll data to support some of the main tenets of the Belief-Sampling Model of survey response. Irish respondents, like their counterparts elsewhere, do not have fixed opinions on many issues and hence are sensitive to small changes in the interview context. This is an important finding as it goes against the commonly held view, as espoused in the Mirror Theory of Opinion Polling, that the public have real opinions on many issues discussed within the media.

Table 4 *Response Option Effects in Attitudes towards the Future of Northern Ireland in the Winter of 1988 and Spring of 1989*

Choice of solution	ESRI				IMS	
	Desirable	Not desirable but acceptable	Unacceptable	Ranking	Desired option	Ranking
Full integration with Britain			–	–	3	⑤
Northern Ireland as an integral part of the United Kingdom **	10	24	65	⑥	–	–
The whole island of Ireland to be part of the United Kingdom again ***	4	3	93	⑦	–	–
A return to majority rule	–	–	–	–	3	⑤
Power sharing between the Unionist and Nationalist communities (with constitutional guarantees to protect the minority)	19	32	49	⑤	29	②
An independent Ulster	–	–	–	–	13	④
A totally independent Northern Ireland *	22	33	25	④	–	–
A Federal Ireland	–	–	–	–	19	③
A Federal Republic of Northern & Southern Ireland	42	33	25	③	–	–
A united Ireland	–	–	–		30	①
A 32-county Republic with one central government	75	13	12	①	–	–
A 32-county Republic with provincial and central governments	48	30	22	②	–	–
N				753–945	1,036	

*   A totally independent Southern and Northern Ireland.
**   Northern Ireland as an integral part of the United Kingdom with civil rights for all.
***   The whole island of Ireland to become an integral part of the United Kingdom with regional governments in Dublin and Belfast.

Note: Encircled numbers refer to the ordered ranking of responses according to popularity.

Question wording:

> To continue with Northern Ireland, I would like you to tell me what you think of the following possible solutions to the present problem. Would you consider each of them to be desirable, not desirable but acceptable, don't know, unacceptable?

ESRI: Survey of Attitudes in Ireland, Mac Greil 1989, question 46.

> Which of the following options, in your opinion, would best help to bring peace to Northern Ireland?

IMS: PMacN/mb.J.11345, April 19 1988, question 20.

Conclusion

The first goal of this chapter has been to show how consideration of public opinion measurement and questionnaire design informs our understanding of what opinion polls can tell us about public opinion. The second objective has been to demonstrate in the Irish context the application of theoretical and methodological insights derived from the academic literature on opinion polling. Until now such a task has rarely been attempted and there is little published work in the field of opinion polling methodology and survey response theory within the Irish social sciences. For the most part opinion poll and academic survey results are taken at face value (that is, adherence to the Mirror Theory of Opinion Polling, or one of its revisions) – a position that I have demonstrated is likely to lead to invalid inferences.

Within this chapter I have shown that different conceptualisations of what takes place during an opinion poll interview strongly determines how one may evaluate public opinion poll results. The contention that opinion poll results directly 'mirror' public opinion, while still influential in many quarters, is based on an unrealistic understanding of how respondents answer poll questions. A review of the opinion polling literature reveals that the mass survey evidence does not support many of the implications of the two main variants of the Mirror Theory of Opinion Polling, where, for example, knowledgeable respondents always express more consistent or truer opinions than their less informed fellow citizens.

Ironically, the more realistic Belief-Sampling Model of survey response indicates on the one hand that opinion polls may not accurately reflect public opinion, but on the other hand shows how the 'problems of polling' illuminates how opinions are formed and recorded during interviews. Moreover, the existence of hard and easy facets of issues and resulting poll questions and responses underscores the merits of the Belief-Sampling Model relative to the Mirror Theory of Opinion Polling.

In the second part of this chapter I have highlighted with six examples how questionnaire format can affect in important ways the opinions measured by Irish pollsters. It should be stressed here that the objective of this chapter has not been to undermine the legitimacy of Irish opinion poll data, but rather to demonstrate its inherent characteristics and provide guidance for more productive interpretations and inferences.

Having outlined in Chapters 1 and 2 the nature of opinion poll and questionnaire design in Ireland, we are now in a position to assess the electoral record of the polls. This is the topic that will be addressed in Chapter 3 with regard to how well Irish opinion poll predictions based on vote intention questions have matched actual election results. An important caveat is required here. Use will be made of the term 'mirroring' public opinion at the aggregate level. If opinion polls correctly predict election outcomes (within sampling error) I will argue that the polls appear to 'mirror' public opinion. This use of the term 'mirror' is different to that implied by the individual-level response processes outlined in the Belief-Sampling Model.

Notes

1 The seminal article establishing attitude measurement in the social sciences was written by L.L. Thurstone in 1928. He made the bold claim that, despite the complexity of views on 'disputed social issues', attitudes and opinions could be measured if certain assumptions were made.
2 Theoretically opinions, attitudes, beliefs and values are distinct concepts; however, in practice with opinion polls these distinctions become reduced to individual responses that relate to immediate events or to long-term orientations. For simplicity, the term 'opinion' will be used here in a generic sense to denote responses to opinion poll questions. For a clear introduction to their interrelationship, see Yankelovich (1991: 120–5).
3 Measurement error should not be confused with sampling error (which was introduced in Chapter 1) as both have different origins and refer to separate and distinct aspects of the opinion polling process.
4 This term derives from Tourangeau, Rips and Rasinski (2000: 178–95). The Belief-Sampling Model is similar in many respects to Zaller's (1992: 42–51) Receive- Accept-Sample (RAS) model of survey response.
5 Converse (1990: 372) has spoken succinctly on this point: 'The two simplest truths I know about the distribution of political information in modern electorates are that the mean is low and the variance is high. Relative to what, given our lack of units of measurement? Relative to naive expectations.'
6 Prior to the 1983 referendum abortion was illegal in the Republic Ireland under the Offences Against the Person Act (1861). The Pro-Life Amendment Campaign (PLAC) sought to ensure that abortion remained illegal in Ireland by amending the Constitution so as to give explicit protection to the unborn. The pro-life lobby saw the passing of the 1983 Amendment as providing a constitutional ban on abortion. However, the legality of this claim remained untested until the X case in 1992.
7 In reality legal abortions are not undertaken in Ireland because of restrictive guidelines created by the Irish Medical Council. Any doctor who is found to be ignoring these professional guidelines though acting within the law would run the risk of seriously jeopardising their career prospects (Hug 1999: 191).
8 The referendum of 2003 following the legal complexity of previous abortion referendums tried to define when life started as the moment of 'implantation' rather than 'conception'. This resulted in a confusing debate about the legality of emergency contraception (the morning-after pill); see Kennedy (2002: 120).

9 This is not strictly speaking correct. Scenarios 1 and 2 derive from the X case of February 1992 and the C case of December 1997. Both law cases ensued from allegations of rape made by young teenagers who subsequently found that they were pregnant. However, these cases were most associated with the legal 'threat of suicide' question.
10 Zaller (1992: 59-61) refers to this idea that individuals feel differently about different aspects of the same issue as 'ambivalence deduction'.
11 Of course public opinion towards issues such as Northern Ireland could have changed in a matter of days after some violent event. In 1978, there were 81 killings and 755 bombs planted in the North. Although the IMS and ESRI surveys were taken four to six months apart there does not seem, in retrospect, to have been any major acts of violence that might explain the opinion difference observed between these two surveys.
12 MRBI/3680/88, *The Irish Times*, 5-6 September 1988, question 11.
13 For an example of priming effects with an issue question, i.e. introduction of the Euro, see Lyons (2003: 11-12).
14 Evidence presented in this sub-section draws from Lyons (2002: 12).

Chapter 3

The Electoral Record of Irish Opinion Polls

> It is literally impossible to interpret opinion poll figures correctly, unless the actual questions, and the background, including previous figures are examined [...] Many observers frequently see the figures as predictive – this, too, is a misinterpretation [...] Another strange misinterpretation is claiming that poll figures had been inaccurate because they were not identical to results of elections, when the poll in question had been conducted anything from a week to three months earlier. This claim implies that public opinion remains static in the face of lively debate.
>
> Jack Jones (2001: 292–3)

One of the key motivations behind the commissioning of opinion polls by the media is to provide estimates of who is likely to be successful in the next general election. In this sense, the vote intention questions contained in all Irish opinion polls attempt to reflect the current levels of support within the electorate if an election were held 'tomorrow'. In Chapters 1 and 2 there was an illustration of the basic criteria that are necessary to provide accurate election poll results. Here I will use these insights to assess the electoral record of Irish opinion polls.

This chapter will introduce and use two new concepts. *Mirror Accuracy* refers to the degree to which the percentage estimates of party support provided in final pre-election opinion polls match with the first preference support observed in actual election outcomes. Estimates that are within random sampling error (± 3 per cent) will be considered accurate, although some reference will also be made to sampling error corrected for design effects (± 4 per cent). In contrast,

Lamp Precision is a measure of the level of correlation between inter-election or non-campaign poll estimates of party support and actual election results. The object here is to evaluate the extent to which the patterns measured in poll data match trends in electoral behaviour. The core idea behind lamp precision is that opinion polls have the potential to estimate the underlying relationships that underpin observed electoral behaviour.[1]

One reason that assessments of polling accuracy are important stems from growing problems evident in opinion polls during recent general elections (McElroy and Marsh 2003, 2007). There are some indications that the problems that led British polling companies in 1992 to underestimate the size of the Conservative vote and overestimate the Labour Party vote are becoming more important in Ireland. In recent elections, such as the 1997 and 2002 contests, Irish pollsters have persistently overestimated Fianna Fáil support in final pre-election polls and underestimated Fine Gael popularity. Curiously, in the 2007 General Election (which will not be examined in this chapter) the polls as a whole underestimated Fianna Fáil support. However, it seems that 'face to face, unlike phone polls, over-state [d] Fianna Fáil support significantly' (McElroy and Marsh 2008:144). On this issue, it is interesting to repeat a point made in Chapter 1 that the quota sampling procedure with face-to-face interviewing that is still used by IMS/Lansdowne and MRBI was abandoned in Britain after 1992 (except in the case of MORI) in favour of telephone or internet polling.

The insights of the Belief-Sampling Model of survey response and the evidence of questionnaire effects presented in Chapter 2 demonstrate that taking vote intention questions at face value – that is, as simple mirrors of public opinion – may result in misinterpretation of the poll results and the drawing of invalid inferences. The fundamental issue of having some understanding of how voters interpret poll questions is a key feature in evaluating the mirror and lamp functions of opinion polls. Chapter 4 will expand on the themes developed here and examine political satisfaction ratings – another core feature of all Irish opinion polls.

In the first section of this chapter I shall describe the characteristics of vote intention questions. The second section will outline the various adjustment procedures that have been used by Irish pollsters to improve the accuracy of their pre-election vote intention items. The following section will assess how well polls track general election outcomes between 1977 and 2002. In the fourth section there will be an investigation of the patterns in partisan responses to vote intention questions during the election cycle. The penultimate section will briefly examine the important question of whether general election campaigns matter using the opinion poll evidence. The concluding section will draw together the empirical findings of this chapter, evaluate the accuracy of Irish opinion polls and assess the implications for our understanding of what mass surveys tell us about public opinion.

Characteristics of Vote Intention Questions

In theory political opinion polling is a straightforward business. A polling company needs to pose only a small number of questions to those citizens who are registered to vote. In this section I will examine two central concerns. First, the Belief-Sampling Model outlined in Chapter 2 warns us to be mindful of the implementation of vote intention questions most especially with regard to question wording and response format. Second, there is the important, though often ignored, issue of how to legitimately interpret vote intention poll items. For example, should the results of all vote intention questions during interelection periods be treated in the same manner, or should we expect campaign poll results to be qualitatively different because of campaign effects? The Belief-Sampling Model suggests that both phases are not comparable, because the contexts are dissimilar and hence the considerations used by respondents to answer vote intention questions changes during the interelection period.

Implementation of the vote intention question

Vote intention questions are asked in almost all Irish public opinion polls and form a core part of a battery of three items that relate directly to party competition and government formation. Consequently, the vote intention item is usually asked first and is followed by a 'forced choice' question that attempts to prompt hesitant respondents to express a preference. It should be noted that IMS and MRBI have asked two other questions (namely preferred government/coalition option and perceived likely winner of the election) closely related to the vote intention item in order to capture some strategic aspects of voting. Nevertheless, the elegance and simplicity of the vote intention question make it an indispensable item for polling companies. For this reason, an evaluation of the vote intention item's strengths and weaknesses is an important first step before empirical analysis. The most obvious place to begin such a task is to examine the format of the question used.

The wording of vote intention questions has been largely constant over time.[2] MRBI has consistently asked its vote intention question after the government and leadership satisfaction items. For many years, IMS adopted a similar strategy. However, in 1993, IMS following the example of Gallup UK (who had changed their policy in 1992) and began to ask the vote intention question first. While the possibility of priming undoubtedly exists it is not clear that MRBI's question order is in reality inferior. The typical wording used by IMS/Lansdowne follows the general format used by Gallup UK between 1943 and 2000 (see King et al. 2001: 2):

> If a General Election were to take place tomorrow, to which Party or independent candidate would you give your first preference vote? IF 'WOULD NOT VOTE/UNDECIDED/ REFUSED' ASK: To which Party or independent candidate would you be most inclined to give your first preference vote? [IMS/Lansdowne, vote intention wording][3]

> If there was a general election tomorrow, to which party or independent candidate would you give your first preference vote? IF 'DON'T KNOW' PROBE AS FOLLOWS – Please think about if for a moment. [MRBI, vote intention wording]

In contrast, MRBI has developed and implemented its own vote intention question, which is similar in the main question text to the IMS/Lansdowne one, but is significantly different in the instructions given to those respondents who give an uncommitted response. This difference between the IMS/Lansdowne and MRBI wording has not been examined in detail in previous research.

In order to investigate this question wording difference I will use the 1992–7 interelection period. During this era there was an almost equal number of IMS/Lansdowne (N=28) and MRBI (N=23) polls and it is possible to assume that the only significant difference between the poll results was the question wording. If we look at the evolution of the 'don't know' polling estimates for both IMS/Lansdowne and MRBI in Figure 7 we see a revealing pattern.

Figure 7 shows there is considerable variation in 'don't know' responses. This is not surprising because sample sizes were some-

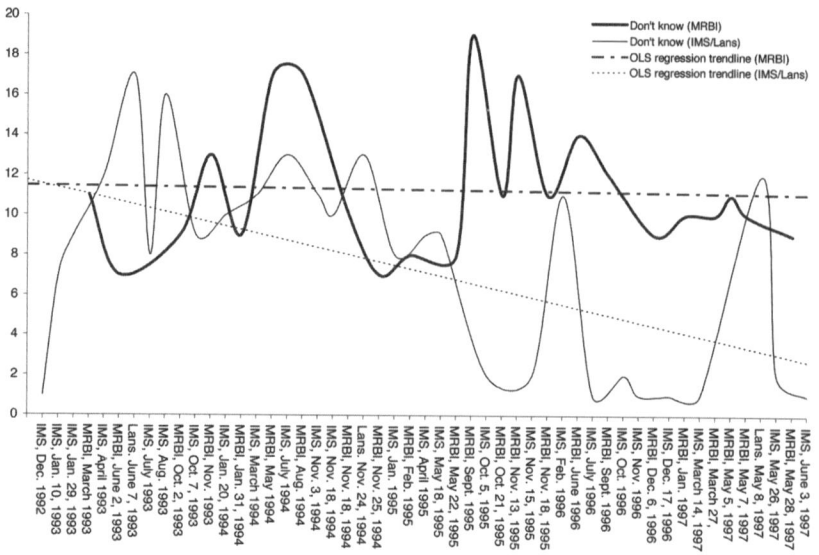

Figure 7 *Investigation of a 'Question Format Effect' for the Vote Intention items used by IMS/Lansdowne and MRBI through Comparison of the Levels of 'Don't Know' in Polls between 1992 and 1997 (per cent)*

Note: the data refers to those respondents in IMS/Lansdowne and MRBI polls during the 1992–7 interelection period whom responded 'don't know' to the vote intention question. As IMS/Lansdowne and MRBI use different question wordings to prompt respondents who replied 'don't know' to choose a party, there is an expectation that this may lead respondents to answer differently. The OLS regression trend lines indicate very different trends over the election cycle implying different question format effects. For IMS/Lansdowne the trend in levels of 'don't know' is downward (despite considerable upsurges in specific polls) while in contrast for MRBI the trend is largely constant – there was no decline in the 'don't know' response rate as the 1997 general election approached.

times small (N ≤70) where the sampling error becomes very large (≥10 per cent). The goal here is to investigate if the information effects surrounding general election campaigns are evident in both the IMS and MRBI vote intention trends. I will return to this topic in the penultimate section of this chapter. A reasonable expectation is that the level of 'don't know' responses will be lowest directly after an election and immediately prior to the subsequent one. Moreover, the number of uncommitted responses will be highest in mid-election periods as political interest is less. Consequently, the trend in 'don't know' responses should follow an inverted 'U'-shaped, or quadratic, trend (note Gelman and King 1993; Holbrook 1996; Alvarez 1997).[4]

The OLS regression lines in Figure 7 indicate very different trends over the election cycle, implying different question format effects. MRBI estimates of 'don't know' fluctuate, but always remain above 6 per cent, while those of IMS/Lansdowne declined as the 1997 general election approached. Such evidence suggests within the Belief-Sampling Model (of survey response) framework that the IMS/Lansdowne vote intention question format 'facilitates' respondents providing 'inclined' answers in the run up to general elections. For IMS/Lansdowne the trend in levels of 'don't know' is downward (despite considerable upsurges in specific polls) while in contrast for MRBI the trend is constant – there was no decline in the 'don't know' response rate as the 1997 general election approached.[5]

The telephone opinion polls undertaken by ICM for the *Ireland on Sunday* newspaper have adopted a third type of vote intention question based on ICM's extensive polling experience in the UK.

> Fianna Fáil, Fine Gael, Labour, the Progressive Democrats, Sinn Féin, Greens, other parties and independent candidates would fight a general election in your area. Which party would be most likely to get your first preference vote at your polling station? [ICM, vote intention wording]

In the UK, some pollsters such as MORI used to ask respondents how they would vote without giving any party options, as is the current practice with IMS/Lansdowne and MRBI. ICM in contrast lists the parties in the question, and this strategy has the important effect in the UK of boosting estimated support for smaller parties such as the Liberal Democrats.

Examining the raw, unadjusted poll data seems most appropriate as each polling company implements different methods to arrive at a final estimate, thereby destroying any strict comparison of the surveying process. The unadjusted poll data for the different questions asked by ICM, IMS and MRBI in the final days of the 2002 general election show that there are differences between the polls, most especially for Fianna Fáil. Effectively these polling companies estimated electoral support for this party to be somewhere between 32 and 42 per cent of respondents and highlight that obtaining good estimates for this party seems to have been a key problem in 2002. In addition, the polling evidence suggests that underestimation of Fine Gael support was a particular problem inherent to the work undertaken by IMS.

Interpretation of the vote intention question

The vote intention question has widespread use cross-nationally as a (proxy) measure of vote choice most often beyond the immediate context of a general election campaign. Research on pre-election (also known as 'trial heat') polling shows that poll estimates of party support far away from an election tend to be the most inaccurate (Gelman and King 1993; Lau 1994; Wlezien and Erikson 2002). This raises the question of the utility of asking vote intention questions that are inaccurate, and perhaps even misleading measures of eventual vote choice.

Within political science there are two perspectives on this question. The first viewpoint, adopting the *Mirror Theory of Opinion Polling* position, asserts that vote intention questions are accurate. This is because there is a constant relationship between fundamental factors such as party attachment, perceived economic performance and satisfaction with government or party leaders, and the responses given to vote intention questions in polls. In effect, in the language of the on-line processing model within cognitive psychology, survey respondents have 'accessible' opinions on vote choice all of the time (Erber and Lau 1990). Consequently, vote intention questions have a legitimate and useful place in all opinion polls.

In contrast, the second perspective, following the logic of the *Belief-Sampling Model*, contends that the accuracy of vote intention questions vary during interelection periods, and are most accurate during general election campaigns where there are strong informational and priming effects (note Kinder 1998). Thus the answers given to vote intention questions vary over time depending on a variety of factors such as media usage and issue saliency (Zaller and Feldman 1992). Therefore, vote intention items are of most research value during campaign periods and have much less reliability as sources of information during interelection periods.

There is relatively little research on this issue in Europe, and none at all in Ireland. Examination of the vote intention question used in Eurobarometer studies by Arceneaux (2006) tends to support the second perspective outlined above. This implies that Irish voters' answers to vote intention questions are probably best seen as 'top of the head' responses that tally more with actual voting behaviour as election day comes closer.[6] This has a very important implication. Responses to vote intention questions beyond election campaigns will *underestimate* the impact of factors that structure party choice on election day. For this reason, Arceneaux argues that the evidence provided by vote intention items will provide a conservative test of any theories examined.

In other words, there is a greater likelihood of concluding that hypothetical party choice responses are not based on a systematic preference structure. Such analytical conservatism comes with a cost. There is the risk of concluding that the responses given to vote intentions are based on whims when this is not really the case. In statistical terms, this problem is known as a 'type II error' (that is, incorrectly accepting the null hypothesis of 'no' vote structuring mechanism).

Adjustments Made to Vote Intention Question Results

The record of pre-election opinion polling in Ireland from its start in 1977 until 1992 was reasonably good where, for example, IMS estimates of support for the two largest parties (Fianna Fáil and Fine Gael) were within two percentage points of the actual first preference vote. MRBI also had a good record during this period, but underestimated Fine Gael support from 1987. However, the record in the 1997 elections marked an important change where the final published figures for both IMS and MRBI markedly overstated (+5 per cent) Fianna Fáil support (Jones 2001: 162–5; McElroy and Marsh 2003: 162). This led MRBI in 1999 to begin publishing 'adjusted' poll estimates of vote intentions, although it abandoned the procedure during the 2002 general election campaign. In this section, we will investigate the logic behind the adjustment of vote intention data and its implications for our understanding of what opinion polls tell us about public opinion.

Polling limits imposed by undecided and unlikely voters

All vote intention questions give the respondent the option of stating a party preference, giving an 'undecided' answer or replying that they will not vote.[7] In the past such uncommitted voters (undecideds and self-confessed abstainers) were either ignored, or allocated proportionately to all parties in the publication of 'committed voter' poll results. What to do with undecided respondents or those who by their own admission are not committed to turning out to vote goes to the heart of what opinion polling is about.

If opinion polling is primarily a process of putting a mirror in front of the face of society, the responses of those who say they are undecided or will not vote are legitimate and relevant pieces of information. On the other hand, if the goal of polling is election prediction, where pollsters want to focus like a lamp on those who will definitely vote and have clear party preferences, then 'undecided' and 'will not vote' responses are a problem if they constitute a substantial number in a sample. It is of course possible to reconcile both perspectives where opinion poll results primarily reflect public opinion during interelection periods, and illuminate the preferences of key segments of the electorate (that is, respondents certain to vote) where prediction is the goal during relatively short general election campaigns.

From an election prediction perspective, undecided respondents are potentially a large source of error in estimating party support from vote intention questions. As this response group is a persistent, and perhaps growing, element in all survey samples, polling companies cross-nationally have felt compelled to find more effective methods of managing this potential source of predictive error. Until the late 1990s, Irish pollsters treated undecided voters in standard ways – ignoring them or allocating them evenly to all parties.

Internationally, other strategies have been tested where the focus has been on measuring the extent to which changes in question wording and implementation can improve the accuracy of poll estimates. Research by Hoek and Gendall (1996) found that various research strategies use of introductory contextual questions as a precursor to eliciting voting intentions, implementation of different question types and adoption of different vote intention question formats, do not result in higher poll accuracy. In fact, having samples where undecided levels are attenuated may lead to less accurate election predictions.

MRBI's adjustment procedure and models of survey response

Since 1997, Irish pollsters have paid more attention to identifying likely and unlikely voters because this was seen to be a key source of error in this general election.[8] To illustrate how efforts have progressed the focus here will primarily be on strategies adopted by MRBI. In June 1997, MRBI conducted an election day poll (not an exit poll) where support for Fianna Fáil was overestimated by 5 percentage points and all the other parties were underestimated.

Analysis of the sample found that the main error occurred among those who had not voted prior to being interviewed.

This 1997 election day survey uncovered a pattern of poll response dynamics that was both surprising and worrying. One subgroup of respondents under-reported their likelihood of abstention from voting by stating insincerely that they would vote for Fianna Fáil. A second subgroup under-reported their likelihood of voting for Fine Gael and other smaller parties or independent candidates. Further research in 1999 combined with a series of constituency level polls showed substantial differences in the response patterns to the standard vote intention question used in national surveys, and the simulated ballots used in constituency polls.[9]

This led to the creation of a new adjustment procedure based on a weighting variable.[10] Effectively, on the basis of a single election day poll conducted in June 1997 MRBI created a profile of those respondents who give misleading answers to survey questions. Using this information MRBI weighted all polls between November 1999 and April 2002 using data collected in June 1997. Such a procedure assumed that the profile of respondents most likely to give inaccurate answers remained constant during all of this time.[11] Moreover, the exact method used to construct this adjustment remains unclear, as MRBI has never specified clearly the methodology used in any of its reports, newspaper commentaries or other publications (for example, Jones 2001). In order to understand and justify their new adjustment procedure MRBI outlined a survey response theory that identified two opinion poll response mechanisms: intentional and unintentional misreporting.

The main problem caused by *intentional* misreporting by respondents is systematic response bias. Deliberate misreporting of turnout derives from well-known social desirability effects, while under-reporting for Fine Gael relates to considerations that are as yet not well understood. *Unintentional* misreporting is based on the assumption that some respondents simply lack sufficient information to answer vote intention questions in a manner that is consistent with their voting preferences. For example, respondents confuse the party allegiance of candidates.[12] According to MRBI such unintentional misreporting results in overestimates for Fianna Fáil.

The MRBI adjustment procedure is an attempt to literally give greater weight to respondents who have 'real' opinions. The thinking behind this strategy fits with the Mirror Theory of Opinion Polling outlined in Chapter 2. From the Mirror Theory perspective, such respondents who give 'top of the head' answers in opinion poll interviews are a problem because they invalidate the premise that opinion poll results reflect true opinions and hence reduce the reliability of pre-election opinion polling.

However, the Belief-Sampling perspective would take a different position. Opinion polls about politics, especially those on election day, prime respondents to give particular kinds of answers that are consonant with the pollster's belief that elections are important – why else would a polling company want to conduct a personal at-home interview about politics? Moreover, for those uninformed about politics, such as the young and disillusioned, the easiest answer to give an interviewer is one from the 'top of the head' where such respondents not unreasonably pick the largest party (Fianna Fáil). This party has been at the centre of government formation after all general elections since 1987.

Assessment of How Well Opinion Polls track General Election Outcomes

The most intuitive way to assess the accuracy of Irish opinion polls is to judge them on the basis of whether they are able to predict the correct level of first-preference support for political parties in their final campaign polls. This criterion may be called *Mirror Accuracy*. Here, the polls are judged on how accurately they mirror the exact percentages of support received by parties on election day. In the next sub-section I will use final pre-election poll estimates to assess the Mirror Accuracy of Irish polls. An alternative view of opinion polls, presented a little later, emphasises the correlation between survey estimates of party support throughout an election cycle and actual voting behaviour. This we may call *Lamp Precision*. Here the objective is to demonstrate through strong correlations ($r \geq 0.7$) that opinion poll results follow the same trends as election results. With lamp precision, opinion polls are seen to reveal important underlying relationships. For example, responses to vote intention questions reveal the link between party attachment (that is not directly measured) and actual voting behaviour.

Mirror accuracy of final pre-election poll estimates

Looking first at the mirror accuracy record, we can see from

Figure 8 the errors in the final campaign polls for all nine general elections between 1977 and 2002 for each polling company that published predictions in the media. IMS/Lansdowne and MRBI are the only companies to have predictions in all of these elections, and their success has been mixed. For example, MRBI was accurate in predicting Fianna Fáil support in the general elections of 1977, 1981 and February 1982 and Fine Gael first preferences in 1987 and 1989. In contrast, IMS/Lansdowne predicted party support exactly in 1977 for Fine Gael and was within one percentage point of the actual result on three other occasions for Fianna Fáil and Fine Gael. However, the accuracy of final poll estimates in the 1997 and 2002 general elections has declined – rather dramatically in the case of IMS, where there was a serious over-reporting of Fianna Fáil support and under-reporting of Fine Gael first preferences.

More generally, Figure 8 illustrates a persistent partisan bias between 1997 and 2002. Of the 21 poll estimates for all nine general elections, Fianna Fáil support was in absolute terms over-reported on 14 occasions and under-reported on just four (November 1982, 1989 and 1992). Fine Gael estimates, on the other hand, were over-reported in absolute terms on seven occasions and under-reported on nine – in fact, such under-reporting was a persistent problem between 1987 and 2002. In the case of the Labour Party, all predictions have been within sampling error (± 3 per cent) of the final outcome, and have quite often been within a percentage point of the officially recorded election result.

Table 5 shows the results of three error estimation measures (average, systematic and non-systematic; see bottom of Table 5 for brief definitions) for the accuracy of Irish opinion polls in all nine general elections between 1997 and 2002 (see Buchanan 1986). These results confirm the impression in Figure 8 that the polls overestimated Fianna Fáil support (by 1.9 per centage points) and underestimated Fine Gael first preferences on average by three-tenths of a percentage point.

If comparison is made between the theoretically expected standard deviations of the pre-election polls and the actual standard deviation of the poll estimates (that is, non-systematic error), the latter should ideally be less than the former. The theoretical standard error for Fianna Fáil support, the largest party during the 1977–2002 period, is 1.6 per centage points and is much less than the non-systematic error estimated for this party (2.4 percentage points; see Table 5).[13]

78   PUBLIC OPINION, POLITICS AND SOCIETY IN CONTEMPORARY IRELAND

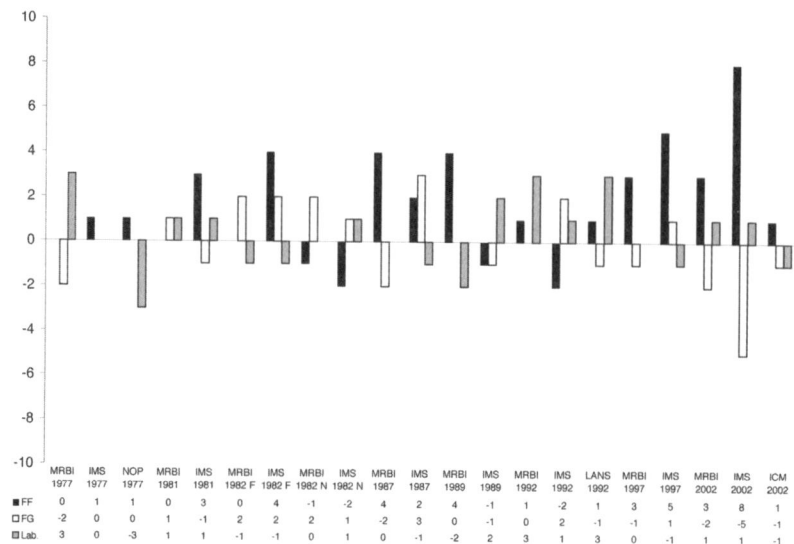

Figure 8 *Absolute Error in Final Poll Predictions of Main Party Support in Nine General Elections, 1977–2002 (per cent)*

Note: Final poll estimates have been based on different criteria. The poll results used are the best estimates published by the polling company in question. Opinion polls from 1977–97 are based on estimates where undecided responses were allocated evenly to each of the main parties, i.e. Fianna Fáil (FF), Fine Gael (FG) and the Labour Party (Lab). Since 1997 attempts have been made to attenuate an over-reporting bias favouring Fianna Fáil through a variety of procedures most of which are concerned with identifying 'likely voters' a common strategy used by pollsters cross-nationally.

The IMS item has had a number of differing formulations, such as: 'If you do vote in the forthcoming general election, which party will you give your first preference vote to? / to which party would you be most inclined to give your first preference vote to?'

The MRBI item is generally: 'If there was a general election tomorrow, to which party would you give your first preference vote? IF 'DON'T KNOW' PROBE AS FOLLOWS – Please think about if for a moment.' For the 2002 general election the poll question was different, in that respondents were given a sample ballot paper with all the candidates in their constituency and asked to fill it in as they would do so on election day.

If we multiply Fianna Fáil's non-systematic error estimate by 1.96, this yields a 'margin of error estimate' of 4.7 per centage points.[14] The theoretical margin of error for simple random sampling as reported by all of the major polling companies for national samples of 1,000 respondents is three percentage points. As noted in Chapter 1, a more realistic margin of error estimate for clustered samples is four percentage points. The Fianna Fáil margin of error estimate derived from opinion polls does not compare favourably with the 3 to 4 per cent margin of error range we would expect from sampling theory.

Table 5 *Accuracy of Twenty Final National Opinion Poll Predictions of First Preference Support for the Main Parties in Nine General Elections 1977–2002 (per cent)*

	Fianna Fáil	Fine Gael	Labour Party
All polls (N = 20)			
Average error	+2.3	+1.4	+1.3
Systematic error	−1.9	+0.3	−0.3
Non-systematic error	+2.4	+1.8	+1.7
IMS polls (N = 9)			
Average error	+3.0	+1.6	+1.2
Systematic error	−2.3	+0.2	−0.6
Non-systematic error	+3.1	+2.2	+1.4
MRBI polls (N = 9)			
Average error	+1.8	+1.3	+1.2
Systematic error	−1.6	+0.2	−0.6
Non-systematic error	+1.9	+1.6	+1.7
Mean actual results	44.1	30.5	10.7
Standard error	1.2	2.0	1.2
Std. deviation	3.7	5.9	3.5

Note: Poll prediction percentages are subtracted from the actual first preference election percentage. Therefore, negative values are overestimates and positive values are underestimates. The error calculations are made for each of the three main parties vote as a share of those with a partisan preference, or as a percentage of the 'government party' vote. The government party measure is interesting for government formation because it refers to the fact that voters have always been faced with the choice of having a Fianna Fáil – or Fine Gael – led single-party government or coalition. This measure predicts who will be the top party and how far ahead they will be of the second party.

Average error is the mean difference between the predicted percentage and the actual first preference vote percentage, ignoring if the error is an overestimate or underestimate. This error measure while intuitive conceals biases such as consistent over or underestimates for particular parties.

Systematic error is the mean difference between the predicted percentage and the actual first preference vote per centage taking into account if the error is an overestimate or underestimate. This error measure reveals poll biases towards specific parties but underestimates the size of the errors, as large overestimates may cancel out equally large underestimates.

Non-systematic error is the standard deviation of the individual errors around the mean of the errors for all nine general elections. This error measure assesses the performance of opinion polls in terms of the deviations that would be expected given sample sizes of approximately 1,000 respondents, after allowing for biases such as non-voters, undecideds, switchers, etc. This measure is similar to the 'margin of error' used in opinion polls, and indicates how widely poll predictions vary discounting systematic error.

Statistical theory would lead us to expect one error (that is, estimates more than one standard deviation from the population mean, with a 95 per cent confidence interval) larger than 4 per cent for Fianna Fáil in every twenty polls. There are, in fact, two polls above this value: the final IMS polls for the 1997 and 2002 general elections. Taking the Irish opinion pollster's less conservative 'industry standard' of 3 per cent, the polls have exceeded this margin of error value on seven occasions in the twenty-one final polls published in the media between 1977 and 2002.

This implies that final campaign polls have a reliability of 65–90 per cent – a figure that contrasts with the industry standard of 95 per cent. Such evidence indicates that the margin of error information provided with campaign polls underestimates their accuracy. Furthermore, the Mirror Accuracy claimed by Irish pollsters is, in reality, less impressive than their claims justify.

Lamp Precision of opinion polls

In the last sub-section I demonstrated the Mirror Accuracy of Irish opinion polls, that is, correctly predicting the actual election results within sampling error. Here, the focus is not on opinion polls accurately estimating the true level of party support in an election, but to see whether the response pattern in vote intention questions is correlated with actual voting behaviour in elections. From this Lamp Precision perspective the absolute differences between poll estimates and actual election results is not a key criterion. The goal is to demonstrate the importance of underlying relationships, that is, whether responses to vote intention questions are strongly correlated to voting behaviour.

Table 6 shows that the polls undertaken nearer to a general election for the three main parties are more strongly correlated with general election outcomes. This is evident both in absolute terms and when comparison is made with the correlations for all dates. This effect is most pronounced for Fine Gael and the Labour Party. Alternatively, as a means of testing the validity of this procedure, polls conducted early in a current election cycle should be more strongly correlated with the previous general election results.

As columns three, five and seven of Table 6 show, this effect is observed and is again more salient in the case of Fine Gael and the Labour Party. Such correlation results indicate that pollsters' vote intention questions explain 76 per cent of the variance of the Fianna

Fáil vote, 98 per cent of the variance of the Fine Gael vote, and 92 per cent of the Labour Party vote.[15] Such results suggest that partisan support is most volatile in the case of Fianna Fáil.

Table 6 *Correlations between Mean Poll Estimates and Actual Election Results for Fianna Fáil, Fine Gael and the Labour Party, 1977–2002*

Days to the election	FF poll estimates – prospective*	FF poll estimates – retrospective**	FG poll estimates – prospective*	FG poll estimates – retrospective**	Labour poll estimates – respective**	Labour poll estimates – retrospective**
0–59	0.87	0.46	0.99	0.46	0.96	0.11
60–149	0.47	0.43	0.96	0.39	0.71	0.46
150–299	0.25	0.08	0.89	0.63	0.66	0.48
300–599	0.75	0.14	0.43	0.35	0.77	0.44
600–999	0.26	0.33	0.20	0.57	0.17	0.88
1,000+	0.58	0.65	–0.31	0.88	<0.01	0.95
All dates	0.47	0.34	0.69	0.53	0.53	0.53

* Correlation between (vote intention) poll estimates and total first-preference support in the next general election
** Correlation between (vote intention) poll estimates and total first preference support in the previous general election

Note: This table refers to nine elections where data for vote intentions include those who replied 'don't know', 'refused' and 'will not vote'. The correlations are based on the mean forecast of all surveys conducted during each countdown period (0–59 days, 60–149 days etc.) for all election years. These mean forecast values for Fianna Fáil, Fine Gael and the Labour Party were correlated with the actual election outcome. A similar procedure was used to calculate mean poll forecasts with actual election outcomes for the previous general election. The table should be interpreted as follows. For Fianna Fáil the Pearson correlation between opinion poll estimates in last 59 days prior to the next general election and opinion poll estimates is 0.87, while the correlation with the previous general election is 0.46

The correlation between all interelection polls and elections at time t and t+1 is given in the final row 'all dates.'

In general, the vote intention estimates within Irish opinion polls exhibit strong correlations (i.e. $r = 0.76$ to 0.98). As the concept of Lamp Precision is based on the degree of correlation between poll estimates and vote intentions, the results presented in Table 6 suggest that Irish polls do track quite well underlying vote structuring factors. In effect, the polling data reveal the power of vote structuring mechanisms such as party attachment. While it is not possible to investigate further the nature of these mechanisms with the data available, it is feasible to look in a little greater detail at the long-term patterns in vote intention poll responses for the three main parties. This is the topic to which I will now turn.

Patterns in Partisan Responses to Vote Intention Questions during the Election Cycle

In our evaluation of the Lamp Precision of Irish opinion polls in the last sub-section I revealed a high level of correlation between vote intentions for particular parties during the election cycle and actual electoral support. In this section I will very briefly extend this analysis and look at how strongly vote intention responses during the election cycle correlate with each other. This is an important question because it reveals if there is a persistent underlying process driving responses to vote intention questions. The results presented in Table 7 reveal that answers to vote intention items in Irish opinion polls follow different patterns for the three main parties.

For Fianna Fáil during most of the interelection period poll forecasts of support are not consistently correlated with one another, indicating that short-term factors are having important effects on poll responses. In fact, Fianna Fáil poll forecasts are more strongly associated with actual voting behaviour (r = 0.87 from Table 7) than with other poll estimates during any phase of the interelection period. This pattern is also true for Fine Gael and the Labour Party. There is, however, one notable exception: poll estimates close to successive elections are strongly correlated (0.84) for Fianna Fáil, suggesting that general election campaigns play an influential role in mobilising vote intentions.

In contrast, poll estimates of support for Fine Gael are more strongly correlated with time, as the second part of Table 7 shows. The figures in the final column indicate that there is an evolution in the pattern within polls for Fine Gael support where early polls in the electoral cycle show little (or negative) correlations with polls undertaken within five months of a general election. The correlations between poll estimates of vote intention for the Labour Party have similar features to those of both Fianna Fáil and Fine Gael. However, vote intentions for the Labour Party are unique in that there is always a positive correlation between poll estimates throughout the interelection period, indicating lower volatility in support.

This evidence builds on the knowledge derived in the previous subsection, where our assessment of Lamp Precision indicated the

Table 7 *Correlations between Mean Interelection Polls Estimates during the Electoral Cycle for Fianna Fáil, Fine Gael and the Labour Party (including 'don't knows'), 1977–2002*

Fianna Fáil			Days before an election			
Days before an election	*0–59*	*60–149*	*150–299*	*300–599*	*600–999*	*1,000+*
0–59	1.00	0.40	0.06	0.60	0.16	0.84
60–149		1.00	0.68	0.47	0.63	0.28
150–299			1.00	0.61	0.63	−0.30
300–599				1.00	0.53	−0.79
600–999					1.00	−0.19
1,000+						1.00

Fine Gael			Days before an election			
Days before an election	*0–59*	*60–149*	*150–299*	*300–599*	*600–999*	*1,000+*
0–59	1.00	0.94	0.89	0.39	0.07	−0.40
60–149		1.00	0.89	0.66	0.34	−0.21
150–299			1.00	0.78	0.68	0.17
300–599				1.00	0.77	0.45
600–999					1.00	0.79
1,000+						1.00

Labour Party			Days before an election			
Days before an election	*0–59*	*60–149*	*150–299*	*300–599*	*600–999*	*1,000+*
0–59	1.00	0.80	0.73	0.87	0.30	0.11
60–149		1.00	0.93	0.96	0.68	0.36
150–299			1.00	0.93	0.70	0.55
300–599				1.00	0.71	0.44
600–999					1.00	0.93
1,000+						1.00

Note: correlations are pairwise with Ns (i.e. number of polls available for analysis) ranging from 5–9 and relate to the responses given in approximately 5,000–9,000 interviews between 1977 and 2002.

importance of some vote-structuring mechanism operating over the long term. Here I have demonstrated that this vote structuring process is most strongly associated with Fine Gael. This contrasts with our Mirror Accuracy results, where we find that polls have trouble dealing with 'shy' Fine Gael supporters. Equally important is the discovery of evidence indicating significant election campaign effects, most especially in the case of Fianna Fáil. Such a finding prompts us to investigate whether Irish general election campaigns matter.

Do Irish General Election Campaigns Matter?

The primary effect of general election campaigns is informational: voters learn more about parties and their policies prior to making a choice on election day (Alvarez 1997). The vote intention questions within Irish opinion polls, while containing valuable information concerning party choice, also give a measure of the level of uncertainty among the electorate about political parties. In short, variation in the level of 'don't know' or 'undecided' is an indicator of public uncertainty about the political choices on offer.

Consequently, vote intention data allow us to examine an important question. Do general election campaigns act as periodic sources of political information? If the signals from political parties such as Fianna Fáil and Fine Gael intensify during election campaigns, and attenuate thereafter, we would expect to see lower levels of uncertainty immediately prior to elections. Mathematically, as I outlined in an earlier section, the expected relationship between the level of uncommitted responses registered in opinion polls and number of days to the next election should be quadratic (inverted 'U'-shape) in nature.

An examination of the evolution of uncertainty concerning party support during the general election cycle shown in Figure 9 demonstrates that there is evidence supportive of the information effects hypothesis where in simple terms election campaigns provide citizens with sufficient information to decide how to vote (see Gelman and King 1993: 433–5; Holbrook 1996: 54–9; Alvarez 1997). As one would expect, there is considerable variation in the poll data which reflects a wide variety of factors such as *house effects* (that is, variance specific to a particular pollster) and coding differences where for certain periods the 'don't know' category and 'will not vote' option seem to have been treated interchangeably. Nevertheless, the effect while weak is present and should be considered a conservative estimate because we have not parcelled out methodological artefacts in this simplified analysis.

This result tallies with the argument that election campaigns provide voters with 'fundamental information' that allows them to vote on the basis of their preferences (Gelman and King 1993; Arceneaux 2006). The data allow us to take one more step where we can try to see when this information effect begins to kick in and have a measurable impact. Our expectation is that this should occur during the election campaign proper, that is, in the final thirty days before an election.

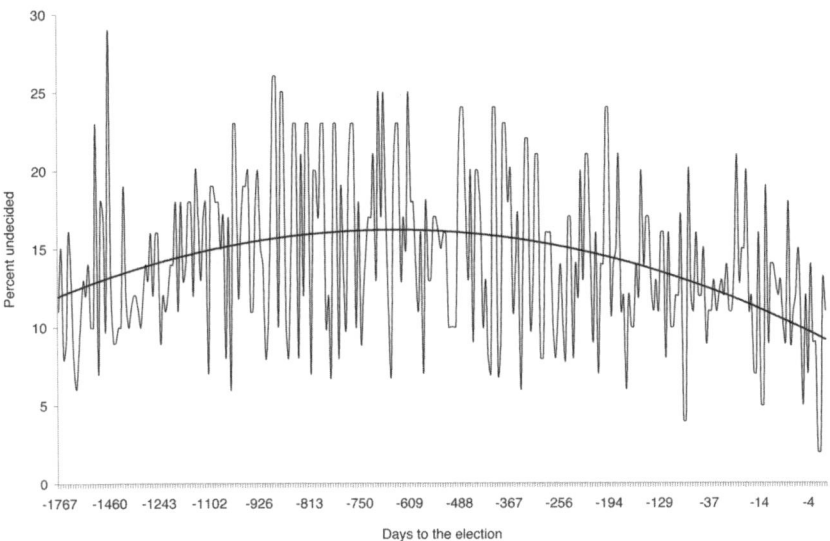

Figure 9 *Evolution of Uncertainty concerning Party Support during the General Election Cycle, 1969–2002 (per cent)*

Note: This dataset refers to those who replied 'don't know', 'undecided' or 'refused' to the vote intention question in 221 opinion polls. Respondents who stated they would not vote are excluded, as it is assumed this was their sincere preference and consequently does not refer to uncertainty about party or candidate choice in a future election. Days to election refers to the number of days from when they poll was undertaken and the subsequent general election. The solid line is a quadratic trend fit ($R^2=0.13$) to these data and relates to a hypothesised relationship discussed in the text.

In Figure 10 the data have been aggregated on the basis of seven time periods, and what we see is a rather surprising result – voter uncertainty in Ireland declines the most prior to the general election campaign. The scale of this effect is limited – 2.5 percentage points – and our indicator is not perfect, but there seems to be a progressive decline from about twenty months before an election until the start of the campaign.

Despite limitations in the data, the message contained in Figure 10 is clear. Irish general election campaigns have limited effects in convincing self-reported undecided voters. If this result is a valid one is confronted with the question: is it possible to see what impact this trend has on party support during general election campaigns?

Figure 11 shows the evolution of party support through the electoral cycle. Labour Party support is largely constant over time,

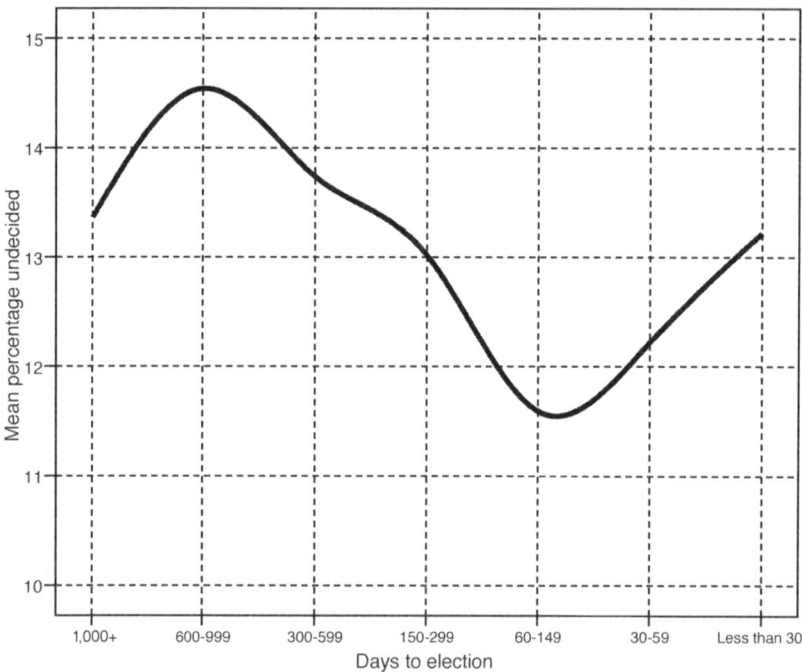

Figure 10 *Decline in Level of Voter Uncertainty concerning Party Support during the General Election Cycle, 1969–2002 (per cent)*

Note: These data refer to the mean level of undecided during six time periods during the general election cycle. As this dataset is derived from a poll of polls (N=221), each of the seven time points is based on survey estimates derived from 5,000–9,000 respondents. The sampling error of these estimates is of the order of 1–2 per cent. In single polls with a thousand respondents sampling error is typically estimated to be 3–4 per cent. This figure represents an aggregation of the data presented in Figure 11, but includes additional poll data relating to elections in 1969 and 1973. Such an aggregation facilitates seeing more clearly when in the general election cycle the decline in respondent uncertainty occurs.

while support for smaller parties and independents increases during the campaign period. The patterns for Fianna Fáil and Fine Gael are surprising for two reasons. First, there is a high level of stability in party support as measured by the vote intention question. Second, change in support for the two main parties peaks in the immediate pre-campaign period (30–59 days). Fine Gael support reaches a high point while that of Fianna Fáil and the 'others' dips, giving the appearance of a drift towards Fine Gael. Such an impression could be illusory. This is because the aggregate data trends do not allow us to accurately track such apparent support flows. Therefore, care in interpretation is required.

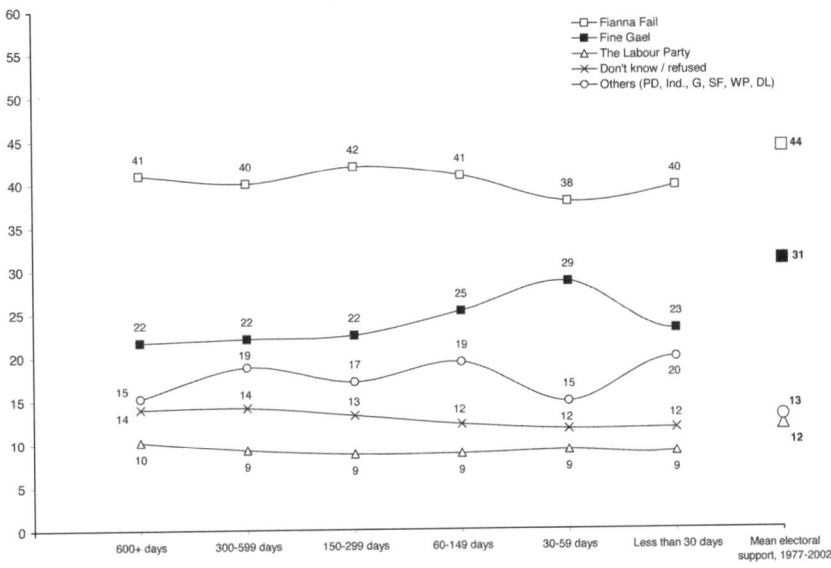

Figure 11 *Evolution of Party Support through the General Election Cycle and Comparison with Actual Election Results, 1977–2002 (per cent)*

Note: These data refers to the mean level of core party support as measured in opinion polls during six time periods during the general election cycle. The line graphs on the left refer to opinion poll estimates, while the dot plots on the right denote mean level of party support among the electorate from 1977–2002.

An inspection of poll estimations of vote intentions for the two main parties during election campaigns reveals little in the way of dramatic changes. There may, in fact, be considerable gross flows with little net change. If examination is made of variation in support for 'others' such estimates seem to be strongly affected, as one would expect, by informational factors. Discussion of informational effects must for the time being remain tentative until a more rigorous analysis can be undertaken.

Conclusion

In evaluating what opinion polls tell us about public opinion a central concern is how well polls match observed behaviour. In this respect, general elections provide an objective external validation where pollsters have traditionally compared their estimates of party support with those witnessed on election day. In this chapter I have developed two concepts – Mirror Accuracy and Lamp Precision – and examined the electoral record of Irish pollsters from two perspectives. These two perspectives fit neatly with the two functions of opinion polls outlined in the introductory chapter of this book.

The empirical analyses presented in this chapter reveal that the Mirror Accuracy of Irish opinion polls exhibits systematic bias, because support for Fianna Fáil is overestimated and support for Fine Gael is underestimated. In contrast, the Lamp Precision criterion suggests that opinion polls actually measure quite precisely attitudinal predispositions that structure electoral behaviour leading to a strong level of correlation ($r \geq 0.76$) between poll estimates of party support and election outcomes between 1977 and 2002. The key implication here is that opinion poll results may not reflect the exact *level of opinion* without error or bias, but poll results do exhibit strong *relationships* between the attitudinal and observed behaviour characteristics of the public.

I noted in Chapter 2 that the conceptualisation of opinion polls as reflecting public opinion revolves around accepting a Mirror Theory of Opinion Polling. With regard to vote intentions during an election cycle this theory of opinion polling is unrealistic, as it assumes that all respondents have 'real' opinions. Many voters in Ireland and elsewhere rarely think about politics beyond election campaigns. The evidence presented in the penultimate section of this chapter would tend to support such a hypothesis. In this respect, the Belief-Sampling Model seems a more realistic perspective.

Significantly, the error and bias components of opinion poll responses have become more important since 1997. One simple reason for the decline in the Mirror Accuracy of polls may stem from the fact that general election campaigns are no longer as effective in informing and mobilising voters as was the case in the past. However, testing such a hypothesis requires further research. In the next chapter we will move beyond political opinions associated with elections and examine what opinion poll results tell us about public satisfaction with government and party leaders.

Notes

1. With regard to use of the term 'accuracy' in this chapter there is no suggestion that vote intention questions asked months or years before an election should match very closely subsequent election results. For mirror accuracy final campaign polls will be compared with election results. The expectation here is that final poll results should ideally be similar to actual voting behaviour. With lamp precision we are interested in relationships and the degree to which poll trends match with electoral trends. Here the term 'precision' refers to how closely both trends are correlated across many elections. Here perfect correlation is treated as a useful standard to make comparisons between political parties.
2. During election campaigns both IMS and MRBI have used sample ballot papers where the candidates and parties on offer in each constituency were presented to respondents. Comparisons of the results from both question types indicate few real differences (McElroy and Marsh 2003: 163). As the party question is consistent over time, this will be the focus of discussion here.
3. The inclusion of 'independent candidates' has only been a feature of IMS polls since 2003.
4. The trends plotted in Figure 7 are plotted as linear trends. In addition, quadratic (second-order polynomial) curves were also plotted (not shown) where the expectation is that the level of 'don't know' responses will be relatively low immediately after one election and immediately prior to the next. During the mid-term period there would be higher levels of uncertainty as the public is paying less attention to politics. The trend exhibited in Figure 9 describing voter uncertainty during a generic election cycle fits this quadratic logic based on information effects.
5. The quadratic trends described in Footnote 4 in relation to Figure 7 indicate that conceptualising information effects as a second-order polynomial function does not fit the data very well ($R^2 = 0.10$ and $= 0.35$ for MRBI and IMS respectively). Figure 10 with data from 221 polls (rather than 51 polls in Figure 7) indicates that a better model would be a third-order polynomial (or cubic) function. Fitting such a model to the IMS data in Figure 7 improves model fit ($R^2 = 0.58$). This strategy has little impact on the MRBI model. Clearly, a cubic rather than quadratic relationship indicates a more complex dynamic model than that presented here and highlights the need for further research.
6. Of course, strictly speaking it is not possible to definitively know that non-campaign vote intention responses are different because there is no means of checking the validity of the answers given. The argument here is based on the assumption that levels of information, on which vote intentions are based, vary in systematic ways through an election cycle.
7. Recording a 'don't know' response occurs after a respondent has been asked to indicate a preference and should they hesitate they are prompted to indicate an inclination. Only after this prompting fails is an undecided response recorded. Poll interviewers attempt to minimise recording non-opinions and generally try to leave 'don't know' options as a last resort.
8. IMS and MRBI have asked intention to vote questions since 1977. These polls consistently overestimate the expected and recalled level of electoral participation. Furthermore, MRBI polls suffer from a question ordering effect where asking intention to turnout after the vote intention question primes the respondent. The success of ICM in the general election and Nice Treaty referendum in producing the best estimates of vote choice suggests that a better strategy is to ask at the outset: (a) probability to participate in next election; (b) vote intention in next election; (c) participation in the last general election and vote choice, and (d) self-description of past electoral participation, e.g. always vote, almost always, etc.
9. Use of simulated ballots items in surveys is not new. It seems to have been developed first by MRBI for a national survey undertaken from 10–18 April 1979 for Fine Gael for the first European Parliament elections (Jones 2001: 26).

10 It should be noted that IMS/Lansdowne and MRBI currently use the term 'core support' in their reports to refer to the preferences of all voters. Party support figures are then adjusted to exclude 'don't knows' (i.e. don't know, will not vote, refused). In a third step a second adjustment is made. For MRBI this involves using its 1997 based weighting scheme on the party support data excluding 'don't knows'. In the case of IMS this final adjustment on party support excluding 'don't knows' is based on reported party preference in the last general election that is weighted to match the actual results of the last election.
11 IMS follow a similar strategy where vote intention data is weighted to match the results of the last general election. This effectively assumes that the structure of party support remains constant between elections.
12 An internal MRBI memorandum by Jones and O'Donoghue (no date) indicates that in constituency poll research 25 per cent could not name any TD in their constituency, 5 per cent could not identify the party to which a TD they named belonged, and 7 per cent incorrectly identified their named TD with a party. Thanks to Maura Murphy of MRBI for this information. Some care in interpretation is required here as inability to match candidates and parties is only important if we are willing to assume that all voters vote for a candidate rather than a party. See also McElroy and Marsh (2003: 163), who found that 7 per cent of respondents in an IMS panel survey (13–28 May 2002) mismatched candidates and parties.
13 The standard error was calculated using the formula pq/n where p is the average first preference support received by Fianna Fáil in the final pre-election polls ($p = 0.46$) with average sample sizes of 1,000 respondents ($n = 1,000$) and $q = 1-p$.
14 Assuming that poll estimates of the true party support follows a normal distribution then it is possible to construct a measure of the spread of the estimats away from the arithmetic mean. The standard deviation is the most commonly used measure of data dispersion. With a normal distribution 95 per cent of the data lies within one standard deviation of the mean. This confidence interval (± one standard deviation from the mean) is often represented as a standard score. In this case the dimensionless quantity 1.96 refers to the confidence interval where 95 percent of the data is located. Consequently, a poll forecast with a reported confidence interval of $p \leq 0.05$ will yield a confidence interval of (2.4 x 1.96) ±4.7 per centage points.
15 The variance explained is calculated by squaring the Pearson correlation (r) value estimated, e.g. the variance of Fianna Fáil vote explained by the poll estimates is $(0.87)^2 = 0.76$

Chapter 4

Satisfaction with the Government, the Taoiseach and Party Leaders

> Satisfaction ratings mean no more, and possibly much less, than the semantics convey. In the wide open spaces of mid-term surveys, they convey the message that electors are generally satisfied with the performance of the party leader or government, and the criterion is far removed from providing any indication whatsoever of voting intentions in an election. In expressing satisfaction, electors are saying that they are happy with the administration and want it to continue in office...
>
> Jack Jones (2001: 97)

In Chapters 2 and 3 it was noted that the prevailing conceptualisation of opinion polls among pollsters and the media is that poll results should ideally reflect public opinion. Consequently, pollsters, in their measurement of political opinions, use phrases such as 'monitoring the political mood' or taking the 'political pulse' of the electorate. This is not to suggest that pollsters have a simplistic view where a single item such as vote intention is seen to mirror all the important details of public opinion towards politics. In September 1982 IMS, for example devised a composite polling measure called the 'Political Index' that was described as 'a summary of the electorate's opinions on key political issues'. This index was composed of six questions and constituted the core battery of items asked in its monthly omnibus polls during the 1980s.[1]

In effect, this strategy adopted by IMS demonstrates that tracking variation in vote intention questions during interelection periods like a 'mirror' is a rather limited exercise. This is because once the media know *what* opinion is towards governments, parties and party leaders they are inevitably drawn to ask *why* it exhibits a particular pattern and *how* it changes over time? Consequently, the interrelated use of government and party leader satisfaction ratings and vote intention items allowed opinion polls to operate as 'lamps' illuminating why the electorate was changing its opinions towards specific parties and politicians. Here I will focus on three poll questions that are asked in almost all opinion polls. These questions investigate vote intention for government parties, satisfaction with government and with the Taoiseach and satisfaction ratings for party leaders.

In this chapter I will examine two main questions. First, is it sensible to view political satisfaction ratings as mirrors of the political mood of the Irish electorate? Second, what is the relationship between political satisfaction ratings and vote intention questions? Here I will enquire if different poll questions help us understand alternative features of political popularity. In a similar manner to Chapter 3, I will attempt to comprehend how poll respondents answer political satisfaction questions during interviews. This will be important in helping us to understand what these specific types of poll questions tell us about public opinion.

In the first section of this chapter there will be a brief methodological discussion of the nature and origins of political satisfaction questions. The second section will outline what the poll results tell us – which governments have been the most popular and which Taoisigh and party leaders have received the highest satisfaction ratings. The third section will look at the relationship between vote intentions for government parties and satisfaction ratings for the government and Taoiseach over the long term. Of course, public opinion is often important because of short-term changes. An example of politically significant short-term effects will be briefly described in section four. The concluding section will endeavour to provide answers to the main questions posed and assess the implications for our understanding of public opinion.

Interpretation of Political Satisfaction Questions

It is important to first consider the origin, nature and purpose of political satisfaction ratings. In this section I will examine government satisfaction rating questions and items that assess the public's approval of the Taoiseach's and main party leaders performance. The goal here is to understand how the public interprets these questions and how they are different (if at all) from vote intention items. Moreover, the discussion of the Mirror Theory of Opinion Polling and the Belief-Sampling Model of survey response in Chapter 2 gives us a useful framework for evaluating these different types of questions. For example, is it reasonable to think that vote intention and political satisfaction ratings during interelection periods are strongly influenced by contextual effects as postulated by the Belief-Sampling Model?

Government satisfaction ratings

The use of satisfaction rating questions in opinion polls has a long history. At an international level, it was Gallup who first developed the question format that is now used in may countries such as Ireland. Satisfaction items form a core part of the 'tracking' (that is, mirroring of public sentiments) which polling companies undertake in the long term. In the UK, Gallup's government satisfaction rating question was first asked in 1946 and has been implemented frequently using the same wording format since 1956.

In Ireland, the first government satisfaction ratings were collected by IMS for *This Week Magazine* in November 1970. It should be noted that IMS is affiliated with Gallup International and hence uses a variety of poll questions that draw on Gallup's extensive experience. MRBI first used a government satisfaction question in a private poll for Fine Gael in April 1973, and has asked this item regularly in its *Irish Times* poll series since October 1982.

The government satisfaction items used by IMS and MRBI as shown below are for practical purposes identical and functionally equivalent. This implies that it should be possible (not withstanding questionnaire and house effects) to combine the responses to these questions to create a more extensive time series charting the evolution in government satisfaction from the 1970s onwards. Plotting trends using government satisfaction data from both polling companies exhibits no significant systematic differences and supports our contention that the IMS and MRBI items are equivalent.

> Are you satisfied or dissatisfied with the way the government is running the country? Response options are: Satisfied, dissatisfied, don't know. [IMS wording]

> Would you say that you are satisfied or dissatisfied with the manner in which the government is running the country? Response options are: Satisfied, dissatisfied, don't know. [MRBI wording]

Unfortunately, Irish pollsters ask questions on approval of the Government's handling of specific policy fields only intermittently. Therefore, it is impossible to see definitively what, if any, policy reasons underpin changes in approval. This is an important limitation as much of the 'new science' of (aggregate) public opinion tracks the electoral consequences of cyclical changes in public policy preferences (Stimson 2004: xvii, 58–95; Stimson 1991; Erikson, MacKuen and Stimson 2002).

MRBI has always asked the government satisfaction question first in their surveys, followed by leadership satisfaction ratings and thereafter vote intention.[2] IMS pursued this strategy until October 1993 when, as noted in Chapter 2, it changed its policy following the example of Gallup UK. Currently, MRBI asks the political satisfaction ratings first followed by the vote intention question. In contrast, IMS/Lansdowne adopt the reverse strategy. Analysis of the polling data for these three items from 1987 to 2005 indicates that this question ordering has very little discernible effect, as the estimates for IMS/Lansdowne and MRBI are very similar for this whole period. Nevertheless, there are two important patterns in the data. On the one hand, prior to late 1993, polling estimates of vote intention for incumbent governments and satisfaction with these same governments were very similar. On the other hand, from 1994 until 2002 government satisfaction ratings were persistently higher than vote intentions for parties in government. It is tempting to attribute such an effect to economic factors (such as opinions associated with the 'Celtic tiger'), but more research is required to test this hypothesis.

More generally, it is important to stress that the different questionnaire formats followed by IMS/Lansdowne and MRBI reflect concerns over question ordering effects – a topic discussed earlier in Chapter 2. The question ordering followed by MRBI adheres to a protocol established by Gallup since 1956 because of fears of a specific question-ordering problem known as the *consistency effect*.[3] This surveying phenomenon relates to the propensity of respondents to give answers to survey questions that are consistent with responses given earlier in an interview (Schuman and Presser 1996: 27–35). With regard to presidential popularity, Sigelman (1981) found that placing this specific item first or last in a questionnaire does not affect the level of approval, but does have an impact on the level of *opinionation* (willingness to express an opinion).

The implication here is that the published results for net government satisfaction in Irish opinion polls are likely to be conservative estimates of approval due to their placement at the start of interviews yielding less opinionated responses. More generally, the importance of questionnaire layout in prompting different considerations for poll responses fits in with the logic outlined in the Belief-Sampling Model.

Satisfaction with the Taoiseach and opposition party leaders

Early versions of the satisfaction with Taoiseach questions asked by MRBI in two polls in 1974 were 'comparative' in nature.[4] The standard 'absolute' wording used today was first implemented by IMS in August 1976, and has been asked in almost all subsequent political opinion polls. The Taoiseach/party leader satisfaction questions generally follow the government satisfaction item. This question ordering may lead to 'consistency' or 'contrast' effects, where the format of the questionnaire shapes the responses given in an opinion poll interview.[5]

For media and political commentators, the Taoiseach and opposition party leader satisfaction ratings are generally interpreted in terms of government satisfaction and vote intention questions. In short, the interrelated responses to the satisfaction and vote intention survey items are envisaged as reflecting *what* public opinion is, and facilitate illuminating *why* voters have particular vote intentions on the basis of levels of satisfaction with the Government and party leaders. The implication here is that those interviewed in opinion polls have 'real' opinions. As we have seen in Chapter 3, responses to vote intention questions vary through the electoral cycle where voters are not always paying the same level of attention to politics and hence their level of informedness varies over time. Consequently, one may posit two different interpretations of public responses to political satisfaction ratings.

Mirror Theory of Opinion Polling The prevailing conceptualisation by Irish pollsters and the media is that responses to Taoiseach and party leader satisfaction ratings are an expression of true and 'sincere' opinions. In this respect, the 'horse race' logic implicit in most media-based polling implies that those who state that they are satisfied with the performance of the Government and the Taoiseach will also express a vote intention for the incumbent party. Likewise, opposition party supporters will be dissatisfied with the performance of the Government and the Taoiseach as their preferred party is not in office.

Belief-Sampling Model If most citizens have only a passing interest in politics for much of the time beyond election campaigns, this implies that many opinion poll respondents may not have opinions concerning the performance of the Government, the Taoiseach and party leaders. Consequently, when faced with an interview question they are compelled to use whatever information is available to construct a response. The expectation here is that context effects will play an important role in the considerations used by respondents to generate an answer. Moreover, we would expect that political satisfaction ratings would show greater variance than vote intention items, as the latter are likely to be based on standing predispositions such as party attachment. In addition, we would expect that the level of uncommitted responses for leaders of smaller parties should be higher than that for leaders of larger parties. The available polling evidence suggests that both of these expectations fit with the data.

However, a definitive judgement on whether the Mirror Theory (where respondents express real opinions) or the Belief-Sampling Model (where those interviewed provide responses on the basis of whatever considerations are prompted by the context of the interview) is the more correct one is not possible. Having only aggregate level data, it is not feasible to know exactly how individual respondents interpret the survey questions presented to them in a face-to-face interview. To simply infer aggregate-level patterns onto the individual level runs the risk of falling foul of the so-called 'ecological inference fallacy', where response patterns observed at the national level can be very different from the relationships revealed in individual-level data (see King 1997: 3–27; Schuessler 1999). Keeping in mind that these poll questions do not have a definitive meaning serves the important function of making us wary of accepting face-value interpretations of what these questions tell us about public opinion. I will now turn to the relationship between vote intention questions and political satisfaction ratings.

Distinction between satisfaction with government and voting intentions

Within political science there has been extensive use of vote intention items and prime minister satisfaction ratings, but not of government satisfaction measures. At first sight this is surprising, as presidential approval and government satisfaction ratings are often the first questions asked in opinion polls across the globe. Nevertheless, government satisfaction results are rarely analysed as a dependent variable, like presidential approval within the political science literature in the United States. In parliamentary systems such as Australia, Britain and Ireland, government lead over the opposition, which is derived from vote intention questions, is used rather than *government satisfaction* ratings to assess government popularity (McAllister 2003; Clarke, Ho and Stewart 2000; Harrison and Marsh 1998).

This important conceptual distinction between vote intentions for government parties during interelection periods and satisfaction with government performance is rarely discussed (note Nadeau, Niemi and Amato 1996; Crespi 1980). Nevertheless, there would seem to be at least four reasons for this distinction:

- Being satisfied with government and voting for government parties are not the same thing. This is because the latter has a behavioural orientation that is influenced by satisfaction with government performance and other factors.
- The concept of government satisfaction in parliamentary democracies is not the same as presidential approval in the US. This difference has an institutional basis. In the US, citizens directly elect the President, whereas in Britain, Ireland and other parliamentary systems it is parties who form governments. Therefore, presidential approval is a direct (electoral) measure, whereas government satisfaction is an indirect one being mediated by party preferences.[6]
- Responses to concrete vote intention items are more valid and reliable measures of government popularity than answers given to relatively abstract government satisfaction questions (note Nannestad and Paldam 1994; Lewis-Beck and Paldam 2000).[7]
- The vote intention and government satisfaction items are different types of survey question. The former is a *decision* measure, where respondents select a single party as their choice for a hypothetical first-preference vote. Such decisions are based on long-term beliefs,

or preferences, and in this respect match with some of the assumptions of the Mirror Theory of Opinion Polling. In contrast, the latter is a *judgement* measure where an interviewee simply indicates whether they are satisfied or dissatisfied (note Lau 2003: 20-1, 43 for a discussion on this distinction). These responses are not based directly on underlying long-term preferences such as party attachment, but based on a running tally of information most likely gleaned from the media. As a result, judgements may be uncorrelated with the original information (for example, party attachment) on which the judgement is based (note Feldman 1995: 263). In short, decisions and judgements are likely to appear inconsistent and judgements will exhibit greater response variance.

If the goal is to get simple 'gut' reactions to incumbent executives' performance the government satisfaction question would seem to be a more appropriate measure, as it is typically asked first in a survey interview. Like the US presidential questions, the Government satisfaction item would seem to be a measure that captures general perceptions about how well the Government is performing. Such questions, as Jones notes in the opening quotation of this chapter, are at best very imperfect indicators of future electoral success (note also Mueller 1970: 19).

These operational insights match with our theoretical expectations. The fourth point above highlights a central feature of the Belief-Sampling Model. The type of poll question and resulting survey response process influences the answers recorded in mass survey interviews. If political satisfaction ratings are judgements based on specific 'bits' of information acquired throughout election cycles, such responses are likely to produce 'noisier' and more inconsistent responses. In contrast, decisions based on long-term predispositions such as party attachment that are reflected in vote intention questions are expected to have lower variance (note Zaller and Feldman 1992). All of this underscores the simple point being made in this chapter – vote intentions for government parties and political satisfaction ratings are different though related phenomena.

Having briefly examined the main characteristics of political satisfaction ratings, it is now time to examine the polling data and investigate what political satisfaction ratings can tell us about political popularity in Ireland.

Popularity of Governments, Taoisigh and Party Leaders

One important feature of opinion poll results is the unique facility they offer for making comparisons between governments, Taoisigh and party leaders across time. In addition, they provide a means of rank ordering governments, Taoisigh and party leaders in terms of popularity. The satisfaction ratings have been used here to construct median values. It would have been preferable to construct 'net satisfaction ratings' (that is, percentage satisfied minus dissatisfied), as this would have given a more accurate picture of public opinion. Unfortunately, missing data make this procedure impossible for all opinion polls that are known to have asked political satisfaction questions. Consequently, it makes sense to use a measure of satisfaction that maximises the number of time points available in order to explore as comprehensively as possible trends over time.

Popularity of successive Irish governments

Figure 12 is interesting as it shows that the two most popular Irish governments were those that presided during the 'Celtic tiger' era of 1994–2002. Moreover, it reveals that the most liked administrations were those that have been in office since 1989. This is a date often interpreted by political and media commentators as the era of Ireland's remarkable transition from 'bust to boom' and the emergence of the process of Social Partnership (note MacSharry and White 2000).

Significantly, the least popular governments were those who presided over the worst phases of an economic recession between 1982 and 1987. This interpretation of the government satisfaction data suggests that economic conditions have played a significant role in mediating popular satisfaction with government. Figure 12 also illustrates an interesting rule of thumb that has been applied to the popularity of US presidents seeking re-election – 'below 50, you lose' (Stimson 2004: 137). The only incumbent Irish governments re-elected in recent times were the Fianna Fáil/Progressive Democrat coalitions, in 2002 and 2007. The first of these three FF/PD coalition governments (1977–2002) was unique in having an average government satisfaction rating above 50 per cent for its entire term of office.

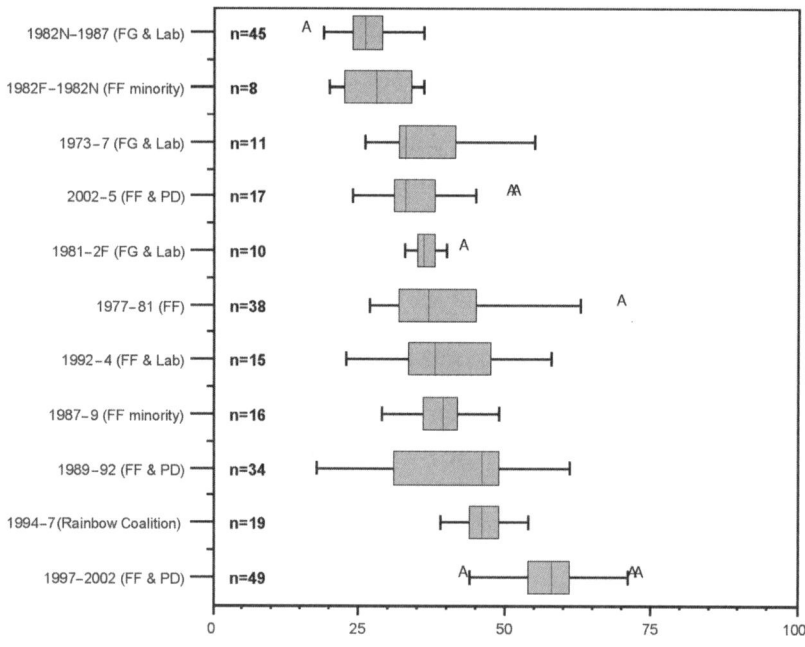

Figure 12 *Boxplots of Satisfaction with the Performance of Irish Governments, 1973–2005 (per cent)*

Note: The data are organised on the basis of median satisfaction rating. The data on the left refer to the number of polls in which the Government was included, e.g. the FF and PD government in office since 2002 has been included in 17 IMS and MRBI polls between June 2002 and February 2005. The vertical dark line at the centre of the boxes is the median. Each box relates to an interquartile range, i.e. the difference between the 25th and 75th percentiles in the data. The lines and whiskers refer to data that lie within two interquartile ranges of the median (or one interquartile range from the edges of the box). The A symbols denote 'outliers', that is, cases 1.5 to 3 box lengths (one interquartile range) from the left or right box edge.

Popularity of successive Irish Taoisigh

It is tempting to think that satisfaction with government and giving a positive rating to the performance of the leader of the Government (that is, the Taoiseach) would go hand-in-hand. The polling data shown in Figure 13 indicate that this can be the case sometimes, for example Ahern's first government (1997–2002).[8]

More often the connection between government and Taoiseach satisfaction is more complex and would seem to depend on

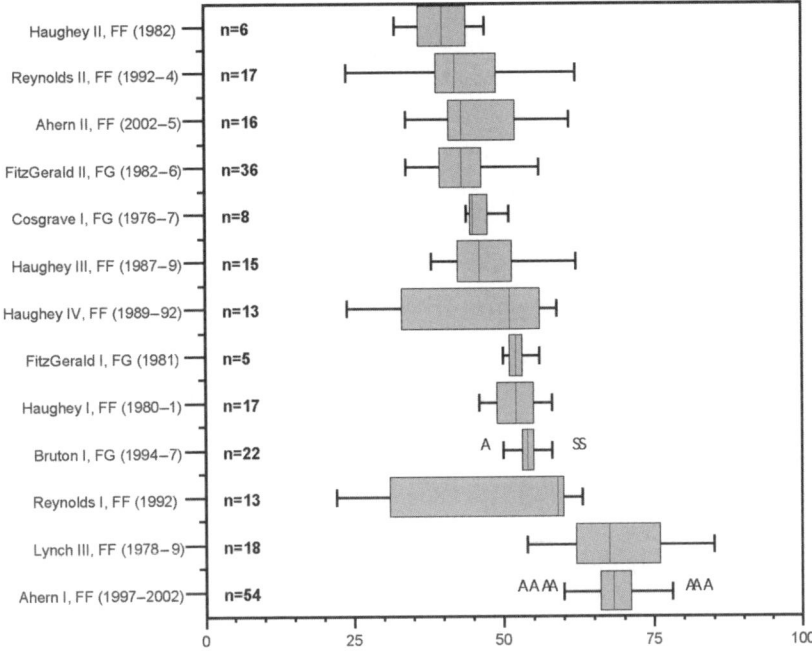

Figure 13 *Boxplots of Satisfaction with the Performance of Successive Taoisigh, 1978–2005 (per cent)*

Note: The data are organised on the basis of median satisfaction rating. The data on the left refer to the number of polls in which a specific Taoiseach was included, e.g. Ahern has been included in 16 IMS and MRBI polls between 2002 and February 2005. The vertical dark line at the centre of the boxes is the median. Each box relates to an interquartile range, i.e. the difference between the 25th and 75th percentiles in the data. The lines and whiskers refer to data that lie within two interquartile ranges of the median (or one interquartile range from the edges of the box). The A symbols denote 'outliers', that is, cases 1.5 to 3 box lengths (one interquartile range) from the left or right box edge. The S symbols (S) relates to 'extremes', i.e. cases that are 3 to 5 box lengths from the left or right box edge.

candidate and context effects (such as the economy). While the minority Fianna Fáil government of 1987 to 1989 was the fourth most popular government, Charles Haughey's third term as Taoiseach has a lower popularity ranking (8). In contrast, Jack Lynch's third term in office as Taoiseach between 1977 and 1979 saw him become the second most popular prime minister recorded by the polls, while his government popularity ranking was lower (number 6). More generally, Figure 13 shows an important pattern.

Irish prime ministers in their first term of office are likely to be more popular on average when comparison is made with subsequent administrations. This pattern holds for Ahern, Reynolds, Haughey and FitzGerald – all Taoisigh who have served more than one term of office for which opinion poll data are available. In partisan terms, Fianna Fáil prime ministers tend to be the most popular or unpopular, while Fine Gael Taoisigh tend to have middling ratings.

Popularity of successive party leaders

One of the key features of parliamentary democracy is the leadership provided by government and effective opposition provided by party leaders out of office. Figure 14 shows a ranking of satisfaction ratings of almost all Irish party leaders since 1976. As can be seen from the number of polls used to estimate the median satisfaction rating, some party leaders have had very different lengths of tenure and this has some influence on the estimates. Fianna Fáil has provided the two most popular party leaders during the last three decades, while Fine Gael has the unenviable distinction of having the two least popular ones.

Garret FitzGerald is the most popular Fine Gael leader examined despite the fact that his second government (1982–7) was the least popular, although he had a middling prime ministerial popularity profile. The Labour Party is interesting in that Ruairi Quinn, who had a relatively brief time as leader, holds the record for being the most popular leader of this party between 1977 and 2005. Dick Spring, one of the longest-serving leaders of the Labour Party (from late 1982 to June 1997) and who led the party to unprecedented electoral success in 1992, has a lower level of overall popularity. This ranking undoubtedly reflects a much broader range of satisfaction ratings ensuing from his long tenure. Therefore, some caution is required in interpreting the median scores and rankings displayed in Figures 12–14.

A key pattern in Figure 14 is the fact that leaders of smaller parties can receive relatively high satisfaction ratings, such as Mary Harney of the Progressive Democrats (PDs) or Gerry Adams of Sinn Féin. What strong satisfaction ratings mean for leaders of small parties would seem to depend on whether they form part of coalition governments (such as Mary Harney and the PDs) and their salience within the media (such as Gerry Adams and Sinn Féin within the Northern Ireland peace process). In general, a common

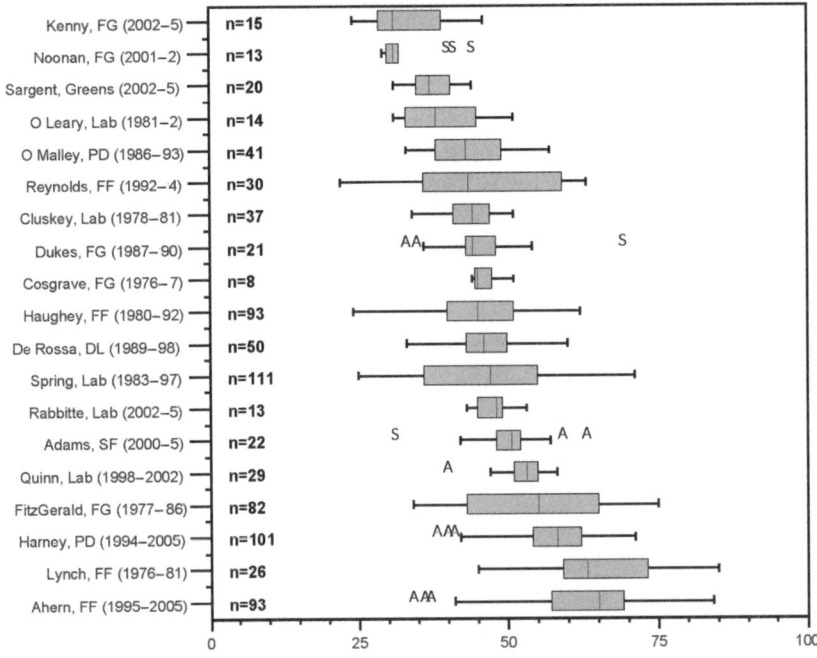

Figure 14 *Boxplots of Satisfaction with the Performance of Irish Party Leaders, 1976–2005 (per cent)*

Note: The data are organised on the basis of median satisfaction rating. The data on the left refer to the number of polls in which the party leader was included, e.g. Ahern has been included in 93 IMS and MRBI polls between 1995 and February 2005. The vertical dark line at the centre of the boxes is the median. Each box relates to an interquartile range, i.e. the difference between the 25th and 75th percentiles in the data. The lines and whiskers refer to data that lie within two interquartile ranges of the median (or one interquartile range from the edges of the box). The A symbols denote 'outliers', that is, cases 1.5 to 3 box lengths (one interquartile range) from the left or right box edge. The S symbols (S) relates to 'extremes', i.e. cases that are 3 to 5 box lengths from the left or right box edge.

characteristic of leaders of small parties and newly elected party leaders (except in the case of Fianna Fáil) is that their low public profile results in a high level of 'don't know' responses and hence low ratings in opinion polls.[9]

In this section I have used opinion poll data in a mirror-like manner to construct rankings of the relative popularity of governments, Taoisigh and party leaders. I have demonstrated that using this method of organising a large volume of data it is possible to compare patterns between different opinions and illuminate like a lamp important and previously little-known interrelationships within Irish public opinion. For example, popular governments are not necessarily associated with popular Taoisigh. Moreover, I have suggested from this simple analysis that opinion poll responses are often shaped by cues from the media, perceptions of economic performance and length of time in office. In the next section, I will build on this work and investigate through time series analysis the long-term relationship between vote intention and political satisfaction ratings.

Long-term Relationship between Key Political Indicators

In order to simplify the analysis undertaken in this section, I will concentrate on public opinion relating to the Government, that is, vote intention for government parties, and satisfaction with the performance of the Government and Taoiseach. It is important first to examine a general profile of these three variables over the entire period for which there are polling data, (late 1977 to early 2005) in order to identify potentially important patterns and trends.

Comparison of leadership satisfaction ratings

One central feature of media commentary on opinion poll results is their emphasis on the competition between party leaders for popularity. There is the 'zero-sum-game' assumption that if the Taoiseach is doing well then the opposition party leaders must be doing badly. Alternatively, there is the view that opposition party leaders compete against each other to provide the most competent alternative to the incumbent Taoiseach. The polling data presented in Figure 15 suggest that this is not a completely accurate picture of how the Irish public answers leadership satisfaction questions.

The most salient pattern in this figure is the common trend exhibited in all of the leadership satisfaction ratings. However, this figure also reveals two important sub-periods: 1978–90 and 1991–2002. This division seems to coincide with the emergence of John Bruton as leader of Fine Gael and Albert Reynolds as leader of Fianna Fáil.

An examination of the correlation between leadership satisfaction ratings shows that for the first sub-period there is significant correlation ($r \geq .5$, $p \leq .001$) between all three ratings. During the second sub-period, the correlation between Fianna Fáil and Fine Gael

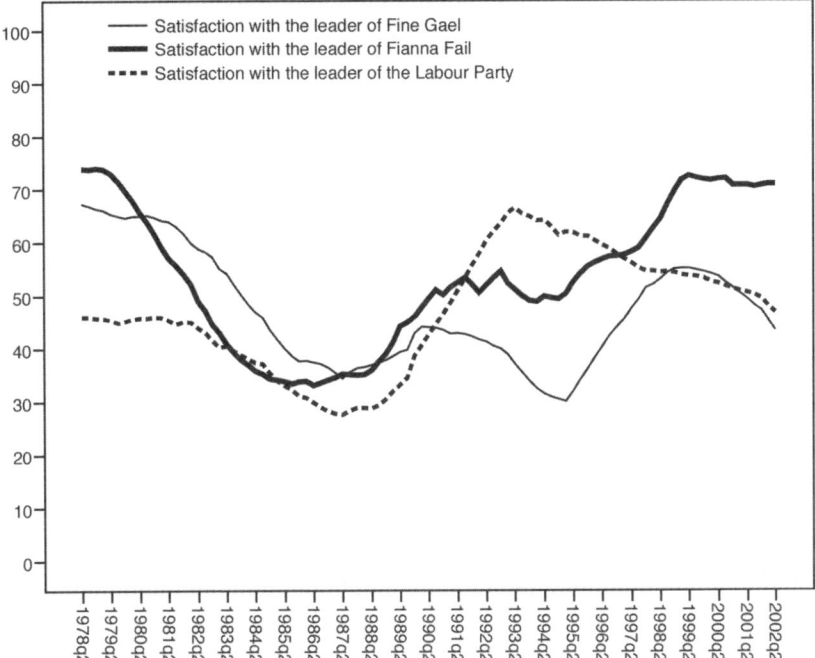

Figure 15 *Comparison of Mean Support for the Three Main Party Leaders in the Republic of Ireland, 1978–2002 (per cent)*

Note: Quarterly data (1978q2–2002q2) have been exponentially smoothed using the Holt et al. (1960) procedure that assumes that there is a linear trend but no seasonal variation (see Mills 1998: 153–63). The polling results have been aggregated to create a quarterly time series. This is a standard econometric procedure to facilitate data analysis.

Would you say you are satisfied or dissatisfied with the way NAME OF PARTY LEADER / TAOISEACH is doing his job as PARTY LEADER / TAOISEACH / TANAISTE ?

Response options are satisfied, dissatisfied or don't know [MRBI wording].

Are you satisfied or dissatisfied with the way NAME OF PARTY LEADER is doing his job as TAOISEACH leader of NAME OF PARTY?

Response options are satisfied, dissatisfied or don't know [IMS/Lansdowne wording].

Correlations between party leader support ratings

Parties	1978–90			1991–2002			1978–2002		
	Corr.	p	N	Corr.	p	N	Corr.	p	N
FF-FG	+0.495	≤0.001	47	+0.499	≤0.001	43	0.345	≤0.001	90
FF-LAB	+0.519	≤0.001	49	−0.125	≤0.001	41	0.416	≤0.001	90
FG-LAB	+0.513	≤0.001	47	+0.081	=0.613	41	0.002	=0.989	88

Note: 'Corr.' refers to Pearson's product moment correlation, 'p' is the significance level and 'N' relates to the number of cases. Calculations based on percentage quarterly data.

leadership ratings remains quite strong (see bottom of Figure 15). However, the leadership ratings for the Labour Party changed in 1990 and precede the remarkable gains made by this party in the general election of 1992 and its time in coalition with Fianna Fáil, which ended abruptly in November 1994.

During the 1990–4 period, Dick Spring's satisfaction ratings effectively exhibited an independent pattern. Thereafter, Labour leadership satisfaction ratings have declined while those of Fianna Fáil and Fine Gael increased (though from very different levels). The party leadership poll data illustrate some remarkable dynamics where the Irish public treated all party leaders in the same manner during the 1980s and differentially in the 1990s. Moreover, since 1999 there appears to be a reversion to a common trend for all leader satisfaction ratings. Whether these series of patterns in the data reflect changing economic conditions or specific political factors requires further research.

Comparison of voting intentions and political satisfaction ratings

The data presented in Figure 16 show two patterns. First, this figure reveals that government and Taoiseach satisfaction ratings are strongly related as they both follow a very similar trend, though at different levels. Second, the general pattern in these three time series seem to be divided into two phases based on key developments in the economy: depression and boom.[10] While this approach is rather informal, the focus of interest is the relative ordering of the three long-term political approval and satisfaction variables. In this respect, one can see in Figure 16 different rank ordering profiles for the vote intention and government satisfaction series during these two phases.[11]

During the 'economic depression' phase (the last quarter of 1980 to the last quarter of 1989), the relative ordering of the key political variables was: (1) satisfaction with the Taoiseach, (2) vote intentions for government parties and (3) satisfaction with government performance. In the following phase where there was the so-called 'Celtic tiger boom', the relative ordering of the three time series switched. From 1990 onwards the ranking was: (1) satisfaction with the Taoiseach, (2) satisfaction with government and (3) expressed vote intentions for government parties.

This pattern in the opinion poll data suggests that it makes sense to think of the economic depression and boom phases as distinct. The implication here is that changing economic conditions have a

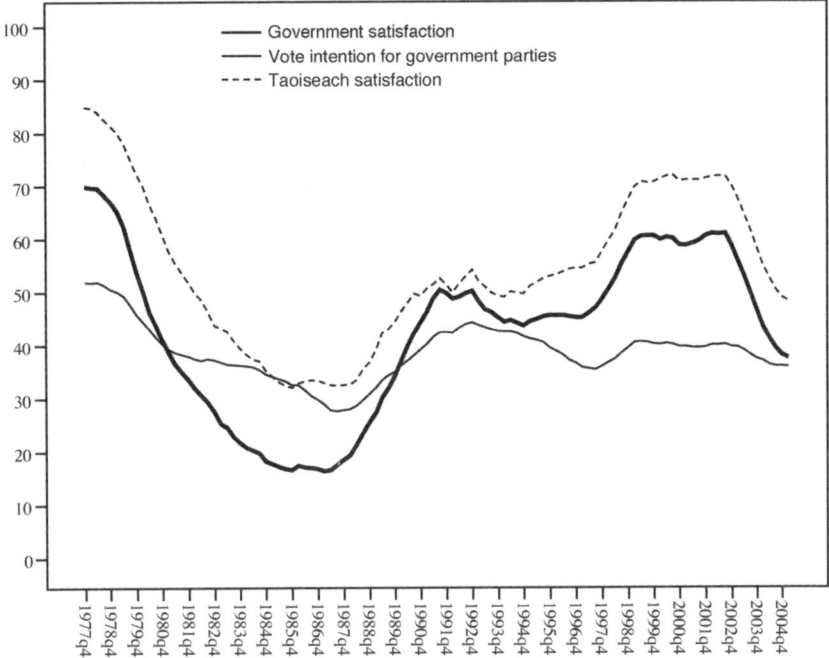

Figure 16 *Comparison of Voting Intentions for Parties in Government with Government and Taoiseach Satisfaction Ratings, 1977–2005 (per cent)*

Note: Quarterly data (1977q4–2005q1) have been exponentially smoothed using the Holt et al. (1960) procedure that assumes that there is a linear trend but no seasonal variation (see Mills 1998: 153–63). As in the previous figure the polling results have been aggregated to create a quarterly time series.

differential impact on political opinions. It seems that public opinion towards the economy translates more easily into political judgements (that is, satisfaction ratings) than political decisions (that is, vote intentions). Of course, such a survey response mechanism makes sense only if one conceptualises government satisfaction and vote intention for government parties as being different polling measures. As we will see in the next subsection, this argument becomes more plausible if we examine the evolution of satisfaction ratings during a generic election cycle.

Evolution of voting intentions and political satisfaction ratings through the election cycle

An examination of the polling evidence shows some important differences in the pattern observed during the interelection cycle. Nevertheless, these differences do follow a logic that relates to both 'partisanship' and 'informational' factors. First, with regard to partisanship, vote intention for the incumbent government as one might expect is less volatile than government satisfaction. The polling data reveal that vote intention for government parties in Ireland follows an inverted U-shape, or quadratic, trend during the election cycle. Such a pattern is in agreement with the 'costs of ruling' argument espoused in the presidential/government satisfaction literature (Mueller 1970; Paldam 1986).[12]

Second, the informational differences between government satisfaction and vote intentions for government parties are evident in Figure 17 from the trend in the countdown to the next general election (end of the tenth decile). The two time series begin at different levels. This dissimilarity probably reflects the fact that government satisfaction and vote intention data are different types of survey question, that is, a judgement and a decision respectively. Thereafter, government satisfaction based on 'gut' reactions fluctuates on the basis of interelection events.[13]

However, as the next general election approaches both vote intentions for incumbent parties and satisfaction with government converge as the voters become more informed in the countdown to Election Day (Alvarez 1997). The slightly higher final level of government satisfaction over vote intentions for incumbent parties may be reflecting the switching of vote intentions in an election campaign, as voters who are satisfied (or dissatisfied) with the Government nevertheless return to their 'normal' party.[14] Regardless of the validity of the explanation put forward here, the main point to be made is that vote intentions for the incumbent government and satisfaction ratings are different. Moreover, this difference is most pronounced outside of election campaign periods. Why this should be the case is the question to which I will now turn.

Analysis of the long-term relationship between the key political indicators

The discussion thus far has illustrated that Irish opinion polls' measurement of political satisfaction ratings and vote intentions

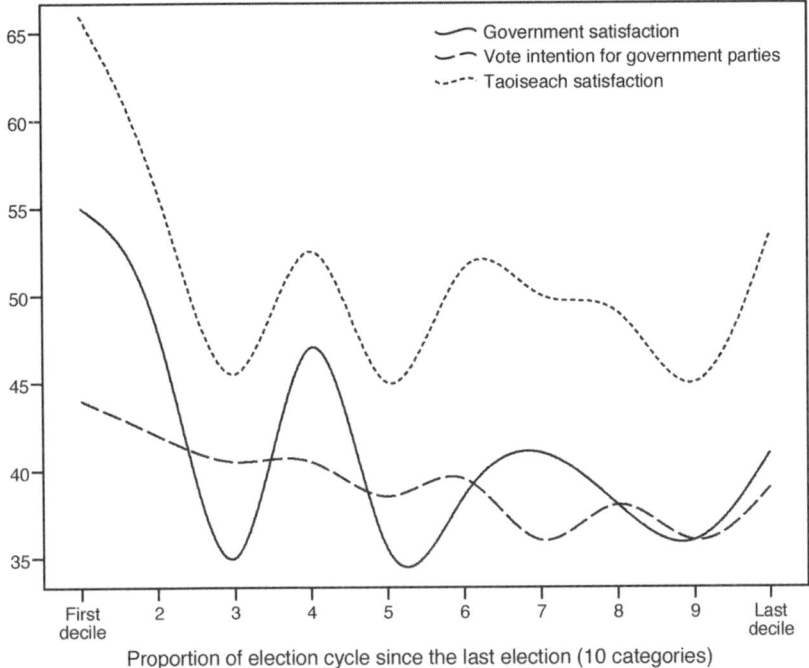

Figure 17 *Comparison of Voting Intentions for Government with Government and Taoiseach Satisfaction Ratings during the Interelection Cycle, 1969–2002 (median percentage ratings)*

Note: As each interelection period is different, ranging from 252–1,806 days, comparison of satisfaction and approval ratings using aggregation of days is inappropriate. For this reason each interelection was divided into deciles and median scores used because these are less affected by outliers than mean values.

towards the incumbent government follow similar trends, but have different levels and have changed their relative ordering (in terms of absolute values) over the last three decades. Such evidence suggests that there are strong relationships between these key political variables and leads us neatly towards consideration of a variety of questions, such as: does vote intention for an incumbent administration determine the level of government satisfaction, or vice versa? Or does satisfaction with the Taoiseach help shape the levels of vote intentions for those parties in power and the level of government satisfaction?

In technical terms, the objective here is to test an interrelated system of models or equations. Each key political measure is both a 'dependent' and 'independent' variable in the overall modelling system.[15] Fortunately, it is possible to investigate causal relationships using the concept of *Granger causality*. The basic intuition behind this concept is that past values of a dependent and set of independent variables can shape the current values of the dependent variable, but not vice versa. This is a key constraint as it allows us statistically to specify and estimate our models (or system of equations). It is important to note that Granger causality does not imply 'causality' according to the common use of the term, but relates to the success of using past values to improve model prediction. I will postpone for a moment a discussion of how to estimate a system of equations to test for Granger causality. It is necessary first to outline one key consideration involved in examining time series data.

An important task in any time series regression analysis is establishing that the variables being investigated are 'stationary', and thereby not likely to yield 'spurious regression' results.[16] This involves checking that the variables being examined are causally related and not just co-trending together. Otherwise we run the risk that all our models and inferences will be misleading. This statistical criterion is called stationarity. Variables are stationary if their mean, variance and covariance with past values (of themselves) does not depend on time, that is, a variable does not increase by some (non)linear function of elapsed time.

Given the strong trends evident in Figure 16, it is not too surprising that none of the political variables are stationary. Therefore, each of these series has a mean or variance that is time dependent (see Mills 1998; Gujurati 1995: 720).[17] A common strategy for making such non-stationary series stationary is to 'first difference' the data, that is, to focus on change per unit time. However, differencing has the drawback of destroying valuable information such as long-run relationships among variables, where the gains of achieving stationarity are outweighed by loss of information (Beck 1991: 67–9; Sanders 2005: 177). I will return to this consideration a little later.

As noted earlier, within this sub-section we are interested not in one, but in three sets of relationships. The main goal is to explore how vote intention for government parties and satisfaction with government and Taoiseach performance are interconnected over time. This implies examining these three sets of relationships *simultaneously*. The simplest methodology within the econometrics literature for undertaking such a task is called Vector Auto Regression (VAR). Within VAR each variable examined is used both as a dependent and independent factor in a series of models estimated simultaneously. In this sub-section we will have three models in our VAR analysis. As noted earlier, this is because we have three variables of interest. For example, in model 1, government satisfaction at time 2 is explained in terms of government satisfaction at time 1 plus Taoiseach satisfaction at time 1 and vote intention for government parties at time 1. Within model 2, vote intentions for incumbent parties at time 2 are explained in terms of vote intentions at time 1 plus government satisfaction at time 1 and Taoiseach ratings at time 1. Model 3 explains Taoiseach satisfaction in terms of past values of this variable plus past values of government satisfaction and vote intentions for government parties.[18] The estimation is undertaken using Ordinary Least Squares (OLS) regression (see Gujarati 1995: 734–54).

In short, VAR has the important advantage of facilitating an investigation of the dynamic relationships among variables without imposing strong *a priori* restrictions, and has the added benefit of allowing an assessment to be made of Granger causality. Technically speaking, as noted earlier, the variables used in such an analysis should be stationary. If they are not they should be differenced in order to make them stationary. Unfortunately, as was also noted earlier this procedure involves a substantial loss of information. Preliminary model testing of our key political variables data using differenced values does (as expected) result in loss of information where all relationships between the three variables disappear. Consequently, a VAR model was estimated with non-stationary variables because the goal is to determine the relationship between the three key political measures, rather than accurate coefficient estimates. Using VAR with non-stationary variables for this limited purpose is considered within the time series literature to be a legitimate exercise (see Freeman 1983: 334; Freeman, Williams and Lin 1989).

The bottom part of Figure 18 shows the results of Granger causality testing carried out after estimation of a VAR model. By undertaking a Granger causality test we are assuming that each of our political variables is strongly determined by the other two, which seems a reasonable assumption given the pattern evident in Figure 16. The Granger test allows us to examine three forms of causality: (a) unidirectional causality, (b) reciprocal causality and (c) independence or no causal relationship.

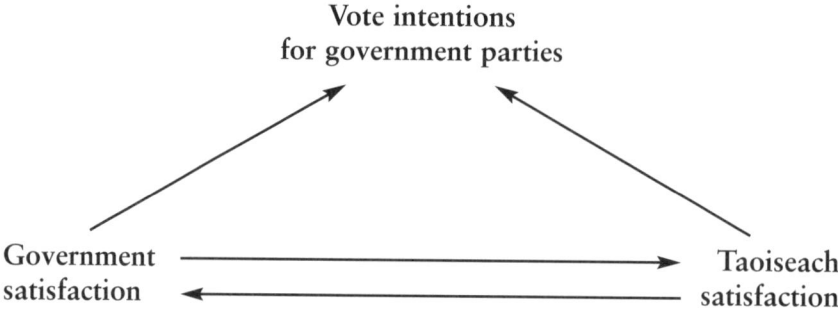

Arrows refer to causal relationships that are significant p≤0.05; see table below for details. Analysis undertaken on quarterly data and refers to polls undertaken between 1982q2 and 2005q1.

Wald tests for causal independence between government approval, government satisfaction and Taoiseach satisfaction, 1978q2–2005q1

	Dependent variables		
Independent variables	Vote intentions for government parties	Government satisfaction	Taoiseach satisfaction
Vote intentions for government parties (d.f. 2)		4.11	.23
Government satisfaction (d.f. 2)	8.64 **		8.66 **
Taoiseach satisfaction (d.f. 2)	7.72 **	7.22 **	
Both variables (d.f. 4)	11.29 **	13.62 **	9.76 **

* $p<0.10$ ** $p<0.05$ *** $p<0.001$ (two tailed test)

Figure 18 *Granger Causal Relationships between Voting Intentions for Government Parties, and Satisfaction Ratings for the Government and Taoiseach, 1978–2005*

Note: In testing for Granger causality the null hypothesis is that the coefficients (plural because of lags) for a specific independent variable are jointly equal to zero. Consequently a series of restricted and unrestricted models are tested. The Wald test assesses whether the unrestricted estimate of a coefficient is significantly different from a restricted estimate using a chi-square distribution where the degrees of freedom equal the number of model restrictions being tested. Here the degrees of freedom correspond to the number of lags for which the Wald tests are calculated. For example, when explaining government satisfaction including past values of government satisfaction (i.e. with two lags) improve model fit significantly [chi-square (108,2) = 8.64, p≤ 0.05].

The basic logic behind the Granger causality test may be illustrated with an example. First, we regress vote intentions for government parties on all lagged vote intention terms (i.e. past poll estimates of vote intention such as those measured three or six months previously).[19] Second, we estimate the first model, but this time we include a lagged independent variable such as government satisfaction. Using a Wald test we then check our null hypothesis that the lagged independent variable does not belong in our regression model because its inclusion does not improve model fit significantly. If we reject the null hypothesis, we conclude that the lagged independent variable (Granger) causes the dependent variable. We can see from the bottom part of Figure 18 that, when predicting vote intentions for government parties including past values of government satisfaction (that is, with two lags), improves model fit significantly [Chi-square (108,2) = 8.64, $p \leq 0.05$].

The results presented in Figure 18 illustrates how well past values of an independent variable impact on predictions of the current values of the dependent variable. These estimates show that both government and Taoiseach satisfaction ratings help shape vote intentions for government parties. However, vote intention for an incumbent government does not Granger cause either government or Taoiseach satisfaction. All three variables are most strongly Granger caused by lagged versions of themselves. These results imply that intentions to vote for government parties are determined by positive perceptions of how well the Taoiseach or government are doing. Nevertheless, the unidirectional (Granger causal) relationships between satisfaction ratings and vote intentions concurs with the argument made earlier in this chapter. Vote intention questions and satisfaction ratings refer to fundamentally different political opinions among the Irish electorate.

Conclusion

At the start of this chapter, I posed two questions with regard to the opinion polling evidence: (a) do political satisfaction ratings mirror the mood of the Irish electorate, and (b) does the interrelationship between responses to vote intention questions and political satisfaction ratings help us illuminate the nature of political opinion in Ireland?

I will now try to summarise the evidence presented in this chapter in formulating answers to these two questions.

With regard to the first question, I have demonstrated, in a similar manner to the analysis undertaken in Chapter 2, that it is important to understand the nature and characteristics of specific poll items. Within the Mirror Theory of Opinion Polling responses to poll questions such as political satisfaction ratings represent stable opinions. However, individual satisfaction items are rarely discussed in isolation. Consequently, if consideration is made of the patterns of responses between vote intention and government and party leader satisfaction ratings, we find that it is not possible to make a definitive interpretation of what the opinion poll data are telling us.

The key reason for this conundrum revolves around the degree to which respondents have knowledge of political developments and are expressing 'true' opinions. This methodological concern goes to the heart of why vote intentions for incumbent parties and government satisfaction ratings are different. Figure 16 reveals that vote intentions for incumbent governments are rarely the same as satisfaction ratings. This implies that satisfaction ratings during interelection periods do mirror the political mood. Yet the 'mood' measured is likely to be based on 'top-of-the-head' responses, according to the Belief-Sampling Model. Evidence consonant with such an interpretation (see Figure 17) shows that political satisfaction ratings exhibit more variance than vote intention responses. The latter, it would seem, are based on long-term predispositions such as party attachment.

In contrast, the pattern in leadership satisfaction ratings across time indicates that the dynamics of public opinion can change substantially. In Figure 15 we saw that the declining political mood of the 1980s affected all party leaders in a similar manner, but in the following decade this pattern changed. This suggests that the factors underlying responses to leadership satisfaction ratings change and the opinion polls have mirrored this fascinating evolution in public opinion.

Turning to our second question, I demonstrated through a simple ranking of the popularity of governments, Taoisigh and party leaders that the polling data reveal important non-obvious features of party politics in Ireland where party leaders and Taoisigh can have different popularity ratings to that of their party, and vice versa. However, there are important interrelationships between these different poll questions. Using time series analytical techniques and the concept of Granger causality, we have found that satisfaction ratings help shape vote intention preferences for incumbent governments, but not vice versa. This fits with our expectations that political satisfaction ratings are judgements (that is, absolute measures where respondents are either satisfied or not) while vote intentions for government parties are decisions (that is, relative measures where parties are ranked). Consequently, these poll questions are qualitatively different.

To summarise, the research results presented in this chapter suggest two things. First, the Irish electorate is a critical one where electoral support for a party or government does not automatically lead to consonant satisfaction ratings. This is the main result from Figure 18. Such a pattern in the polling data is unexpected if one thinks that vote intentions form the foundation for political satisfaction ratings. However, the data presented in Figure 16 show that the vote intention trend has often been different from that of the satisfaction ratings. These two poll series refer to different aspects of public opinion.

Second, although vote intention responses are based on relatively stable opinions they are subject to change. The results in Figure 18 reveal that vote intentions for government parties are influenced by satisfaction in the performance of the Taoiseach and his cabinet. One might speculate in this respect that changing economic circumstances have strongest direct effects on political satisfaction ratings (political judgements) and weaker indirect effects on vote intentions (political decisions). In short, political satisfaction ratings appear to mediate the influence of economic change on vote intentions. Whether or not this mechanism is correct, such thinking does highlight the opportunities for further research into what drives political satisfaction ratings in Ireland and how such ratings influence vote intentions.

In Chapters 2 and 3 I have examined the core questions asked in all Irish opinion polls. In the remaining chapters I will switch attention to substantive issues – the liberal agenda, Northern Ireland and opinions towards the economy and European Union. These chapters are different in the sense that there is significantly less polling information and use will be made of other sources of public opinion data. Notwithstanding these data considerations, many of the theoretical and methodological concerns examined in chapters 1 to 4 will form central elements in the work undertaken in the next four chapters.

Notes

1 These six political index questions related to: (a) satisfaction with government performance; (b) satisfaction with the performance of the main party leaders; (c) preferred outcome of any forthcoming general election, i.e. desire for a change of government; (d)

views as to whether or not there should be a general election now; (e) voting intentions, and (f) preference for Taoiseach.
2 During general election campaigns government satisfaction questions are not asked. This is to reduce the risk of confusing respondents when the Dáil has been dissolved.
3 Comparison of surveys where the government satisfaction item was asked first with polls where it was asked later in an interview reveals no significant differences beyond what might be expected from sampling error.
4 'I would like to ask you to think about how Mr Cosgrave has done as Taoiseach, and how you think Mr Lynch would have done, over the past twelve months. Please look at the card and tell me which of these statements comes nearest to your opinion in this respect? SHOW CARD. 1) Mr Cosgrave has done better then Mr Lynch would have done; 2) Mr Lynch would have done better than Mr Cosgrave has done; 3) Both equal; 4) No opinion / don't know. MRBI/500/74, March 1974, question 5; MRBI/530/74, October 1974.
5 Schuman and Presser (1996: 27) make reference to the types of questions that result in question ordering effects. They argue that there can be 'part-part' and 'part-whole' combinations of pairs of questions. For example, does government satisfaction also logically imply satisfaction with the Taoiseach (whole–part item combination)? Or are government and Taoiseach satisfaction merely two specific indicators of a general 'political mood' factor where differential responses are to be expected (part–part combination)? While there is no research on this topic for Irish polls, raising this question has the merit of encouraging researchers to be more explicit as to how they interpret these standard poll questions.
6 This argument loses some force in systems where there are coalition governments because vote intention measures of government approval lose direct meaning, especially during interelection periods. In addition, the growth of presidential-style prime ministers would seem to reduce the position of parties in the minds of voters.
7 However, within the Vote and Popularity (or VP-function) literature government popularity and vote intention are sometimes treated synonymously. During interelection periods, responses to vote intention questions in opinion polls represent simple judgements of government performance, and are not complicated by the actual act of voting that is seen to be influenced by a whole range of other factors (note Paldam 1991: 16).
8 Comparison of the relative ranking of governments (n=11), Taoiseach (n=13) and party leaders (n=19) is formally incorrect due to the different number of cases. Here this type of comparison is used informally to indicate large differences in relative popularity.
9 Use of a net satisfaction measure (per cent satisfied minus dissatisfied) might make some difference here where most respondents give a 'don't know' response. For those with an opinion, many may be satisfied with the performance of leaders of small parties given the limited resources under which they operate, etc. However, our interest here is overall public opinion; consequently the simple measure adopted seems most appropriate.
10 There are polling data from 1969, but most are sporadic until late 1977. In order to create a time series that would give a reasonable picture of overall trends, thus avoiding often quite large fluctuations due to short-term factors, the data was aggregated into quarterly time periods. In effect this involves using a poll of polls where estimates are based on samples of between 1,000 and 8,000 respondents (median=2,967). Such a procedure provides more confidence in the trends observed.
11 The trends presented in Figure 16 represent the percentage responses of all those interviewed rather than those who had an opinion, where opinion change comes not only from those changing their mind, but also changes in the number of respondents giving 'don't know' responses.
12 Examination of vote intention for the incumbent government used a poll of polls (i.e. all available poll data aggregated on the basis of time within the election cycle). A quadratic model fit for this data explains 97 per cent of the variance. Similar quadratic model fits

were fitted for government and Taoiseach satisfaction ratings. However, this relationship is less strong as model fit is 68 per cent and 43 per cent respectively.
13 Some care is required in making interpretation of the peaks and troughs evident in Figure 16, because this graph refers to a generic election cycle where the data that are used to construct this figure are based on polling data that are likely to be clustered around elections and other politically significant events such as referendums, crises, etc. For this reason, specific peaks and troughs may not be generic, but specific in nature due to the clustered nature of the polling data.
14 Without panel data the only means of exploring this question would be to apply an ecological inference technique to aggregate-level survey data, where the transition rates of various subgroups could be estimated (Penubarti and Schuessler 1999). Such an analysis lies beyond the scope and goals of this chapter.
15 A dependent (or outcome) variable is what is to be explained, it 'is hypothesised to be caused by, or 'dependent' on, one or more independent variables'. In contrast, an independent (or explanatory) variable is hypothesised to influence and hence help explain changing values of the dependent variable (King, Keohane and Verba 1994: 77; Seawright and Brady 2004, pp. 273–313).
16 In simple terms, two variables measured over time might have a similar trend, but this is not evidence that they these variables are causally related to each other, as they may both be correlated with a third factor. In order to avoid such 'spurious' effects it makes sense to parcel out the trend components first and then examine causal relationships (for details see Mills 1998: 63ff).
17 The Dickey–Fuller Generalised Least Squares approach is a more robust test than the original Dickey Fuller and Phillips and Perron test and is considered within the econometrics literature to be a more appropriate test for unit roots.
18 Here, for simplicity, each dependent variable is lagged by one time period. Quite often longer lag periods are chosen leading to more complex models with many parameters. The number of lags chosen is determined by various statistical (likelihood ratio) tests that help the researcher determine the correct model specification. Lagging is used to deal with the problem of serial correlation in the error terms.
19 Granger tests can be sensitive to the number of lags included in a model. Here a variety of likelihood ratio tests were used to find the most appropriate lag length to handle serial correlation in the error terms as VAR assumes that error terms are uncorrelated.

Chapter 5

Public Opinion towards the Liberal Agenda

> Each discussion began with a specific theme – abortion, divorce, contraception – but the underlying agenda related to something more profound and fundamental: what kind of people we were, what we wanted to become, and who was standing in the way of progress and change.
>
> John Waters (1991: 82)

In the first four chapters of this book I have concentrated on outlining and critically evaluating key general features of the Irish opinion poll data. Furthermore, in Chapters 3 and 4 there has been an exploration of what the core questions asked in all opinion polls tell us about public opinion in Ireland. It has been established that a critical aspect in examining the mirror and lamp functions of opinion polls revolves around understanding how respondents answer questions during opinion poll interviews. In addition, our discussion of the Mirror Theory of Opinion Polling and the Belief-Sampling Model has shown that different conceptualisations of the poll response process strongly determines how we evaluate opinion poll data.

In this chapter, I will build on the lessons and insights gained in the first four chapters and start an examination of the four major themes and substantive questions outlined in the introduction to this book. I will first look at the 'liberal agenda'. This agenda is also known in academia as the 'liberal–conservative cleavage'. This particular cleavage has been one of the most prominent within Irish society since 1981 and was the basis for what was arguably one of the most divisive elections (the abortion referendum of 1983) since the foundation of the Irish State (Hug 1999: 154).[1]

Debates between liberal and conservative visions of Irish society have for the most part been undertaken within the context of referendums on abortion and divorce. Here government-proposed amendments to the Constitution require the consent of the electorate for ratification. These debates on abortion and divorce have highlighted important underlying divisions within Irish public opinion, but have surprisingly not involved major interparty conflict. For this reason, the liberal–conservative cleavage is unique in being a 'subliminal' source of conflict within Irish politics (Sinnott 2002: 815).

The strategies adopted by Irish political parties during the various abortion and divorce referendum campaigns have varied considerably. These have ranged from abstention from debate in order to avoid serious internal rifts (for example Fianna Fáil in the divorce referendum of 1986) to heavy campaigning (for example Fine Gael and the Labour Party in the divorce referendum of 1995). Nevertheless, the constitutional requirement that there be referendums on these moral issues ensures that the electorate is the final arbiter. For this institutional reason public policy-making on liberal agenda issues has involved public opinion playing a more important role that would normally be the case where legislation emanates from the Irish parliament (Oireachtas).[2]

In this chapter I will not examine broader explanations and theories of why values, often based on religious teachings, have tended to evolve in advanced Western societies. This is not to suggest that the general sociological processes of Modernisation and Secularisation are unimportant.[3] For practical reasons, I will concentrate in this chapter on public opinion towards the liberal agenda as the polls and the media have devoted considerable attention to this topic. In this respect, this chapter will try to answer two main questions. First, if opinion polls can be said to reflect public opinion, what kind of picture do we get – a declining conservative and increasingly liberal public or something more complex? Second, there will be an attempt to try to use the available opinion poll data to illuminate 'why' public opinion has exhibited particular patterns using cohort analysis and comparison of different question types.

In the first section of this chapter there will be a brief description of the opinion poll data. This will be followed by an overview of the literature on public opinion towards the liberal agenda and the main debates within this field of research. The third section will very briefly outline the logic of using a hard/easy distinction when examining liberal agenda poll questions. The following section will assess the importance of liberal agenda issues for the Irish public and this will be followed by an examination of the long-term trends in responses to hard and easy questions relating to abortion and divorce. Section six will briefly look at if there has been opinion change on liberal agenda issues, and the following section will trace the source of opinion change through cohort analysis. In the final section there will be some concluding remarks relating to the two questions raised at the start of this chapter.

Opinion Poll Data

One central feature of media-commissioned polling data in Ireland, as noted in earlier chapters, are their electoral focus. This is particularly evident in the number and type of poll questions relating to the liberal agenda. In fact, nine out of ten of all questions relating to moral issues refer to referendums on abortion and divorce. For this reason, this chapter will focus primarily on the abortion referendums of 1983, 1992 and 2002, and the divorce referendums of 1986 and 1995. There are fewer than a dozen poll questions relating to contraception and homosexuality, both important domains where groundbreaking legislation was introduced in the 1980s and 1990s.

Fortunately, academic surveys such as the European Values Survey (1981, 1990 and 1999), the International Social Survey Programme series of surveys (1985–present), the Irish Social and Political Attitudes Survey (2002) and the first Irish National Election Study (2002) also have a number of questionnaire items on Irish public opinion towards abortion, divorce, homosexuality and euthanasia. However, such data will be used primarily in this chapter to supplement and to extend the insights provided by media-commissioned polls undertaken by IMS, Lansdowne and MRBI.

The questions asked by these three polling companies regarding public opinion towards divorce and abortion are of three main types. The first are vote intention questions. These are the most numerous and enquire how respondents proposed to vote in the various referendums. These questions were often specific in nature relating to the actual text of proposed amendments to the Constitution. The second type were what might be best described as general questions, where those interviewed were asked whether they favoured legalising abortion and divorce, and under what circumstances. The third main group of questions relate to the impact of referendum campaigns and occasionally sources of influence on moral questions. In addition, there is a smaller number of poll questions on a variety of topics such as voter turnout and desirability of having referendums on moral issues.

Literature on the Liberal Agenda

The two most polled issues on the liberal agenda have been abortion and divorce. This is because both have been the subjects of seven referendums. Given the use of this direct democratic mechanism as a basis for policy-making in these two areas, it is not surprising that a good deal of the liberal agenda literature emphasises the central role of public opinion. In this respect, much of the argumentation portrays the Irish electorate sending 'signals' to political elites demanding more or less liberal social policies. In this respect, public opinion is not seen to be the source of public policy-making as it simply accepts or rejects proposals made by government in referendums. As a result, public opinion on liberal agenda issues is treated as the battlefield where the influence of key pressure groups is observed. This has the unfortunate consequence of reducing public opinion, and by implication citizens, to the role of pawns in the grand strategies of pressure groups or competing socio-historical forces. In briefly reviewing an extensive literature I shall highlight four broad strands of research on the liberal agenda.

Culture war

The first strand emphasises that support for the liberal agenda is seen to divide Irish society into two opposing camps – Past Ireland and Modern Ireland (Waters 1991: 82–3).[4] The socio-historical forces underpinning this conflict relate to a more complex interaction of pressures coming from the Catholic Church, those wanting Ireland to be more pluralist, advocates for a united Ireland and those wishing to resist secularising trends. Here public opinion is seen to be subject to an endogenous mechanism of change where the link between Catholicism, identity and definition of community is weakening through a process largely driven by generational replacement (note Girvin 1986; Lee 1989; Hesketh 1990; Coulter 1997). While the available polling data cannot test such a historically rich thesis, this perspective does suggest that we should expect to find strong divisions on the basis of age and location (urban/rural) primarily where the old and rural dwellers should constitute the most conservative sections of opinion on issues such as abortion and divorce.

Church and State

A second and related strand centres on the clash of 'Church and State'. Within this line of research, it is argued that public policy on liberal agenda issues has been strongly determined by the natural law doctrine within the Catholic Church and the fact that the majority religion in the Republic of Ireland is Catholicism (see Hug 1999: 1–2). Resistance to legalising abortion, divorce, contraception and homosexuality was justified as protecting the moral, and hence social, order. From this perspective, the liberal agenda was seen to represent attempts to weaken the family and its role as a fundamental pillar of social order. The contention here is that conservative pressure groups in the early 1980s attempted to use public opinion to copper-fasten the legal ban on abortion and resist efforts at legalising divorce (Hug 1999: 5; note also Whyte 1980; Inglis 1998b: 77–94).[5] Consequently, the emergence of a liberal agenda in Ireland is seen from this perspective to represent a shift within public opinion away from one based on collective responsibility to one centred on individual rights. In opinion polling terms, the expectations from this perspective are that the younger, more highly-educated cohorts will be more liberal in outlook and more likely to favour legal provisions for abortion, contraception, divorce and homosexuality. In addition, we should expect, following the 'devotional revolution thesis' and its emphasis on the emergence of a rural Catholic middle class in the late-nineteenth century, to see significant differences on the basis of social class, where the lower classes and farmers would tend to be more conservative and fearful of change than all others.

Ethnocentrism

The third strand emphasises the historical origins of the liberal agenda debates and argues that moral conservatism is a facet of a much broader force founded on 'ethnocentrism'. For example, Garvin (1988) contends that the key values that underpin contemporary Irish political culture were created in the nineteenth century following the famine, where a fundamentalist form of Catholicism emerged during a 'devotional revolution' (note Larkin 1972). As a result, Catholic piety became intertwined with social status, definitions of what it meant to be Irish, and idealist visions for the Irish State following independence (Inglis 1998b: 93). For those who defined Irish identity in terms of Catholicism and the rural community ideal, the emergence of a liberal agenda was perceived as something that would destroy what it meant to be Irish.[6] With such absolutist reasoning there could be no pluralism of values within Irish society (O'Carroll 1991: 58–68). The legalisation of abortion and divorce amounted to nothing less than the changing of Irish identity. While this form of argumentation is largely value-based, one would expect following this ethnocentrist logic to see important opinion differences on the basis of age, location of residence and social class. Supporters of liberal agenda issues are most likely those least entwined in Ireland's traditionalist heartland, that is, young, highly educated urbanites.

Referendum campaign effects

The final 'campaign' strand of research on the liberal agenda focuses specifically on public opinion and voting behaviour during referendum campaigns. Here one may identify two types of argument: a dynamic perspective and a structural one. According to Darcy and Laver's (1990) referendum dynamics account of the 1986 divorce referendum, the dramatic change in public opinion (30 percentage points) during this two month campaign resulted from two factors. The first factor was a divisive referendum where political parties withdrew from active debate fearing permanent splits within their own ranks. The second factor relates to the style of campaigning. The 1986 referendum campaign was mainly shaped by local community leaders who had a primarily Catholic and conservative orientation. Darcy and Laver note that these dynamics have occurred on a number of occasions in local referendums in the United States, and are typified by rapid opinion change in a conservative direction where support for changing the status quo rapidly evaporates. The implication here is that opinion change will be uniform across all subgroups, although this effect will be weaker among those living in urban areas and among the higher social classes due to their relative insulation from local community leaders.

An alternative, structural explanation for public preferences towards liberal agenda issues is that public opinion is not simply composed of 'yes' or 'no' components, but is actually made up of three groups – 'liberals', 'pragmatists' and 'conservatives'. This argument appeared first in Kennelly and Ward (1993: 130) and was later expanded by Richard Sinnott in a series of publications (Sinnott et al. 1995; Sinnott 1995a: 234–48, 2002: 819). According to the structural explanation, each group was seen in the referendums of 1983, 1986 and 1992 to have support from about 30 per cent of the public. The main difference between each group was not only the direction of opinions, but also the intensity of opinion. While the liberals and conservatives were firm in their convictions, it was the pragmatists that were susceptible to campaign effects.[7] As the available data (opinion polls and election results) do not allow estimation of opinion intensity, it has been hypothesised that specific groups, (that is, farmers and the working class) would constitute the most conservative elements within Irish public opinion. Moreover, it was suggested that Fianna Fáil supporters would be more conservative than either Fine Gael or Labour Party identifiers.

This brief overview of the literature relating to the liberal agenda has one common feature despite its diversity. All of the explanations are group-based where there is no individual-level mechanism, or theory, as to who supports or opposes liberal agenda reforms. In a sense this is convenient, as it matches with the fact that the available opinion poll data are also at an aggregate level. However, this should not be taken to mean that individual-level explanations could not be constructed. Furthermore, we have seen that almost all of the perspectives reviewed are observationally equivalent in that they suggest that there should be differences of opinion towards abortion and divorce on the basis of age, location and social class; although Sinnott (1995) suggests that partisanship may also be important. In the next section, I will demonstrate that opinion poll questions on liberal agenda issues need to be interpreted with care.

Hard and Easy Opinion Poll Questions on the Liberal Agenda

The cataloguing of opinion poll questions on the basis of whether they refer to hard or easy facets of an issue is a recurring theme in this book. This broad distinction of the 'hardness' of public opinion makes considerable sense in light of the history of the divorce, abortion and contraception issues (Hug 1999). In each of these domains, public opinion in principle favoured legal reforms to match the social reality and norms prevalent within Ireland after 1970. These are represented in polls by the response pattern to 'easy' questions where support for legal reforms was quite high. However, when specific policy details were proposed, significant segments of the public frequently set aside their desire for a more liberal society and adopted conservative stances. Consequently, with hard poll items levels of support for or against divorce and abortion were more evenly matched. This pattern, which we will see later in figures 20 and 21, is almost a defining feature of opinion poll results relating to the abortion and divorce referendums.

In this respect, Chrystel Hug, in her book *The Politics of Sexual Morality in Ireland* (1999), notes that opinion polls and academic survey evidence on attitudes towards homosexuality in Ireland are strongly influenced by both the context in which questions were asked and the format of the survey question implemented. Hug makes the important point that Irish public opinion appeared to be 'more absolutist when it came to abstract questions', such as 'homosexuality is never justified', and more tolerant when discussing specific policies, such as gay marriage.[8]

Such inconsistency in the pattern of opinion poll responses makes little sense from the Mirror Theory of Opinion Polling. However, using the Belief-Sampling Model such inconsistency is less puzzling, as there is the recognition that different questions and contexts lead respondents to use different considerations in giving answers during opinion poll interviews. This raises the issue of what mechanisms would lead us to observe such different responses to substantively related poll questions. In this respect, I argued in Chapter 2 that differential responses to hard and easy facets of an issue are likely to be conditioned by specific factors. Within this chapter I will make the case that age is one of the most important conditioning variables on liberal agenda issues because it serves as a proxy indicator for differential socialisation. Such an expectation stems from the literature review outlined earlier, where we noted that the older age cohorts are likely to be the most conservative.

Consequently, by distinguishing between hard and easy facets of liberal agenda issues we are in a better position to see if opinion polls can mirror public opinion in this domain. Moreover, by having theoretical expectations as to why public opinion is divided on hard questions I will use cohort analysis to illuminate what processes help explain opinion stability and change. As we will see, the age variable can have an impact on liberal agenda opinions through two distinct mechanisms: generational replacement and 'true' opinion or intra-cohort change. Within this chapter, I will attempt to ascertain which of these two mechanisms of opinion change has been the most influential.

Before introducing the cohort analysis results, it is necessary first to illustrate the importance of liberal agenda issues for the Irish public. I will undertake this task in the next section. In the following section I will demonstrate, using poll questions asked over many years, the importance of distinguishing between hard and easy responses to survey items dealing with opinions on the provision of abortion and divorce in Ireland.

Importance of Liberal Agenda Issues within Irish Public Opinion

While the issues of abortion, divorce and contraception figure prominently in histories and analyses of contemporary Ireland, it is none the less an empirical question as to whether these issues were considered important by citizens. The polling evidence available for scrutiny shows that when respondents were asked about the 'most important issue' facing the country, or the most important issue in the next general election, liberal agenda issues were spontaneously mentioned by fewer than one in ten of those interviewed. Rather than outline the relative importance of the various issues on the liberal agenda, I will adopt a practical strategy and focus on public opinion towards abortion and divorce. This is because of the prominence of these issues in the media and the fact that there are a considerable number of poll questions relating to abortion and divorce stretching back to 1974.

The opinion polling evidence suggests that the first abortion and divorce referendums did not stem from a public demand for constitutional change. If an examination is made of support for having a referendum on abortion we can see that the Irish public were divided on this question during the 1980s. Significantly, as Figure 19 illustrates, the first referendum had an important information effect as the number responding 'don't know' declined considerably between 1983 and 1992.

Figure 19 also shows the importance of specific events such as the X case in 1992 and the C case in 1997. Ironically these legal cases, which highlighted the need for legislation, preceded declines in support for a referendum to address the issue.⁹ The failure of successive governments to enact legislation following the abortion referendum of 1983 forced the Irish judiciary to make public policy in this area (Hug 1999: 168–72; Kennedy 2002: 115).

In short, the Supreme Court's decision in the X case in February 1992 made continued government inaction on the abortion issue untenable. The general consensus among contemporary expert commentators was that another abortion referendum was necessary to clarify the situation. This led to the unprecedented decision to hold three abortion referendums on the same day as a general election in November 1992. Ironically, this unprecedented election did not 'solve' the abortion issue, and in fact only serves to highlight the enduring nature of the abortion question. In the next section I will try to assess from the available polling data the long-term trends in attitudes towards both abortion and divorce.

Long-term Trends in Responses to Hard and Easy Questions on Divorce and Abortion

While the question of legalising divorce has never been a central issue in election campaigns, it none the less has been a recurring topic of interest within the media since opinion polling started in 1970. Fortunately, some of the earliest media-commissioned polls contain questions examining Irish public support for changing the constitutional ban on divorce. Such poll data allows us to assess if Irish public opinion has changed on this issue since 1970, when divorce was first mooted, to the removal of the constitutional ban in 1995.

Here I will use the distinction between 'hard' and 'easy' poll questions introduced in Chapter 2.[10] To briefly recap, it is argued in this book that the public do not have single overarching opinions on many issues, but have views on different facets of an issue that are based on a variety of considerations. This conceptualisation is based on the insights of the Belief-Sampling Model of survey response that was also discussed in Chapter 2. More precisely, 'hard' questions are those that relate to the means by which a policy will be implemented and, in the case of issues like abortion and divorce, refer typically to consideration of constitutional amendments. In contrast, 'easy' questions relate to policy goals where there is little reference to the means by which a policy will be undertaken, or many of its consequences.

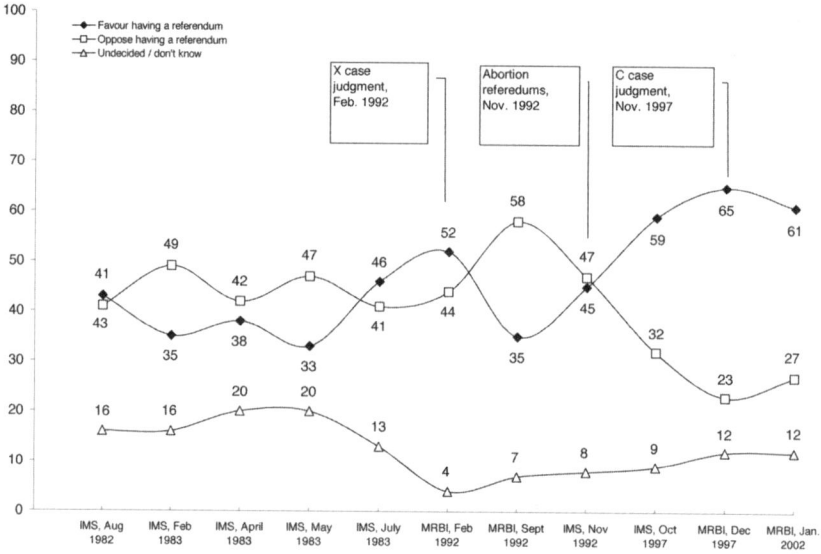

Figure 19 *Popular Support for a Constitutional Referendum on Abortion in the Republic of Ireland, 1982–2002 (per cent)*

Note: The poll estimate for December 1997 is not based on a direct question but on opinion towards what should be done following the C case of November 1997.

Examples of poll questions used to construct this time series:

> Do you think there ought to be a referendum on this issue [abortion] or not? IMS/Omnibus, 10 August 1982, question 9.

> The recent Supreme Court decision interpreting the 1983 Pro-Life Amendment to the Constitution appears to allow for the possibility of abortion being carried out in Ireland in certain circumstances (including the likelihood of suicide by the mother). Some people favour a referendum to revise or replace the 1983 Amendment in such a way as to rule out any possibility of legal abortion in Ireland under any circumstances. Others are opposed to such a referendum. What is your opinion? IMS/2S.156, 02/05/92, Independent Newspapers, question 11.

> Some people feel a referendum should be held to put an article into the Constitution placing a total ban on abortion. In your opinion should such a referendum be held? MRBI/4080/92, 25 September 1992, *The Irish Times*, question 11.

> The government has decided to hold a referendum on abortion. Its main aim is to change the decision reached in the X case by removing the threat of suicide as a grounds for abortion. It will also protect the unborn from the time of implantation, rather than conception. Do you, or do you not, believe the referendum should be held? MRBI/5860/02, 22 January 2002, *The Irish Times*, question 9.

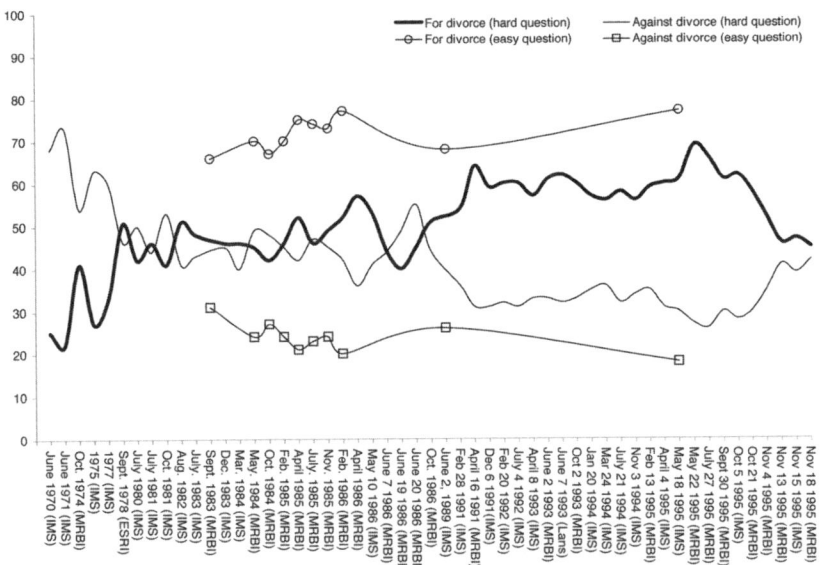

Figure 20 *Comparison of Hard and Easy Facets of Public Opinion towards Legalising Divorce in the Republic of Ireland, 1970–95 (per cent)*

Note: The question format relating to support for changing the constitutional ban on divorce changed over time. The first divorce referendum took place on June 26 1986 and the second one on November 24 1995.

Examples of hard questions:

As you know, divorce is not legal in Ireland, but a legal separation, where neither party is free to remarry is in certain circumstances, permitted. Do you feel that divorce, as say in England, should be legalised here, or do you feel that it should never be legalised here? Please look at this card, and tell me which of these statements best describes your opinion. SHOW CARD G. MRBI/500/74, October 1974.

As you probably know, the Irish constitution contains an article prohibiting divorce. A referendum is to be held to remove the ban from the constitution, and in its place to provide – through the Courts – for the possibility of divorce in the following circumstances. SHOW CARD AND READ OUT. (1) A marriage has failed. (2) The period of failure is at least five years. (3) There is no reasonable possibility of a reconciliation. (4) Dependent spouses and children are provided for. In the Referendum, will you vote for or against this change? MRBI/3440/86, 29 April 1986, *The Irish Times*, question 7.

SHOW CARD B. On this card is set out the proposed amendment to the Constitution on which people will be asked to vote on November 24th. Please read the proposal carefully. If you do vote in the Referendum, will you vote in favour of the amendment or against? IMS/CMC/ SOS/ld/J.5S-357, 5 October 1995, question 11.

Examples of easy questions:

> Divorce is not legal in Ireland, but a legal separation, where neither party is free to remarry is permitted. Do you feel that divorce should be permitted in certain circumstances or do you feel it should never be permitted here in Ireland? MRBI/3290/84, 10 May 1984, *The Irish Times*, question 7.

> In the situation where irretrievable breakdown of a marriage is established and five years subsequent to separation have elapsed – are you in favour or opposed to divorce being permitted in that situation? IMS/CMC/SOS/ld/J.5S-228, 18 May 1995, *Sunday Independent*, question 11.

The evidence presented in Figure 20 illustrates opinion change where a majority were against legalising divorce for most of the 1970s. Between 1978 and April 1986 public opinion towards divorce was evenly divided, and this was an important backdrop to the first divorce referendum. Despite the electorate voting against legalising divorce in 1986 the opinion poll data suggest that thereafter a majority of the Irish public supported removing the ban on divorce.

Apart from the dramatic opinion changes noted by Darcy and Laver (1990) and Jones (2001: 75–80) during the 1986 campaign, another key pattern evident in Figure 20 is the dissimilarity between campaign and non-campaign poll results. One explanation of this difference is that non-campaign poll responses were made in the context of 'easy' questions, as they did not involve any immediate consideration of public policy. In contrast, opinions expressed during divorce referendum campaigns were answers to 'hard' questions as the proposed changes to the Constitution involved consideration of specific concerns such as rights of succession, ensuring standards of living for first and second families where parents were divorced, and the potential cost to the taxpayer of 'abandoned' families (see Hug 1999: 64).[11]

The changing form of the poll questions asked also fits with the discussion of the survey response process described in Chapter 2. The Belief-Sampling Model alerts us to the likelihood that with a changed context (that is, referendum and non-referendum periods or different survey items and response options), answers to poll questions will be based on contrasting sets of considerations and information. If we compare the trends in hard and easy question responses towards legalising divorce as shown in Figure 20, we see that responses to easy facets of the divorce question appear to represent minimum and maximum levels of public opinion on either side of this issue. Moreover, although the poll data for easy questions are much shorter the trend for supporting legal reform seems to have grown between 1983 and 1995 (from 66 to 77 per cent), while opinion opposed to lifting the legal ban on divorce declined (from 31 to 18 per cent).

A similar trend in the hard and easy facets of the abortion issue, is evident in Figure 21. The constitutional amendments proposed for abortion in 1983, 1992 and 2002 revolved around the central question of whether there should be a complete ban on abortion in Ireland.

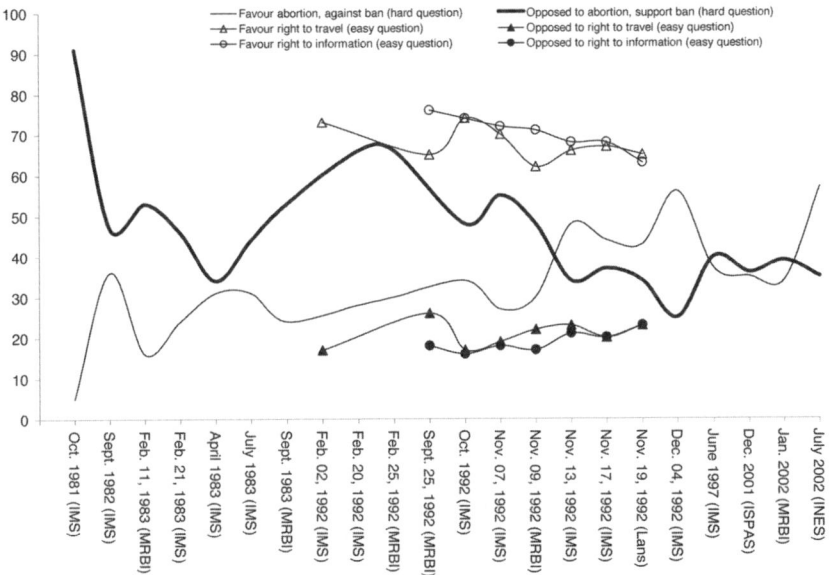

Figure 21 *Comparison of Hard and Easy Facets of Public Opinion towards Legalising Abortion in the Republic of Ireland, 1981–2002 (per cent)*

Note: The question format relating to support for changing the constitutional ban on divorce changed over time. The first abortion referendum took place on 7 September 1983: the second set of referendums coincided with the general election of 25 November 1992. The most recent abortion referendum took place on 6 March 2002.

Examples of hard questions:

The following is the proposed amendment to the constitution. The state acknowledges the right to life of the unborn and, with due regard to the equal right to life of the mother, guarantees in its laws to respect, and, as far as practicable, by its laws to defend and vindicate that right. Would you vote yes, to include the amendment in the constitution, or no, not to include it? MRBI/3210/83, 1 September 1983, question 9.

The wording on the Ballot Paper on the Right to Life/Abortion issue will be – SHOW CARD – 'It shall be unlawful to terminate the life of an unborn unless such termination is necessary to save the life, as distinct from the health, of the mother where there is an illness or disorder of the mother giving rise to a real and substantial risk to her life, not being a risk of self-destruction'. Will you vote 'yes' to put the amendment in the Constitution, or 'no' not to put it in? MRBI/4090/92, 9 November 1992, *The Irish Times*, question 15.

The Government is holding a referendum on abortion on March 6. Its aim is to change the decision reached in the X case by removing the threat of suicide as a grounds for abortion. It will also protect the unborn from the time of implantation, rather than conception. If the referendum were held in the morning, would you vote – 'yes', in favour of the changes proposed by the government, or 'no', against the changes proposed by the Government? MRBI/5860/02, 22 January 2002, *The Irish Times*, question 10.

Examples of easy questions:

And the Referendum will also be to decide if women going abroad for abortions should have access to information about the facilities available. In that referendum, do you intend to vote for or against access to information? MRBI/4080/92, 25 September 1992, *The Irish Times*, question 10a.

How will you vote in the forthcoming abortion referendum in relation to the first amendment – the Freedom to Travel? IMS/CMC/SOS/Id/J.2S349, 13 November 1992, question 14.

The X and C cases, as noted earlier, led the Irish judiciary to create public policy allowing limited abortion in the absence of any legislation coming from successive governments following the first abortion referendum in 1983. Figure 21 also reveals that support for a complete ban on abortion declined from February 1992, following the X case. While support for limited abortion increased, it seems that by 2002 the conservative and liberal elements in Irish public opinion were evenly matched. In the abortion referendum of March 2002, the Government's proposal to allow limited abortion to save the life of the mother was rejected by a tiny margin (0.84 per cent of the votes cast, see Kennedy 2002). Such evidence shows that the abortion issue remains the most divisive liberal agenda question in Ireland.

While the substantive subject of abortion has been divisive, other facets of this issue relating to 'freedom of travel' to have an abortion outside Ireland and the 'right to information' about abortion services elicited majority support when they were debated and voted on in late 1992. Again, if we compare the trends in hard and easy responses to the question of changing the legal status of abortion as shown in Figure 21, we see that responses to easy questions (that is, opposing freedom of travel or availability of abortion information) appear to represent minimum and maximum levels of public opinion on either side of this issue.[12]

In general terms, Figures 20 and 21 exhibit similar patterns. By focusing on the hard facets of the divorce and abortion issues we see that about 30 per cent of the Irish public supported a liberal stance, with a further 30 per cent adopting a conservative position, while the remainder were undecided. With regard to the easy facet of the divorce and abortion issues about 70 per cent have consistently supported legal reforms, while 20 per cent have taken a conservative position and opposed any liberal changes. Thus, within this section we have seen that public opinion towards liberal agenda issues is marked by patterns of both stability and change. Of equal importance has been our demonstration that opinion polls can be used to mirror public opinion. However, this is a delicate task requiring careful interpretation of how respondents answer specific types of poll questions. Nevertheless, it has been established that such a task is possible and yields valuable insights into the nature of public opinion. In the next section I will address more directly the key concern within the liberal agenda literature, which is the identification of change in values within Irish society.

Change in Public Opinion Towards the Liberal Agenda

The polling evidence presented in the previous section relating directly to divorce and abortion referendums indicates that the Irish public has become more liberal since 1970. In this respect, Figures 20 and 21 suggest that in the early 1990s about one in five of the Irish public was conservative, that is, opposed divorce and abortion, while about seven in ten were willing to support some legislative reform.[13] This trend towards greater liberal opinions on a variety of moral issues is also evident in academic survey evidence shown in Figure 22. Using ten-point scales that investigate the extent to which the Irish public believed certain human actions are 'never or always justified', it is possible to chart the median position of the Irish public from 1981 to 2002.

We can see from Figure 22 that in 1981 public opinion was strongly conservative on almost all issues – homosexuality, prostitution, abortion, euthanasia and suicide – where the median public stance was that these types of human action were 'never justified'. In contrast, opinions towards divorce were more liberal. Such liberalism increased between 1981 and 1999; however, even on this issue the Irish public never came close to stating divorce was 'always justified'.

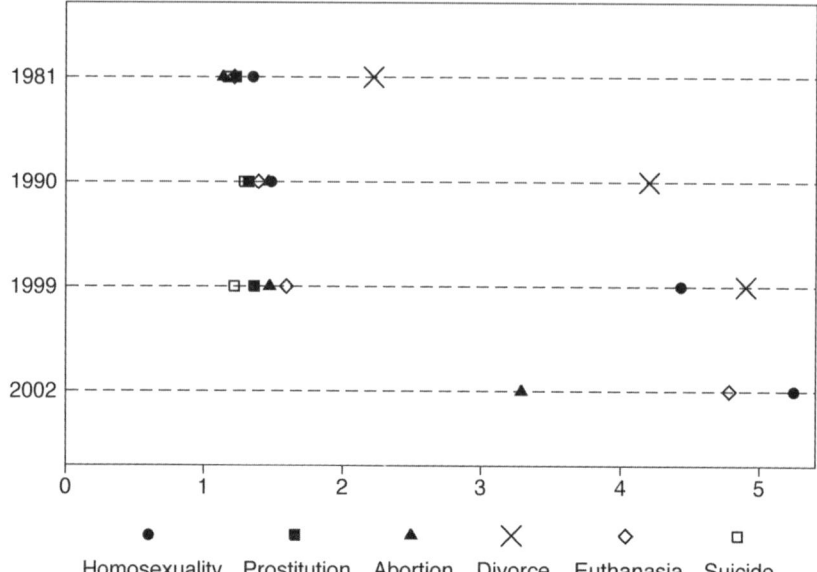

Figure 22 *Change in Position within the Irish Public on certain Liberal Agenda Issues (10-point scale; 1 = Never Justified; 10=always justified)*

Sources: EVS 1981, 1990, 1999 and ISPAS 2001/2. The question text used was as follows: People who agree fully with the statement [e.g. abortion is never justified] on the left would give a score of '1'. People who agree fully with the statement [e.g. abortion is always justified] on the right would give a score of '10'. Other people would place themselves somewhere in between these two views. Where would you place yourself on these scales?

As this is an ordinal scale an interpolated median measure is employed, which locates the median by linear interpolation between respective category boundaries (van der Eijk 2001). The data for ISPAS was composed of 11-point scales; this data was recoded where points 0 and 1 were combined. For the sake of clear presentation, confidence estimates for the data points in this chart are not shown, and the scale has been reduced (i.e. 1–5) to improve clarity.

One could argue that the questions used to construct Figure 22 were 'easy' questions, as they relate in principle to particular moral positions. Nevertheless, this question format led respondents, perhaps through priming (a whole range of issues such as cheating on taxes, joyriding, spouses having an affair and accepting a bribe were also investigated), to adopt 'black and white' moral positions. However, I noted earlier that 'always/never justified' survey questions seem to raise in the minds of Irish respondents considerations of the consequences of greater liberalism in society, rather than principles such as tolerance (see note 8).

The homosexuality issue is interesting in that public opinion became much more liberal during the 1990s. This change seems to have followed the passing of legislation on this issue in June 1993 by the Irish government. Furthermore, unlike legislation on divorce and abortion, legal reform of the law on homosexuality did not involve a referendum.[14] This distinction is important because had there been a referendum on this issue it would most likely have failed. A Lansdowne poll of June 1993 clearly shows that Irish public opinion did not support liberalising the law relating to homosexuality in Ireland, although there were strong differences on the basis of age, region, urban/rural residence and class. Only one in three (34 per cent) supported legalising homosexual acts between adults aged 17 years or more.[15]

Nevertheless, during the 1990s (as Figure 22 demonstrates), Irish public opinion became more liberal in nature, which suggests greater levels of toleration. This lessening of conservatism in the EVS data was limited to divorce and homosexuality – both were subject to groundbreaking legal reforms in the mid-1990s. All other issues remained characterised by strong conservative opinions. This differential pattern in Figure 22 suggests that government-led legal reforms can precede the emergence of more tolerant opinions on moral issues. It would seem therefore that legislation can, in some circumstances, shape attitudes. We have to be careful here, as the data for 2002 show growing liberalism for the abortion and euthanasia issues despite the fact that there have been no significant legislative reforms in these areas over the last decade.

Such trends nevertheless raise the question: what has been the mechanism of opinion change in Ireland on liberal agenda issues over the last three decades? In order to address this question I will focus in the next section on age, a key-conditioning variable in the expression of opinions on liberal agenda issues. More specifically I will illustrate through the use of cohort analysis the relative importance of two fundamental mechanisms of opinion change associated with age: generational replacement and intracohort effects.

Cohort Analysis of Opinion Change on Liberal Agenda Issues

Within this book, one of the major objectives is to investigate public opinion in Ireland and how it has changed since 1970. We have already seen in the introductory chapter how opinions towards legalising divorce changed dramatically over a few months in 1995. A similarly dramatic process had occurred in the previous divorce referendum campaign in 1986. During these two relatively brief election campaigns the Irish electorate changed its mind. This is not the only way in which public opinion change can take place; opinion change may also occur, although individual citizens and subgroups remain constant in their views. Such things are possible because all populations are constantly changing.

On a typical day in the Republic of Ireland in 1989, 85 citizens died and 142 were born. In the general election, of 24 May 2007, most of the 51,000 born in that famous year, when the Berlin Wall fell, were eligible to vote as they turned eighteen. According to the Central Statistics Office, during 1989 the population actually decreased, as more people died and emigrated than were born. However, the 1988–90 period was exceptional as it is the only one in recent decades to exhibit population loss. In general, over the last three decades most of the loss from the Irish adult population resulted from death. Within the social sciences, the natural process through which a society is continuously changed is known as *generational replacement*.

This natural biological process can have far-reaching consequences determining whether public opinion is marked by stability or change. Moreover, as noted above, generational replacement can affect overall public opinion in ways that at first sight seem counterintuitive. Through the process of birth and death public opinion changes because there is a transformation in the 'public', where younger age groups start with opinions different from those of their parents and grandparents. In this sense, the older generations die without ever changing their opinions and younger generations replace them having embraced different values from the outset.[16] How does this process of opinion formation and change occur?

Socialisation and period effects

There are two main answers put forward to explain differences of opinion across the generations. The first explanation is based on the process of socialisation, where each citizen learns their values and opinions from their family, peers, school environment and the media. This perspective emphasises that opinions learned when young leave an imprint on the individual that often lasts a lifetime, and it becomes difficult to change opinion as a person ages. The second explanation relates to the impact of great events on an age group (or cohort). These period effects (also known as intracohort change) have the power to shape the opinions of specific groups throughout the life cycle. Unlike the socialisation explanation, the period effects model argues that older citizens can change their opinions because of the impact of 'history-making' events (see Glenn 1977: 61–4; Mayer 1992: 147; Firebaugh 1997: 22).

In this section I will try to assess whether generational replacement or opinion (intracohort) change within the Irish adult population explain most of the variation we observe in European Values Surveys (EVS) data relating to liberal agenda issues. Unfortunately, use of IMS, Lansdowne and MRBI polls for this task is impossible as it is necessary to be able to track the same age cohorts through successive polls (for example, 20–29-year-olds in 1981 who were 30–39 in 1991). The age categories used in poll reports and the timing of questions does not facilitate such a task.

With regard to the data used within this chapter, it is important to note that some care is required when interpreting the cohort analysis estimates produced. This is because they are based on sample sizes that are relatively small (175–300 respondents) and may consequently have fairly large sampling errors (6–10 per cent). In the absence of larger datasets or different sources of polling data on the same issue, there is limited scope to deal with this limitation on the analysis undertaken. Therefore, trends that exhibit change of less than 10 per cent should be interpreted with caution, as they may be due to sampling error.

It is important to keep in mind that the socialisation and period effects explanations of public opinion change are based on an important assumption, that is, the process of ageing (or life-cycle effects) does not have a significant impact on the opinion change observed. For example, I do not expect citizens to have liberal views on abortion when they are young and to become progressively more conservative as they age. Life-cycle effects are special in the sense that they relate to opinion changes at the individual level that are rarely a source of observed opinion change at the social level because the effects are most often offset by changes due to generational replacement. In the next sub-section I will examine whether life-cycle effects are a significant source of opinion change.

Life-cycle effects as a source of opinion change

The existence of life-cycle effects is predicated on observing two patterns in the data. First, there should be significant and persistent differences between cohorts who are at different stages in the life cycle. Second, while age may be correlated with opinions towards liberal agenda issues such as abortion, the opinions within each age group must move in a direction that brings them closer to the pattern observed in older cohorts (see Mayer 1992: 178–84). Thus, if differences in opinions towards abortion are due to ageing, then all cohorts should increasingly state that abortion is never justified as they grow older.

When we look at the relationship between age and belief that abortion, divorce, euthanasia and homosexuality are never justified, we observe that all these liberal agenda issues are correlated with age.[17] Such evidence is consistent with an ageing effect. The data presented in Figure 23 demonstrate opinion change for the same cohorts as they progress through the life-cycle.[18] The interpretation of these charts is straightforward. If there were no opinion change for a specific cohort, this would be represented by a flat line (for example cohort 8, for the 'homosexuality is never justified' chart at the bottom of Figure 23). In contrast, if there were a conservative opinion change the lines would rise (showing an increase on the 1981 estimates). However, with a liberal opinion change the lines would fall (exhibiting a decrease on the 1981 estimates). For the very youngest and oldest cohorts I have estimates for only two time points.

In general, the patterns evident in the three charts represented in Figure 23 reveal that there are persistent dissimilarities between the different birth cohorts. However, for the most part opinions through the life cycle tend either to remain largely constant or to become more liberal (except in the case of homosexuality for the oldest age cohort in 1981 and 1990). This seems to be especially true in the case of opinions towards divorce. One rather surprising feature in this figure is that the opinions expressed in the 1990 wave of EVS were the most liberal. This gives the impression in Figure 23 that there was a 'conservative swing' in the older age groups (cohorts 3, 4 and 5) in 1999.

Why this should have occurred is not entirely clear, although Fahey, Hayes and Sinnott (2005: 127) argue that this pattern may be evidence for a life-cycle effect. Whatever the source of this conservative swing, there is sufficient evidence in Figure 23 to justify the assumption that life-cycle effects are not a significant source of opinion change. I will now turn to the important question of whether the evolution in public attitudes towards liberal agenda

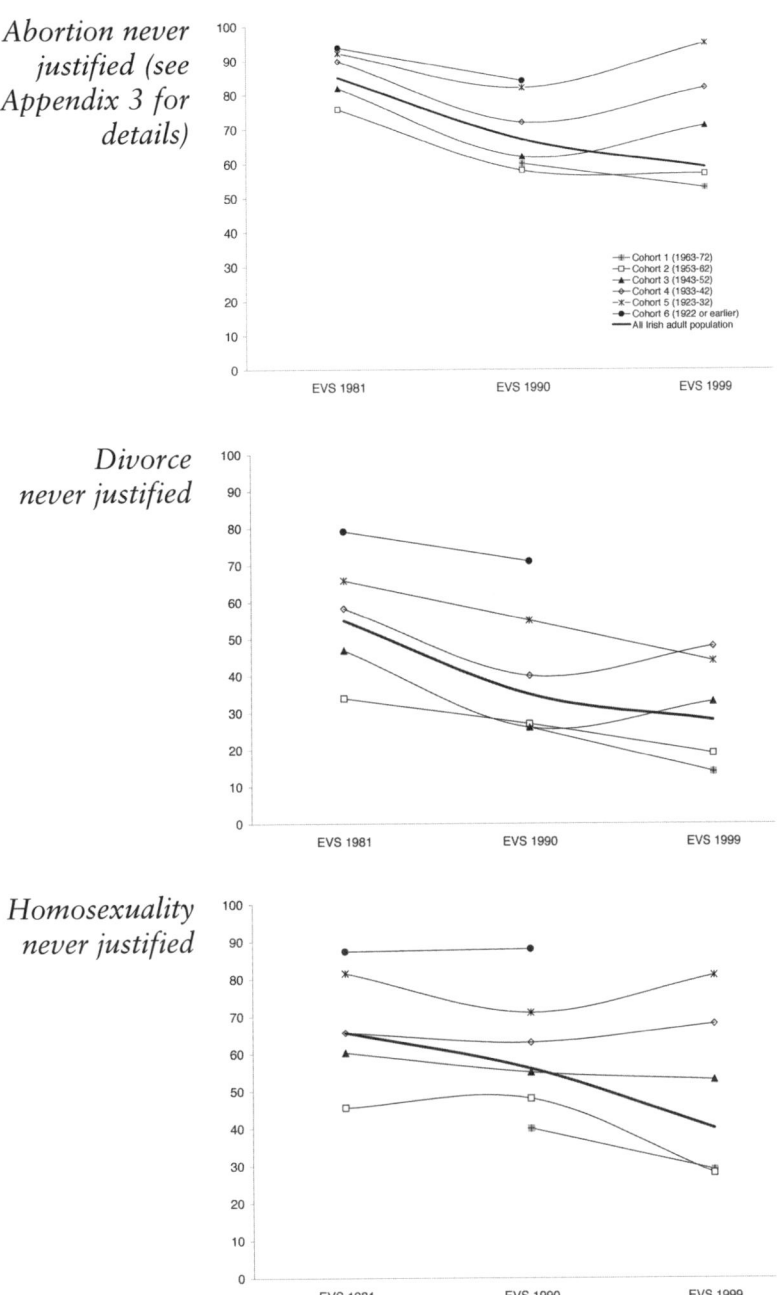

Figure 23 *Percentage in Six Birth Cohorts who felt that Abortion, Divorce or Homosexuality were 'Never Justified' in the Republic of Ireland in 1981, 1990 and 1999, European Values Survey (per cent)*

issues resulted from the changing composition of the Irish adult population, or from intracohort effects where citizens changed their minds.

Impact of generational replacement and intracohort change on opinions towards abortion

I argued earlier that two important mechanisms of public opinion change are: (a) generational replacement – where evolving attitudes are based on the changing age composition of the public, and (b) intracohort change – observed opinion change where people of all ages have changed their mind. In order to demonstrate these two distinct sources of opinion change, I will use a detailed example to illustrate how it is possible to make estimates of these different sources of change.

In 1981, 1990 and 1999 the European Values Survey asked, using a ten-point scale, whether or not abortion is always or never justified. Taking points 1 and 2 on this scale I will examine the trend in responses to those adopting the most conservative stance (that abortion is never justified). In 1981, 85 per cent of the Irish public thought abortion was never justified; nine years later in 1990 this had fallen to 67 per cent; by 1999 this figure had declined once more to 59 per cent. The data shown in Table 8 reveal that the drop in strong conservative opinion against abortion under any circumstances resulted from the operation of two mechanisms of change.

The first of these mechanisms is evident in the fact that of the four birth cohorts (cohorts 3, 4, 5 and 6 in Figure 20) present in all three waves of the EVS, all but one registered a decline (on the level recorded in 1981). While 1990 appears to be the most 'liberal' year, with a resurgence of conservatism in 1999, the trend for the 1981–99 period is one of decline in strong conservative opinions. If we assume that all three surveys had representative samples, the evidence presented in Table 8 demonstrates that the Irish public underwent a process of intracohort change where opinions towards abortion being 'never justified' softened.

The second mechanism is related to the observation that younger cohorts such as those born after 1972 were much less likely in 1999 (35 per cent in contrast to a total figure of 59 per cent) to say abortion was never justified than all other birth cohorts. Moreover, the youngest age cohort grew from zero to 26 per cent of the EVS sample in 1999, while the two oldest age cohorts declined from 28 per cent of the sample in 1990 to 21 per cent in 1999. From such evidence it seems reasonable to think that the replacement of older Irish citizens by younger ones has had a significant impact on total public opinion towards abortion.

Table 8 *Public Support for the View that Abortion is 'Never Justified' in the Republic of Ireland, 1981–99*

Cohort	1981 responses			1990 responses			1999 responses		
	Percentage saying 'never justified'	Percentage of sample	N	Percentage saying 'never justified'	Percentage of sample	N	Percentage saying 'never justified'	Percentage of sample	N
1. 1973–81	–	–	–	–	–	–	35	26	248
2. 1963–72	–	–	–	60	25	247	53	21	196
3. 1953–62	76	21	241	58	19	193	57	18	173
4. 1943–52	82	22	251	62	18	178	71	15	140
5. 1933–42	90	16	185	72	16	158	82	10	94
6. 1923–32	92	15	170	82	12	118	95	11	103
7. 1913–22	93	14	156	84	10	104	–	–	–
8. 1903–12	90	12	132	–	–	–	–	–	–
TOTAL	86	100	1,135	67	100	998	59	100	954

Source: data derived from calculations on the European Values Survey waves of 1981, 1990 and 1999.

In short, the evidence presented in Table 8 highlights that both generational replacement and intracohort change contributed to an evolution in public opinion towards abortion during the 1980s and 1990s. The question now arises: which of these two processes had the greater impact on public attitudes towards abortion? In order to find an answer to this important enquiry, I will estimate the effects of generational replacement by seeing what public opinion would have looked like if there had been no population change. I will do this by holding the composition of the Irish population constant, but allowing the opinions within cohorts to change.

Therefore, one needs to eliminate the effect of opinion change from total change observed in order to see the impact of generational replacement. The basic logic may be represented as follows:

Opinion change   Actual opinion   Actual opinion
due to generational   =   change plus change   −   change only*
replacement   due to generational
                                        replacement

* Also known as intracohort change. All change here relates to opinions measured at two time points that are sufficiently far apart for detectable generational replacement effects to occur (≥ 4 years).

Table 9 demonstrates how this procedure is implemented using census and survey data. In the first column of this table I have noted down the population distribution in 1981 as derived from the census of that year.[19] In the second column we have the percentage in each cohort who stated in 1990 that abortion is never justified. In the third column we multiply the cohort distribution in 1981 by the percentage cohort attitude towards abortion in 1990, and then sum across all cohorts.

Table 9 *Estimation of the Effects of Generational Replacement on Public Opinion towards the View that Abortion is 'Never Justified', 1981–90*

Age cohorts	1981 population distribution (1)	1990 response percentage (2)	Population distribution in 1981 × EVS response in 1990 (3)
18–29	0.21	59.51	12.36
30–9	0.22	57.51	12.51
40–9	0.16	62.36	10.12
50–9	0.15	71.52	10.93
60–9	0.14	82.20	11.47
70+	0.12	84.00	10.08
TOTAL	1.00	66.73	67.48

A: Total percentage in 1981 who stated abortion is never justified = 86
B: Total percentage in 1990 who stated abortion is never justified = 67
C: Total absolute change between 1981 and 1990 (B minus A) = 19
D: Change due to generational replacement (B [66.73] minus Total Dist. 1981 × Response 1990 [67.48]) = 0.75
E: Percentage change due to generational replacement (C/D * 100) ≈ 4%
F: Change due to intracohort change (C minus D) = 18.25
G: Percentage due to intracohort change (F/C*100) ≈ 96%

Note: Abramson (1983) and Mayer (1992) have used this methodology to examine party identification and opinion change in the United States. Some care is required with this procedure as the estimates produced are based on sample sizes that are relatively small (175–300) and may have fairly large sampling errors (6–10 per cent). In the absence of larger datasets or different sources of polling data on the same issue, there is limited scope to deal with this limitation on the analysis undertaken.

This sum (66.73 per cent) is our estimate of what public opinion towards abortion would have been in 1990 had there been no change in the composition of the Irish population since 1981. If we subtract this figure from the actual total opinion recorded by EVS in 1990 (66.73 − 67.48 = −0.75 points), we can calculate the impact of generational replacement. The details of our algebraic estimates are shown in Table 9. Looking at the calculations beneath this table, we see that there was a 19 per cent decline (the estimate labelled 'C') in support for the view that abortion is never justified between 1981 and 1990. From our simple calculations we know that 0.75 points (4 per cent) are due to generational replacement and 18.25 points (96 per cent) may be attributed to the Irish public 'changing its mind', that is, intracohort change.

In summary, most of the change in opinion regarding abortion recorded in the European Values Surveys of 1981 and 1990 was due to period effects. It would appear that the discussion of abortion in the 1983 referendum campaign and thereafter led the Irish public to soften its stance on the abortion issue. This implies that the imprint of socialisation processes with regard to liberal agenda issues such as abortion is not an indelible one. Opinion change can occur with core beliefs due to the influence of history-making events. Using the methodology demonstrated in Table 9, we are now in a position to assess the contributions of generational replacement and intracohort change on Irish public opinion towards a number of liberal agenda issues. Furthermore, given that there are three waves of EVS I will track these mechanisms of opinion change for the 1980s and 1990s to trace when most change occurred.

Comparison of sources of opinion change on four liberal agenda issues

The data presented earlier in Figure 23 and the results presented in the last sub-section indicate that different age cohorts do have different opinions on liberal agenda issues. Successive cohorts tend to be more liberal in orientation. Thus with generational replacement Irish public opinion will become more liberal over time. However, Figure 23 also reveals that many cohorts have become less conservative on abortion, divorce and homosexuality during the 1980s and 1990s. Table 9 revealed that for abortion the decline in conservatism was mainly (96 per cent) due to opinion (intracohort) change between 1981 and 1990. This evidence suggests that Irish public opinion has become less conservative, though perhaps not necessarily liberal, in nature. In this sub-section I will examine four liberal agenda issues and estimate sources of opinion change between 1981 and 1999 using the same methodology demonstrated in Table 9.

These results are presented in Table 10. The almost two-decade period for which there have been three waves of EVS has been broken into two phases (1981–90 and 1990–9) to see if opinion change exhibited different characteristics in the 1980s than in the 1990s. In addition, an overall measure of change between 1981 and 1999 was estimated.[20] The results in Table 10 reveal that the main source of opinion change on liberal agenda issues between 1981 and 1999 has been intracohort (or 'true' opinion) change. This means that changing opinions within cohorts due to period effects (e.g. referendum campaigns, media reporting of the X case, etc.) has been more important than generational replacement.

Table 10 *Comparison of the Effects of Generational Replacement and Intracohort Change on Public Opinion towards Four Liberal Agenda Issues in Ireland, 1981–99 (European Values Survey)*

Survey Question	Time period	Total change in public opinion*	Change due to generational replacement	Change due to intracohort change	% change due to generational replacement	% change due to intracohort change
Abortion	1981–90	19	1	18	4	96
	1990–99	8	3	5	36	64
	1981–99	26	3	23	10	90
Divorce	1981–90	20	1	19	6	94
	1990–99	8	2	6	27	73
	1981–99	27	2	25	8	92
Homosexuality	1981–90	9	1	8	15	85
	1990–99	17	2	15	15	85
	1981–99	26	3	23	11	89
Euthanasia	1981–90	14	5	9	39	61
	1990–99	7	2	5	23	77
	1981–99	21	2	19	7	93

*Sub-period values do not always sum correctly due to rounding errors. The exact questions used here are given in Appendix 3 and relate to behaviour which respondents were asked to rate on a scale as being always or never justified. Those who chose points 1 and 2 on the ten-point scales (where 1 = never justified and 10 = always justified) were coded as having a 'never justified' opinion. All opinion change noted was negative, i.e. a decline in conservative responses. In order to keep the presentation simple absolute differences are given in this table. The estimates for 1990–9 periods are based on the population census of 1991, whereas the other two time periods are based on comparison with population distributions in 1981. For this reason, summing the combined opinion and demographic effects for 1981–90 and 1990–99 will not match with the 1981–99 estimates.

As Figure 23 shows, many of the older cohorts retained essentially fixed opinions on abortion and homosexuality. In comparative perspective, a similar analysis of liberal agenda issues in the United States from the late 1960s to the late 1980s found that generational replacement rather than intracohort effects was the major source of change in American public opinion (Mayer 1992: 156).

However, the results in Table 10 highlight that (a) timing and (b) the domain of opinion change were important. If we look at the timing of opinion change we observe from the top section of Table 10 that, on the abortion issue, most opinion change between 1981 and 1990 came from intracohort effects. However, between 1990 and 1999 the importance of generational replacement increased significantly. A similar pattern is evident for the divorce issue. The fact that there were high-profile referendum campaigns during the 1980s on abortion and divorce appears to have spurred higher levels of opinion change, leading to generational replacement accounting for the lower portion of total change during this decade.

In contrast, during the 1990s divorce and homosexuality were the subjects of legislative reforms and in this decade intracohort change was the dominant process of opinion change. However, with the divorce issue about a quarter of the total opinion change noted (27 percentage points) was due to generational replacement. More generally, these results imply that legislative initiatives have played an important role in the evolution of public opinion by stimulating public discussion and hence opinion (intracohort) change.

Table 10 also reveals that the pattern of opinion change has been similar for all four issues where intracohort change has predominated. Euthanasia is a useful example of a liberal agenda issue that has had very low prominence within the media since 1981 and hence little public debate. Nevertheless, the process of opinion change on this issue has become increasingly based on intracohort rather than generational replacement effects.

Overall, the cohort analysis results presented in Table 10 suggests that Irish public opinion became less conservative on these four liberal agenda issues between 1981 and 1999. Moreover, most of the opinion change observed has resulted from citizens changing their mind. On average, nine-tenths of the change observed in Table 10 is due to intracohort effects and one-tenth is due to population change. This evidence supports the view that Irish public opinion became more liberal during the 1980s and 1990s.

Conclusion

At the start of this chapter I outlined two general questions as to what opinion polls might tell us about public opinion in Ireland on liberal agenda issues. With regard to the first question, which asked if opinion polls can mirror public opinion, I have demonstrated that it is possible to use polls for such a task. However, care is required because liberal agenda issues such as abortion and divorce have distinct facets that must be kept separate in order to make valid inferences. In this respect, I have built on the hard and easy distinction in opinion poll questions introduced in Chapter 2. This conceptual distinction has been applied in Figures 20 and 21. These figures show that considerations of principle (easy facet) and policy (hard facet) have had very different levels of support. In addition, these figures reveal that public opinion change has been primarily concentrated on hard facets of these issues. This important finding implies that the public has been genuinely engaged in the debate on these moral questions stemming from successive referendum campaigns. In summary, our task of carefully reflecting public opinion on the abortion and divorce issues has revealed that Irish public opinion on key moral questions has become more liberal.

Moving on to the second question posed at the outset of this chapter, why has public opinion on liberal agenda issues changed? Discovering that there has been opinion change on some liberal agenda issues has spurred us to find techniques that allow us to illuminate some of the details of these processes. For this reason, I have used a simple cohort analysis methodology to estimate whether the opinion change observed was primarily the result of generational replacement or actual opinion (intracohort) change. The identification of age as being a key variable conditioning opinion change on liberal agenda issues stemmed from our brief review of the literature on this topic. The main finding from our cohort analysis results shown in Table 10 is that the primary mechanism of opinion change in Ireland on liberal agenda issues between 1981 and 1999 was intracohort change. In short, Irish public opinion has become more liberal since 1981.

Beyond considerations of the opinion polling aspects of the research undertaken in this chapter, the results presented have three important implications for the broader study of value change in Ireland. First, the change in liberal–conservative values has resulted primarily from period effects, that is from history-making events such as referendum campaigns, rather than from the demise through population replacement of 'traditional Ireland'. In theoretical terms, this shows that thinking of value change as being primarily based on socialisation processes leads to an overly static view of attitudinal change. Moreover, the division between 'old' conservatives and 'young' liberals derived from a socialisation account of value change oversimplifies social reality.

Second, the fact that the abortion and divorce issues have hard and easy facets highlights that Irish public opinion towards such issues has never been monolithic, but has always been based on different considerations. Consequently, while strong advocates of conservative and liberal positions may have dominated media debate, public opinion was composed of citizens who did not have immutable positions because their opinions have always been based on a variety of considerations whose relative importance has evolved over time.

Third, the fact that legalising divorce and homosexuality has coincided with an increasing liberal orientation within Irish public opinion is an intriguing finding. Such an association suggests that public opinion on moral issues is influenced by institutional factors and the laws passed by government. The main implication here is that public opinion may support increasingly liberal social policies after it has been shown that such legal reforms do not lead to a decline in social order. In short, public opinion tends, for sensible reasons (fear of unknown consequences), to be conservative though not closed-minded on liberal agenda matters. However, we should not overestimate the importance of institutional factors, as opinions towards abortion and euthanasia where there have been no legal reforms have also witnessed important shifts towards a more liberal public stance.

In the next chapter, we will turn our attention to an issue that has figured prominently in the media and public agenda: the Northern Ireland question. This issue, like the liberal agenda, has undergone dramatic changes since opinion polling began in 1970.

Notes

1   The liberal agenda is a term given to campaigns led by reformers such as Mary Robinson (President of Ireland 1990–7) and Senator David Norris and a variety of specific interest groups (see Hug 1999). Their goal was to change Irish law so that abortion, contraception, divorce and homosexuality were no longer illegal. The law in these areas had been

justified on the basis of the Catholic Church's concept of 'natural law' and supported on a majoritarian principle.
2 According to Sinnott (2002) there have been eight liberal–conservative referendums amending the Irish Constitution (Bunreacht na h-Éireann): delete the special position of the Catholic Church (1972); prohibit the legalisation of abortion (1983); permit divorce (1986, 1995); abortion, right to information (1992); abortion, right to travel (1992); and restrict the availability of abortion (1992, 2002).
3 There is a considerable literature based on these topics using a variety of approaches. Some of the most recent literature is based on analysis of EVS and ISSP survey data. See Whelan (1994); Hornsby-Smith and Whelan (1994); Whelan and Fahey (1994); Hardiman and Whelan (1998); Cassidy (2002); Fahey (2002); Ward (2002); Coakley (2005a): 44–8, 62–3; Fahey, Hayes and Sinnott (2005): 30–56, 114–39a.
4 Some commentators such as Waters (1991, 1997) and Fennell (1989) argue that the main division within Ireland on the liberal agenda and a whole range of other economic and political issues centred on differences between the elites based in Dublin 4 and its environs ('the D4 set'), and the rest of (mainly) rural Ireland.
5 The link between Church and State was not just simply a conjunction of Catholic teachings with legislation and public policy. It had also had a strong ideological component where public opinion favoured public policy that complemented Catholic teachings. In this sense the liberal agenda represented a challenge not only to the position of the Catholic Church but also to significant sections of public opinion that genuinely supported the status quo (note Inglis 1998b: 252).
6 Strong ethnocentrism is often associated with prejudice towards those considered to be 'outsiders' and attitudes suggesting intolerance and possibly authoritarianism (Raven and Whelan 1976; Mac Gréil 1980, 1996).
7 One weakness of this argument, which claims to be a more parsimonious explanation than that of Darcy and Laver (1990), is that there is no convincing mechanism put forward to explain why pragmatists voted 'no' to divorce in 1986 and 'yes' in 1992 on the substantive abortion question. The main reason for this weakness is that the empirical analysis is based on aggregate-level election results and regression models using census data (social class indicators), there is no direct opinion poll evidence identifying the pragmatist section of public opinion and illustrating that this group is defined by less intensely held opinions.
8 Here it seems that ISSP questions asked in 1994 on gay marriage elicited considerations based on tolerance and respect for the privacy of people's sexual lives – an easy facet of the homosexuality question. However, the general question of homosexuality being always or never justified was, in contrast, a hard issue, because it raised in respondents' minds considerations of the consequences of allowing homosexuality to be an open feature of Irish society and fears of breakdown in traditional norms and values primarily based on Catholic teachings (see Hug 1999: 229–32).
9 The X case refers to a Supreme Court judgment in February 1992 that overturned an earlier ruling that prohibited a 14-year-old rape victim from being allowed to travel to Britain for an abortion. The court ruled that abortion was legal where there was 'a real and substantial threat to the life of the mother' (Kennedy 2002: 115). In an IMS poll on 19–20 February 1992, 64 per cent disagreed with the High Court ruling forbidding travel for an abortion and 66 per cent agreed that the 1983 abortion amendment to the constitution needed revising (IMS/CMC/mc/J.2S087, Independent Newspapers, questions 7–8). Similar support favouring abortion occurred after the C case judgment; see MRBI/4620/97, 10 December 1997, question 10.
10 In Chapter 2 I elaborated four criteria for assessing the hardness of poll questions. In this chapter the focus will be on which poll questions were asked (i.e. context criterion) and whether the poll questions asked outlined the consequences of expressing a specific response (i.e. consequences criterion).
11 One could argue that, in the 1970s, all poll questions towards divorce might have been

'easy' questions since there was little likelihood of a referendum on this issue. Nevertheless, the polling data in Figure 21 suggest that respondents saw changing the constitutional ban on divorce as being qualitatively different from discussions on the merits of divorce in principle.

12 It should be noted that support for the right to information and travel declined during the 1992 abortion campaign, where the liberal side declined by 8–13 percentage points and the conservative side gained by 5–8 percentage points. As noted earlier, this represents a general feature of liberal agenda referendums – liberal support tends to decline during such campaigns.

13 These figures are rough estimates as more exact figures depend on question format and timing (close to a referendum or not). In general, there is support for unrestricted abortion among 5 per cent or less of the Irish public. A similar number adhere to a strongly conservative position and think that abortion is never justified.

14 Government legislation ensued rather reluctantly from a European Court of Human Rights ruling of 1988 following a case taken by (Senator) David Norris some years earlier. A similar process was required to change the law in Northern Ireland.

15 Hug (1999: 229–32) notes that opinion polls and academic survey evidence on attitudes towards homosexuality in Ireland are strongly influenced by question format effects. Hug made the point that opinions were 'more absolutist when it came to abstract questions' and more tolerant when discussing specific policies such as gay marriage.

16 This type of investigation, known as cohort analysis, can be very technical in nature because of a variety of methodological issues that arise when trying to explain opinion change in cross-sectional survey data. Here the analysis used is kept as simple and straightforward as possible. For an introduction to cohort analysis see Glenn (1977), Converse (1976), Abramson (1983), Firebaugh (1992, 1997).

17 Using Pearson product moment correlation, where age is measured in years and justification of the various liberal agenda issues is a ten-point scale (1=never justified, 10=always justified), the correlations observed in EVS 1981, 1991 and 1999 are broadly similar. For example, in EVS 1999 the correlations with age were as follows: abortion ($r= -0.3$); divorce ($r= -0.4$); euthanasia ($r= -0.3$) and homosexuality ($r= -0.4$), and all were significant ($p \leq 0.001$).

18 As the final EVS wave is not exactly a decade after the second one, this represents a limitation in the use of this data for cohort analysis. However, the EVS dataset is the only dataset available that is suitable for this of type analysis and gives us a rare picture of inter-generational opinion change on liberal agenda issues. Fahey, Hayes and Sinnott (2005: 125–9) have conducted a similar type of analysis where they examine both cohort differences and life-cycle effects. In the analysis undertaken here, we concentrate on illustrating and comparing the impact of intracohort and generational replacement effects – a question that Fahey, Hayes and Sinnott do not pursue.

19 It should be noted that simply using the population composition in 1981 for later time points does not facilitate estimating the full effect of generation replacement. This is because we ignore the complexity of taking into account the differential death and emigration rates of different cohorts. For the sake of simplicity, we will ignore these complications and 'freeze' the population in order to make a simple estimation of the likely impact of generational replacement. Abramson (1983) and Mayer (1992) follow a similar strategy.

20 In general, most cohorts are based on nine-year spans to match the length of time between European Values Surveys (i.e. 1981, 1990, 1999). However, for the youngest cohort an 18–29 span was used so as to be able to match with the published 1981 Census data – a consideration necessary for estimation of cohort effects. Fahey, Hayes and Sinnott (2005: 126–9) adopted a different strategy and ignored the 18–24 year olds in order to have a perfect match. The position adopted here is that this involves a loss of valuable information. Despite these different operationalisations, the substantive results from both research approaches are the same.

Chapter 6

Public Opinion in the Republic of Ireland towards the Northern Ireland Question

> All issues have intrinsically simple and complex facets; which particular facets predominate at a given time is an empirical question.
>
> E.G. Carmines and J.A. Stimson (1980: 81)

The liberal agenda issues examined in the last chapter were defined in political terms by the fact that it was the actions and opinions of the public that led political elites. The best example of this phenomenon is family planning. Widespread use of artificial contraception preceded public policy in this area by two decades. In contrast, the Northern Ireland issue appears to be one where it is successive governments who have led the public. One could argue that the liberal agenda and Northern Ireland issues follow different dynamics because of the role of the Catholic Church – an organisation that has been content to leave the Northern Ireland question as a prerogative of government. However, both the liberal agenda and national question are similar as no general election campaign since 1970 (when opinion polling began) has been shaped by policy stances on these issues (Sinnott 1995a: 178; Marsh and Sinnott 1999: 164; Garry et al. 2003: 126–7).

In this chapter I will investigate, within the limitations imposed by the polling data, the evolution of public opinion in the Republic of Ireland towards the Northern Ireland question. In the construction of opinion trends we will once again demonstrate that not all poll questions are the same and much care is required in using and interpreting movements in public opinion. In effect, the mirror and lamp functions of opinion polls that may be used to help us conceptualise more clearly what polls tell us about public opinion need careful construction – the data do not speak for themselves. Consequently, in this chapter methodological considerations will shape not only the type of data that will be presented for investigation, but also the inferences and conclusions we may draw from these data.

Substantively, this chapter will try to show what opinion poll results on the Northern Ireland question tell us more generally about Irish public opinion. Given the sweeping political changes that have occurred with the peace process, this raises some intriguing public opinion questions. For example, can we now say that the Northern Ireland issue is settled within Irish public opinion where there is an acceptance of the new political situation in the north? Or does popular sentiment towards the Northern question exhibit considerable stability where profound political changes have not, as yet, led to equally large changes in public opinion? These are some of the topics that will be addressed here.

This chapter will start with a brief inventory of the polling data available and a discussion of which substantive issue areas are amenable to analysis. The second section will present a short discussion of previous research in this field and this will be followed by an outline of how poll questions on Northern Ireland will be broadly categorised in this chapter and why. The substantive analysis extends from sections four to six where poll data on Irish public opinion towards constitutional issues, political initiatives in the search for peace, and long-term trends will be introduced. In the final section I will draw together the evidence presented and attempt to answer both the specific questions posed and the more general issue of what opinion polls can tell us about public opinion towards Northern Ireland. As in all the substantive chapters, we must first start with the foundations of our public opinion analysis and address – what are the data?

Opinion Poll Data

The Northern Ireland question is considered by students of politics using a variety of methodologies to be one of the most important issues within the Republic of Ireland.[1] An examination of the type and range of survey questions asked by IMS, Lansdowne and MRBI since the 1970s shows that most poll questions relate primarily to political initiatives. In fact, if one plots the level of violence using a variety of measures such as number of fatalities per year against the annual level of surveying, one notices that the level of opinion polling on the Northern Ireland question in the Republic did not follow the officially recorded level of violence as one might expect.

Opinion polling on the Northern question peaked in the Republic (and in Northern Ireland) during the referendum campaign on the Belfast/Good Friday Agreement in 1998. This fits in with the general pattern noted in previous chapters that opinion polling in Ireland is strongly driven by media interest in electoral politics. This implies that media-commissioned opinion polls will primarily provide a political perspective on Irish public opinion towards Northern Ireland. If an examination is made of all the poll questions asked on this topic since 1970, one discovers that the scope for assessing opinion change is restricted.

Fortunately, trend series can be constructed for four sets of questions. The first series deals with opinions on Articles 2 and 3 of the Irish Constitution. These provisions asserted the Republic's claim of future sovereignty over the entire island of Ireland. The second series deal with public aspirations towards achieving a united Ireland, while the third series examines opinions towards the withdrawal of British troops from Northern Ireland. The last series investigates public preferences towards the border between Northern Ireland and the Republic. Substantively, these time series are similar in that they measure facets of more general preferences towards the preferred constitutional status of Northern Ireland.

However, as will be seen later these time series do not consist of the same types of poll questions and considerable care is required when interpreting the trends exhibited by these data. In this chapter two other sets of poll questions will be investigated. The first examines the salience of the Northern Ireland question within public opinion in the Republic since the 'Troubles' began. The second set of items deals with public opinion towards the most important peace initiative – the Belfast/Good Friday Agreement of 1998. Prior to presenting these opinion poll trends and results, it is important first to summarise previous research in this field.

Literature on Public Opinion towards Northern Ireland

The two most important analyses of public opinion towards the Northern Ireland question have adopted a comparative perspective. The first piece of research introduced the concept of a 'concurring majority'. Here an attempt was made to discover, using opinion poll data from Britain, Northern Ireland, and the Republic of Ireland, whether there was a consensus within public opinion in these three jurisdictions as to a solution to the Northern Ireland question (Rose, McAllister and Mair 1978). The second major piece of research in this field undertaken almost twenty years later by Hayes and McAllister (1996), and later updated following the fundamental changes brought about by the Belfast/Good Friday Agreement of May 1998, adopted a similar comparative strategy (see Fahey, Hayes and Sinnott 2005: 89–93).

A key feature of these research papers is the difficulty of assembling similar poll questions in order to chart trends in public opinion. Given the focus of this chapter the Hayes and McAllister (1996) article is of most interest as they elaborate clear hypotheses regarding trends in public opinion change towards the Northern Ireland question in the Republic. They argue, from IMS and MRBI opinion poll data relating to support for a united Ireland, British troop withdrawal from Northern Ireland and attitudes towards Articles 2 and 3, that Irish public opinion regarding Northern Ireland has gone through three distinct stages (Hayes and McAllister 1996: 74–5).

In the first stage from 1968 to the late 1970s there was strong public support for a united Ireland and the possibility that this could occur in the short term. The second, much shorter stage between 1981 and 1984 saw a 'strengthening in support for unity' as the British government was seen to be unable to formulate effective policies to deal with nationalist grievances. The third stage commenced with the Anglo-Irish Agreement of 1985, and coincides with the emergence of the peace process. According to Hayes and McAllister (1996), evidence of this three-stage evolution in public opinion in the Republic over the last two decades is manifest in three trends: support for a united Ireland, retention of constitutional claims over Northern Ireland and preference for British troop withdrawal have all declined.

In this chapter an attempt will be made to examine this thesis using a more extensive set of polling data where the focus will be on the Republic of Ireland. Moreover, a preliminary examination of the survey data suggests that poll questions relating to Northern Ireland follow a similar general pattern to that identified in Chapter 5. Within that chapter I demonstrated the importance of distinguishing between 'hard' and 'easy' facets of an issue.

Hard and Easy Opinion Poll Questions Relating to the Northern Ireland Question

According to at least one account, public opinion played an important restraint on negotiations during the early phases of the peace process (Trumbore 1998). If an attempt is made to assess what public opinion in the Republic of Ireland favoured, one finds a bewildering array of poll questions that come in a variety of formats. In order to reduce this complexity to manageable proportions, this chapter will consider opinion poll questions concerning Northern Ireland on the basis of their 'hardness', a concept introduced in Chapter 2.

It makes much intuitive sense to view opinion towards Northern Ireland and the poll questions used to measure such opinion from this perspective. At its simplest the Northern Ireland question can be reduced within the Republic of Ireland to desiring a united Ireland. However, if the question posed deals not with desires for a united Ireland, but with how to achieve a peaceful solution to the violence in the north, the considerations involved are much harder to reconcile. Hayes and McAllister (1996: 77) make a similar argument, noting that the 'complexity of Irish public opinion towards Northern Ireland' is based on both principle (easy) and practical (hard) political and economic considerations.

Although one might expect that different facets of the Northern Ireland question will result in different levels of support among public opinion in the Republic, it is more difficult to see why this might be the case. Carmines and Stimson (1980), who developed the hard and easy distinction, argued that the basis of differential response profiles stemmed from the impact of conditioning factors. Preliminary investigations (see Figure 27 presented later in this chapter) of the poll data on Northern Ireland show that the age variable does help to explain the hard and easy distinction that is presented a little later in Figure 25. This implies that the process of socialisation has discernible effects on opinions towards Northern Ireland. Unfortunately, due to insufficient data, it is not possible to undertake a cohort analysis in a similar manner to that undertaken in Chapter 5 to examine this effect.

Importance of the Northern Ireland Issue in Public Opinion towards Politics in the Republic of Ireland

An important preliminary task is to see whether the Irish public regards the Northern Ireland question to be an important one. Recent research using a number of academic surveys has shown that the Northern Ireland issue remains important, although its dominance appears to be declining (see Marsh et al. 2001: 168–70; Fahey, Hayes and Sinnott 2005: 25; Garry 2006; Kennedy and Sinnott 2006). Indeed, respondents have been specifically asked on a number of occasions in IMS and MRBI polls if the Northern Ireland question is important to them.

The poll data show that in 1979 Northern Ireland was considered to be an 'important problem' by three in four of those interviewed. By 2002, the next time point for which there are data, the Northern Ireland question was still seen to be important by 68 per cent of respondents.[2] Given the political history of the Republic of Ireland there is strong reason to think that voters differentiate between the major political parties on the question of Northern Ireland (Sinnott 1995a: 164–5).

Fortunately, there is survey evidence available (comparable polls in 1978 and 2002) that allows us to investigate two aspects of the partisan nature of the Northern Ireland question in the Republic. First, has the Irish public's preference for a united Ireland evolved over the last three decades? Second, have public perceptions of parties' positions on Northern Ireland changed since the 1970s? An analysis of these data indicates that the median position of the Irish public on seeking a 'united Ireland now' or 'abandoning this aim altogether' has become more 'centrist', as have the perceived positions of all the main parties. However, it is possible to go 'behind' these poll estimates and examine the degree to which all of those interviewed in a poll express the same perceptions of where the parties lie on the question of a united Ireland. Examining the data presented in Table 11 one finds a significant decline in the coherence of Irish public opinion.[3]

Looking at popular sentiment towards the Northern Ireland question from a different perspective, the opinion poll evidence shows that Fianna Fáil has been persistently seen as the party most competent to deal with Northern Ireland. A number of surveys undertaken around the last general election in May 2002 show that voters who expressed 'nationalist' opinions were most likely to support Sinn Féin and Fianna Fáil (Kennedy and Sinnott 2005;

Garry 2006). However, if we look at the importance of the Northern Ireland issue in making a vote choice in recent general elections we find that its influence, derived from self-reports, declined from 14 per cent in 1997 to 4 per cent in 2002.

Table 11 *Results of Agreement Measure Estimations using the Davis and Sinnott (1978) and INES (2002) Survey Results to Estimate Self and Party Placements on Preferences for a United Ireland*

Survey/ placement	Agreement measure	Interpolated median	Arithmetic mean	Standard deviation	Variance	Mode
Davis and Sinnott (1978)						
Self-placement	0.32	2.85	3.06	1.73	2.99	3
Fianna Fáil	0.51	2.42	2.61	1.37	1.88	2
Fine Gael	0.42	3.08	3.31	1.47	2.16	2 & 3
Labour Party	0.33	3.46	3.65	1.60	2.55	3
INES (2002)						
Self-placement	0.04	3.50	3.22	1.97	3.86	1
Fianna Fáil	0.17	3.16	3.11	1.81	3.29	1
Fine Gael	0.23	3.90	3.80	1.77	3.12	4
Labour Party	0.34	3.86	3.75	1.63	2.65	4
Green Party	0.30	3.95	3.91	1.69	2.86	4
PD	0.24	3.70	3.54	1.77	3.15	4
Sinn Féin	0.73	1.11	1.64	1.58	2.48	1

Note: Calculations are based on van der Eijk's (2001) measure of agreement for ordered rating scales (A) to create estimates of preferential and perceptual agreement. The agreement measure indicates the degree to which there is preferential agreement among the public on a united Ireland, where zero represents no agreement and one perfect agreement. This procedure is described in more detail in Chapter 5. The survey data examined here is based on a seven-point scale where '1' refers to 'insist on a united Ireland now' and '7' implies 'abandon the aim of a united Ireland altogether'. The scales for 2002 were rescaled to a seven-point ones to facilitate comparison with the Davis and Sinnott survey of 1978.

It is undoubtedly true that this difference between the 1997 and 2002 poll results reflects dissimilar concerns during these two election campaigns, and is not evidence of a long-term shift in public opinion. Nevertheless, such data does show that the Northern Ireland issue has played only a minor role in recent general elections, and is not a consistent feature of electoral politics. In addition, the Irish National Election Study (2002) shows that the Northern Ireland issue (as represented by support for a united Ireland and considered to be very or fairly important by 67 per cent of respondents) was less important than all the other issues examined, namely taxation (88 per cent), the environment (83 per cent), the EU (73 per cent) and abortion (70 per cent).[4] Of course, public opinion towards Northern Ireland need not be linked to electoral concerns for it to be politically important. In the next section I will examine the Northern Ireland question from an aspirational or irredentist perspective.

Constitutional Issues and Status of Northern Ireland

Public opinion towards the constitutional future of Northern Ireland has been investigated within Irish opinion polls since 1970 primarily in terms of the four trend series described earlier, that is, opinions towards retaining or repealing Articles 2 and 3; support for a united Ireland; removal of the border, and redeployment of British troops out of Northern Ireland. The objective here is to examine the polling evidence available, and see whether public opinion on these four interrelated topics has changed in the last three decades. This task is not a simple one because in many cases particular poll items were asked once. For this reason, the polling data on the desired future status for Northern Ireland is composed of a set of questions dealing with the same substantive theme, but with different question and response formats. Because of these methodological difficulties, no attempt will be made here to chart support for different constitutional options that have been proposed over the years.[5]

As we will see, use of such survey evidence requires considerable caution as trends constructed from these data exhibit much variance. Ironically our inability to determine opinion change over time yields valuable information on the survey response process itself and the apparent 'malleability' of Irish public opinion in responding to various question–response formats. As discussed earlier, one of the key distinctions that can be made in the presence of such response effects is an identification of 'hard' and 'easy' questions.

Articles 2 and 3 of Bunreacht na h-Éireann

Within the Republic of Ireland a key contribution to the peace process in the north has been a willingness on the part of governments and the public to modify constitutional claims over Northern Ireland. Public opinion poll questions have been asked on the issue of retaining or amending Articles 2 and 3 of the Irish Constitution since 1974. These poll questions are unfortunately not consistent.

Initially, opinion polls asked two distinct items: first, whether there should be a referendum on Articles 2 and 3, and second, how the respondent would vote in such a referendum. The question format changed in the 1990s, when removing the claims in Articles 2 and 3 was linked with efforts to support the emerging peace process in Northern Ireland.

An early poll undertaken by MRBI in late 1974 showed that four in ten favoured having a referendum, although only 11 per cent would have voted to remove these provisions. However, 61 per cent favoured having a 'united Ireland today', thus realising the aspirations inherent in Articles 2 and 3. Later, in April 1998, the survey data show that 61 per cent were prepared to vote 'yes' to amend Articles 2 and 3. In a follow-up question, 20 per cent saw Articles 2 and 3 as a 'justifiable claim', while 51 per cent stated that it was a 'justifiable claim, but could be given up for peace in Northern Ireland'.

The important implication here is that responses to Articles 2 and 3 poll questions were strongly determined by contemporary events. This may help to explain the pattern evident in Figure 24, which is predominantly one of fluctuation with no clear trend. Unfortunately, such fluctuation is composed of both question format and political context effects. Both are endogenously related, as different question formats reflect changed political realities at different junctures in time. As noted earlier with regard to the Belief-Sampling Model of survey response, this is a characteristic element of opinion poll responses that involve different considerations.

For these reasons, it is difficult to determine that opinion towards Articles 2 and 3 has really changed as Hayes and McAllister (1996: 79) assert. Generally, the more recent data from the European Values Survey of 1999 suggest that support for the aspirations inherent in Articles 2 and 3 may have declined by about 20 per cent since 1974, but was still important for 30 per cent of the Irish public in 1999. This is consonant with the argument put forward by Hayes and McAllister. However, the very dramatic changes in support for retaining Articles 2 and 3 between 1995 and 1999 indicate that while the impact of the peace process is important, there is still significant support for a united Ireland which rises and falls depending on context. This implies that the three-stage evolution in Irish public opinion towards the north outlined by Hayes and McAllister may not be so clear-cut.

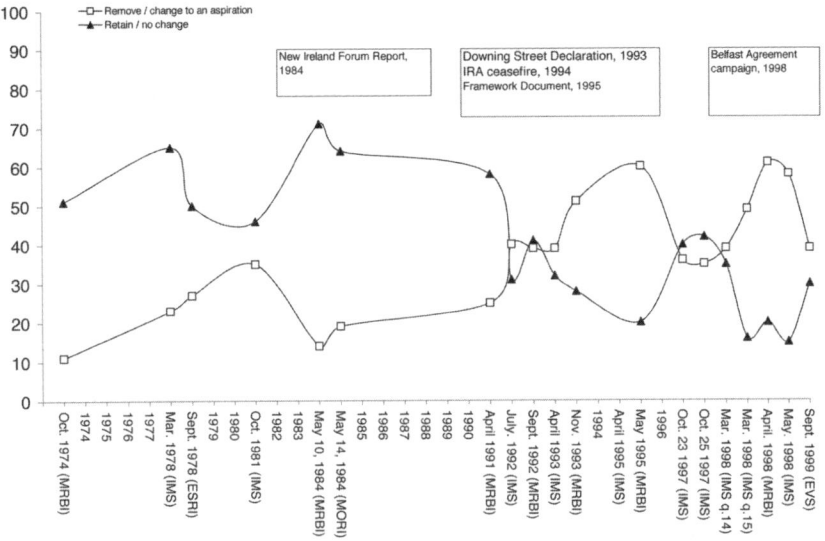

Figure 24 *Public Opinion towards Proposals to Make Changes to Articles 2 and 3 of the Irish Constitution, 1974–99 (per cent)*

Note: examples of poll questions asked on proposals to amend Articles 2 and 3:

Should the Irish parliament and people make a gesture to the people in the north by withdrawing the territorial claim to the six counties in the constitution? (IMS: JN780, Table 10a, Northern Ireland: a survey of prevailing attitudes in the Republic of Ireland (Dublin: A survey commissioned by Panorama / BBC); Rose, McAllister and Mair (1978: 35); 2–9 March 1978).

Articles 2 and 3 of the Constitution state the Republic's claim to jurisdiction over the island of Ireland. Are you in favour or not in favour of the claim contained in these articles? MRBI/3950/91, 16 April 1991, *The Irish Times*, question 10.

Articles 2 and 3 of our Constitution assert a legal claim to the territory of Northern Ireland. It has been suggested that they should be amended to confirm our acceptance that there will be no change to the existing constitutional status of Northern Ireland except by peaceful means and with the consent of a majority in Northern Ireland. Do you think Articles 2 and 3 should be left as they are, or do you think they should be amended as outlined? IMS: CMC/SOS/id/8S-181, 26 March 1998, *Sunday Independent*, question 14.

Support for a united Ireland

In the search for peace in Northern Ireland many different constitutional options have been discussed, and these have formed the basis of a wide range of opinion poll questions since 1968 (see Rose, McAllister and Mair 1978; Mac Gréil 1980, 1996; Jones 2001). Our chief interest here relates to preferences for a united Ireland, the most consistent option in all the poll questions available, where two basic types of survey item have been implemented. The first type comprises easy questions about the principle or symbolism of having a united Ireland. In contrast, the second type consists of hard questions where preferences for a united Ireland were linked with other considerations such as finding a 'solution' to the violence in the north or supporting the 'peace process'.[6]

Figure 25 illustrates clearly as hypothesised that the level of support exhibited in easy questions is considerably higher than that observed for hard items. As expected, hard and easy trends are essentially parallel, indicating in absolute terms that both trends refer to different facets of the same issue. Substantively, this figure illustrates considerable opinion stability on the question of a united Ireland if one compares the first and final figures in both series.

Poll questions that deal with symbolic ends, such as a united Ireland, are much easier for the public to provide answers to in survey interviews than programmatic policies to achieve desired goals such as peace and political stability.[7] One can see this general effect in two ways. First, in the Davis and Sinnott survey of 1978 those interviewed were asked many different types of questions on Northern Ireland. In all cases, responses for (easy) symbolic goals yield higher positive results than those dealing with difficult (or hard) choices such as constitutionally-based peacemaking. Second, when the Irish public have been asked whether or not they would be prepared to pay higher taxes for a united Ireland a majority have responded negatively. Moreover, a majority saw unification in 1984 as likely to make the Republic worse off financially.

This evidence suggests that great care must be taken in interpreting answers to questions that address the creation of a united Ireland. Dissimilar question types posed to the *same* respondents yield significantly different response patterns. In summary, the polling data do not provide definitive evidence that public opinion towards the aspiration of a having a united Ireland has changed since 1968 as Hayes and McAllister (1996) argue. Moreover, the

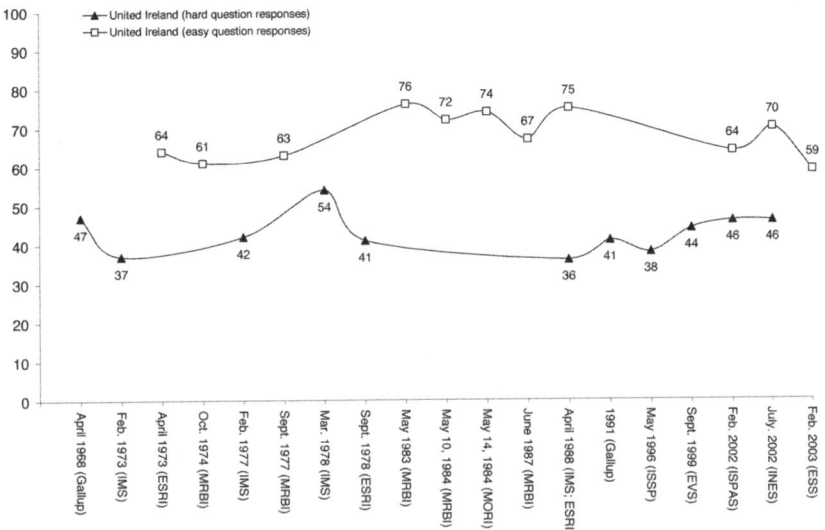

Figure 25 *Comparison of Hard and Easy Facets of Public Opinion Support for a United Ireland in the Republic of Ireland, 1968–2003 (per cent)*

Note: The top line refers to poll questions that simply asked respondents their personal preferences for a united Ireland. The bottom line is based on responses to questions where the future status of Northern Ireland was discussed with reference to a variety of political solutions, of which a united Ireland was just one choice. Given the question format, these 'hard' and 'easy' questions are represented as different time series.

Example of a hard question:

Which of the following options, in your opinion, would best help to bring peace to Northern Ireland? IMS: PMacN/mb.J.11345, Independent Newspapers, 8–10 April 1988, question 20. Response options: Full integration with Britain; A return to majority rule; Power sharing between the Unionist and Nationalist Community (with constitutional guarantees to protect the minority); An independent Ulster; A federal Ireland; A united Ireland.

Example of an easy question:

Personal reaction to a United Ireland today? Very much in favour, somewhat in favour, not really in favour, very much against. MRBI/530/74, Report of a Survey for 7 Days/RTÉ; Table 9; Rose, McAllister and Mair (1978: 35); 2 October 1974.

three stages identified on the evolution of public opinion are not apparent in the poll data examined.

Attitudes towards the border and partition of the island of Ireland

While preferences towards Articles 2 and 3 and the goal of a united Ireland were aspirational in nature, it could be argued that opinions towards the border and partition reflected a concrete reality. Consequently, preferences towards reunification of the island of Ireland through removal of the border should, logically speaking, be related. A summary of the poll questions shown in Table 12 reveals that items were rarely repeated, so it is not possible to definitively say that opinion towards partition has remained stable, or has changed since 1970. The general impression is that the importance of the border has probably declined, because the border as an issue has become subsumed under other concerns such as creating peace between the two communities in Northern Ireland.

The suspicion here is that the border issue has evolved from an easy question in the 1970s to a hard question in the 1990s. In other words, in 1970 support for removing the border was equated directly with achieving a political settlement through the creation of a united Ireland. However, by the 1990s compromising on the border issue was seen to be one way in which the Republic could promote peace within Northern Ireland. It would seem that the history of bloodshed within Northern Ireland from 1968 led citizens in the Republic to realise that removal of the border was likely to lead to even greater levels of violence. Consequently, the 'border issue' became a hard facet of the Northern Ireland question, as it involved confronting the trade-off between desiring a united Ireland and promoting peace.

From this perspective, we would expect to see, with the emergence of the peace process, a decline in support for removal of the border between the 1970s and late 1990s. The polling evidence presented in Table 12 supports this contention, as the belief that there would be 'no peace until partition ends' declined by 21 per cent between 1978 and 1999. Moreover, only 4 per cent thought in 1995 that the border was an 'obstacle to better relations between North and South'. This is not to suggest that the border is symbolically unimportant to the Irish public. As of 1996 it 'mattered' to 54 per cent of those interviewed. However, as an issue it has declined in importance since the 1970s. Part of the reason seems to be that a majority (57 per cent in 1978) have accepted since the 1970s that ending partition will not solve the Northern Ireland problem.

Table 12 *Summary of Public Opinion in the Republic of Ireland towards Ending Partition, 1970–2001 (per cent)*

Survey & question type	End partition	Notes
		General support for ending partition (easy questions)
May 1970 (IMS)	70	Prefer border to go
June 1972 (ESRI)	78	Government should work to end partition
Mar. 1978 (IMS)*	58	Border will go
Sept. 1978 (ESRI, q.159)*	73	Border will eventually disappear
Sept. 1978 (ESRI, q.93)	72	No peace until partition ends
Sept. 1978 (ESRI, q.96)	40	Disagree that the Northern Ireland problem cannot be solved by ending partition
Sept. 1999 (EVS)	51	No peace until partition ends
		Policy preferences towards ending partition (hard questions)
May 1970 (IMS, q.9b/c)	57	Can be achieved by negotiation
	14	Prefer border to go using violence if necessary
April 1995 (IMS)	4	Border an obstacle to better relations between North and South
Feb. 1996 (MRBI, q7)	47	Border matters but not prepared to use violence
	7	Border matters prepared to use violence
	42	Border does not matter

* The 15 per cent discrepancy between these two questions asked in the same year is surprising and is likely to be the result of a priming effect as the IMS question occurred at the start of the interview (q.2), while in the ESRI survey it came after 67 questions relating to Northern Ireland problem (q.159).

In this respect, it is not surprising to see from an examination of responses to poll questions asked between 1978 and 2001 on how long it would be until the border was dismantled that the modal (most popular) response given was 'never'. Moreover, since 1983 between two-thirds and three-quarters of the Irish public estimated that removing the border would, at the very least, be a long-term prospect.

In short, the opinion poll evidence shows that since 1970 a majority in the Republic have favoured a united Ireland. However, only a minority think that partition is likely to end in the near future. Moreover, since 1970 an even smaller minority (7 to 14 per cent) have been willing to use violence to attain such an objective. Overall, the polling evidence relating to the border indicates that it has become less important to the Irish public, though still symbolically important for a (bare) majority. This pattern fits with the Hayes and McAllister thesis of opinion change, although whether this occurred in (three) stages or continuously across time is not clear from the data available.

Public Opinion towards British Troops in Northern Ireland

Public opinion in the Republic of Ireland towards the presence of British troops in Northern Ireland has changed since the violence began in the late 1960s. Initially in 1970 these troops were seen as stabilising the political situation where the Stormont government had lost control and Northern Ireland was moving rapidly towards full-scale civil war. However, there has been majority support for the principle of withdrawal since at least 1978 once the Irish public perceived British troops as an occupation force. According to Hayes and McAllister (1996: 76), political developments during the 1980s and 1990s changed public opinion in the Republic of Ireland 'by weakening support for Irish unity and underpinning support for constitutional options, most notably a continued British presence in Northern Ireland'.

The survey evidence presented in the previous sub-section suggests, in contrast, that public support for a united Ireland in the Republic has remained remarkably stable despite all the political changes. A similar pattern is evident in public opinion towards the withdrawal of British troops from Northern Ireland. Figure 26 shows that majority support for troop withdrawal has been a salient feature of Irish public opinion since the 1970s, although the level of support seems to have declined from about three in four in 1978 to approximately six in ten in 2002.[8]

Hayes and McAllister (1996) are correct in identifying a significant change in 1987 and 1988. Whether such a change is connected with a surge in violence in 1987, and infamous events such as the Enniskillen 'Remembrance Day' bombing, is impossible to ascertain from the existing poll data.

Overall, the poll evidence on troop withdrawal reflects both changing political circumstances and perhaps also changing opinions. Given such causal endogeneity within the data being examined, it is impossible to identify (without additional information or a different research strategy) whether there has been true opinion change on this issue, as Hayes and McAllister have contended (see Manski 1995: 4;

King, Keohane and Verba 1994: 185–95). It is to the question of changing political circumstances, and an assessment of public opinion towards initiatives leading eventually to the peace process, that I will now turn.

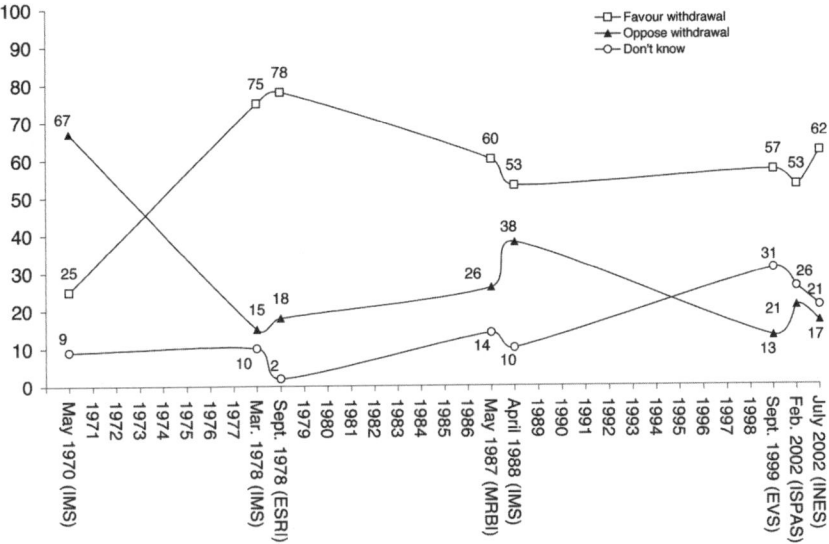

Figure 26 *Public Opinion towards Proposals for the Withdrawal of British Troops from Northern Ireland, 1970–2002 (per cent)*

Note: The data do not always sum to 100 per cent due to rounding error. Here are some examples of the poll questions asked on this issue:

Do you think that British troops should leave Northern Ireland or not? IMS: JN:1452 RJA/mec, Creation Group Ltd., 25 May 1970, question 8.

The British Government should remove the British army from the streets in Northern Ireland? (Survey on Attitudes Towards Social & Political Issues, ESRI, July–September 1978, question 138).

Which of these statements comes closest to the way you yourself feel about the presence of British Troops in Northern Ireland? IMS/PMacN/mb.J.11345, Independent Newspapers, 8–10 April 1988, question 21. British Troops should withdraw from Northern Ireland immediately; British Troops should withdraw from Northern Ireland within five years; British Troops should remain within Northern Ireland until a settlement is reached; British Troops should not be withdrawn from Northern Ireland.

I will now read out some more statements. Please tell me to what extent you disagree or agree with each statement. SHOW CARD A2. Statement 4: The British Government should declare its intention to withdraw from Northern Ireland at a fixed date in the future. Irish National Election Study (INES) 2002. This survey was undertaken by the ESRI in the summer of 2002, question A12(3).

Political Initiatives and the Search for Peace

From a public opinion perspective, the opinion poll evidence presented suggests that on 'easy' questions, such as the principle of wanting a united Ireland opinions in the Republic have been stable. However, with 'hard' questions, relating to solutions to the conflict and endorsing specific policies, public opinion has changed in dramatic ways where, for example, the aspirations of Articles 2 and 3 were amended through referendum in 1998.

One plausible interpretation of this difference in public opinion hinges on the fact that although Northern Ireland has remained an important aspirational (that is, an easy issue) question it has played little role as a 'hard' electoral issue in general election campaigns. This is because the policy positions, as opposed to the perceived competence, of the main political parties in the Republic on the Northern Ireland question have been identical.[9] In short, the Northern Ireland question, as noted earlier, is primarily an irredentist aspiration in the Republic. As a result, successive Irish governments have been able to lead public opinion and negotiate compromise agreements without strong fear of being punished electorally.

The general thrust of public opinion towards peace initiatives, starting with the Anglo-Irish Agreement (1985), the Hume–Adams dialogue, the Downing Street Declaration (1993), the Framework Document (1995) and the paramilitaries' ceasefire, was public support for any strategy that had the potential to end the violence. In the next sub-section I will concentrate on the Belfast/Good Friday Agreement as this peace initiative, unlike all the others, directly involved public opinion with the undertaking of a referendum in May 1998.

Public opinion during the Belfast/Good Friday Agreement campaign

By January 1998, it seemed that the strategy for peace being adopted by the British and Irish governments would involve profound changes within Northern Irish politics stemming from a new constitutional settlement (for details see Cox et al. 2002; Elliot 2002). While the Irish public supported moves towards a solution by both governments, there was nevertheless general scepticism concerning the timescale; fewer than one in ten thought there would be agreement by May 1998.

Public support for the Belfast/Good Friday Agreement followed different trends on either side of the border. In the Republic, support for the agreement increased by 25 per cent between 26 March and 18 May. In contrast, in the north, support for the Agreement declined initially, and then increased slightly close to polling day. The different campaign dynamics on either side of the border are not surprising. This is because both referendums, while ostensibly about supporting the peace process, were in reality bound up with different considerations.

The opinion polls undertaken by IMS and MRBI in the Republic during this period focused primarily on vote intentions and four main issues: support for amending Articles 2 and 3; release of paramilitary prisoners; the link between decommissioning of weapons and participation in political negotiations, and perceptions of the referendum campaign. The 'yes' side dominated the campaign, where the resources of all the major parties, government and media reiterated a simple message (Mansergh 1999: 127). That simple message stated that amending Articles 2 and 3 was a vote for peace. 'No' campaigners were portrayed as 'hardcore' nationalists who still believed that violence would ultimately lead to a united Ireland.

In effect, those who wanted a 'yes' vote turned the referendum issue into an 'easy' one, where the 'hard' question of whether amending Articles 2 and 3 circumscribed in some manner aspirations towards a united Ireland was not debated. Moreover, the division of poll questions on the Northern Ireland question into hard and easy types may be interpreted as an 'evolution', where an initially hard question evolved into an easy one.[10] The 'yes' campaign was careful not to allow the referendum of May 1998 to be defined as a trade-off between 'a united Ireland' and 'peace at all costs'.[11]

If this interpretation is correct, the expectation would be that those with the greatest political experience – that is, the older age cohorts – should exhibit the greatest attitudinal change during the campaign. This is because their initial position reflected most accurately the 'hard' facet of the question being posed in the referendum. The opinion poll data show that the Belfast/Good Friday Agreement campaign had an impact on all voters. However, for the older age cohorts (50–64 years and 65+) the campaign effect seems to have been greatest (see Figure 27).

This evidence implies that the Hayes and McAllister thesis of opinion change over three distinct phases remains unproven. What we do know is that there was a pronounced campaign effect. However, Figure 24 indicates that such an effect was gone a year later, when the European Values Survey asked about support for having changed Articles 2 and 3. In fact, public opinion towards these constitutional provisions returned to levels evident a decade earlier when the peace process was in its infancy.

One important question stemming from the Belfast/Good Friday Agreement referendum is: has Irish public opinion towards the hard and easy facets of the Northern Ireland question changed in recent times?

Long-term Trends in Responses to Hard and Easy Questions

One could argue that voting in the Belfast/Good Friday Agreement referendum was primarily a vote for the 'peace process'. This interpretation implies, in contrast to Hayes and McAllister (1996: 78), that there was no 'dramatic decline in support for retaining Articles 2 and 3'. What we witnessed instead was a *different* pattern of responses to *different* question types.

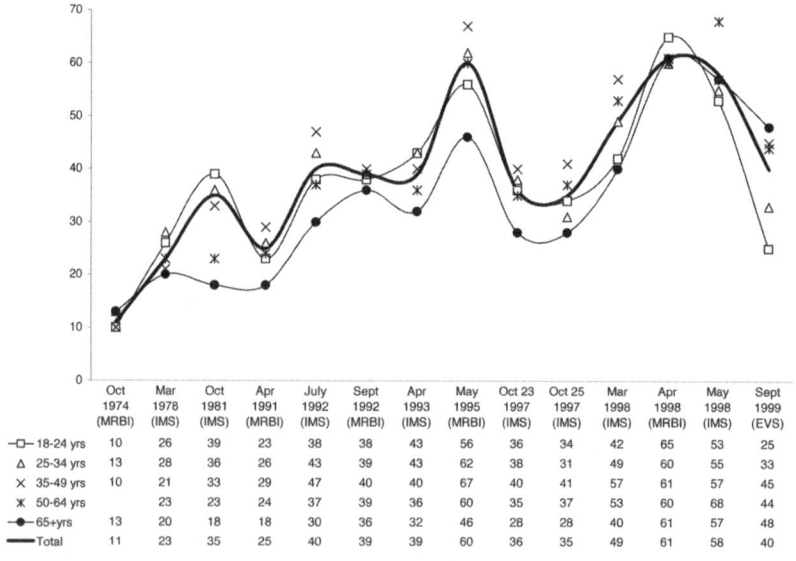

Figure 27 *Public Opinion among Different Age Cohorts towards Proposals to Make Changes to Articles 2 and 3 of the Irish Constitution, 1974–99 (per cent)*

Note: that the data refers to the percentage of those interviewed that supported making amendments to Articles 2 and 3. In the MRBI poll of 1974 only data for those aged 50+ years was reported, and this estimate is represented here for convenience in the 65+ category. See Figure 24 for examples of poll questions used to construct this time series.

A simple age cohort analysis, shown in Figure 27, lends support to this interpretation. The process of opinion change was practically the same for all age groups; where one might have expected that the older cohorts to have been less in favour of change, this was not the case.

In light of the hard and easy question distinction used in this chapter, the strong swings evident in Figure 27 may be seen as reflecting different facets of this specific issue. Amending Articles 2 and 3 was an easy question when linked to peacemaking, but was otherwise a hard question. If this poll question distinction is a useful one we should expect to see less variance (sharp swings) in opinion poll questions that are defined to be either easy or hard.[12] Those opinion poll questions dealing with support for a united Ireland facilitate testing this expectation within the limits of the available data. Looking at the cohort response profiles to easy questions one sees little change in support within age subgroups. In fact, total support for the principle of a united Ireland was at the same level in 2001 as it was in 1974 (61 per cent).

An examination of the trend series of hard questions, in contrast, shows a total increase in support for a united Ireland (36 per cent in 1988 to 46 per cent in 2002). It seems that the oldest age cohort was most strongly influenced by the Belfast/Good Friday Agreement campaign. Moreover, the distinctive profiles exhibited by responses to hard and easy questions confirms that the logic outlined in Chapter 2 based on distinguishing between different facets of an issue is a useful research strategy.

Conclusion

In this chapter we have seen how a changing political situation impacts on public opinion. This raises some important theoretical issues. How is one to interpret substantively similar opinion poll questions when the political context within which these questions have been asked changes considerably over time? These concerns relate directly to how we conceptualise respondents' answers to opinion poll questions. In Chapter 2, where I described the Belief-Sampling Model, it was noted that changing context leads citizens to use different considerations and information in providing answers during opinion poll interviews. In effect, when this process occurs we do not witness opinion change, but see the emergence of different facets of opinion on the same issue. Use of the concept of hard and easy question types reinforces this assessment, as trend series divided according to this criterion show considerable stability. This helps us answer the two questions posed at the start of this chapter.

Our first question asked whether the Northern Ireland issue was settled within Irish public opinion. There are two answers to this enquiry. First, in terms of the easy facet of the Northern issue there is still stable majority support for a united Ireland. From this perspective, public opinion on the Northern question was settled with partition in 1922; since this time irredentist sentiments have held sway. Second, the hard facet also shows opinion stability. Presumably, given the experience of the Northern 'Troubles' since 1968, the Irish public favours peace if there has to be a trade-off between having a united Ireland or a cessation of violence. Taking both the hard and easy facets of opinion towards Northern Ireland separately yields the important finding that public opinion in this domain is characterised by stability. Furthermore, this dual patterning within the data reveals why it has been possible for successive Irish governments to build a peace process even though one consequence of this course of action appears at first sight to sacrifice the long-term irredentist goals of the Irish electorate. The key public opinion lesson to be learned from the Belfast/Good Friday Agreement referendum is that separation of principles from policy lies at the heart of the peace process in the Republic. Whether a similar mechanism operates within Northern Ireland is an intriguing project for further research.

Turning to the second question posed at the outset, I asked whether political events surrounding the peace process have been ahead of public opinion in the Republic. Again, our distinction of poll questions on the basis of hard and easy facets is crucial here. With regard to an easy facet of the Northern question, such as desiring a united Ireland, public opinion in the Republic appears to lag behind political developments and is inconsistent with the fact that a majority of the electorate supported amending Articles 2 and 3 in 1998. However, taking the trend in responses to hard facet questions we see that public opinion *pre-dates* the profound political changes that came with the peace process. In short, the Irish public have no single view on the Northern Ireland question and are best conceptualised as having a set of opinions based on different considerations. For these reasons, one must conclude that the Hayes and McAllister thesis of change in Irish public opinion occurring in three distinct phases is not strongly supported by the data presented in this chapter.

While many of the headlines in the Irish media in the 1990s were dominated by events in Northern Ireland, there were also profound changes taking place within the Republic. For the first time since independence, the Irish economy developed into a remarkable success story that made it the exemplar state within the European Union. In the next chapter, we will turn our attention to public opinion towards the economy and inquire whether public opinion is best characterised by stability or change.

Notes

1. Evidence for this comes from four sources. One stream of research has examined the attitudes of party elites (Sinnott 1984, 1986, 1989). A second stream has employed 'expert surveys' (Laver and Hunt 1992; Laver 1998; Benoit and Laver 2006). In contrast, a third stream has used 'party manifesto' data (Mair 1986; Budge, Robertson and Hearl 1987; Budge et al., 2001; Garry and Mansergh 1999; de Vries, Giannetti and Mansergh 2000). Finally there are the results from mass survey research (Hardiman and Whelan 1994: 153; Sinnott 1995a: 160–6; Fahey, Hayes and Sinnott 2005: 25).
2. This estimate derived from INES may suffer from priming and potentially represents an overestimation. Before being asked this importance question respondents would have answered ten questions relating to Northern Ireland and more specifically seven items relating to self and party placement on a united Ireland scale.
3. These measures of agreement (A) within public opinion are based on procedures described in van der Eijk (2001). With regard to self-placement on the united Ireland scale, the measure of agreement declined from A = 0.32 in 1978 to A = 0.04 in 2002. Perceptions of the positions of Fianna Fáil and Fine Gael also exhibit decline, unlike the Labour Party, which has remained stable.
4. These data are taken from INES questions B44.8b, B44.9a, C7 and C26.
5. For comparison of public opinion in the Republic of Ireland towards different solutions to the Northern Ireland question see Rose, McAllister and Mair (1978), Davis and Sinnott (1979), Mac Gréil (1980; 1996) and Jones (2001).
6. In the definition of hard and easy questions given in Chapter 2 the emphasis was on different question texts; the focus here is on the response options offered to respondents, i.e. the consequences criterion. Of course, an examination of the questions shows that in practice the difference between hard and easy questions stemmed from the way the poll questions were asked. The key point here is that respondents were forced into considering specific alternatives and not simply allowed to respond 'yes' or 'no' to a general question.
7. This differential level of opinionation across survey question types and categories is of fundamental importance. Recent research on this topic by Alvarez and Brehm (2002) and Althaus (2003) has shed important light on what surveys tell us about public opinion. Discussion of this issue will be addressed more directly in the concluding chapter.
8. In fact, mean support (21 per cent, 1978–2002) for those who favoured a British troop presence is not much different from the mean number who gave given non-committal responses (16 per cent) to these poll questions. In effect, this poll item is best regarded as a proxy indicator for 'pro-irredentist nationalism' (Fahey, Hayes and Sinnott 2005: 23–5).
9. The Northern Ireland issue is similar to the race issue in the United States as it formed the

basis around which party competition crystallised in the 1920s. However, as the Northern Ireland issue has lost much of its salience there is the possibility that through a process of 'issue evolution' a new issue could rearrange the Irish party system along different cleavages (Carmines and Stimson 1989).

10 This contrasts with the issues of abortion and divorce. In Chapter 5 we saw that easy questions based primarily on principles derived from Catholic Church teachings, evolved into hard questions of policy during successive referendum campaigns.

11 Here the hardness of the poll questions relates to the context criterion outlined in Chapter 2. The key point here is that support for the principle of a united Ireland remains popular amongst the Irish public. Interpretation of the decline in support for Articles 2 and 3 in 1998 must be interpreted in the context of the Belfast/Good Friday Agreement campaign.

12 It was noted earlier in Chapter 2 that 'easy' questions refer to principles or goals (e.g. desiring a united Ireland) while 'hard' poll items refer to policies to achieve desired goals (e.g. supporting the peace process by removing Articles 2 and 3 of the Irish Constitution in a referendum in May 1998).

Chapter 7

Economic Opinion in Ireland and Left–Right Orientation

> The left–right dimension seems to have a relatively unclear meaning for the Irish public. Both the partisan and ideological components are weak in Ireland, our persistent deviant case.
> R. Inglehart and H. D. Klingemann (1976: 270)

There is little doubt that the Northern Ireland peace process and ratification of the Belfast/Good Friday Agreement in May 1998 were history-making events. Nevertheless, the patterns evident in the opinion poll data are much less dramatic. In fact, by separating the hard and easy facets of the Northern Ireland issue one observes considerable stability in opinion over time. For many commentators, changes in the Irish economy during the 1990s were no less dramatic. Within this chapter an examination will be made of economic opinion in Ireland using the concept of 'left–right.'

In comparative terms, Ireland is a unique and valuable case study of public opinion towards the economy as it is one of the few small open markets that have managed to go from 'bust' to 'boom' in the space of a decade. For this reason alone, one would expect to see considerable changes in public opinion towards the economy as perceptions evolved with a rising economic tide. If an examination is made of a number of opinion poll questions implemented by IMS, Lansdowne and MRBI since 1974 relating to the economy, two-thirds of the items asked refer to government budgets, public policy and confidence in the economy. The remaining questions deal with specific economic topics such as unemployment, taxation and inflation.

What is perhaps most surprising from an international perspective is that the concept of left–right plays almost no role in the formulation of opinion poll questions in Ireland. This is an important finding as it indicates that Irish pollsters are content to 'mirror' economic opinions on specific policy proposals such as increasing public spending, changing the level of taxation, and so on. There has been much less effort on the part of Irish pollsters to ask *why* the Irish public has particular economic preferences.

In many countries, the logic underlying opinions towards a multitude of economic questions is understood in terms of economic left–right orientation. For this reason, left–right self-placement questions have been asked frequently and used as a means of illuminating public policy preferences, vote intentions and satisfaction ratings. In Ireland, things are different, as pollsters discovered in the 1970s that the Irish public see the world in a manner that is inconsistent with a left–right ideological perspective. Such 'inconsistency' represents a concrete example of the key puzzle identified in the introductory chapter where public opinions on different facets of the same issue appear at first sight to be inconsistent. In Chapter 2, I introduced the useful tool developed within the framework of the Belief-Sampling Model of categorising poll questions as being either 'hard' or 'easy'. From this perspective, the apparently inconsistent responses to poll questions stem from different considerations. As I have demonstrated, this has been a key theme in Chapters 5 and 6 and will also play an important role here.

We will start our investigation of economic opinions in Ireland by briefly describing the main characteristics of the available data. In the second section there will be a brief literature review and an examination of how economic left–right orientation in Ireland has changed since 1976. This will be followed by an exploration of the Eurobarometer evidence on left–right in Ireland. In section four I will present a parsimonious model of how left–right self-placement changes over time. In the subsequent section, the focus will be on assessing the stability of opinion patterns, that is the overall response profile, regarding left–right self and party placements. In the penultimate section the economic preferences of the Irish public will be looked at in terms of so-called 'tax and spend' questions asked in IMS and MRBI polls. Thereafter, there will be some concluding remarks.

Opinion Poll Data

This chapter and the next are different from previous ones in that significant use will be made of Eurobarometer survey data. In this respect there will be a strong emphasis on the left–right self-placement question that has been included in most Eurobarometer surveys since the early 1970s. Moreover, perceptions of the positions of political parties on this dimension will be taken from a variety of sources including the European Election series of surveys. One of the main reasons for this strategy of extending the range of data used beyond media-commissioned opinion polls is that the number of consistent questions asked by IMS, Lansdowne and MRBI on economic issues is much less than the number asked about liberal agenda issues and Northern Ireland. I will, however, use the invaluable series of questions asked by Irish pollsters on the topics of taxation and proposals for social spending. It is fortunate that IMS asked a number of questions on a variety of topics associated with left–right in an early poll in September 1976. The results of this survey give us a benchmark in charting subsequent changes recorded in academic projects such as the first Irish National Election Study (summer 2002). Before presenting what the polls tell us about left–right orientation and public opinion towards the economy, it is important first to discuss briefly how well the left–right concept applies in the Irish context.

Literature on the Left–Right Concept and Application in the Irish Context

While the concept of economic left–right is widely understood by political commentators, it is appropriate at this point to provide a definition of what this concept means to Irish pollsters. The only example of a domestic polling definition of left–right is given in an IMS poll report written in September 1976. IMS defined 'left' as being associated with socialism, where such an orientation 'seeks to bring about greater justice and equality by a redistribution of wealth and extensive state expenditure and intervention'. In contrast, 'right' was stated to be 'a non-dogmatic belief in the virtues of private enterprise and private property, accompanied by good housekeeping and minimal state intervention' (IMS 1976: 10).[1]

As I will show a little later the left–right concept, when explained in this manner, had no meaning for three in ten respondents. Moreover, in the ISPAS survey of 2001/2 one in four declared that the concept of left–right was 'not important' for them, while another 14 per cent 'did not know.' These basic poll results lead to the compelling question: why does left–right have such little meaning in Ireland? The existing academic literature on this topic suggests at least five different answers to this important question.

- The concept of economic 'left–right' is typically used within political science to explain the sources of division and competition in society (Lipset and Rokkan 1967). In this respect, the process of industrialisation is seen to have created the foundations for class-based party competition. Ireland is a 'deviant case' within Europe because it evolved from an agrarian to a post-industrial economy in a single step, thereby bypassing the industrialisation process and its socio-political consequences.
- There is a long-standing weakness of left-wing parties in Irish electoral history. One of the main explanations for this weakness is that the Labour Party did not participate in the first post-independence elections when voters became socialised into voting on the basis of criteria that do not deal with left–right interests and concerns (Farrell 1970: 487).
- Party competition in Ireland does not exhibit any significant policy differences, or polarisation, and has little power in explaining vote choice (Sinnott 1995a: 160–4; Gilland Lutz 2003: 49–55; O'Malley and Kerby 2004: 43–8; Laver 2005: 204–8).
- According to the polling evidence, party support in Ireland is not *strongly* based on class (Whyte 1974: 647–6). This 'politics without social bases' thesis has been re-examined and qualified in subsequent research by: McAllister and O'Connell (1984); Laver (1986a, b; 2005: 197–8); Breen and Whelan (1994); Sinnott (1995a: 181–8); Evans and Sinnott (1999: 436–452) and Garry (2006).
- Political discourse in Ireland is not structured by left–right debates. Consequently, the political cues used by the Irish electorate in making electoral choices or assessments of public policy do not reflect a value system consonant with an economic left–right ideology. As a result, responses to left–right academic survey questions are inconsistent (Fogarty 1984: 68, 72; Hardiman and Whelan 1994a: 163; Kennedy and Sinnott 2006; Fahey, Hayes and Sinnott 2005: 140-50).

The first two arguments are concerned with the impact of historical processes that are not of direct interest here. However, the issues raised in the final three arguments are based on evidence derived from a variety of mass survey projects.[2] As the focus in this chapter is on public opinion I will concentrate on the attitudinal (final) stream of the literature outlined above. In this respect, our task is to see what

Irish opinion poll data tells us about economic opinions and their consistency with the concept of left–right. In the next two subsections I will outline what the earliest known opinion poll dealing with left–right attitudes discovered in 1976. Thereafter, I will reveal what surveys undertaken in 2001 and 2002 tell us about this topic.

Left–right orientation in Ireland in 1976

The earliest and most extensive examination of left–right orientation in a media-commissioned opinion poll in Ireland was undertaken during August and September of 1976 by IMS for RTÉ (Radio Telifis Éireann: Irish State Television). As noted earlier, this poll shows that three in ten of those interviewed were unable to place themselves on a left–right scale. There was a large gender difference, with 39 per cent of females and 21 per cent of the male respondents refusing to give answers to the left–right self-placement question. Moreover, there were large differences among females: the net left–right score for housewives was 6.4, whereas for all other females it was 2.9.

Overall the results of the IMS poll of 1976 show two important patterns. First, very few respondents identified themselves as leftwing. It seems that the centre-left category may have fulfilled the role as the left-wing anchor (or most extreme) point on the IMS fivepoint scale where just 2 per cent identified themselves as left-wing. Second, the centre and 'don't know' categories encapsulated a majority of the public. Both of these groups were similar in favouring more spending on social welfare. In short, left–right orientation, although having some peculiar features, was not entirely absent in Ireland in the 1970s.

In the IMS survey, understanding of the left–right concept was related to social class, level of education and age. If we target those who were able to place themselves on the IMS five-point left–right scale, we see from examining the poll data that the concept did have some application. Taking opposite ends of the spectrum, Labour Party identifiers were most left-wing, while those supporting more government control of industry were most right-wing. Such results are inconsistent in part because of a questionnaire problem.[3] Nevertheless, belief that government spending on social services should be cut and selfidentification as a 'conservative' were rightist stances.

This evidence suggests that ambiguity in the conceptualisation of left–right in Ireland is a long-term feature of public opinion. However, the IMS poll data do highlight that a majority of those interviewed in 1976 were right-wing in orientation. Perhaps the most surprising result from this poll is a gender difference where men were (relatively speaking) more left-wing than women. Nevertheless, not all women had the same views. Married women were most right-wing, while unmarried females were more left-wing than men. Also, higher levels of political activism such as giving money to a party or working for a political candidate were associated with being strongly right-wing.

Left–right orientation in Ireland in the early twenty-first century

Recent research has identified two separate dimensions relating to economic left–right orientation (Fahey, Hayes and Sinnott 2005: 140–61; Kennedy and Sinnott 2005). These two dimensions have been described as 'economic equality' and 'government intervention' (or economic liberalism). The mean position of the Irish public is leftist with regard to economic equality and rightist towards government intervention in the economy.[4] This lack of consistency may be interpreted in two ways. First, Irish citizens do not see the world in simple left–right terms. Support for equality may be traced to traditional Catholic thinking, but there is a rejection of the idea that government should be the agent to bring this about. Second, the questions used to investigate the left–right concept are capturing different considerations from respondents because there is no strong tradition of left–right ideological political discussion in Ireland. The argument to be put forward here combines elements of both of these insights by using the concept of 'hard' and 'easy' questions introduced in Chapter 2, and applied earlier in Chapters 5 and 6.

To briefly summarise, opinion poll questions relating to the economy differ from one another in their degree of hardness. Within the economic domain 'easy' questions refer to policy goals and principles such as 'equality of income' and 'freedom to create wealth' or desirable situations such as low taxes and prices and high standards in the provision of social services. In contrast, 'hard' questions deal with the means to achieve these policy goals, such as preference for lower taxes and consequent reduction in spending on social services. The responses to poll questions on the same issue, but relating to different facets (hard/easy) will yield different and apparently inconsistent response patterns. This is because as the Belief-Sampling Model contends responses are based on different considerations. However, *ceteris paribus* one would expect the most knowledgeable portion of the public to understand most clearly the 'hard' aspects of the left–right concept.[5]

As noted earlier, left–right self-placement questions are not asked in media-commissioned polls. Consequently, I will make use of the Irish Social and Political Attitudes Survey (winter 2001/2) and the first Irish National Election Survey (summer 2002) to assess contemporary left–right opinions.

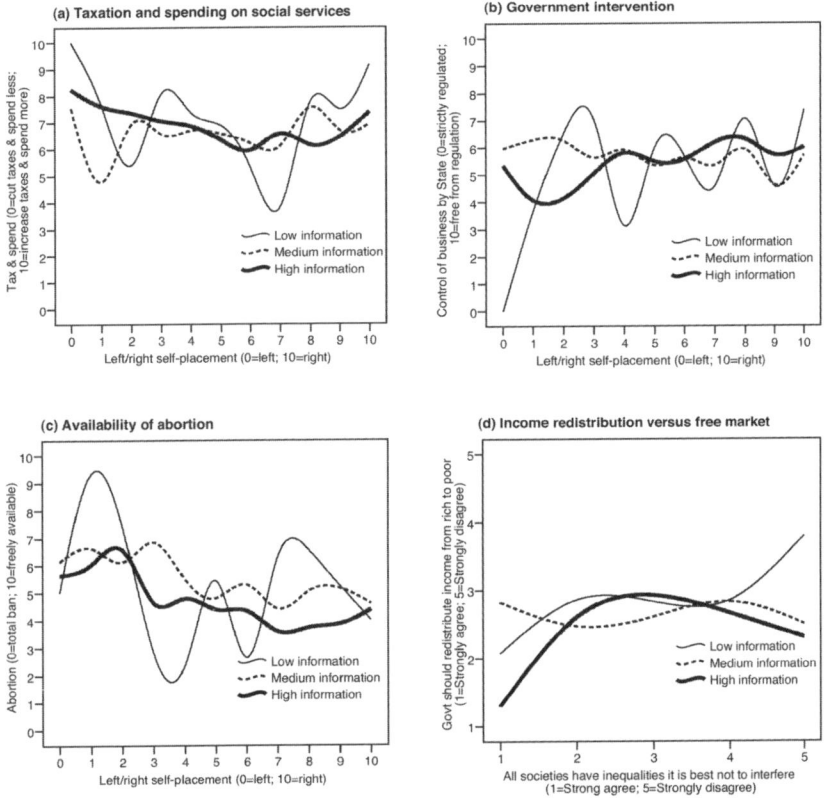

Figure 28 *Comparison of Left–Right Self-Placement and Opinions Associated with Left–Right Ideology in Ireland, 2001–2 (mean scores)*

Source: INES, questions B44.1, C25_1, C27_1. Level of political knowledge / information is derived from questions E39.1–5 where those who answered 4-5 items correctly were coded as 'high information', while those with 2–3 correct answers were coded as 'medium information' and the rest were denoted as 'low information'. In the cases of the 'tax and spend' and 'abortion' scales, there were also follow-up items asking about the importance of the issue for the respondent. Using this variable yielded roughly similar patterns to level of political information. The data for chart (c) is taken from ISPAS, questions E23.1 and E23.7.

According to the standard interpretation of left–right, those on the left will favour greater spending on social services even if this means higher taxes, and will also favour government intervention into the economy. If we inspect the data presented in windows (a) and (b) of Figure 28 we observe that a majority of the Irish public favour increased social spending, regardless of left–right orientation and level of political knowledge. A broadly similar pattern exists for government intervention in the economy, where a majority of the public favour a 'balanced' stance (points 4 to 6 on the 11-point scale), although there is a perceptible left–right orientation for the high information segment of the public. In general, respondents treat 'tax and spend' and 'government intervention' items as easy questions. Consequently, for the Irish public there is no 'hard' trade-off as the logic of the left–right concept implies.[6]

Window (c) reveals, as previous research has argued, that economic left–right orientation in Ireland is influenced by considerations of liberal agenda issues such as abortion (see Hardiman and Whelan 1994a: 163). Significantly, the 'hard' issue of abortion shows a much stronger level of consistency with left–right self-placement. Moreover, this pattern exists for all levels of political knowledge, although the relationship for the more highly informed exhibits less variance. As we saw in Chapter 5, abortion is a 'hard' issue over which the public has definite opinions, and there is an understanding that a pro-life or a pro-choice stance has real consequences, as indicated in public opinion in the X and C law cases in 1992 and 1997.

If we look at the data presented in window (d) of Figure 28 our expectation, according to the left–right concept, is that public preferences should exhibit a diagonal trend going from top left to bottom right. In fact, we see a pattern that is largely absent of any ideology – the public, regardless of level of information, favours a centrist position on wealth redistribution and government intervention to reduce income inequality. Here it seems many respondents were equivocal and could see the merits of both statements and hence picked 'middle of the road' responses, thus avoiding the hardness of the questions intended by the survey designers (note Alvarez and Brehm 2002: 124–48).

Importance of left–right orientation and other values

One explanation for the failure to find consistent answers between left–right self-placement questions and answers to other survey items may result from respondents not seeing this concept as having any importance for them. As a result, commercial opinion polls and academic mass surveys mirror this simple fact. When asked directly if this was the case in late 2000, almost four in ten of those interviewed in the cross-national Asia Europe Survey (ASES) survey stated that the concept of left–right was 'not important'.[7] Moreover, this was the majority response (52 per cent) for those aged 18–24 years.

If we look at the left–right concept in terms of partisanship at least half of all partisans in Ireland in late 2000 were centrist (that is, of no definite left–right position), or did not think left–right was important. However, for those who did state that left–right was 'important' the ideological complexion among party supporters makes sense; for example, Sinn Féin, Green and Labour Parties supporters are leftist while Fianna Fáil and Fine Gael supporters are rightist. It is also interesting to note that there were some significant demographic differences on the importance of left–right. For example, men rather than women saw the concept of left–right as being important. It seems that the gender difference noted in the IMS survey of 1976 persists.

The main general finding from the previous subsection is that the concept of left–right in Ireland, as represented by self-placement questions, does not help us predict positions for a wide range of issues within the domain of economics and beyond. One might argue that perhaps Irish respondents have problems with being asked direct left–right questions and use of self-placement scales. It is possible, using the ASES survey and a statistical technique called 'principal component (factor) analysis', to see whether the latent pattern in responses to many questions typically connected with a left–right orientation can provide some evidence of an underlying left–right structure to Irish public opinion.[8]

The main idea here is that some concepts such as left–right cannot be measured with single questions, but are more appropriately examined using a variety of indicators. Our expectation is that if left–right is an important dimension in Ireland it should be represented as a single factor, which explains a relatively large proportion of the total variance in the data. The results of our principal components analysis in Table 13 reveal that it is possible to identify five underlying factors within Irish public opinion. Egalitarianism explains most variance (almost 15 per cent), but this is not much stronger than any of the other latent factors identified. In short, the

Table 13 *Principal Component Analysis of the Major Value Dimensions in Irish Society, October–December 2000 (ASES survey)*

	Rotated factor				
Variables	Egalit- arianism	Chauvin- ism	Postmat- erialism	Economic liberalism	Internat- ionalism
Everyone should have the right to express his opinion even if he or she differs from the majority (q208b)	**0.754**	0.076	0.035	−0.276	0.129
Competition is good because it stimulates people to develop new ideas (q306a)	**0.681**	−0.086	−0.067	0.096	−0.019
People should be allowed to organise public meetings to protest against the Government (q208c)	**0.681**	0.076	0.155	−0.162	0.146
The Government should take responsibility for ensuring that everyone either has a job or is provided with adequate social welfare (q306b)	**0.539**	−0.029	0.289	0.378	−0.272
Ireland should limit the import of foreign products (q208a)	0.031	**0.761**	0.196	0.045	−0.096
Foreigners should not be allowed to buy land in Ireland (q208d)	0.131	**0.675**	−0.137	0.286	0.053
Ireland's television should give preference to Irish-made films and programmes (q208f)	−0.106	**0.651**	0.090	−0.131	0.132
A good environment is more important than economic growth (q412b)	−0.060	0.063	**0.808**	−0.112	0.075
Incomes should be made more equal (q412a)	0.258	0.107	**0.660**	0.144	−0.014
Individuals should strive most of all for their own good rather than for the good of society (q412g)	-0.049	0.209	0.136	**0.671**	−0.046
Society is better off when businesses are free to make as much profit as they can (q306g)	−0.127	−0.104	−0.176	**0.654**	0.259
For certain problems international bodies such as the UN should have the right to enforce solutions (q208e)	0.181	0.089	−0.061	−0.019	**0.801**
With regard to most of the big problems we face, what the IRISH government decides doesn't make much difference (q306c)	−0.064	−0.019	0.304	0.341	**0.555**
Total	1.94	1.56	1.41	1.38	1.17
Percentage of the total variance explained	14.92	11.98	10.87	10.64	8.97
Cumulative percentage of variance explained	14.92	26.90	37.77	48.41	57.38

Note: This principal component analysis was undertaken using varimax rotation. The Kaiser–Meyer–Olkin Measure of Sampling Accuracy (KMO) is 0.64, which indicates no significant problem with small partial correlations among the variables. The Bartlett test of sphericity shows the correlation matrix is not an identity one and factor analysis is appropriate (Chi-square approx. = 1080.31, p<0.001). The Asia Europe Survey (ASES) was a cross-national survey implemented by the Gallup organisation in nine European and nine Asian countries between October and December of 2000. The project was funded by the Japanese Ministry of Education and directed by Professor Takashi Inoguchi, Graduate School of Public Policy, Chuo University, Tokyo, Japan.

results shown in Table 13 show that there is no overarching economic left–right dimension and that 'egalitarianism' and 'liberalism' (i.e. anti-government intervention) are both consistent underlying values of the Irish public. In fact, analysis of a variety of recent academic surveys underscores the difficulty of empirically identifying key cleavages highlighted in the literature on Irish political culture (see Coakley 2005a: 64–7).[9]

The evidence presented in Table 13 suggests that the Irish public's underlying value system is 'morselised' where different beliefs and values such as equality and liberalism are applied in different policy domains (Lane 1962: 353; Hochschild 1981: 237). In this respect, the hardness of questions inherent in the left–right concept does not form part of the considerations used by respondents in answering questions during poll interviews. As a result, academic surveys and opinion polls are, by reporting 'inconsistent' answers, mirroring public opinion. Consequently, the utility of the left–right concept to shine a lamp on the structure of opinions on a wide variety of issues would seem to be much weaker in Ireland than elsewhere.[10]

Eurobarometer Evidence on Left–Right in Ireland

In the last section we saw using specific surveys undertaken in 1976 and later in 2001–2 that the left–right concept works only to a limited degree in Ireland. Here comparison of answers to left–right self-placement questions with other relevant survey items was used as a means of cross-validation. The strategy adopted will be to focus on the evolution of responses to left–right self-placement questions over time. In short, has left–right opinion in Ireland changed between 1973 and 2004? If left–right has meaning in Ireland one would expect responses to self-placement questions to mirror economic change. Economic change in Ireland since 1970 has been dramatic where the economy has experienced a series of recessions followed by unprecedented growth in the 1990s.

As noted earlier, media-commissioned opinion polls almost never ask left–right self-placement questions. Fortunately, Irish polling companies have implemented the left–right self-placement probe in EU Commission-sponsored 'standard' Eurobarometer surveys undertaken biannually in Ireland since 1973. As the left–right concept is considered to summarise underlying values that change only slowly over time, there is the expectation that the trend in the self-placement

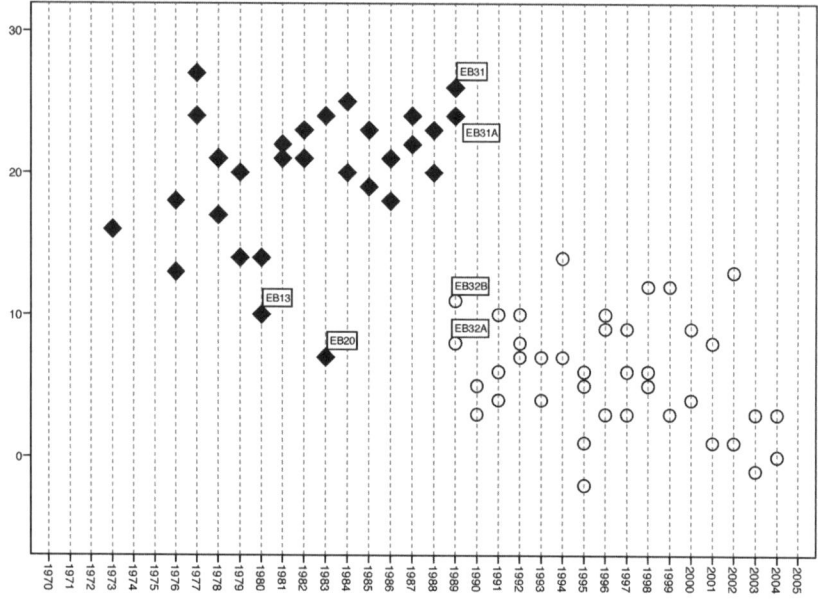

Figure 29 *Evolution of Net Change in Left–Right Self-Placement in Ireland, 1973–2004 (per cent)*

Source: Eurobarometer cumulative trend file 1971-2002 and recent Eurobarometer reports. Net left–right score was calculated as follows: Right per cent minus Left per cent where Left refers to respondents who chose points 1–4 on the scale and Right those who selected points 7 to 10. A net rightist score is thus positive as shown in this figure while a net leftist one would be negative. If an OLS regression line is passed through all of these data the total fit (R^2) is 0.54, with a slope = –0.47 However, if we only model the pre-1990 data, R^2=0.12 and the regression line exhibits a slight positive trend. In contrast, analysis of the post-1990 results in a model fit of 0.16 and has a slight negative trend. This division of the left–right time series corresponds to the changeover in Eurobarometer polling from IMS (September 1973 to July 1989) to Lansdowne (October 1989–May 2004). It should be noted that EB31 and EB31A are separate surveys; EB32A and EB32B were a single survey with a split questionnaire (A and B) design. This figure shows that there can be very large variations in left–right measurements within single years (e.g. 1983, 2002).

questions should exhibit considerable stability. The Irish data are surprising in this respect. Responses at the 'mid-points' of the ten-point left–right scale underwent large changes from October 1989 onwards where the modal (most popular) response shifted dramatically from point 6 to point 5 on the scale. If the ten-point scale data are aggregated to 'left' (1–4), 'centre' (5–6) and 'right' (7–10) categories, the key change is a growth in centrist responses in the late 1980s and decline in right-wing answers with support for a leftist orientation remaining largely constant. More recently, since about 2000 or 2001 there has been an increase in the number of interviewees giving non-committal answers, i.e. 'don't know'/refused.

Figure 29 shows net change of left–right orientation and illustrates the distinctiveness of the response patterns before and after 1989. The net scoring system weights the difference between right- and left-wing answers by centrist and 'don't know' responses. This strategy has the effect of reducing the net difference where many respondents pick centrist or 'don't know' options. Figure 29 indicates that there are effectively two clusters in the data, separated by a dramatic change in July–October 1989, yielding contrasting trends for the two sub-periods. Overall the data suggests a progressive move leftwards towards the centre, a process that accelerated in the 1990s.

These results raise an important question: should the left–right time series be treated as a single unit, or as two separate series? In other words, is the change in opinion real or the result of some other possibly methodological process? If we look at the evolution of all points on the Eurobarometer left–right scale we witness a dramatic shift in the modal response. There is a sharp change from point 6 to point 5 in 1989. This adjustment is suspicious as it makes little sense in polling terms. It is true that the pre-election budget of 1989 cut the standard and top rates of tax for the first time in twenty years. However, one could argue that only in a public with a finely-tuned sense of left–right could such a change be meaningful.

Moreover, from a methodological perspective there was an important reorganisation in Eurobarometer polling around the time of the dramatic changes noted. Between September 1973 and July 1989, IMS had the contract for undertaking Eurobarometer polls. Thereafter, Lansdowne Market Research undertook this work until May 2004. Part of the reason for the change in contract appears to have resulted from concerns over survey quality across the EU.[11] In the construction of a Eurobarometer trend, file researchers at MZES (University of Mannheim, Germany) state in their file documentation that some of the technical aspects of the Eurobarometer surveys undertaken prior to 1990 such as weighting were 'country specific, idiosyncratic'. The implication here is that the significant change in response patterns noted in Figure 29 are methodological in nature.

In order to pursue this question of whether the swing to the left evident in Eurobarometer is real or methodological, a comparison was made with the European Values Survey (EVS) results for 1981, 1990 and 1999. Figure 30 shows that EVS has a significantly higher estimate than contemporary Eurobarometer polls for point 6 on the left–right self-placement scale in 1990 and 1999.

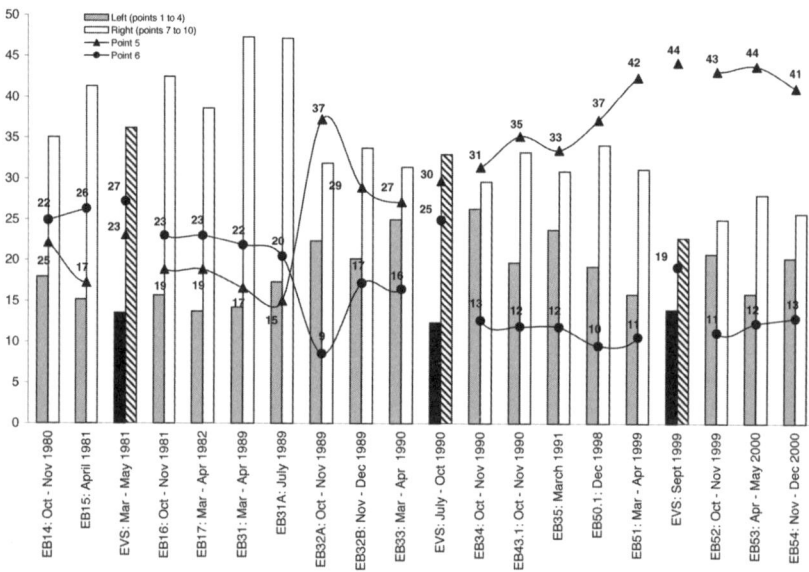

Figure 30 *Comparison of Left–Right Self-Placement Scales Implemented in Eurobarometer and European Values Surveys in 1981, 1990 and 1999 (10-point scale: Left=1, Right=10)*

Source: Eurobarometer cumulative trend file 1971-2002 and European Values Survey (EVS) datasets. Net left–right score was calculated as follows: Right per cent minus Left per cent where left refers to respondents who chose points 1–4 on the scale and right those who selected points 7–10. In order to distinguish EVS from Eurobarometer, leftist responses in EVS are indicated by a black bar while rightist ones are denoted by an oblique striped bar. As points 5 and 6 are of central interest, these are indicated by separately by lines with a dark circle or triangle respectively.

It should be noted that EVS and Eurobarometer were undertaken by IMS in 1981 and that both survey projects elicited similar response patterns during the 1980–2 period. Thereafter, EVS has been undertaken by the Economic and Social Research Institute (ESRI), which, as noted earlier in the introductory chapter, is primarily involved in academic surveying. Moreover, in 1990 the EVS estimate for left-wing responses (12 per cent) is about half that of contemporary Eurobarometers (25 per cent in EB 33 and 26 per cent in EB 34). The evidence presented in Figure 30 suggest three main findings.

First, there are house effects (deriving from different surveying procedures used by IMS/Lansdowne and the ESRI, see note 12) in the measurement of left–right self-placement as the EVS results for 1990 and 1999 are different to Eurobarometer polls for the same period. Second, the results in the first Lansdowne Market Research Eurobarometer survey, EB 32A, are anomalous when compared to contemporary polls. Third, the emergence of point 5 as the modal response category appears to be a real effect as it is evident also in EVS estimates. Overall, the data suggest a decline in right-wing self-identification and steady support for a left-wing stance. In addition, this decline in right-wing identification is associated with quite a high number of EVS respondents picking point 6 on the left–right scale. Taken together the evidence presented in Figure 30 indicates that the swing to the left noted in Eurobarometer is methodological in nature, but is ironically associated with a real shift leftwards which is picked up in EVS.[12]

In order to ascertain what could account for the sharp changes associated with the change in polling company between EB 31A and EB 32A, enquiries were made with Lansdowne Market Research. Later there was also some consultation with the German Social Data Archive in Cologne, which has the most complete archive of Eurobarometer documentation available.[13] Surprisingly, the records describing the questionnaire, use of show cards and so on indicate no differences between the IMS and Lansdowne surveys. The implication here is that the effect may be related to variation in interviewing protocols, which have not been fully documented. For example, there may have been differing policies regarding attempts to convert non-responses. However, the overall non-response rate for the left–right item from 1977–July 1989 and October 1989–late 2002 are rather similar (i.e. 15 and 19 per cent respectively).[14] In conclusion, it is not possible to pinpoint exactly the source of the methodological artefact observed.

Impact of Economic Changes on the Left–Right Orientation of the Irish Public

In the last section we found that net left–right position in Ireland changed significantly from the late-1980s, just as the economy evolved from depression to unprecedented growth. The implication here is that the left–right orientation of the Irish public might have changed as the economy went from recession to unprecedented expansion and growth. However, we also found evidence suggesting that this apparent change in net left–right orientation may in part be an artefact of the Eurobarometer polling process. In this section, I will investigate whether the change in net left–right orientation of the Irish public is best explained in terms of economic factors or as a methodological artefact.

The argument put forward here is that it is unreasonable to think that the Irish public would have had detailed knowledge of Irish economic development. It seems more realistic to suppose that public attention would have been focused on prominent factors that impinge on the citizen: level of income tax paid to the Government and unemployment rate. For much of this period, inflation was low (3 per cent or less after 1986), so this variable most likely had little effect. Having outlined two key economic factors that might influence the left–right position of the Irish public, it is necessary to explain more clearly *why* these variables should have an impact and *how* they are related to left–right self-placement (that is, is there a positive or negative relationship?).

Specifying the model

In the last paragraph it was argued that citizens' knowledge of the economy is limited. While very few of the Irish public could have stated in a poll interview that the unemployment rate in 1988 was 16 per cent, all would have known that the jobless number was very high and that a desired goal was to reduce this rate. This notion of a fully informed public is useful in thinking about the relationship between public opinion and economic conditions. In other words, if the public were fully-informed and behaved according to the logic of left–right orientation it should be possible to say how net left–right orientation will alter with changes in unemployment and taxation – both factors likely to be salient to most citizens.

In the regression model of change in left–right orientation, the dependent variable is scored as the net percentage selecting a left-wing position (points 1 to 4 on the left–right self-placement scale) minus a right-wing (points 7 to 10) one. Simple graphical analyses indicate that the public became less right-wing where the net left–right score for the public has become has declined from −27 percentage points (that is, net right-wing in 1977) towards 0 (that is, a balance between left and right in 2004). Thus the trend away from the right towards the centre (a movement to the left) observed in the Eurobarometer time series implies a positive trend for the net left–right orientation of the Irish public given the coding scheme used. The expectations or hypotheses to be tested may be summarised as follows:

H.1 For methodological reasons there will be a negative relationship between net left–right position and the switch from IMS (1977–88) to Lansdowne (1989–2004) where IMS is associated with more rightist responses and Lansdowne leftist ones.

H.2 With high unemployment rates the net orientation of the public will be rightist and will become more leftist when the level of unemployment declines. Thus the expectation is that there will be a negative relationship between net left–right orientation and unemployment rate.

H.3 When the tax rate is high the Irish public will adopt a right-wing stance, and conversely when taxes are low will exhibit a more leftist position. This implies a negative relationship between net left–right position and level of taxation.

I will now outline the underlying logic with regard to each of the three explanatory variables. In the previous section I discussed and investigated the idea that the change in net left–right orientation among the Irish public as represented in the Eurobarometer data is a methodological artefact. For reasons that are unclear, IMS elicited higher levels of right-wing responses than Lansdowne Market Research. In order to take account of this effect surrounding the change of survey company for Eurobarometer in 1989, I will model this factor as a simple dummy variable where a value of '1' is used for IMS (1977–88) and '0' thereafter for Lansdowne Market research.[15] This is the basis for the expectation expressed in the first hypothesis.

In the early 1980s, Ireland had high levels of inflation and unemployment. However, inflation was brought under control relatively quickly while unemployment remained a persistent problem for another decade. According to a once-influential line of thinking in economics and politics, governments are often faced with a trade-off between reducing either unemployment or inflation.[16] In this respect, one may argue that once inflation is not a problem support for government policy will orient towards reducing unemployment the other key economic issue (Stigler 1973; Hibbing and Alford 1983; Hibbs 1987). The expectation is that when unemployment is high the public will be more rightist, i.e. supportive of business friendly policies that are expected to boost employment. In contrast, when unemployment declines the public will become more leftist and favour policies such as increased spending on healthcare, etc. because in a sense these policies can now be afforded. Consequently, in our second hypothesis it is expected that there should be a negative relationship between level of unemployment and the Irish public's net left–right self-placement.

The impact of income tax was also particularly important in Ireland during the period examined. The main reason is that a majority of Irish voters (70 per cent) earned less than the mean income and yet many of them paid direct income tax at the highest rates.[17] Consequently, during the 1980s and 1990s there was a decline in the 'progressivity' of the tax system, where those on lower incomes saw their rate of taxation increase while those on high incomes witnessed a reduction (Ruane and O' Toole 1995: 142–5; note also FitzGerald 2004). Our expectation expressed in H.3 is that if a majority of citizens pay higher rates of income tax (56 per cent in 1994) the public is more likely to move to the left with a reduction in the high tax rate. This may seem rather perverse because at a personal level one would expect that if a person pays lots of tax they would expect high standards in public services, that is, typical left-wing policies. One may posit two reasons for this relationship.

First, if we look at the individual level, citizens who are paying a high rate of taxation will adopt a rightist stance for self-interested reasons because they desire a higher level of income that would ensue with a lower taxation rate. Second, from a collective or national perspective if many more people are employed, due in part to a reduction in personal income tax, there is more public money to spend on social welfare and public health.[18] Preferences for such spending are most often associated with a leftist stance. This shift to the left in public preferences can occur with the virtuous cycle that defined the 'Celtic tiger' economy – low inflation, decreasing unemployment and decreasing income tax levels as the tax base increases and the number claiming social welfare declines.

Regression analysis

In the regression analysis undertaken it was considered prudent, because of the potential methodological problems associated with points 5 and 6, to exclude these data from analysis. However, a net left–right score weighted for 'centre' (points 5 and 6) and 'don't know' responses yields similar results to those reported in Table 14.

In Table 14 models 1 to 3 show that movement in the Irish public's left–right position reflect change in surveying company, level of unemployment and prevailing high tax rate. In model 4, most of the hypothesised relationships are observed. However, it is interesting to note that in the combined model the unemployment and high tax rate variables have negative coefficients, as predicted, but that these coefficients are not statistically significant.[19] The fact that tax rate is not statistically significant matches with the pattern exhibited in Figure 28(a), where we found that there is no relationship between opinions on taxation and increased public spending and left–right self-placement.

In general, the results of the regression models suggest that the movement to the left in Irish public opinion is primarily explained by methodological changes. Such evidence undermines the view that in Ireland net change in left–right orientation at an aggregate level is strongly shaped by contextual factors. Moreover, the conventional conception that responses to left–right self-placement questions in surveys reflect a long-standing value orientation that shapes political opinions and vote choice is problematic. Changes in survey methodology as we have seen in this section can be an important source of variation in left–right estimates. Such methodological effects have important consequences on any inferences one would like to make from such survey data.

In the next section an examination will be made of the stability in response patterns to left–right survey items, rather than the specific responses given. The goal here is to see whether the way in which the Irish public has answered these items has changed over time.

Table 14 *Regression Analysis of Net Change in Left–Right Self-Placement on the Eurobarometer Ten-Point Scale in the Republic of Ireland, 1977–2004*

	Model 1	Model 2	Model 3	Model 4
Constant	−5.41 ***	12.02 *	3.30	0.95
	(0.85)	(6.55)	(4.33)	(3.86)
IMS implements EB survey (1977–88) where rightist responses predominate	−1.04 ***			−9.97 ***
	(1.33)			(1.13)
High tax rate as percentage of mean income		−0.76 **		−0.16
		(0.24)		(0.22)
Unemployment as a percentage of the total workforce			−1.02 **	−0.24
			(0.33)	(0.23)
AR(1) to control for serial correlation in residuals	0.12	0.67 ***	0.74 ***	<.01
	(0.19)	(0.10)	(0.10)	(0.18)
Adjusted R-squared	0.78	0.76	0.76	0.84
S.E. of regression	3.01	3.13	3.10	2.55
Log likelihood	−66.44	−67.51	−67.28	−60.81
Durbin-Watson statistic	1.91	2.03	2.21	2.30
Inverted AR Roots	0.12	0.67	0.74	<0.01
Mean dependent variable	−9.96	−9.96	−9.96	−9.96
S.D. dependent variable	6.35	6.35	6.35	6.35
Akaike information criterion	5.14	5.22	5.21	4.88
Schwarz criterion	5.29	5.37	5.35	5.12
F-statistic	45.92	41.51	42.42	34.78
Prob. (F-statistic)	<0.01	<0.01	<0.01	<0.01
Breusch–Godfrey Serial Correlation LM(2) Test:	0.50	0.21	0.49	5.47
	(0.78)	(0.90)	(0.78)	(0.06)
ARCH Test:	0.14	0.04	0.42	0.11
	(0.71)	(0.84)	(0.52)	(0.74)
White Heteroscedasticity Test:	0.04	2.28	3.64	1.30
	(0.83)	(0.32)	(0.16)	(0.94)
Ramsey RESET Test (F statistic):	<.01	NA	NA	0.48
	(0.99)			(0.50)
N (adjusted endpoint for AR1 estimation):	27	27	27	27

* $p \leq 0.10$ ** $p \leq 0.05$ *** $p \leq 0.001$ (two tailed test)

Note: The dependent variable is net left–right self-placement, i.e. percentage left (1–4) minus percentage right (7–10) on Eurobarometer scale. Survey data taken from Eurobarometer trend file (1973–2002) and updated to 2004. Economic data is taken from Leddin and Walsh (1999), Reidy (2000) and the Central Statistics Office (CSO). Analysis based on OLS regression using an AR 1 procedure to model serial correlation in the error term. NA refers to a near-singular matrix, as the powers of the fitted values in the RESET test are highly collinear.

Stability of Opinions on Left–Right Self-Placement and Party Placement in Ireland

A fundamental feature of public opinion is the degree to which the public, or segments thereof, share the same preferences and perceptions (McCloskey et al. 1960). Such a common orientation goes to the heart of whether or not a society is held together by consensus or fragmented by cleavages. Given the primacy attributed to left–right divisions in influential theories of political systems, such as that of Lipset and Rokkan (1967), poll questions on left–right self- and party-placement offer a unique opportunity to examine the degree of

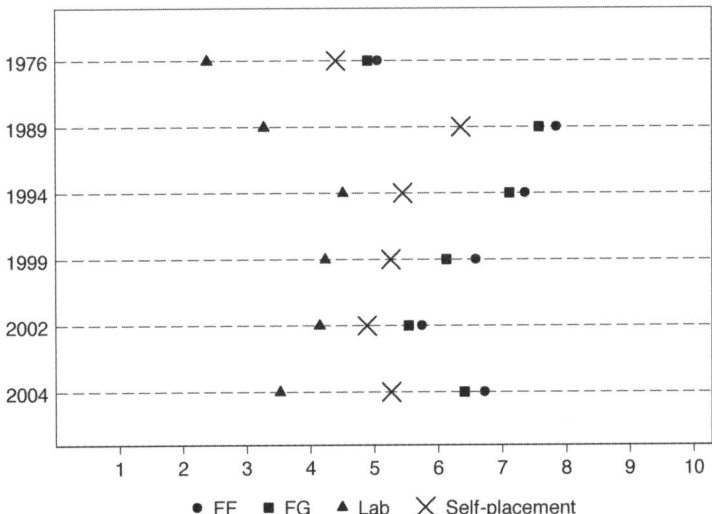

Figure 31 *Left–Right Positions of the Main Parties and Public in Ireland on the Basis of Public Perceptions, 1976–2004 (10-point scale; Left = 1, Right = 10)*

Sources: IMS August 30 – September 8 1976, EES 1989 (EB 31A), EES 1994 (EB 41.1), EES 1999, INES 2002, EES 2004.

Note: Interpolated median scores are used because finite ordered rating scales such as the standard left–right one often have biased measures of central tendency and dispersion if mean and standard deviation estimates are used (Herrera, Herrera and Smith 1992; Huber and Powell 1994). For this reason an interpolated median measure is employed, which locates the median by linear interpolation between respective category boundaries. The left–right scales for 1976 and 2002 were rescaled and recoded as appropriate for comparison with the standard ten-point scale used in European Election Studies. For the sake of clear presentation confidence estimates for these data points are not shown. Reproduced with permission from Kennedy, Lyons and Fitzgerald (2006: 793).

common agreement as to the basis of political competition in Ireland. One of the main assertions made about left–right orientation is that it can be seen as 'organising and simplifying a complex political reality' where the 'concept is sufficiently general that as new issues arise they can be fitted into the framework' (Inglehart 1990: 287–8, 293).

Fortunately, the IMS poll of August–September 1976 asked a series of questions on both left–right self-placement and perceptions of the left–right positions of the three main political parties. This provides a baseline for investigating change in the following three decades.[20] Examination of the evidence presented in Figure 31 illustrates a remarkable level of consensus during this period, with the Labour Party always to the left of the public's median position and Fine Gael and Fianna Fáil always to the right. The relative ordering of the public and parties remained constant, although the absolute median positions have changed. Such results suggest that while there may be movement of net opinion towards the left or right there is, nevertheless, constancy.

The data presented in Figure 31 lead us to consider the question that stability in the ordering of parties is based on a consistent view among the Irish public. In other words, is there agreement within public opinion over where the public itself lies on a left–right scale and is there consensus over where the parties lie on this scale? Here we encounter an important methodological consideration when using ordered rating scales. Use of simple summary statistics such as the mean and standard deviation in ordered rating scales is affected by the fixed number of categories used in such scales, and by differences in the location of central tendency in observed scale distributions.[21] This implies that mean estimates of left–right scale placements can be misleading if consideration is not made of the distribution of responses. In this respect, van der Eijk (2001) has argued that the standard deviation reflects not only dispersion but also skewness, and is therefore inappropriate as a measure of dispersion (or its inverse: agreement or consensus).

For this reason, use will be made of van der Eijk's (2001) measure of agreement for ordered rating scales (A) to create estimates of preferential agreement and perceptual agreement. The former relates to the desired balance between left–right in Irish society, while the latter denotes common agreement as to where the main political parties are located on this dimension.[22] The results of estimating van der Eijk's agreement statistic (A) are shown in Figure 32. Here the general pattern seems to be one of change in public opinion.

Consequently, while the relative ordering of parties on a left–right dimension has remained constant since 1976, the coherence of public opinion has declined. With regard to perceptual agreement, Ireland is not unique in this respect. Public agreement on the left–right position of parties has been declining in many other EU-15 member states (see Oscarsson 2002). Whether this is a long-term trend (pre-1989) or is related to key historical events such as the fall of communism is unknown and requires further research.

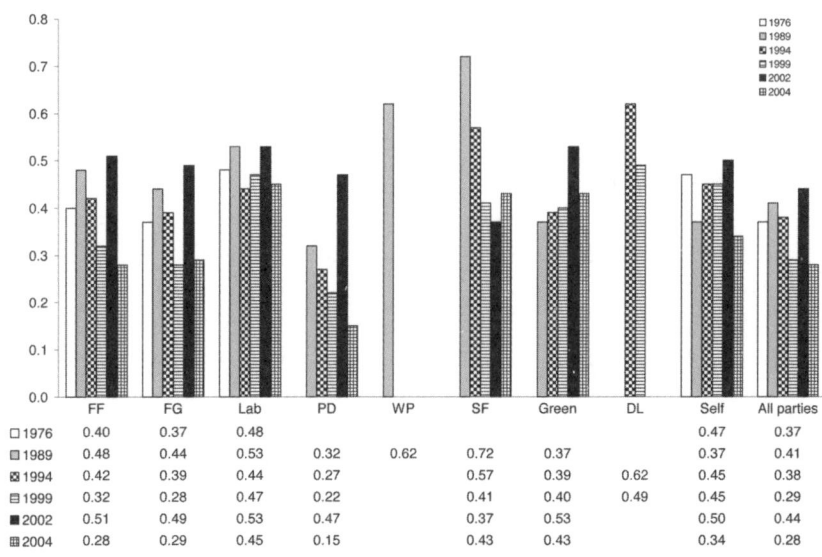

Figure 32 *Perceptual and Preferential Agreement on Parties and the Public's Left–Right Positions in Ireland, 1976–2004*

Sources: IMS 30 August– 8 September 1976, EES 1986 (EB 31A), EES 1994 (EB 41.1), EES 1999, INES 2002, EES 2004. Perceptual measures for specific parties and for all parties in specific years (a systemic measure) were estimated using van der Eijk's (2001) agreement 'A' statistic and related software. Preferential measures for respondents' left–right self-placement (denoted as 'Self') were calculated similarly.

One interesting pattern in Figure 32 is that the level of perceptual and preferential agreement is highest in 2002, where the data come from a post-general election study (INES). The effect is also present to a lesser degree in 1976 in a survey undertaken months before the

1977 general election. The different patterns in the 1976 and 2004 agreement estimates suggest that contextual effects relating to timing in the electoral cycle and most recent election type may have some impact on measures of preferential and perceptual agreement.[23] In the next section I will try to assess whether Eurobarometer's mirroring of left–right orientation over such a long period concurs with the other polling evidence available.

Opinion Poll Evidence on Irish Citizens' Attitudes towards Level of Taxation and Public Spending

In the previous sections we have seen that left–right orientation at an *aggregate* level exhibits considerable stability. Change in orientation, as measured in Eurobarometer, does occur, however, it does not involve a significant move to the left or right but variation in emphasis at the centre, and appears to reflect factors related to the surveying process and changing levels of unemployment. In this section an examination will be made of key questions from IMS, Lansdowne and MRBI polls that refer to the Irish public's views on the relationship between level of taxation and public spending. This is a concrete topic often operationalised in Likert scale items (where respondents give a 'strongly agree' to 'strongly disagree' response to a statement).

One could argue, in terms of the left–right concept, that public preferences for lower levels of taxation are indicative of a right-wing stance and increased public spending a left-wing one. However, the empirical evidence presented earlier in Figure 28(a) and model 5 of Table 14 demonstrates that attitudes towards taxation in Ireland are not strongly correlated with left–right self-placement. Therefore, in discussing Irish public opinion towards taxation it seems appropriate not to refer to these attitudes as being strictly speaking indicative of a left- or right-wing orientation.

As noted earlier, Irish pollsters do not use left–right self-placement questions to assess economic opinions. The most consistent topic examined that relates to general economic orientation is attitude towards increased levels of taxation. Moreover, from pollsters' and media companies' perspective, taxation is an important topic because citizens tend to have reasonably strong opinions about the amount of tax they pay to the Government. This is because all citizens are directly affected by (direct or indirect) taxes, whereas unemployment affects a subset of the public. Moreover, the question of whether the public favours increased taxation in order to pay for more spending on health, education and social welfare is often seen as a reasonable indicator of the general economic orientation of the public. As noted in Chapter 2, poll questions which simply ask 'Do you favour more public spending?' or 'Would you like tax cuts in the next budget?' are not very useful, because such 'easy' questions imply no economic consequences and ignore the reality that (cost/benefit) trade-offs are a fundamental feature of economic life.

The poll results shown in Table 15 refer to questions asked by pollsters that attempted to elicit what the Irish public would choose if it had the choice between increasing public spending (IPS) or keeping the level of taxation as low as possible (KTL). In most cases, these were hard questions where the respondent had to choose one option or the other, where consideration had to be made of the consequences of either course of action. However, there were some 'easy' questions, which provide us with the opportunity to see whether this distinction is important in assessing economic opinions. In addition to allowing us judge Irish public preferences on the left–right dimension, there is the possibility of investigating whether the shift to the left in the late 1980s and 1990s noted earlier might also be evident in these poll data.

Question 1 in the first row of Table 15 shows the impact of discussing increased spending in the absence of any mention of how such a policy might impact on level of taxation or government borrowing (see also question 5 for a similar effect). Such evidence suggests that easy questions based on desired goals (questions 1 and 5) elicit different responses to hard poll questions where respondents have to consider difficult trade-offs. In this respect, introduction of the term 'tax' into a poll question produces fairly predictable results. If the Irish public is offered a choice between increased public spending or a cut in taxation, the most popular response has always been to reduce taxes.

Question 13 in Table 15 appears to indicate an important change in orientation. However, there is reason to think that this effect may be more apparent than real, because tax rates were reduced significantly during the 1990s. Between 1991 and 2001 the highest rate of income tax fell from 52 to 42 per cent, and the lowest rate from 29 to 20 per cent. Therefore, the option of sacrificing 'further tax cuts', which were at an already-historic low (since 1977), may not have been perceived in the same way as it was in the past. Subsequent poll questions indicate that a net pro-low taxation stance prevails, and the data in

Table 15 *Opinions towards Taxation and Spending in the Republic of Ireland, 1976–2003 (per cent)*

No.	Date	Cut or not increase taxation	Increase spending	DK	Majority view*	Notes
1	Aug.–Sept. 1976	11	51	7	IPS	Stay the same 31%. No mention of increased taxation
2	July–Sept. 1978	51	46	1	KTL	Prepared to pay more tax to run a united Ireland (reverse coding)
3	Jan. 1987	63	29	7	KTL	Reduce tax and cut expenditure
4	July 1988	51	16	30	KTL	Cut expenditure or raise taxes
5	Oct. 1988	20	66	2	IPS	Reduce poverty and tax 'better-off' people more**
6	Dec. 1988	48	49	3	?	Cut tax or reduce poverty
7	June 1989 (q10)	43	36	21	KTL	Cut taxes even if this means cuts in spending on health, education and social welfare
8	June 1989 (q11)	58	33	10	KTL	Cut expenditure only way to reduce unemployment in long term. No mention of taxation. However, possible priming from previous question
9	June 1991	63	30	7	KTL	Higher taxes for more jobs (reverse coding)
10	Dec. 1992	62	26	11	KTL	Against increased borrowing in principle
11	Jan. 1993	41	54	5	IPS	Spend more on social services even if it increases government borrowing. No mention of increasing taxation
12	Mar. 1998	67	22	12	KTL	To regain national competitiveness government should increase taxes and cut spending (reverse coding here)
13	May 2001	20	74	6	IPS	Sacrifice further tax cuts for a better health service
14	May 2002	59	12	16	KTL	Increased public spending to be paid for by options other than increased taxes, e.g. borrowing from abroad, selling state industries or none of these (12%); reverse coded
15	Sept. 2003	48	38	14	KTL	To pay for existing public services government should cut spending, i.e. not increase taxes or borrow more money (reverse coded)
16	Oct. 2003	50	40	10	KTL	Increase taxes to improve public services

*   Net effect refers to whether the majority view was to keep taxes low (KTL) or increase public spending (IPS).
**   This item had two parts. In the first respondents were asked whether they were in favour of spending more money to reduce poverty (88 per cent agreed). In the second part, the issue of increasing taxation for the 'better-off' to help fund this policy resulted in 66 per cent agreeing.

Note: 'Reverse coding' is used here to construct a dataset from questions with varying formats and response options. In each case the question relates to cutting spending or increasing taxation. For comparability the responses to these items have been reversed, i.e. increase taxes implies support for more spending while cut spending or borrow more money implies not increasing taxation. This procedure is not ideal but does facilitate making some comparison between different poll questions over time to see whether there is opinion stability on the more general orientation towards taxation and spending. Details of all questions numbered 1 to 16 are in Appendix 2.

Table 15 concur with evidence from successive waves of the European Values Survey that the Irish public remains consistently against increasing taxation to fund additional public spending.

Overall, the data presented in Table 15 suggest that the Irish public has been consistently in favour of a low tax regime when faced with the 'hard' choice between choosing increased spending and keeping taxes low. However, when easy questions are posed the public adopts a pro-spending stance. Such a pattern of responses reinforces the message delivered in previous chapters that distinguishing between hard and easy facets of an issue is important when interpreting public opinion poll trends. From a scholarly perspective, the apparent inconsistency between the rightist 'keep taxes low' trend in Table 14 and the leftist shift noted in the Eurobarometer left–right self-placement data indicates that the considerations used by respondents underpinning these two data series are different. Such inconsistency is puzzling from the perspective of the Mirror Theory of Opinion Polling. However, within the Belief-Sampling Model framework such discrepancies reflect key features of how respondents formulate answers during poll interviews.

Conclusion

In this chapter I have investigated what opinion polls and academic surveys tell us about Irish public opinion towards the economy. Moreover, I have undertaken this task using the concept of left–right orientation. Specific questions on economic issues asked in IMS,

Lansdowne and MRBI polls primarily aim to mirror public opinion. In contrast, left–right self-placement items aim to illuminate the nature of attitudes and values by showing a logical interconnection between survey responses on a wide range of issues that can be explained by means of an underlying ideology.

The data from Eurobarometer charting the evolution of left–right self-placement since 1973 indicate a swing towards the left-of-centre after 1989. Unfortunately, there are methodological problems with these data where a change in surveying company in 1989 matches with a net shift leftwards in Irish public opinion. This suspicion is confirmed in a regression analysis. However, the left–right self-placement data in the European Values Survey of 1990 suggests the change might be real.

Examination of the application of the left–right ideology concept in an IMS poll in 1976 and academic surveys in 2001/2 show very mixed results. Left–right orientation is not entirely absent, but it does not always exhibit the expected relationships. The pattern in response to left–right issue questions suggests that survey interviewees tend to treat them as easy questions where the public favours both government intervention into the economy to ensure greater equality and greater economic freedom to facilitate the creation of wealth. There is no perceived trade-off between these competing goals (within the logic of the left–right concept), even among the highly informed. Only in the case of the salient issue of abortion did the left–right orientation behave as expected, and here it occurred regardless of level of political knowledge.

However, when respondents are faced with hard questions that make sense to them, as outlined in Table 15, they consistently adopt a 'keep taxes low' stance. More generally, the prevailing pattern appears to be that the Irish public is leftist on some easy questions and rightist on hard ones. This 'inconsistent' response pattern can, however, be explained with the framework of the Belief-Sampling Model. Here the argument is that the considerations used by respondents to answer these types of questions do not reflect the logic of left–right because those interviewed are giving 'top-of-the-head' answers.

Much would seem to depend on context. For example, the data presented in Figure 30 mirror change in self and party placements, but no change in relationships. The public is always in the middle, with the Labour Party to the left, and Fianna Fáil and Fine Gael on the right. In addition, public perceptions of decline in economic growth since 2000 may have resulted in a rightward shift and the disappearance of the relationships outlined in (model 5) Table 14. In summary, the polling and survey data indicate that changes in economic opinions and values in Ireland over the last three decades have been mainly a matter of degree. The Irish public has been consistently against increases in taxation to support, for example, higher spending on social services, although it supports leftist principles and goals.

In the next chapter I will investigate a substantive issue which, unlike the liberal agenda, Northern Ireland and the economy, has been characterised as being a low-salience issue for both the Irish media and the public. This may seem a little surprising, as there have been six referendums relating to Ireland's membership of the European Union since polling began and Ireland has been the recipient of large amounts of EU structural funding. Nevertheless, Irish public opinion towards the European integration project is important, and this was perhaps best exemplified during the ratification process for the Nice Treaty during 2001 and 2002.

Notes

1 It should be noted the format of this IMS left–right self-placement question is different from the standardised measures used in Eurobarometer (1973) and the first Irish National Election Study (2002). Nevertheless, the IMS question from 1976 is the only domestic left–right measure available for the 1970s and seems to capture the underlying concept of interest.
2 Of course some of this literature, such as the final two points, does not so much answer why left–right has relatively little meaning, but highlights particular manifestations of this broader question.
3 In the IMS poll report this item was stated to be problematic. It seems that respondents interpreted the term 'control' in different ways. The original intention of more government control over industry did not equate with the government establishing more state-owned enterprises or vice versa. Cross-tabulation of this variable with party allegiance and political orientation suggests otherwise. For this reason, IMS felt the results from this question were unreliable.
4 Kennedy and Sinnott (2005) in their analysis of ISPAS (2001/2) found that 10 per cent of the Irish public have right-wing values on an economic equality scale while 12 per cent have left-wing values on a government intervention scale.
5 This hard/easy distinction should occur elsewhere. However, in the UK this distinction is absent as support for equality correlates with government support for industry. In this respect, the pattern prevailing in Ireland may not be unique, but is none the less not typical of advanced industrial economies with stable political systems.
6 In Chapter 2 we noted in our definition of hard poll questions that respondents' consideration of the consequences of the policy preferences preferred was important. For example, a respondent who favours tax cuts and sees no connection to a decline in public spending provides a qualitatively different answer from respondents who understand that there is often a trade-off between policies. This is the basis of the consequences criterion applied here.

7   In this international survey the Irish public ranked 11th out of 17 in seeing the left–right concept as being important. Here are the rankings in ascending order, with the percentage who stated left–right was important in parentheses: Indonesia (14); Singapore (18); Taiwan (18); Japan (23); United Kingdom (27); Sweden (34); Ireland (34); Portugal (41); Greece (43); Germany (43); France (44); Spain (44); Malaysia (46); Italy (49); Thailand (53); Philippines (63) and South Korea (64). These data suggest that Ireland is not very different from political systems that are typically seen in left–right terms, e.g. the UK and Sweden.

8   Principal Components Analysis is a statistical method for transforming a large set of correlated variables into a smaller set of uncorrelated variables, or factors. This data reduction procedure makes data management and inference easier and removes problems of multicollinearity. Using a mathematical procedure called 'rotation' it is possible to see if the latent variables or factors identified are strongly correlated with one another (see Lewis-Beck 1994).

9   There are some differences as to the definition of these dimensions. Garry (2005), using the 2002 Irish National Election Study (INES), identifies the four dimensions as 'egalitarianism', 'moral conservative', 'pro-environment' and 'nationalist'. Fahey, Hayes and Sinnott (2005), using EVS data, identify these four dimensions, also. In contrast Kennedy and Sinnott (2005), using ISPAS data, enumerate six dimensions: the four outlined along with a 'pro-integration' and '(economic) intervention left'.

10 This is of course an empirical question, which will not be pursued here, as our key interest is what Irish polls tell us about economic opinions. This is nonetheless an important topic for future research because Irish opinions towards the economy may be more similar to those in other European countries than past comparisons of left–right survey data (as noted in the opening quote of this chapter) suggest.

11 In fact the change from IMS to Lansdowne was part of a change in consortium, as it is a consortium of polling agencies that undertake Eurobarometer (EB). From 1970 to 1989 this consortium was the Gallup-led European Omnibus Surveys (EOS) group. Thereafter, EB was undertaken by polling companies associated with the INRA (Europe) Coordination Office. Since the autumn of 2004 (EB62.0), Eurobarometer surveys have been implemented under the direction of Taylor Nelson Sofres (TNS).

12 European Values Surveys (EVS) are implemented by the ESRI, which has a methodology different from those of IMS and Lansdowne. The former uses a probability sampling technique whereas the latter two organisations use a quota-based design. This gives greater confidence that the changes noted are not purely methodological artefacts as they are evident in two different sources for the same period. Moreover the left–right self-placement question has always been asked towards the end of Eurobarometer interviews where there is no apparent evidence of a question-ordering effect.

13 Special thanks in this respect are due to Mr Richard Waring, Lansdowne Market Research; Professor Michael Marsh, Trinity College Dublin, and Dr. Meinhard Moschner, Social Data Archive, Cologne, Germany.

14 There has been a steadily growing level of non-response to the left–right item since the early 1990s.

15 Figures 29 and 30 show that in late 1989 there was a simultaneous change in survey company and a dramatic change in left–right responses. This causes a problem using an annual dataset. One could code the change over as occurring in either 1988 or 1989. Alternatively, one could ignore 1989 altogether as being a 'mixed' case. Here it was decided to adopt the conservative strategy and make 1988 the cut-off point. Regardless of how this variable is coded the substantive results are the same as those reported in Table 14, except that the high tax rate has a positive non-significant coefficient when 1988 is not used as the cut-off point.

16 This is based on the Phillips curve which essentially demonstrated empirically that there is a trade-off between unemployment and inflation. This idea was influential among

economists and policy-makers in the 1960s, but lost influence thereafter as the relationship predicted by the Phillips curve could not explain stagflation (high unemployment and inflation) in the 1970s.

17 The taxation variable used here is the 'marginal tax rate', i.e. percentage of mean income, as this facilitates comparison over time.

18 As the data analysis undertaken in the next sub-section uses aggregate or national level data it makes most sense to use this collective reasoning as a basis for our third hypothesis (H.3).

19 The diagnostic statistics shown in the bottom part of Table 14 indicate that there are no significant problems in the OLS regression models with serial correlation in the error terms, autoregressive conditional heteroscedasticity, heteroscedasticity in the residuals and incorrect model specification.

20 Survey data to examine this question are rare. Poll items of this type have only been asked once in media commissioned polls (i.e. IMS poll for RTE, August–September 1976). Fortunately, this question has been asked in all European election studies since 1989 and in the first Irish National Election Study (INES) in 2002.

21 For example, if the mean is located towards the end of a scale (or anchor points) a few cases at the opposite end of the scale will have a strong impact on the estimated standard deviation because of the large difference from the mean. In less skewed distributions distance from the mean is attenuated, thereby yielding a smaller standard deviation.

22 In simple terms this measure decomposes empirical (survey question response) distributions into 'modal', 'uniform' or 'semi-uniform' ideal types, where an average measure of agreement is calculated from these constituent parts weighted by the proportion of cases they represent. The agreement measure has a value of –1 where there is strong disagreement (perfect bimodality), 0 indicates a uniform distribution where there are equal levels of support to all points on the scale, while +1 indicates strong agreement (perfect unimodal distribution). For details see van der Eijk (2001).

23 These differences may also have a methodological origin, as the IMS poll of 1976 used a five-point scale, the various European Election Studies have used a ten-point scale and INES (2002) adopted an eleven-point one. Moreover, not all polls used the same mode of interviewing. INES is also unique in that the left–right questions were part of a 'drop-off'. One could argue that this created an important methodological artefact in the data. While there may be something in this conjecture, the Eurobarometer survey undertaken during the same period illustrates a similar change with previous surveys. The implication here is that the general election campaign of 2002 had an effect on how the Irish public answered left–right questions. This is suggestive of an informational effect similar to that discussed in Chapter 3.

Chapter 8

Irish Public Opinion towards the European Union

> Stage one: Look, this is just scare mongering by troglodyte isolationists. It's not going to happen.
> Stage two: It's just a proposal and it's not going to affect us that much.
> Stage three: It's too late now. You voted for that three years ago.
> Breda O'Brien, *The Irish Times*, September 2000

While the Irish public may have been one of the most ardent supporters of European integration, though perhaps one of the least informed in the early 1990s, by the end of the decade there were signs of growing unease (Sinnott 1995b: 9). As a series of referendums brought forward integration initiatives of increasing ambition, Irish referendum debates tended to focus on economic considerations, although other issues such as neutrality and abortion have also been important. Nevertheless, the Irish electorate have supported referendums largely on the basis of government advice with few major party divisions towards the European Union (Sinnott 2002: 820–4). As the opening quote suggests, far-reaching policies such as Economic and Monetary Union (EMU) never seemed to be debated in public. Moreover, some members of the electorate were shocked to discover they had in fact been ratified in previous referendums. By June 2001, with the first Nice Treaty referendum, public acceptance of the elite goal of being a 'psychological insider within the integration process' appeared to change.[1]

It was at this point that Irish public opinion towards the European Union assumed considerable importance when the Irish electorate rejected the Nice Treaty. This 'no' vote was seen to jeopardise enlargement of the EU. There was considerable shock as Irish public opinion, when measured in Eurobarometer surveys, had always been strongly positive towards European integration. While a second Nice Treaty referendum campaign reversed the decision of June 2001, an MRBI poll of June 2005 indicated that the Irish public were even more negative towards the Constitutional Treaty than they were to the Nice Treaty (Sinnott 2005), and were prepared, like their French and Dutch counterparts, to vote 'no'. Such evidence suggests that Irish public opinion towards the EU has changed since 1972, when 83 per cent of the seven in ten citizens who voted supported accession.

In fact, a cursory examination of all EU referendum results (ignoring the extraordinary circumstances surrounding the first Nice Treaty poll in June 2001) reveals that support for integration declined by about 20 percentage points between 1972 and 2002 and citizen participation in such referendums dropped by an equal amount. The electoral evidence suggests that there is growing disengagement from the European integration project in Ireland and perhaps the emergence of an anti-EU sentiment. One of the questions addressed in this chapter is whether similar trends are present in the opinion poll data.

Within this chapter our attention will be focused on two key topics: public opinion surrounding EU referendums, and citizen support towards European integration in Ireland since accession in 1973. In addressing these two topics there is also a division of data whereby IMS, Lansdowne and MRBI poll results will be used to examine public opinion in EU referendums and Eurobarometer data will be used to study general attitudes towards integration. I will not investigate public opinion relating to European elections as this topic has been examined elsewhere (Sinnott 1995a: 250–78; van der Eijk et al. 1996; Reif and Schmitt 1980; Reif 1984).

As in previous chapters an attempt will also be made to evaluate what opinion polls tell us about Irish public opinion. Here I will concentrate on two particular questions. First, what are the limitations of using single poll questions as a means of reflecting opinions towards a complex issue such as the European integration project? Second, how is it possible to make sense of the interrelated structure of opinions measured in surveys? In searching for answers to these two questions I will employ an innovative statistical technique based on the work of James A. Stimson, an American political scientist, who has written extensively on public opinion and electoral change in the US. Using his methodology, we will be able to look in greater detail at the evolution of public sentiment towards the EU in Ireland between 1973 and 2002.

In the first section of this chapter there will be a brief overview of opinion polling questions on the European integration project since 1970. The second section will examine public opinion in the six EU referendums held in Ireland. The third section will investigate using Eurobarometer data Irish public opinion towards the general process of European integration between 1973 and 2002. Here I will map opinions towards the integration project and also test some hypotheses as to the foundations of these attitudes. In the concluding section an appraisal will be made of what Irish opinion polls tell us about public attitudes towards integration.

Opinion Poll Data

Most of the opinion polling relating to citizens' attitudes towards European integration have been undertaken biannually by the European Commission since the early 1970s. Within Ireland these polls were carried out by IMS until July 1989, and thereafter have been undertaken by Lansdowne Market Research. While the Commission and other EU institutions have undertaken these polls for internal use, these mass surveys have been used extensively by academics and have in addition been the basis for many European Parliament Election Studies. In comparison to this rather large long-term surveying enterprise, the amount of purely 'domestic' polling has been much less extensive. An examination of the inventory of question types reveals that there is not a consistent policy of asking poll items relating to the EU on a regular basis. Generally speaking IMS, Lansdowne and MRBI ask questions relating to European referendums and focused most attention on the first European Parliament elections in 1979. The remaining questions address a wide range of issues, some of which touch on particular domestic concerns such as the impact of further integration on neutrality and abortion. The lack of any frequent polling on attitudes towards the EU limits any generalisations that may be inferred concerning changing attitudes. For this reason, use will be made of Eurobarometer data in the penultimate section of this chapter.

Opinion Poll Results and Referendum Voting Behaviour

There have been six EU referendums in the Republic of Ireland. For all of these exercises in direct democracy there has been at least one opinion poll. The primary focus in many of these surveys was estimation of likely voting behaviour. Questions on reasons for vote choice and impact of the referendum campaigns do provide valuable contextual information. However, the format used in these poll items is not consistent. Consequently, it is difficult to trace trends in opinions on specific referendum related issues over time.

Accession to the EEC, 1972

In early November 1970, thirty months before joining the so-called 'Common Market' (European Union), there was the first domestic opinion poll on the issue of European integration. This IMS survey was important in showing that public support for Irish accession to the European Economic Community (EEC) was rather mixed. The IMS polling data reveals that a plurality (48 per cent) approved of membership, while almost one in four had no opinion, or did not know. A similar pattern of support for accession was recorded in a second poll in June 1971. All of these poll results occurred before the campaign to join the EEC had taken place. In the referendum on 10 May 1972 there was a high turnout (71 per cent) with 83 per cent voting in favour of membership. One of the key reasons for the jump in public support for membership must have involved persuading almost the entire 'don't know' group (26 per cent) to vote in favour.[2]

The IMS poll of 24–5 April 1972 is interesting in that it is the only empirical evidence of the impact of this referendum campaign. The first question in this survey asked respondents what they thought the result of the referendum would be. Two in three believed that the referendum would be passed, while one in five thought it would fail.[3] The groups who were most positive about the outcome were the ABC1 classes (81 per cent), those living in Munster (77 per cent), the young aged 21–34 years (71 per cent) and men (71 per cent). According to this poll, three in four stated they would 'definitely' participate in the referendum, with another 17 per cent stating they would 'probably be voting'. These estimates tally well with the actual turnout figure.

The Single European Act Referendum, 1987

In May 1987, there was a referendum on the next phase of European integration, the Single European Act (SEA). During the campaign MRBI undertook one survey on 14 May for *The Irish Times*. The poll results indicated that the referendum would be carried by a comfortable margin (two to one approximately). Nevertheless, the high level of uncertainty (39 per cent) suggested that turnout would be low. On the day, turnout was 44 per cent, 29 percentage points lower than turnout in the general election, which had taken place some three months earlier (see Gallagher 1988; Jones 2001: 87–8). This pattern of perceived lack of knowledge accompanied by low turnout became a key feature of subsequent Euro-referendums and was to play an important part in the failure of the first Nice Treaty referendum some fourteen years later (see Sinnott 2001, 2003).

The Maastricht Treaty (on European Union) Referendum, 1992

The next EU referendum held in Ireland occurred on 18 June 1992 on the Treaty of European Union and brought forward important institutional changes along with a timetable for Economic and Monetary Union (EMU). Politically the Maastricht Treaty ratification process was a watershed. Danish voters rejected the treaty while the French electorate passed it by a wafer-thin margin (51.05 per cent in favour), while in the UK the Conservative government of John Major was almost defeated (note Franklin, van der Eijk and Marsh 1995). In contrast, for the Irish public one of the main concerns was a promise of almost nine billion euro of structural funding that would be 'secured' with ratification of the treaty.

A unique feature of the Maastricht Treaty referendum was that during the campaign on 2 June news of the rejection of the Treaty by the Danish electorate emerged. According to a Lansdowne poll conducted between 29 May and 8 June this development had an impact on some segments of the Irish electorate. Using respondent's stated voted intentions the Danish 'no' vote appears to have motivated undecided voters (as measured in the pre-2 June sub-sample of the Lansdowne poll) to side with the 'no' camp. As a result, support in favour of the treaty declined by 8 percentage points after the Danish rejection on 2 June while opposition increased by 12 points.[4]

A simple difference of proportions test on the pre- and post-2 June sub-samples of the Lansdowne poll shows that the impact of the

Danish 'no' vote on Irish public opinion was associated with (though not necessarily caused by) an increase in anti-Maastricht support and a decline in undecideds (see Appendix 4). Equally interesting was the dramatic increase in those who expressed concern over the possibility that Ireland might be moving towards a liberal abortion regime. In general, most of the post-Danish referendum trends appear to have been negative ones from the Irish government's perspective. However, such an assessment must remain tentative, as there are insufficient polling data to test this interpretation more carefully.

In the European Commission's post-referendum survey over one-third (37 per cent) of those who voted in favour of the treaty did so 'with reservations'.[5] Voters claimed that one of the reasons for this situation, and a 43 per cent abstention rate in the referendum, was that 44 per cent of the respondents felt only 'vaguely aware of the issues' or reported that they did 'not know what the treaty was about'.[6] All in all, one of the key features of the Maastricht referendum was voter confusion and lack of knowledge (note Holmes 1995).

The Amsterdam Treaty Referendum, 1998

This referendum was overshadowed by the simultaneous poll on the Belfast/Good Friday Agreement (note Mansergh 1999; Gilland 1999). Despite the historical significance of the Northern Ireland Agreement voter participation was about the same (56 per cent) as that for the Maastricht Treaty, where the socio-demographic and attitudinal patterns of voter abstention were similar. MRBI undertook a single poll relating to the Amsterdam Treaty referendum campaign, while IMS asked questions in two polls. However, most information on the referendum comes from two post-election surveys undertaken by Lansdowne Market Research. Here I will focus on the poll undertaken in early August for the European Commission Representation Office in Ireland.

According to the results of the Commission-sponsored poll four in ten voters reported that their reason for participation stemmed 'mainly because of the Northern Ireland Agreement', while only one in twenty stated that it was 'mainly because of the referendum on the Amsterdam Treaty'. For a plurality (47 per cent), both referendums were seen as being equally important. This survey evidence suggests that slightly more than half of those who claimed to have voted on 22 May 1998 would have participated in a referendum dealing solely with the Amsterdam Treaty. This would have implied a turnout rate of about 33 per cent – a figure very close to the actual turnout rate in the subsequent (first) Nice Treaty referendum in June 2001.[7]

The polling data suggest that if there had not been concurrent referendums the difference in support between the 'yes' and 'no' camps would have been 73 per cent in favour and 20 per cent against. These estimates may be misleading for two reasons. First, over-reported turnout in this poll was 9 per cent. Second, this estimate assumes that those who reported that both referendums in May 1998 were equally important would have turned out to vote. Both of these factors highlight the difficulties that pollsters and researchers face when dealing with respondents reports that are subject to significant levels of inaccuracy.

This post-election survey also revealed that there was 'core' opposition to integration among one in five Irish voters (21 per cent) – these were self-identified 'no' voters in the Lansdowne poll. One of the implications from this polling figure is that if most Eurosceptic voters actually vote and overall turnout declines to about one in three, then 'no' voters have a real opportunity to constitute a majority in the final referendum result.

The First Nice Treaty Referendum, 2001

There were two public opinion polls published during the first Nice Treaty referendum campaign; both of these were commissioned by *The Irish Times* and undertaken by MRBI.[8] Although the Nice Treaty was undoubtedly important in terms of enlargement and institutional reform, there is relatively little survey information on how the campaign developed. This perhaps reflects the general complacency that the referendum would be passed, despite general lack of interest in the issue among politicians, the media and electorate (O' Mahony 2001). In the first MRBI poll, where interviewing took place on 14–15 May, there was slender majority support (52 per cent) for the Nice Treaty, with 27 per cent not knowing how (or if) they would vote, and a little over one-fifth (21 per cent) stated they would vote 'no'.[9] In the second poll, at the end of May, about one week before the referendum, a plurality (45 per cent) declared support for the Treaty with 28 per cent against and the remaining 27 per cent undecided. In this second poll the only subgroup to show majority support for the Nice Treaty were Progressive Democrat supporters (65 per cent), who accounted for about 3 per cent of the electorate. The greatest drop in support was among women, where those in favour of the treaty fell from 50 to 40 per cent. However, the total proportion replying 'don't know' remained constant.

One of the key issues of the campaign was neutrality and the possible implications of Ireland being part of a European Common Foreign and Security Policy (CFSP). Half of the Irish public favoured participation in the EU's Rapid Reaction Force for 'peace enforcement' or 'peacemaking'. However, 40 per cent also favoured strengthening neutrality even if this implied less involvement in CFSP. Such evidence suggests that Irish public opinion towards CFSP has both an easy facet (support for the principle of neutrality) and a hard facet, where there is recognition of the benefits of involvement in the EU's foreign and defence policy. This apparent inconsistency in Irish public opinion is a topic that I will address more directly a little later.

In general, the poll evidence suggests that the key factor behind the failure of the first Nice Treaty referendum was perceived lack of knowledge. Almost two in three (64 per cent), stated that they had at best only a vague idea of what the Treaty was about. The importance of this lack of knowledge factor was evident in attitudes towards EU enlargement where 41 per cent said they were in favour, while 15 per cent were against, but 43 per cent were undecided. Moreover, this perceived lack of information was the most frequent reason (44 per cent) given by respondents for not participating in the referendum (Sinnott 2001: ii–v; Lyons 2002: 7–9; Coakley 2005b: 105).

The Second Nice Treaty Referendum, 2002

The second Nice Treaty referendum campaign had six polls, four MRBI surveys, one Lansdowne and one ICM poll. This greater media interest in the referendum was indicative of the political importance of this election, in light of the failure of the first referendum (see Hayward 2003; Laffan 2003: 20–6).

One major factor that seemed to be important for participation in this election was perceived understanding of the Treaty. According to the ICM poll, almost three-quarters (72 per cent) of those who felt that they had a 'very/fairly good' understanding stated that they were certain to vote. In contrast, fewer than four in ten (39 per cent) of those who stated that they did not have a good understanding of the Treaty were certain to participate in the referendum. Furthermore, the available survey evidence reveals that the perceived information deficit about the Treaty was only effectively dealt with during the second Nice Treaty campaign.

However, the IMS post-referendum survey for the European Commission Office in Ireland indicates that very few sources of information, such as the 'National Forum on Europe', referendum leaflets and door-to-door canvassing, were judged to be useful by a majority (75–85 per cent) of the electorate. Examination of the reasons given by respondents as to why they were not in favour of the Nice Treaty are difficult to ascertain, because it is not easy to compare across polls as each polling company had its own question wording and specific response format.[10] The questions asked by IMS and MRBI have very different response patterns. The general impression is that issues such as neutrality, loss of funding or benefits and job losses were the main reasons behind not supporting the Treaty in both referendums. However, the polling evidence does not point to one key reason that alienated voters from supporting the treaty.

In this section I have used IMS, Lansdowne and MRBI opinion poll results to examine opinions towards European integration during referendum campaigns. In almost all cases these canvasses were characterised by major party support of integration, with the exception of the Labour Party, which campaigned against accession in 1972 but changed its position thereafter.[11] Nevertheless, as noted earlier, participation in EU referendums and support for the integration project has been declining since 1972. However, as we will see in the next section, the standard questions asked in Eurobarometer since 1973 suggest that Irish public opinion towards the integration project has been strongly positive since the 1980s.

Unfortunately, the polling data relating to EU referendums do not contain standard question formats to allow us to chart trends towards integration from this electoral perspective. However, it is known that issues such as neutrality, abortion and economic considerations have been important, although it is unclear which aspects of the integration project have most impact on Irish public opinion. In the next section we will move beyond referendum campaigns and investigate general opinions towards the EU, and how these have evolved over time.

Public Sentiment towards the European Integration Project

Irish polling companies have not investigated general opinions towards the process of European integration on a frequent basis. For this reason, it is difficult to address important questions such as: 'has the Irish public's attitudes towards the European Union changed over time?' In this section I will examine this question using Eurobarometer – a biannual series of surveys undertaken in Ireland since 1973. These surveys have inquired into attitudes towards the process of integration, and also specific institutions and policies. The EU issue, like the other substantive topics examined, may not be encapsulated by a single overarching judgement, but is made up of facets. In a similar manner to previous chapters I will demonstrate here some of the hard and easy facets of the EU issue, and what this tells us about Irish public opinion.

Hard and easy facets of opinion towards the EU

The only domestic Irish opinion poll series on general orientation towards integration relates to a choice between supporting efforts to 'unite fully with the EU' as opposed to thinking that Ireland should do all it can to 'protect its independence from the EU'. This particular item is an example of a hard question as it forces respondents to make a choice between two desirable goals.[12] Examination of the results of this series of questions between 1996 (there is also a very early measure for 1978) and 2005 as shown in Figure 33 reveals that support for integration among Irish citizens is critical, and does vary over time.

This implies that there is no single opinion on the EU, but a number of opinions based on different considerations. Significantly, during the final week of the first Nice Treaty referendum campaign in June 2001 'protecting independence' became the plurality view (see Sinnott 2001, 2002; Lyons 2002, 2003). The disadvantage of this measure is that it is a single opinion poll item, and may elicit specific response patterns. It would be preferable to have a number of measures that tap into different hard and easy facets (as discussed in earlier chapters) of the underlying orientation towards European integration.

Fortunately, Eurobarometer has four standard questions asked in many of its surveys since 1973. Within the literature on public opinion towards integration these four standard survey questions have been considered as providing utilitarian and affective measures of support (Lindberg and Scheingold 1970: 38–63). This utilitarian/affective distinction in survey questions about the EU matches with the hardness concept developed in Chapter 2, and implemented in the last three chapters. Eurobarometer questions that tap the

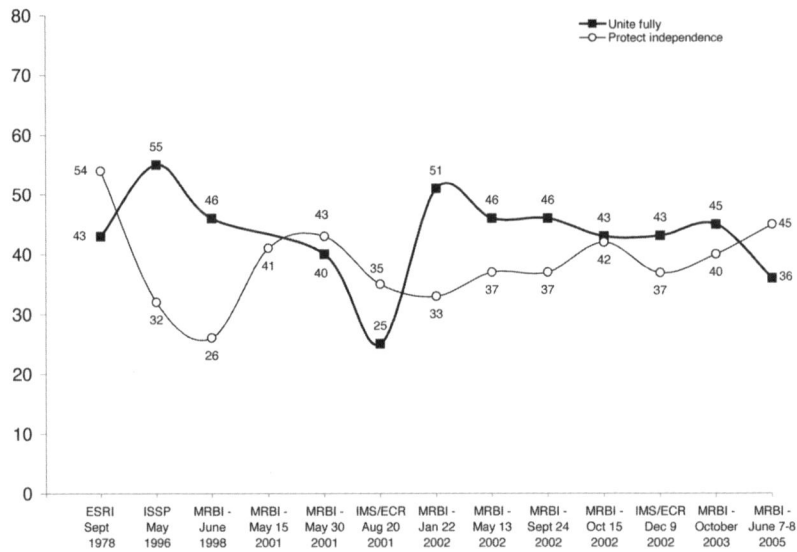

Figure 33 *Popular Support for European Integration in Ireland, 1978–2005 (per cent)*

Note: This figure is based on data from the following: 'Our position as a distinct and independent nation is threatened by our membership of the EEC.' The response options were: (1) Strongly disagree; (2) Moderately disagree; (3) Slightly disagree; (4) Slightly agree; (5) Moderately agree; (6) Strongly agree; (7) Don't know / No reply. ESRI Survey, July–September 1978, question 36 (see, Davis and Sinnott 1979); All agree/disagree responses aggregated as appropriate; ISSP May 1996, MRBI June 1998, MRBI 15 May 2001, MRBI 23 January 2002, MRBI 24 September 2002, MRBI 15 October 2002, MRBI October 2003, MRBI 7–8 June 2005, IMS/ECR 30 August 2001 and IMS/ECR 10 December 2002. The question wording used was: 'Which of the following statements comes closest to your view of Ireland's status within the EU?' SHOW CARD (1) Ireland should do all it can to unite fully with the EU, (2) Ireland should do all it can to protect its independence from the EU, (3) No opinion/don't know. The mean/median non-committal response (don't know/no opinion) for the entire period is 17 per cent, with a peak of 40 per cent in August 2001 and a minimum of 3 per cent in 1978.

affective aspects of integration are 'easy' in the sense that they refer to favouring the principles behind the creation of the EU, whereas utilitarian questions deal with evaluations of policy or institutional performance, that is, a 'hard' facet.

If we now examine the four standard Eurobarometer questions (see Figure 34 for the question format) it seems sensible to see EU membership as a 'good thing' and that there are 'benefits from membership' as representing hard, or utilitarian, facets of opinion towards integration. In contrast, support for efforts to 'unify western

Europe' represents an easy facet. The 'dissolution' item has no clear interpretation within the literature, although its pattern in Figure 34 suggests that it elicits responses most similar to hard questions.[13]

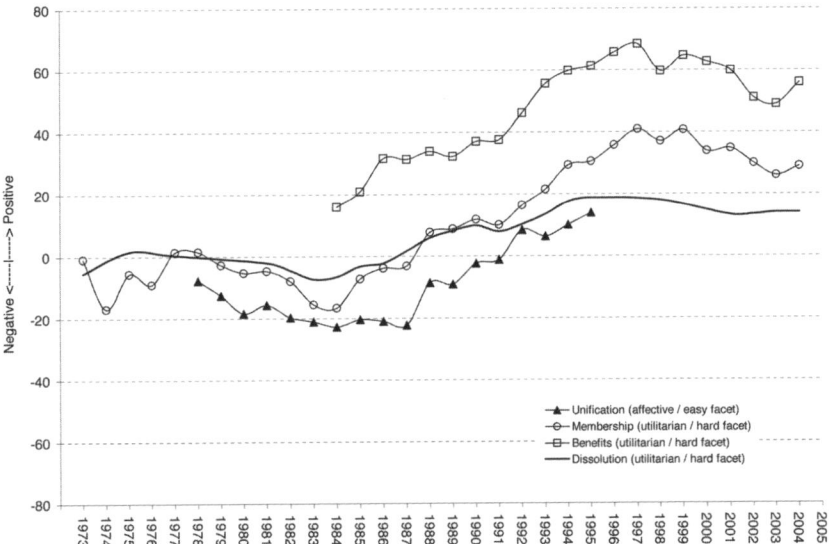

Figure 34 *Net Support for European Integration in Ireland in Comparison to the EU Average, 1973–2004 (per cent)*

Source: Mannheim Eurobarometer trend file 1970–2002 and Eurobarometers 58.1–62.0. Net scores constructed by subtracting negative integration responses from positive ones and weighting the difference by the non-committed response rate (i.e. don't knows, no answer or DK/NA) so as to take account of situations where significant proportions are uncertain and refuse to answer the survey question. Net positive scores indicate that Ireland is above the net EU average while negative ones vice versa.

The net average EU score for all four measures is 0 per cent with 'positive' being above this value and 'negative' below.

The four standard Eurobarometer questions are:

UNIFICATION: In general, are you for or against efforts being made to unify Western Europe? (1) For very much; (2) For; (3) Against; (4) Against very much (5) DK/NA.

MEMBERSHIP: Generally speaking, do you think that IRELAND'S membership of the European Community (Common market) is...? (1) A good thing; (2) Neither good nor bad; (3) A bad thing; (4) DK/NA.

BENEFITS: Taking everything into consideration, would you say that IRELAND has on balance benefited or not from being a member of the European Community (Common Market)? (1) Benefited; (2) Not benefited; (3) DK/NA.

DISSOLUTION: If you were told tomorrow that the European Community (Common Market) had been scrapped, would you be very sorry about it, indifferent or very relieved? (1) Very sorry; (2) Indifferent; (3) Very relieved; (4) DK/NA.

Figure 34 shows that net support for integration in Ireland began to move beyond the European average in 1984 and increased until 1997. This figure also shows that there is an ordinal (interaction) relationship between these indicators, as they follow the same pattern but operate at different levels of support, and the trends in these time series (excluding the 'dissolution' measure) do not overlap.

An equally important implication of the pattern in Figure 34 is that the relative popularity of hard and easy facets for the Northern Ireland question and liberal agenda issue is opposite to that observed for the EU data. In other words, the EU issue is different because it is the 'hard' facet that is most popular. What does this mean? The evidence presented suggests that for the Irish public the goals of the integration project (such as creating a 'united Europe') are more controversial than the policies it pursues. This may stem from fears that European integration will undermine Irish sovereignty and culture (note Coakley 2005b: 108–10). In this respect, Figure 34 reveals that to date support for integration in Ireland is primarily based on a willingness to sacrifice national values for utilitarian ends.[14]

If we assume that the ordinal relationship between the four indicators in Figure 34 demonstrates the existence of an underlying sentiment towards the EU this opens up important possibilities for understanding public opinion. In previous chapters I have kept the hard and easy facets of an issue separate. In this chapter I will advance beyond this position by exploiting the opportunities inherent in Eurobarometer data, and explore the interrelated opinion structure underpinning sentiments towards the EU. In order to achieve this objective one must have a method of measuring this underlying sentiment.

Developing a measure of popular sentiment towards the European Union

Our ability to estimate a measure of general sentiment towards the European Union is constrained by the limits of the available data. As noted earlier, domestic Irish polling data are insufficient to construct any measure of general orientation. Even within the much more extensive Eurobarometer dataset, apart from the 'membership' question no other item has been asked at least once a year since 1973. In effect, within Eurobarometer what we have is a considerable number of 'mini-series' that exist for sub-periods, many of which overlap one another. Ideally, we would like to be able to construct a single measure of public opinion towards the EU that incorporates all the survey data available. Such a measure would provide us with the most comprehensive assessment of the structure of public opinion towards the EU.

James A. Stimson, an American political scientist, in a series of influential books and articles has developed a statistical technique for creating a comprehensive measure of public opinion.[15] In his work, Stimson has used this technique to investigate whether public opinion shapes policy-making within the American political system. Rather than dealing with public preferences for specific policies, Stimson argues that the political importance of public opinion can be reduced to an underlying value, or prevailing 'public mood'. In the United States, the prevailing public mood is seen to reflect desires for more or less liberal policy-making. Here our interest is the EU, so the core underlying value that drives specific opinions towards the Union is seen to be a general predisposition, or sentiment, for more or less integration.

In his research, Stimson developed a procedure that facilitates obtaining a comprehensive measure of the 'public mood' (see Stimson 1991: 33–60, 129–32 for details). His methodology is based on maximising the amount of information that can be gleaned from multiple overlapping series of opinion poll questions relating to a single underlying core value (such as liberalism). In essence, the goal is to construct a latent or underlying factor that shares the same variance over time as all of the 'mini-series'. Technically speaking, we would like to implement a longitudinal 'factor analysis'. Stimson has developed a 'dyadic recursion' algorithm that does this task by capturing the shared variance across many different individual time series (Erikson, MacKuen and Stimson 2002: 199–202; Stimson 2004: 77).[16]

The intuition being pursued here is that changing opinions towards the European Union will be evident in the responses to a wide range of questions on integration, and the goal is to see whether these individual trends all move in the same direction at about the same points in time. If European integration has little importance for the Irish public then we would expect to see no trend, that is, a flat line with small random fluctuations.[17]

Using the Mannheim Eurobarometer trend file (1973–2002), an underlying time series measure was constructed from 45 different questions relating to different aspects of the European integration issue. The questions selected were asked on at least three separate occasions and deal with attitudes towards the integration project, common policies and trust in EU institutions. For each of the series of 45 questions the Irish public's net response was coded as the percentage that gave a pro-integration answer divided by the percentage that gave either a pro- or anti-integration response. Thus neutral, non-committed, don't know and no reply responses are excluded from the calculation of the EU sentiment measure (see Erikson et al. 2002: 197).

Items asked in Eurobarometer that related to general political factors such as party attachment, vote intentions, sense of political efficacy, national identity, left–right self-placement and post-materialism were ignored. In addition, questions relating to media use, level of political interest and political discussion were also excluded. In short, all trend questions asked in Eurobarometer not dealing specifically with the process of integration were excluded.

The expectation here is that this latent factor relates to a general sentiment towards the European Union and process of integration. The results of this longitudinal 'factor' analysis are shown in panel (a) of Figure 35. In this figure there are three sentiment measures. The dimension 1 series is based on the expectation that there is a single general sentiment towards the EU. This dimension explains that 44 per cent (44.3) of the total variance observed in the Eurobarometer survey questions is common to this underlying EU sentiment measure.[18]

The remaining 56 per cent of the total variance is due either to question-specific attitudes or to error. It would seem that most of the attitudes and public debate about the EU is aligned along dimension 1. An examination of which factors are most strongly positively or negatively correlated with dimension 1 does not give a completely clear picture, as respondents may be interpreting the questions in a manner that is not entirely consonant with scholarly expectations. However, dimension 1 would seem to relate to intergovernmental versus federal (that is, common policy) aspects of integration. Panel (a) of Figure 35 indicates that general support for integration has increased over time in Ireland, most dramatically after 1984. More generally, the analysis undertaken here suggests that seven in ten Irish citizens support an intergovernmental approach to the EU and fewer than one in three favour a federalist style of integration.

Looking at these results in terms of the Belief-Sampling Model, it seems that the questions asked in the Eurobarometer survey prompt Irish respondents to focus on national or intergovernmental aspects of EU membership and representation rather than on the policy-

(a) Including the four standard Eurobarometer questions

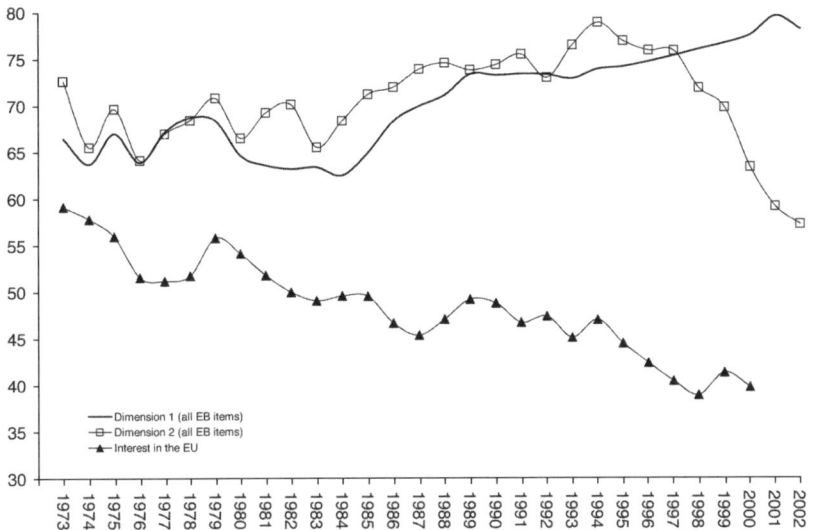

(b) Excluding the four standard Eurobarometer questions

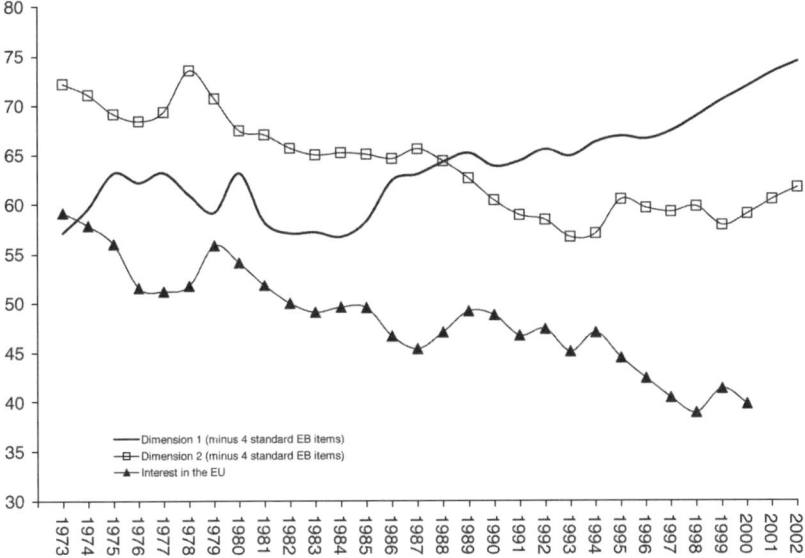

Figure 35 *Public Sentiment and Interest towards the European Integration Project in Ireland, 1973–2002 (per cent)*

making aspects of EU institutions, which produce legislation that has effect across all member states. Moreover, the academic view that it is contradictory for respondents to support the integration process but be unhappy about its common policy aspects is inappropriate. The Irish public favours more integration but wants the EU to do less common policy-making. In short, Irish public opinion towards European integration is ambivalent.

As noted earlier, dimension 1 explains less than half of the total variance. Therefore, not all responses to the Eurobarometer questions follow dimension 1. There are no strong expectations about what other general feature of public opinion might help explain common movement in answers to survey items relating to the integration project. Adopting an inductive approach it is possible to estimate a second dimension within the data.[19] In theoretical terms, the expectation is that any second dimension in public opinion towards European integration should have a different cross-time or temporal pattern from dimension 1. We can observe from panel (b) of Figure 35 that this is consistently the case only after 1994. It would seem that unease with the EU emerged in Ireland in the mid-1990s and that this feeling increased dramatically from 1997. This is an interesting finding as it suggests that fears within Irish public opinion about the integration project emerged before the Nice Treaty rejection in June 2001.

Examination of panel (a) of Figure 36 illustrates that many of the same variables associated with the intergovernmental pole of dimension 1 also exist for dimension 2. However, on the federal or common policy pole there are differences between both dimensions. For dimension 1, common policies for industry, workers, data protection and the importance of the European Parliament are the least pro-integration stances.

In contrast, with dimension 2 it is common policies on asylum, immigration, science, unemployment, the Single Market and Irish MEPs orientation towards Europe, rather than national orientation, which seem to be most important. Interestingly, the differences between dimensions 1 and 2 would seem to have a strong temporal aspect, as demonstrated in Figure 34.

It was noted earlier in our discussion of public opinion in EU referendums that a key issue was level of citizen awareness of the integration process. In this respect it is possible with half a dozen Eurobarometer questions to estimate an EU interest/awareness measure in a similar manner to dimensions 1 and 2. The third

(a) Including the four standard Eurobarometer questions

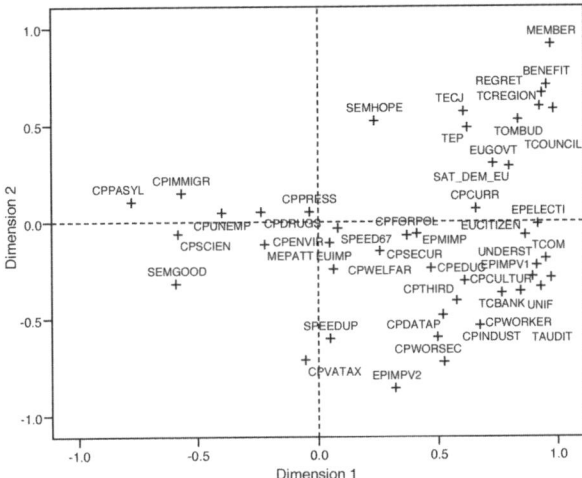

(b) Excluding the four standard Eurobarometer questions

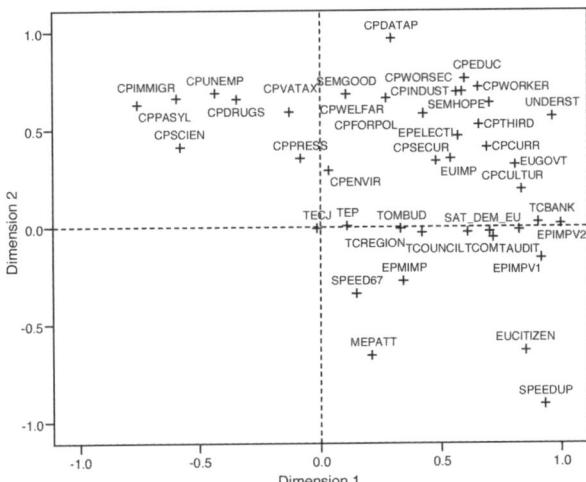

Figure 36 *A Two-Dimensional Representation of Popular Sentiment in Ireland towards the EU and the Process of Integration, 1973–2002*

Note: The loadings on the two dimensions are derived from Eurobarometer survey preference questions. Loadings are correlations between individual item time series and the derived underlying EU sentiment measure. See Appendix 4 for details of the variable abbreviations used in this figure. Both axes have a range of +1.0 to –1.0. Because of the difference in level of explained variance, the vertical axis in both figures is out of scale and over-represents the relative importance of dimension 2 in comparison to dimension 1. The axis scaling used has the advantage of facilitating observation of all the time series and their relative orientation in this two dimensional space.

(bottom) line in panel (a) of Figure 35 demonstrates that interest and awareness among the Irish public in the integration project declined substantially (19 points) between 1973 and 2000.

If we look more closely for a moment at panel (a) of Figure 35 we see two surprising patterns. The overall sentiment measure indicates that support for the integration project has generally been increasing with time. In contrast, interest and awareness of the EU has been declining over the same period. Significantly, the peaks in interest/awareness match years when the EU was prominent in the media, that is, following accession in 1973, during years when there were European Parliament elections and EU referendums (Single European Act 1985, Maastricht 1992), and when Ireland held the Presidency of the European Council (1975, 1979, 1984, 1990, 1996). One important consequence of the trends presented in Figures 33 and 34 is that use of the standard Eurobarometer questions to measure popular support for integration in Ireland may be giving an overly positive perspective on public attitudes towards the EU.

Decisions about which variables should be included in the estimation of the sentiment measure are important.[20] As the contribution of each series to the overall sentiment measure is weighted by their frequency, those questions asked most often will have the strongest impact on the estimation procedure. Consequently, it is sensible to consider that the four most frequently asked measures of support for integration (unification, membership, benefit and dissolution) might be colouring our EU sentiment measure. This suspicion seems to be well founded. Panel (b) of Figure 35 demonstrates that removal of these four key indicators from the overall sentiment measure yields attenuated levels of support for integration.

Equally important is the fact that the pattern observed is very different. Looking at panel (b) of Figure 36, one observes that along dimension 1 opinions on common policies such as asylum, immigration, science, unemployment and taxation contrast with support for a common currency, an EU government and wishing for a faster rate of European unification. Here there seems to be a division in support for policies or developments that enhance the EU level of decision-making.

In contrast, dimension 2 of panel (b) of Figure 36 indicates that Irish public opinion differentiates between common policies organised at the European level between member states and overtly Europeanist ideas such as thinking of oneself as a European citizen, wanting the speed of integration to increase and thinking Irish MEPs should support things that are good for Europe as a whole rather than the short-term interests of Ireland.[21] It seems that the main difference in the two EU sentiment measures represented in panel (b) of Figure 36 relates to whether specific opinions concerned with speeding up the process of unification and identifying oneself as a European citizen with common policy-making are conjoined. For dimension 1 these two aspects of the integration project are linked, while in dimension 2 they are separate.

If we consider this difference in terms of the trends exhibited in Figure 35 that derive from contrasting opinion structures as demonstrated in Figure 36, this has an important impact on our understanding of the evolution of Irish public opinion towards the EU. The evidence presented shows that construction of an EU sentiment measure, without the four standard Eurobarometer items, demonstrates that unease with the integration project started in Ireland in 1978. In contrast, if use is made of all the available Eurobarometer measures the point at which unease becomes evident is much later: 1994. This difference in timing conveys very different interpretations of the long-term dynamics of generalised support for European integration in Ireland. What we do know for certain is that by the time of the first Nice Treaty referendum (June 2001) doubts about the direction of the EU were important.

Overall our attempts to construct an EU sentiment measure using as many questions asked in the Eurobarometer series of polls as possible has indicated the presence of important trends and raised some fascinating questions about the impact of survey question format on our ability to generalise about developments in public opinion. Furthermore, we have the puzzling finding that while general sentiment towards the EU has been increasing, interest and awareness have been declining.

What moves popular sentiment towards the European Union?

What is clear from the Eurobarometer survey evidence presented so far is that opinions and general sentiment towards the European Union in Ireland have changed over time. One may posit that the main reason for this opinion movement relates to the impact of economic factors, as the integration project was for many years primarily driven by economic goals. Perhaps the most widely examined economic variables influencing attitudes towards integration are factors such as level of unemployment, inflation and net receipts, or payments, from the European Union (note Gabel 1998a, b). An alternative approach within the scholarly literature on European integration has been to show that awareness and interest in the EU are associated with being favourable towards the integration project (Inglehart 1970; Blondel et al. 1998; McLaren 2002). In the next sub-section I will build a simple aggregate-level model of support for European integration in Ireland between 1977 and 2004 using variables that broadly reflect these two perspectives within the literature.

Model of Support for European Integration
Looking first to economic explanations of support for integration, the strategy adopted at this juncture is to treat each of the dimensions estimated earlier as a dependent variable. In other words, the goal here is to examine the general argument prevalent within the literature on public support for integration that citizens' sentiment towards the EU is influenced by economic factors and interest or awareness in the EU. We can specify our expectations in the following four hypotheses:

H.1 Public sentiment towards the EU is influenced by the level of unemployment. When unemployment rates are declining, public sentiment towards the EU will be more positive, as the integration project is judged to yield tangible benefits.
H.2 Public sentiment towards the EU is also shaped by price levels. When the rate of inflation is low positive public sentiment towards the EU will be greatest.
H.3 Direct gains from the EU, such as the transfer of monetary funds for national and regional development, will also be associated with increased positive sentiment towards the integration project.
H.4 Higher levels of interest or awareness in the European integration process will be associated with increased levels of positive sentiment towards the EU.

In summary, the first three hypotheses suggest that public sentiment towards the integration project will be positive for (hard) utilitarian reasons, while the remaining one suggests that opinions are based on a feeling of being informed about the integration process.[22] Also included in all models is a linear trend variable that captures the growth in experience of the public towards European integration. This variable also serves the useful function of accounting for variance that is a linear function of time, and would otherwise become part of the error term, thereby introducing increased levels of serial correlation in the error terms of the models estimated.

As noted in Chapter 4, regression models of time series data require caution because of collinearity or spurious regression problems and serial correlation among the error terms. Differencing these data (using annual change rather than current values) removes the collinearity problem, but runs the risk of underestimating the statistical relationships. However, ignoring collinearity problems creates the danger of over-estimating effect magnitudes. The strategy adopted here to deal with these problems is to use an Ordinary Least Squares regression technique where serial correlation in the error terms is modelled as an autoregressive (AR 1) process. Diagnostic test results shown in the bottom part of Table 16 suggest that this strategy is a reasonable one.[23]

I noted earlier that the annual values in our EU sentiment measure seem to be sensitive to the presence of the four key questions asked in almost all Eurobarometer polls to investigate public attitudes towards integration. In order to investigate this effect, four dependent variables were tested in the regression modelling results reported.[24] In models 1 and 2 of Table 16 there is an examination of the first dimension(s) extracted for the EU sentiment measure, where model 1 includes all Eurobarometer questions while model 2 excludes the four standard measures. Models 3 and 4 follow a similar strategy, with the second extracted dimensions. Please note that in model 3 the dependent variable includes all Eurobarometer items, while model 4 excludes the membership, benefits, dissolution and unification series of questions.

The results shown for model 1 in Table 16 reveal that a more positive orientation towards the European Union is associated with falling unemployment and inflation. However, budgetary transfers from Brussels do not appear to have a strong impact on the Irish public's orientation towards the EU. Moreover, interest or awareness in the process of integration is positively ($p < 0.10$) associated with support for the integration project. Our suspicion that length of time since membership might have an impact on public support for integration is well-founded. It seems that positive sentiment towards the EU increased by about a half a point (0.42) per year following accession.

Table 16 *Regression Analysis of the Influence of Key Economic Indicators and Interest in the EU in Sentiment towards European Integration in the Republic of Ireland, 1973–2000*

	Models include all Eurobarometer survey question		Models excluding four standard Eurobarometer items	
	Model 1	Model 2	Model 3	Model 4
Constant	52.12 ***	34.19 *	62.98 ***	86.35 ***
	(10.98)	(17.90)	(13.50)	(10.83)
Unemployment (per cent of total workforce)	−0.53 **	0.02	−0.37	−0.24
	(0.18)	(0.25)	(0.24)	(0.17)
Inflation (per cent annual change in CPI)	−0.26 *	−0.39 *	−0.02	0.00
	(0.13)	(0.22)	(0.18)	(0.14)
Net receipts from the EU (× 10 million Euro)	0.02	0.05 **	−0.01	−0.01
	(0.01)	(0.02)	(0.02)	(0.01)
Interested or aware of the integration project	0.36 *	0.69 *	−0.01	−0.20
	(0.21)	(0.35)	(0.26)	(0.20)
Years since accession 1973	0.42 **	0.02	0.40 *	−0.60 **
	(0.18)	(0.28)	(0.22)	(0.17)
AR(1) to control for serial correlation in residuals	0.55 **	0.34	0.48) **	0.48 **
	(0.21)	(0.23)	(0.21)	(0.22)
Adjusted R-squared	0.90	0.62	0.77	0.90
S.E. of regression	1.54	2.59	1.94	1.51
Sum squared residuals	47.23	134.23	75.64	45.49
Log likelihood	−45.86	−59.96	−52.22	−45.35
Durbin–Watson statistic	1.95	1.55	1.83	1.62
Inverted AR Roots	0.55	0.34	0.48	0.48
Mean dependent variable	69.81	71.20	63.36	63.77
S.D. dependent variable	4.87	4.22	4.07	4.80
Akaike information criterion	3.92	4.96	4.39	3.88
Schwarz criterion	4.25	5.30	4.72	4.21
F-statistic	40.11	8.17	15.64	40.49
Prob. (F-statistic)	<0.01	<0.01	<0.01	<0.01
Breusch–Godfrey Serial Correlation (LM2) Test:	0.27	3.77	2.67	4.84
	(0.87)	(0.15)	(0.26)	(0.09)
ARCH Test:	0.51	1.05	2.89	0.80
	(0.47)	(0.31)	(0.09)	(0.37)
White Heteroscedasticity Test:	12.51	9.88	16.78	10.85
	(0.25)	(0.45)	(0.08)	(0.37)
Ramsey RESET Test (F-statistic):	0.81	0.61	1.14	1.86
	(0.38)	(0.45)	(0.30)	(0.19)

* p ≤ 0.10   ** p ≤ 0.05   *** p ≤ 0.001 (two tailed test)

Note: Analysis based on an OLS regression using an AR 1 procedure to model serial correlation in the error term. Standard errors are in parentheses. The dependent variable in model 1 is dimension 1 of the total sentiment towards the EU measure using all 45 items as shown in panel (a) of Figure 35. In model 2 the dependent variable is dimension 2 estimated from all the Eurobarometer items. Within models 3 and 4, there is a similar procedure of examining two extracted dimensions, where the four core measures asked in almost all

Eurobarometer surveys that are used as measures of general attitudes towards integration (membership, benefit, dissolution and unification items) are excluded from the sentiment measure used in the analysis as illustrated in panel (b) of Figure 35. Model 3 refers to dimension 1 and model 4 refers to dimension 2.

In model 2, which examines the second dimension of EU sentiment, we observe that declining inflation and receipt of more funds from Brussels combined with interest/awareness in the integration project are important. The main differences between models 1 and 2 stem from: (1) the impact of unemployment and (2) linear growth in support for integration following accession. The different patterns here would seem to be strongly influenced by the dynamics illustrated in panel (a) of Figure 35, where dimension 2 (unlike dimension 1) exhibits a sharp decline after 1994, and hence follows a similar track to that observed for interest and awareness of the EU.

Models 3 and 4 are similar in that they do not include the four standard Eurobarometer measures; they highlight that exclusion of these items demonstrates quite clearly that respondents interpret the standard items in an economic way. Moreover, economic factors and expressed interest or awareness of the activities of the EU do help explain the contrasting trends revealed in panel (b) of Figure 35.

It would seem from this evidence that interpretation of public sentiment towards the process of European integration is strongly influenced by the type of survey questions asked. This important finding suggests that Eurobarometer surveys are providing a more economic perspective on popular opinion towards the EU than is often realised. The question of which measure of EU sentiment (including or excluding the four standard questions) is superior in terms of validity and reliability is not something that can be easily answered. This is because one would need an independent source of public opinion data to benchmark these two different operationalisations of popular sentiment towards the EU. Such work represents an important line of future research.

Conclusion

Within this chapter I have used two sources of polling data to examine Irish public opinion towards the European Union since 1970.

Broadly speaking the polling results from IMS, Lansdowne and MRBI have allowed us to mirror the opinions of the Irish electorate during each of the six European referendums held in Ireland. Unfortunately, due to the relative scarcity of data and methodological problems with some of the poll questions used, it has not been possible to track public opinion across different referendums. For this reason, the second part of this chapter has been devoted to exploring in a mirror- and lamp-like manner public opinion towards the EU using the Eurobarometer series of surveys. In this respect a lot of ground has been covered, and perhaps I have raised as many questions as I have been able to answer. Let me now try to review the progress that has been made.

At the start of this chapter I posed two questions. The first question enquired about the limitations of using single poll questions as mirrors of public opinion. Unlike in previous chapters it has been possible through the combined use of media-sponsored poll data and results from Eurobarometer surveys to illustrate the benefits of having multi-question measures of a single orientation or mood within the public. The evidence from the referendum campaigns, where single question measures are used, reveal how little we know about public attitudes towards integration. The electoral data indicate decline in support and interest in the EU, yet the extant media-commissioned polling information provides little insight into this trend. Moreover, as Coakley (2005b: 107–8) cogently argues, the standard questions asked in Eurobarometer suggest increasing support for integration – a fact that runs counter to Euro-referendum trends. Such evidence suggests that public opinion towards the EU, which is for many Irish citizens a low-salience issue, are best conceptualised as deriving from different considerations. Moreover, the research undertaken in this chapter highlights the benefits, and also the difficulties, of using multi-question methods to track and mirror public opinion on different facets of an issue.

The second question put forward at the outset was: how is it possible to make sense of the interrelated structure of opinions measured in polls and surveys? The key innovation in this chapter has been to demonstrate the use of a methodology that gives us the capacity to combine many different kinds of questions, often asked intermittently, to construct an overall public opinion sentiment measure. In constructing such a measure I have shown that Irish public opinion towards European integration appears to have a broadly intergovernmental–federal structure.

In attempting to explain the EU sentiment measure estimated using as many of the questions asked in Eurobarometer as possible, we have discovered that inclusion of the four standard measures asked in almost all Eurobarometer polls makes a big difference. Inclusion of such items means that it is possible to explain much of the variation in Irish public sentiment towards the EU in terms of economic factors, that is, declining rates of unemployment and inflation combined with increases in net payments from the EU are associated with a positive orientation. Significantly, the level of public interest in the EU is also important. However, when the four standard Eurobarometer questions are excluded from our EU sentiment measure, neither our economic nor interest variables have any significant impact. The implication here is that, while economic and informational factors are undoubtedly important in shaping sentiment towards integration, this is not the complete picture.

While the process of European integration may have a low salience within Irish public opinion, it nevertheless has important political consequences. The experience of the Nice Treaty referendums highlights that public support for the European integration project is not automatic. Moreover, the results of the Constitutional Treaty ratification process in France and the Netherlands in the early summer of 2005 confirm this fact on a wider European stage. The analysis undertaken in this chapter demonstrates that public opinion towards the EU cannot be reasonably summarised in a single survey question. This chapter has attempted to make a contribution in this respect by demonstrating a more realistic means of conceptualising and measuring public opinion on this important issue.

Notes

1. This perspective, quoted from Halligan (2000: 29), neatly summarises the Irish government's general strategy within the European integration project from accession in 1973.
2. This is a conservative estimate, as it does not include the 29 per cent who did not vote.
3. 'As you know, there will be a referendum (or general vote) throughout the country on May 10th when everyone will be asked to vote on the Common Market. What do you think will be the result of this referendum? Do you think it will be a vote for Ireland going into the Common Market, or a vote against Ireland going into the Common Market?' IMS J.1832, Independent Newspapers Ltd., 24–5 April 1972, question 1.
4. For a comparative analysis of the Maastricht referendums in Denmark, France and Ireland see Franklin, Marsh and McLaren (1994); Franklin, Marsh and Wlezien (1994).
5. 'How did you vote in the referendum – in favour of or against the Maastricht Treaty?' (1) In favour of; (2) Against; (3) Cannot remember; (4) Refused. If voted in favour, 'Did you have any reservations or not regarding your decision to vote in favour of the Maastricht

Treaty?' Lansdowne Market Research, Commission of the European Communities, AM/RB 2L-188, 20–8 August 1992, question 2a–b.
6 'By the date of the referendum (June 18th) how good was your understanding of the issues involved? Please use this card to choose the most appropriate phrase.' (1) I had a good understanding of what the treaty was all about; (2) I understood some of the issues but not all that that was involved; (3) I was only vaguely aware of the issues involved; (4) I did not know what the treaty was all about. Lansdowne Market Research, Commission of the European Communities, AM/RB 2L-188, 20–8 August 1992, question 5.
7 If one were to assume that about half of those who voted mainly because of the Northern Ireland Agreement would have voted in any case on the Amsterdam issue, estimated turnout would be at a similar level (in the low forties) to the Single European Act referendum in 1987 and the stand-alone European Parliament elections of 1984 and 1994. Such evidence indicates that apathy towards integration is not a new feature of Irish public opinion; its origins may be traced back to the mid-1980s.
8 There were items on the other two referendums on the accession to the International Criminal Court and abolition of the death penalty. These issues were relatively uncontroversial and were ratified by the electorate.
9 'As you may know, three Referendums are being held on June 7th next on a number of issues. For each of the Referendums shown on this card, I would like you to tell whether you are likely to vote Yes or No [or No opinion]? SHOW CARD. (a) The Nice Treaty, which provides, among other things, for enlargement of the number of countries in the European Union...' MRBI/5577/01, 14–15 May 2001, question 7.
10 For example, MRBI in its September 2002 survey, read out a series of six statements about the Nice treaty with which the respondent could agree or disagree. IMS got interviewers to code from a set of nine pre-codes issues that influenced the voting decision. Three responses were coded. ICM focused on those who intended to vote 'no' and asked them to pick form a series of five statements that best matched their reason for voting 'no'. In contrast, the IMS/ECR post-referendum polls involved interviewers noting down verbatim reasons for respondents vote choice. These were later coded into ten categories.
11 This is not to deny that smaller parties such as the Greens and Sinn Féin have consistently opposed further integration during EU referendum campaigns.
12 This trend question is not entirely consistent or frequently repeated and must be interpreted with caution (see Appendix 4). This question is defined as hard following the definition outlined in Chapter 2, as respondents are forced to consider the costs and benefits of supporting integration, i.e. the consequences criterion, and this is reflected in the format of the question used.
13 There is an extensive literature on the interpretation of these Eurobarometer trend items and more generally how to operationalise popular support for European integration. See Eichenberg and Dalton (1993); Gabel and Palmer (1995); Niedermayer (1995); Anderson and Reichert (1996); Deflem and Pampel (1996); Anderson (1998); Eichenberg (1998); Gabel (1998a, b); Carey (2002); McLaren (2002); Rohrschneider (2002); Steenbergen and Jones (2002); Marks and Hooghe (2003); Brinegar, Jolly and Kitschelt (2004).
14 Issues where the goals rather than the means are controversial are not uncommon. Examples would include the issue of racial integration in America, and equal treatment for women and men and equality regardless of sexual orientation, thus allowing gay marriage. For many of these types of issues traditional values clash with changing expectations and expanded views of equality (note Stimson 2004: 33–7).
15 Stimson in collaboration with Robert S. Erikson and Michael B. MacKuen, has pioneered work over the last two decades on creating a unified model of political behaviour in the United States. In this respect, the work of Stimson represents the cutting edge of research into aggregate public poll analysis and its interconnection with the political system.
16 It is important to keep in mind this procedure uses aggregated (i.e. total public opinion)

data. There is no mapping of the structure of individual level opinions as in conventional principal component (factor) analysis.

17 It is possible that there are in reality many unrelated dimensions each tapped by different questions. The expectation is that public opinion is not driven by a multitude of values, but is likely to be structured by one or two core values or factors. If this assumption is not true the underlying factor(s) identified will explain little of the overall variance. The software used for this analysis can search for a maximum of two underlying factors.

18 The variance explained is based on an eigenvalue estimate of a dimension extracted divided by the total variance for the entire Eurobarometer survey results matrix. Survey questions are weighted by their frequency within the total period examined where more frequently asked items have greater weight. In order to put these estimates into perspective it should be noted that a liberal policy mood measure for the US constructed for the 1952 to 1996 period using 133 series (1,610 different questions) explains 37.8 per cent of the total variance (Erikson et al. 2002: 201–3).

19 Following extraction of the first dimension, each time series is regressed on dimension 1 in sequence in order to estimate that portion of each questions' variation not shared with dimension 1. Thereafter, this estimated residual variation is subjected to a dimensional analysis. The true mean and variance of dimension 2 is under-identified. Consequently, the mean value of dimension 2 is set to the mean of dimension 1 and the variance of the second common factor is defined to be the 'fraction of the first dimension standard deviation in proportion to its explanatory power' (Erikson et al. 2002: 208).

20 This may represent a limitation of the Stimson methodology where the trend in the questions asked most frequently may dominate the overall trend observed. On this general issue of bias Mayer (1992: 123, n. 19) notes that Stimson's algorithm may also exaggerate small changes in public opinion. In short, care is required in interpreting and evaluating the sentiment measure.

21 Dimension 1 of the EU sentiment measure estimated (excluding the four standard Eurobarometer measures) explains 34 per cent of the total variance, while dimension 2 explains 17 per cent. More than six-in-ten (63.9 per cent) respondents, between 1973 and 2002, chose a pro-EU answer. However, one in -three (36.1 per cent) expressed unease or opposition towards the integration project. These are not hugely different to the per centages reported earlier for the dimensions extracted using all Eurobarometer items.

22 Unemployment relates to an average annual percentage as estimated in the Labour Force Survey. Inflation is the annual change in the Consumer Price Index. This data is taken from figures published by the Central Statistics Office. Net receipts from the European Union (millions of Euro) were taken from annual reports published by the European Commission.

23 As the goal here is an exploratory one, lagged dependent variables were not included in the regression models as independent variables. This is to minimise the risk of attenuating the potential impact of the economic variables (see Achen 2000).

24 A bivariate time series regression model of the two dependent 'first dimension' variables yields a positive coefficient (0.45, p=0.009, DW=1.72, adjusted R-square=0.92; the model also includes AR(1) (and years since accession variables), suggesting that inclusion of the four standard Eurobarometer items in an EU sentiment measure has important consequences. The two sentiment measures tap into different facets of public opinion.

Conclusion

> The ultimate values of politics and economics, the judgments on which public policy is based, do not come from special knowledge or from intelligence alone. They are compounded from the day-to-day experience of the men and women who together make up the society we live in. That is why public-opinion polls are important today.
>
> G. H. Gallup and S. F. Rae (1940: 266)

In this concluding chapter the main goal is to outline the implications of the research presented in this book. For this reason, the objective here is to provide some answers as to what opinion polls tell us *in toto* about Irish public opinion. At the outset of this study I introduced a metaphor to help us understand more clearly what opinion polls can tell us about public opinion. This metaphor of the 'mirror and the lamp' has also been employed to draw attention to the purpose of opinion polls.

In Chapter 2 I argued that the prevailing media and polling philosophy of 'ascertaining and simply reporting the facts' (the Mirror Theory of Opinion Polling) involves assuming that poll respondents always have 'true opinions'. Much polling research since the 1930s suggests that this is an unrealistic assumption. The process of opinion polling is not a simple matter of asking questions to a representative sample, recording the answers, tabulating the results and presenting them in the media in easily-understandable charts.

Frequently within this book I have stressed the importance of not taking poll results at face value. In Chapter 2 I formalised this insight by stating that opinion poll results are the sum of expressed *opinions* plus *error* within the process of providing a response and *bias* within the polling methodology itself. In practice, this means that opinion poll data can only be properly evaluated by examining the questionnaire used, understanding the sampling procedure employed and comparing the poll results with previous or contemporary surveying data. Therefore, as I have argued repeatedly in this work, the polling data never speak for themselves – poll results have meaning only through interpretation.

One of the objectives of this research has been to outline and demonstrate some methods for the interpretation of opinion poll questions asked in Ireland, evaluating the polling methodology employed and outlining the key themes addressed in such polls. It is surprising, given the ubiquity of poll and survey results and their availability in Ireland since 1970, that there has been to date no academic book-length treatment of this topic. This situation is all the more surprising given the consensus among social scientists that Irish society has been transformed in fundamental ways in the last three decades. Almost all agree that public opinion has changed, and yet there have been no comprehensive studies of what the opinion poll data tells us about this process. This book has tried (a) to fill this gap; (b) contribute to a greater understanding of Irish society; and (c) provide some guidance on interpreting and drawing inferences from poll data.

This concluding chapter is structured as follows. The opening section will discuss the evidence presented on how opinions on different facets of the same issue are often inconsistent – a pattern that is a key puzzle within Irish public opinion. In the second section I will address the three main questions about the nature of Irish public opinion posed in the introductory chapter. The following section will review the utility of conceptualising opinion polls as providing a mirror and lamp on public opinion. The fourth section will outline the lessons learned in this book regarding what opinion polls can tell us about public opinion. Suggestions for future research are made in the penultimate section, and thereafter there are some concluding observations.

A Key Puzzle: Hard and Easy Facets of Public Opinion

A central puzzle of this book has been that public opinion towards specific issues such as abortion, divorce and Northern Ireland are characterised by what appear at first sight to be inconsistencies. In

Chapter 2 I developed from the Belief-Sampling Model of survey response the notion that many issues have hard and easy facets, and that poll questions tap into these differences. The existence of inconsistent responses to different facets of an issue represents an opportunity to develop a greater understanding of the process of survey response, and also of the nature of public opinion.

The simultaneous presence of hard and easy facets for a variety of issues reveals that the Irish public do not always have single all-encompassing views on specific topics. In effect, different poll questions, or indeed the same poll question in a different historical context, elicit different considerations from respondents and hence different answers. I demonstrated the utility of the hard/easy distinction (or degree of hardness) in all of the substantive chapters of this book. For example, Chapter 5 reveals that support for the principle of a complete ban on legalising divorce and abortion (easy facets) shows considerable stability. In contrast, public opinion towards legislating on these issues (hard facets) has exhibited much more variation over time.

In addressing this public opinion puzzle through use of the hard/easy concept I have highlighted a central theme within all public opinion research – the importance of citizen knowledge. A central debate within public opinion since the 1960s has been the assertion made by Converse (1964) that most citizens answer survey questions on political issues in a largely random manner because they are uninformed. Our demonstration of knowledge effects on different facets of the same issue reveals that this Non-Attitudes Model (introduced in Chapter 2) oversimplifies the nature of the survey response process. In short, interpretation of opinion poll results and understanding what they tell us about public opinion necessitates having some insight into how respondents provide answers during poll interviews.

The What, How and Why Questions of Irish Public Opinion

At the outset of this book I formulated three questions that I hoped to answer in my investigation of Irish opinion polling data. In effect, the 'what' question refers to the mirror function of polls, while the 'how' and 'why' questions refer to a potential lamp function. The strategy here is to provide, through brief examples from the research undertaken in chapters 1 through 8, answers to these 'big' questions.

What is public opinion in Ireland on a variety of issues?

In this book there has been an exploration of public opinion relating to political matters, the liberal agenda, Northern Ireland, the economy and the European Union. In Chapter 3 opinion poll data were used to construct a portrait of how vote intentions for the three main parties evolve during a generic election cycle, and how this matches with electoral behaviour. We revealed that public opinion prior to elections is different from that observed during interelection periods. This effect appears to be greatest *prior* to general election campaigns, implying that the 'information effects' hypothesis of Gelman and King (1993) works somewhat differently in the Irish case.

Political satisfaction ratings also exhibit some interesting characteristics: satisfaction ratings for party leaders, the Government and vote intentions for government parties all co-vary together. This implies that during mainly interelection periods there is a political 'mood' that causes all the key political indicators to rise and fall together. In historical terms, it is important to note that the lowest political ratings occurred during the economic recession of the 1980s.

More generally, public opinion in Ireland in the domains analysed may be summarised as follows. On moral issues the Irish public has become more liberal on questions such as legalising divorce and homosexuality. This is not to deny that there are still strong public divisions on issues such as abortion. With regard to Northern Ireland the Irish public favours the peace process, but still aspires to a united Ireland. In economic matters, public opinion towards the economy is centrist in orientation and baulks at suggestions of increasing taxation to improve social services.[1] Yet the Irish public does favour policies that promote greater equality. For this reason, opinions associated with the concept of left–right orientation in Ireland do not appear to follow a pattern evident in much cross-national research.[2] Furthermore, Irish public opinion towards the European Union is in overall terms positive. Nevertheless, there is some suspicion that this may be a feature of the specific questions implemented most frequently in the standard Eurobarometer surveys.

How does Irish public opinion evolve over time and what factors help explain opinion stability and change?

One of the main reasons underlying interest in public opinion polls is the contention that Irish citizens' opinions have changed since

1970. Throughout this book I have demonstrated that evaluating whether public opinion has changed is not a straightforward task. In Chapter 2 it was noted that opinion poll measurement often comes with bias and error. As a result, questionnaire effects can give the appearance of opinion change where the poll results are reflecting, for example, priming or question order effects.

Moreover, in Chapter 3 it was revealed that responses to vote intention questions evolve during the election cycle as interest in politics waxes and wanes. Hence the undecided rate in polls follows a particular (quadratic/cubic) pattern, as does the accuracy of poll estimates, and the correlation between poll data and actual voting patterns. In addition, use of the hard/easy concept for distinguishing between different facets of an issue highlights that comparison of poll questions requires considerable care. I noted in Chapter 6 that use of opinion poll results on different facets of an issue to construct a single trend series can be misleading.

In Chapter 5 I made the important point that opinion change measured at the aggregate level in mass surveys can stem from at least two sources. First, citizens do in fact change their opinions because of historically important events (that is, period effects giving rise to intracohort change). Second, there is opinion change because the 'public' changes due to generational replacement. Here the opinions of older cohorts literally die out and are replaced by the different opinions of a new generation. If all public opinion change is explained by generational replacement this means there is no opinion change at the individual level. There are of course more complicated patterns of opinion stability and change, but these two mechanisms suffice to explain the patterns observed in the data examined.

Why does Irish public opinion exhibit certain patterns?

While the primary goal of most IMS, Lansdowne and MRBI polls is to mirror public opinion, there is nevertheless always some aspiration to explain why certain opinions prevail. In Chapters 5 and 6 it was revealed that many of the explanations of public opinion towards the liberal agenda and Northern Ireland reflect the impact of age. Here the effects of socialisation would appear to be particularly important. In both of these chapters I demonstrated that opinions do differ systematically on the basis of age. Moreover, through simple cohort analysis in Chapter 5 it was possible to estimate how much observed opinion change was due to variation in the socialisation processes (represented by opinion differences among younger and older age cohorts) and how much was due to the impact of events (period effects). In this chapter, it was discovered that most opinion change on liberal agenda issues resulted from intracohort effects where the imprint of socialisation processes is not indelible.

The evidence presented in Chapter 7 shows that opinion change can be obscured by technical features of the surveying process, where changes in surveying company were accompanied by an alteration in responses to the left–right self-placement question. Moreover, this chapter also reveals that the inconsistency in polls may be accurately mirroring public preferences, that is, leftist on economic equality issues and what would be considered rightist on trade-offs between increased taxation and social spending.[3] In this respect, an imbroglio of methodological, conceptual and theoretical issues highlight once again the care and caution required when dealing with mass survey data.

In Chapter 8 I demonstrated that, although electoral support for integration declined significantly between 1972 and 2002, Eurobarometer measures of public support for the EU illustrate a sharp increase. Nevertheless, the evidence presented showed that Eurobarometer estimates of support for integration are tapping primarily into economic sentiments. As a result the standard Eurobarometer measures may be giving us a biased view of Irish public opinion towards the EU. Moreover, this empirical finding may help to explain the contrasting trends noted between the electoral and survey data. Overall the evidence presented in this chapter underscores the need for caution when interpreting single-item measures of opinions towards complex issues such as the EU.

The Mirror and Lamp Conceptualisation of Opinion Polls

Within this book considerable use has been made of the idea of conceptualising opinion polls as providing a means of describing and analysing public opinion. These mirror and lamp functions are not completely distinct and separate, but address different characteristics of the polling process. Comparison of commercial and academic surveys helped us to see that decisions relating to questionnaire design and frequency of surveying underscore the important fact that polls are designed with specific functions in mind. In general terms, commercial polls published in the media aim primarily to mirror public opinion on a frequent basis. In contrast, academic polls focus on illuminating the interrelationship between attitudes and values, and do so relatively infrequently (annually or less often).

In Chapter 2 I linked the mirror function of opinion polls to conceptualisations of how respondents answer questions during poll interviews. Here I contrasted the Mirror Theory of Opinion Polling with the Belief-Sampling Model, and tried to demonstrate that viewing the function of opinion polls as mirroring the preferences within society has important consequences for what opinion polls can tell us about public opinion. On many occasions within this research I have demonstrated that the Mirror Theory of Opinion Polling yields an unrealistic view of how citizens answer poll questions.

When examining the electoral behaviour of the Irish public and the results of opinion polls in Chapter 3, there was an extension of the mirror/lamp conceptualisation of mass surveys through the introduction of the concepts of mirror accuracy and lamp precision. These concepts proved very useful in directing the research strategy adopted. Furthermore, we discovered that Irish opinion polls in mirror accuracy terms suffer from bias, while our investigation of lamp precision highlighted important partisan differences and shed light on the dynamics of how party support evolves during the election cycle.

Within the four substantive chapters I made strong use of another important distinction – hard and easy questions – and demonstrated that in order for polls to reflect public opinion effectively, considerable care is required when interpreting mass survey questions. Furthermore, such research highlighted that understanding that issues have different facets not only improves a researcher's ability to mirror public opinion, but also explains why different facets exhibit different levels of support. In Chapter 8 I went one step further and illustrated through the use of multi-question measures of public sentiment towards the European Union how construction of complex 'mirrors' offers the possibility of shining a much more powerful lamp on the profile of public support for integration.

Overall, the policy of conceptualising opinion polls as mirrors and lamps of public opinion has shown itself to be a fruitful strategy for three reasons. First, it helps to summarise in a succinct manner the key functions of opinion polls and how they are connected to public opinion. Second, this conceptualisation of opinion polls has the distinct merit of providing a framework for structuring research – operationalising the dictum that 'good questions make good science'. Third, this perspective underscored the importance of seeing opinion polls and the polling process in an interrelated way, where assessment of data quality involves having an appreciation of how respondents answer questions during poll interviews.

What can Opinion Polls tell us about Irish Public Opinion?

The central question addressed in this book is the connection between opinion polls and public opinion. This is a fundamentally important consideration because of the association in Ireland since 1977 of opinion poll results with 'public opinion' and their perceived legitimacy as being a 'voice of the people' (note Blumer 1948; Rogers 1949; Bourdieu 1979; Converse 1987; Herbst 1993). Even if one is willing to accept this conflation of mass survey results with public opinion, there still remains the key question of how to interpret poll results.

One common perspective – the Mirror Theory of Opinion Polling – simply takes poll results at face value, where survey questions are seen as providing factual information that mirrors the true opinions of the public. The big assumption here, as I noted in Chapter 2, is that respondents when interviewed do have 'real' opinions. There is much evidence to suggest that this is an unrealistic assumption where respondents quite often provide answers to poll questions from the 'top of their head'. In short, there is a danger in making a simple association between opinion poll results and public opinion. The weaknesses of the polling process cannot simply and uncritically be attributed to 'public opinion' writ large (note Albig 1956).

These are no mere idle academic or technical preoccupations, because the concept of public opinion lies at the heart of all forms of democratic governance (MacKinnon 1828; Bryce 1888; Dahl 1989; Habermas 1962; Cutler 1999). If opinion polls suggest that citizens have little interest in public affairs and lack a basic knowledge of politics, should this be used as a basis for concluding that democracy is an ineffective form of governance? It is when we consider the role of opinion polling from this perspective that we see how important it is to understand what opinion polls tell us about public opinion.

Within this book I have examined this general question within the context of the opinion polling process in the Republic of Ireland. For this reason the scope of this book has concentrated on the fundamental task of mapping out the capacity of Irish opinion polls to measure public opinion. As I noted in the Introduction, this involves consideration of four key components of the polling process.

Data component

The potential of opinion polls to tell us useful things about public opinion depends critically on the nature and extent of the polling data that are publicly available for scrutiny. In this book I have highlighted that the vast bulk of the polling data in Ireland exists in the form of *aggregate*-level reports that are primarily oriented towards eliciting vote intentions in the next general election and current levels of satisfaction with the Government and party leaders. In this respect, much of what we can learn about public opinion from polls has a strong electoral hue and relates to subgroups within society. As such, Irish opinion polls function as a mirror of limited scope and as a lamp of limited power when measuring public opinion. However, media-commissioned opinion polls are complemented by a growing number of academic survey datasets. With such data it is possible to construct and test individual level explanations, thereby providing answers as to why *individuals* hold specific attitudes.

Methodology component

A defining feature of what opinion polls can tell us about public opinion comes from the technical aspects of survey sampling and questionnaire construction. The findings from Chapters 1 and 2 indicate that the sampling error quoted in Irish polls is an overly conservative estimate of the likely error margin. Moreover, the record of the polls in making election predictions exhibits very significant bias for the 1997 and 2002 general elections. These methodological problems and related issues of polling accuracy reveal important concerns that have not been fully addressed by Irish pollsters. In this respect, issues such as adjusting vote intention estimates to correct for bias in misreported turnout and party choice remain thorny problems. Equally worrying has been the manner in which constituency-level polls have been reported in the media. Between 1999 and 2002 these polls were portrayed as simulations of the electoral system, predicting voter transfer patterns and likely candidate eliminations during specific counts. There seemed to be little understanding within the media of the technical problems associated with such polling enterprises.

More generally, the evidence presented in this book suggests that the poll data published in newspapers do not contain sufficient information to allow readers to properly evaluate the results. Typical issues of poll quality address questionnaire layout, type of question asked, response format employed and the coding scheme used for the classification for verbatim responses. One simple solution to this problem would be to place all of the relevant technical details and more extensive poll results on an internet website which interested citizens could consult. Such a strategy would underscore the professionalism and integrity of polling and media companies in their laudable endeavour of putting opinion poll results in the public domain as a service to citizens.

Substantive component

The type and range of issues examined in opinion polls determine what mass surveys can tell us about public opinion. Since the introduction of random sample polling by Gallup in the United States in the 1930s, public opinion polls, have been strongly associated with political issues. Irish polls like their counterparts elsewhere, have embraced this conceptualisation of public opinion polling. Consequently, the four substantive topics examined in this book – the liberal agenda, Northern Ireland, the economy and the European Union – have all been the subject of referendums or have been key issues in general election campaigns.

A typical strategy within polls is to use opinions on substantive issues to explain why there is observed change in vote intentions and political satisfaction ratings, that is, to explain increases or decreases in the levels recorded in the standard poll items. While the key advantage of opinion polls over academic surveys is their immediacy in measuring opinions close to important events, this focus on current events comes at a price. Commercial polls, unlike academic surveys, rarely measure underlying value orientations. However, I have shown that through careful examination of media-commissioned polling results it is nonetheless possible to learn quite a lot about the nature of Irish public opinion.

Theoretical component

Apart from election results there are very few readily available sources of information on what citizens think about issues of public concern. In this respect, opinion poll results not only reflect *what* public opinion is, but potentially tell us important things about *why* public opinion exhibits certain characteristics. By contrasting the Mirror Theory of Opinion Polling and the Belief-Sampling Model of survey response, we learned that the implicit and naive assumption that poll results represent 'true opinions' does not match with the capacities of real citizens. Therefore, our exploration of how respondents answer different kinds of poll questions reflects on varying levels of interest and knowledge about current affairs. I have built on this fact and developed the idea that poll questions that address different facets of an issue can be rated on the basis of their relative 'hardness' into two broad categories – hard and easy questions.

The evidence that has been presented to support this perspective gives us insight into the nature of public opinion. For example, the evidence presented in Chapter 7 demonstrates that there is no strong underlying opinion structure (such as a left–right ideological orientation) that links in a coherent manner many different opinions towards the economy. In short, the research in this book shows there is rarely a single 'public opinion' on an issue; rather, there are opinions on different facets of the same issue, and quite often these are qualitatively different in nature. Consequently, the 'inconsistency' within opinion poll data mirrors a fundamental feature of public opinion.

What's to be Done?

Much of the work undertaken in this book has been based on illustrating what IMS, Lansdowne and MRBI opinion polls tell about public opinion in Ireland. Where appropriate, academic surveys have been used to supplement this data and assist in our attempt to understand the results from the media-commissioned polls. In mapping out the data from these commercial surveys a lot of territory has been covered, and I have raised a number of questions for future research. In this respect, the following five topics represent some of the issues that promise to be fruitful lines of inquiry:

- A key message in this book has been that opinion poll data should not be taken at face value. In Chapter 2 I outlined a number of questionnaire design effects. There is undoubtedly scope for more

research in this area, as there has been little previous published work on this topic in Ireland.
- In Chapter 3 I examined changing levels of vote intentions for parties across the whole electorate. However, changing patterns of support among subgroups were not addressed. Future work to remedy this deficiency should explore the class basis of support for political parties in Ireland, as it has been over two decades since the last opinion poll-based study (Laver 1986b).
- The accuracy record of the polls examined in Chapter 3 suggests the need for more research on strategies that underpin vote intention estimates. The poll record suggests systematic bias in the results produced by IMS and MRBI for Fianna Fáil and Fine Gael. This is a fundamentally important opinion polling issue, and is likely to be the subject of 'internal' research in the run-up to future general elections.
- The time series analysis results in Chapter 4 suggest that political satisfaction ratings are more likely to be determined by economic factors than vote intentions for government parties. Testing the idea that economic conditions have a much stronger impact on government satisfaction than vote intentions for government parties would represent an extension of previous work by Borooah and Borooah (1990) and Harrison and Marsh (1998).
- In addition, more detailed future research could use subjective (for example, perceived improvements in household finances over the last year) rather than objective economic indicators such as unemployment rates. This proposal is based on research in the UK and elsewhere that has found that what the public think about the economy may be more important than what is 'objectively' happening (Sanders 2005: 176). In short, does the 'feel-good' factor have important effects on vote intention and political satisfaction ratings in Ireland over the long-term?

Of course, the scope for further research on public opinion increases dramatically once one begins to consider the opportunities offered by a growing number of academic surveys. For example, with the Eurobarometer dataset it would be interesting to extend the time series analysis undertaken in Chapter 8 to include many more member states, and assess the degree to which the patterns of support for integration in Ireland prevails elsewhere. Such an endeavour might prove to be a productive extension of current research on citizens' perceptions of EU institutions and the integration project.

Moreover, application of the cohort analysis techniques introduced in Chapter 5 to the study of support for integration offers some important research opportunities. For example, are changing attitudes towards the EU primarily driven by real opinion change or by generational replacement? Such work would shed light as to why many European citizens were unenthusiastic about ratifying the Constitutional Treaty, despite its endorsement by member state governments.

Concluding Remarks

Opinion poll results play an important role within Irish society by providing a conduit through publication in the media for communication between citizens and their political representatives. Therefore, opinion polls complement the electoral process by giving a voice to citizens during interelection periods. As Gallup and Rae argued in the opening quotation to this chapter, opinion polls do have a unique potential to highlight to elites the desired goals and values in society, without necessarily claiming to have definitive answers on specific policy-making questions. Of course, the opinion polling process is part of a two-way flow of communication.

Quite often the sentiments expressed in poll results are acknowledged as a signal of public satisfaction or disquiet. However, there have been two occasions where political leaders have disliked the message carried in opinion polls and decided to change the law on opinion polling. The immediate motivation behind the Government's most recent attempt to ban pre-election polls in June 2001 (undertaken within one week of a by-election defeat where there had been criticism of a TG4/MRBI constituency poll) appeared to stem from wanting to 'shoot the messenger' when faced with unpalatable electoral messages (see Jones 2001: 298–302).

Fortunately, flaws in the proposed legislation led to an abandonment of the plan. Such episodes reveal that Article 40.6.1° of Bunreacht na hÉireann (the Irish Constitution) that guarantees citizens the right to freely express opinions in public is not fixed in stone. New legislation regulating opinion polling has the potential to undermine this important constitutional provision and facet of Irish liberal democracy.

However, some Irish pollsters' recent practice of claiming to be able to simulate an election count within a constituency poll using just 400 respondents undermines the credibility of legitimate polling.

This is an example of Gresham's law (of monetary economics), where 'bad' polls have the capacity to drive 'good' ones from the market (Yankelovich 1991: 23). In short, the potential of opinion polls to speak to us about Irish public opinion requires a critical understanding of what polls can and cannot do. The bottom line is that not all opinion polls are the same and poll results do vary in quality. It is hoped this book contributes in some small measure to increased understanding of this important fact.

Notes

1. The data presented in Figures 29, 30 and 31 suggests a centre-left orientation, as the modal response on left–right self-placement scales since late 1989 has been point 5 where left=1 and right=10. More generally, a plurality of respondents have always chosen a centrist option, i.e. points 5 and 6 on the left–right 10-point scale.
2. However, whether the Irish attitudes on issues associated with the left–right concept are significantly different to those measured elsewhere is an important question that could not be addressed within the constraints imposed on a chapter-length treatment of general attitudes towards the economy. Nevertheless, it is undoubtedly an important topic for future research and a reappraisal of Ireland's reputation as a *sui generis* case in comparative political research.
3. Care in interpretation is required here; as panel (a) of Figure 28 shows, there is little correlation within Irish public opinion between left–right self-placement and position of level of taxation and level of public spending. The term 'rightist' here refers to a conventional scholarly analysis.

References

Abramson, P. R. *Political Attitudes in America* (San Francisco: Freeman, 1983).

Achen, C. H. 'Mass Political Attitudes and the Survey Response', *American Political Science Review*, 69 (1975) pp.1218–23.

Achen, C. H. 'Why Lagged Dependent Variables can Suppress the Explanatory Power of Other Independent Variables', paper presented at the annual meeting of the Political Methodology section of the American Political Science Association (Washington DC, 2000).

Albig, W. *Modern Public Opinion*)New York: McGraw-Hill, 1956).

Althaus, S. *Collective Preference in Democratic Politics: Opinion Surveys and the Will of the People* (Cambridge: Cambridge University Press, 2003).

Alvarez, R. M. *Information and Elections* (Ann Arbor University of Michigan Press, 1997).

Alvarez, R. M. and Brehm, J. *Hard Choices, Easy Answers: Values Information, Information, and American Public Opinion* (Princeton Princeton University Press, 2002).

Anderson, C. J. and Reichert, M. S. 'Economic Benefits and Support for Membership in the EU: A Cross-national Analysis', *Journal of Public Policy*, (1996), 15, 231–49.

Anderson C. J. 'When in Doubt, Use Proxies: Attitudes Towards Domestic Politics and Support for European Integration', *Comparative Political Studies*, 31(5), (1998), pp.569–601.

Arceneaux, K. 'Do Campaigns Help Voters Learn? A Cross-national Analysis', *British Journal of Political Science*, 36(1), (2006), pp.159–73.

Beck, N. 'Comparing Dynamic Specifications: The Case of Presidential Approval', *Political Analysis*, 3, (1991), pp.51–88.

Benoit, K. and Laver, M. *Party Policy Positions in Modern Democracies* (London: Routledge, 2006).

Blondel, J., Svensson, P. and Sinnott, R. *People and Parliament in the European Union: Democracy, Participation and Legitimacy* (Oxford: Oxford University Press, 1998).

Blumer, H. 'Public opinion and public opinion polling', *American Sociological Review*, 13(5), (1948), pp.542–9.

Borooah, V. and Borooah, V. K. 'Economic performance and political popularity in the Republic of Ireland', *Public Choice*, 67, (1990), pp.65–79.

Bourdieu, P. 'Public Opinion Does Not Exist', in Matelart, A. and Siegelaub, S. (eds), *Communication and Class Struggle* (vol. 1). (New York: International General, 1979, pp. 124–30).

Bradburn, N. M. 'Presidential Address: A Response to the Nonresponse Problem', *Public Opinion Quarterly*, 56, (1992), pp.391–97.

Breen, R. and Whelan, C. T. 'Social class, class origins and political partisanship in the Republic of Ireland', *European Journal of Political Research*, 26, (1994), pp.117–33.

Brehm, J. *The Phantom Respondents: Opinions Surveys and Political Representation* (Ann Arbor, University of Michigan Press, 1993).

Breslin, A. and Weafer, J. *Religious Beliefs, Practices and Moral Attitudes. A Comparison of Two Irish Surveys, 1974–1984.* (Maynooth: Council for Research and Development, 1985).

Brinegar, A., Jolly, S. K. and Kitschelt, H. 'Varieties of capitalism and political divides over integration', in, Marks, G. and Steenbergen, M. R. (eds), *European Integration and Political Conflict*. (Cambridge: Cambridge University Press, 2004, pp. 62–92).

Bryce, J. *The American Commonwealth*, 2 vols (Indianapolis, Liberty Fund (1888) 1995).

Buchanan, W. 'Election predictions: an empirical assessment', *Public Opinion Quarterly*, 50(2), (1986), pp.222–7.

Budge, I., Robertsonm D. and Hearl, D. *Ideology Strategy and Party Change: Spatial Analyses of Post-War Election Programmes in 19 Democracies (*Cambridge: Cambridge University Press, 1987).

Budge, I., Klingemann, H. D., Volkens, A., Bara, J. and Tannenbaum, E. *Mapping Policy Preferences: Parties, Electors and Governments: 1947–1998* (Oxford: Oxford University Press, 2001).

Carey, S., 'Undivided Loyalties: Is National Identity an Obstacle to European Integration?' *European Union Politics*, 3, (2002), pp.387–413.

Carmines, E. G. and Stimson, J. A. 'The Two Faces of Issue Voting', *American Political Science Review*, 74(1), (1980), pp.78–91.

Carmines, E. G. and Stimson, J. A. *Issue Evolution: Race and the Transformation of American Politics* (Princeton: Princeton University Press, 1989).

Cassidy, E. G. (ed.), *Measuring Ireland: Discerning Values and Beliefs* (Dublin: Veritas, 2002a).

Cassidy, E. G. 'Modernity and Religion in Ireland: 1980–2000', in, Cassidy, E. G. *Measuring Ireland: Discerning Values and Beliefs*. (Dublin: Veritas, 2002b, pp.17–45).

Clarke, M. D., Ho, K. and Stewart, M. C. 'Major's Lesser (not minor) effects: prime ministerial approval and governing party support in Britain since 1979, *Electoral Studies*, 19(2), (2000), pp.255–73.
Coakley, J. 'Society and political culture', in, Coakley, J. and Gallagher, M. *Politics in the Republic of Ireland*, 4th edition (London: Routledge/PSAI Press, 2005a, pp.36–71).
Coakley, J. 'Irish public opinion and the new Europe', in, Holmes M. (ed.), *Ireland and the European Union: Nice, Enlargement and the Future of Europe* (Manchester: Manchester University Press, 2005b, pp.94–113).
Colwell, R. 'Telephone Polling – Fear of the Unknown', *The Sunday Business Post*, (23 May 2004, p. 12).
Converse, P. E. 'The Nature of Belief Systems in Mass Publics', in, Apter, D. E. (ed.), *Ideology and Discontent* (Glencoe: Free Press, 1964, pp. 206–61).
Converse, P. E. 'Attitudes and Non-attitudes: Continuation of a Dialogue', in, Tufte, E. (ed.) *The Quantitative Analysis of Social Problems* (Reading, MA: Addison-Wesley, 1970), pp.168–89.
Converse, P. E. *The Dynamics of Party Support: Cohort-Analyzing Party Identification* (London: Sage Library of Social Research, vol. 35, 1976).
Converse, P. E. 'Changing Conceptions of Public Opinion in the Political Process', *Public Opinion Quarterly*, 51, (1987), S12–24.
Converse, P. E. 'Popular Representation and the Distribution of Information', in, Ferejohn, J. A. and Kuklinski, J. H. (eds), *Information and Democratic Processes* (Urbana University of Illinois Press, 1990, pp. 368–88).
Coulter, C. '"Hello Divorce, Goodbye Daddy": Women, Gender and the Divorce Debate', in, Bradley, A. and Valiulis, M. G. *Gender and Sexuality in Modern Ireland* (Amherst University of Massachusetts Press, 1997), pp. 275–98.
Cox, M., Guelke, A. and Stephen, F. (eds), *A Farewell to Arms? From 'Long War' to Long Peace in Northern Ireland* (Manchester: Manchester University Press, 2002).
Crespi, I. 'The Case of Presidential Popularity', in, Cantril, A. W. (ed.), *Polling on the Issues* (Washington DC: Seven Locks Press, 1980), pp. 28–45.
Curtin, R., Presser, S. and Singer, E. 'The effects of response rate changes on the index of consumer sentiment', *Public Opinion Quarterly*, 64(4), (2000), pp.413–28.
Cutler, F. 'Jeremy Bentham and the Public Opinion Tribunal', *Public Opinion Quarterly*, 63, (1999), pp.321–46.
Dahl, R. A. *Democracy and its Critics* (New Haven, CT: Yale University Press, 1989).
Darcy, R. and Laver, M. 'Referendum dynamics and the Irish Divorce Amendment', *Public Opinion Quarterly*, 54, 1, (Spring 1990), pp.1–20.

Davis, E. E. and Sinnott, R. *Attitudes in the Republic of Ireland Relevant to the Northern Ireland Problem* (Dublin: ESRI Paper No. 97), 1979.

Deflem, M. and Pampel, F. 'The myth of postnational identity: Popular support for European unification', *Social Forces* 75(1), (1996), pp.119–43.

Eichenberg, R. C. 'Measures, Methods and Models in the Study of Public Opinion and European Integration, 1973–1977', paper presented at the American Political Science Association meetings (Boston, 1998).

Eichenberg, R. C. and Dalton R. J. 'Europeans and the European Community: The Dynamics of Public Support for European Integration', *International Organisation* 47(4), (Autumn 1993), pp.507–34.

Eijk, van der, C. 'Measuring Agreement in Ordered Rating Scales', *Quality and Quantity* 35(3), (August 2001), pp.327–41.

Eijk, van der, C., Franklin, M. N. et al., *Choosing Europe? The European Electorate and National Politics in the Face of Union* (Ann Arbor University of Michigan Press, 1996.

Elliot, D. 'The use of substitution in sampling', *Survey Methodology Bulletin* 33, (1993), pp.8–11.

Elliot, M. (ed.) *The Long Road to Peace in Northern Ireland.* (Liverpool: Liverpool University Press, 2002).

Erber, R. and Lau, R. R. 'Political Cynicism Revisited: An Information Processing Reconciliation of Policy Based and Incumbency Based Interpretations of Changes in Trust in Government', *American Journal of Political Science* 34(1), (1990), pp.236–53.

Erikson, R. S., MacKuen, M. B. and Stimson, J. A. *The Macro Polity* (Cambridge: Cambridge University Press, 2002).

Evans, G. and Sinnott, R. 'Political Cleavages and Party Alignments in Ireland, North and South', in, Heath, A. F., Breen, R. and Whelan, C. T. (eds) *Ireland North and South: Perspectives from Social Science* (Oxford: Oxford University Press, 1999, pp.419–56).

Fahey, T. 'Is Atheism Increasing? Ireland and Europe Compared', in, Cassidy, E. G. *Measuring Ireland: Discerning Values and Beliefs.* (Dublin: Veritas, 2002), pp. 45–66.

Fahey, T. and Williams, J. 'The Spatial Distribution of Disadvantage in Ireland', in, Nolan, B., O' Connell, P. J. and Whelan, C. T. *Bust to Boom? The Irish Experience of Growth and Inequality* (Dublin: Institute of Public Administration, 2000), pp. 223–43.

Fahey, T., Hayes, B. C., Sinnott, R. *Conflict and Consensus: A Study of Values and Attitudes in the Republic of Ireland and Northern Ireland* (Dublin: Institute of Public Administration, 2005).

Farrell, B. 'Labour and the Irish Party System: A Suggested Approach to Analysis', *Economic and Social Review* 4, (1970), pp.477–502.

Feldman, S. 'Reliability and Stability of Policy Positions: Evidence from a Five-wave Panel', *Political Analysis* 1, (1989), pp.25–60.

Feldman, S. 'Answering Survey Questions: The Measurement and Meaning of Public Opinion', in, Lodge, M. and McGraw, K. M. (eds) *Political Judgment: Structure and Process* (Ann Arbor University of Michigan Press, 1995), pp. 249–70.
Fennell, D. *The Revision of Irish Nationalism* (Dublin: Open Air, 1989).
Finnegan, R. B. and McCarron, E. T. *Ireland: Historical Echoes, Contemporary Politics* (Boulder: Westview, 2000).
Firebaugh, G. 'Where Does Social Change Come From? Estimating the Relative Contributions of Individual Change and Population Turnover', *Population Research and Policy Review* 11,(1992), pp. 1–20.
Firebaugh, G. *Analyzing Repeated Surveys* (Thousand Oaks, CA: Sage [University series on quantitative applications in the social sciences, series no. 07–005], 1997).
FitzGerald, G. 'Tax System Exacerbates our Social Inequality', *The Irish Times*, 6 November 2004, p. 14.
Fogarty, M., Ryan, L., and Lee, J. *Irish Values and Attitudes: The Irish Report of the European Values Study System* (Dublin: Dominican Publications, 1984).
Franklin, M. N., Marsh, M. and McLaren, L. 'Uncorking the Bottle: Popular Opposition to European Unification in the Wake of Maastricht', *Journal of Common Market Studies*, 32(4), (1994), pp.455–72.
Franklin, M. N., Marsh, M. and Wlezien, C. 'Attitudes Towards Europe and Referendum Votes: A Response to Siune and Svennson', *Electoral Studies*, 13(2), (1994), pp.117–21.
Franklin, M. N., van der Eijk, C. and Marsh, M. 'Referendums Outcomes and Trust in Government: Public Support for Europe in the Wake of Maastricht', *West European Politics*, 18, (1995), pp.101–17.
Freeman, J. R. 'Granger Causality and the Time Series and Analysis of Political Relationships', *American Journal of Predicted Science*, 27(2), (1983), pp.327–58.
Freeman, J. R., Williams, J. T. and Lin, T. M. 'Vector autoregression and the study of politics, *American Journal of Political Science*, 1989, 33(4), 842–77.
Gabel, M. J., 'Public Opinion and European Integration: An Empirical Test of Five Theories', *Journal of Politics* 60, (May 1998a), pp.333–54.
Gabel, M. J. 'International Economics and Mass Politics: Market Liberalization and Public Support for European Integration', *American Journal of Political Science* 42, (July 1998b), pp.936–53.
Gabel, M. J. and Palmer, H. 'Understanding Variation in Public Support for European Integration', *European Journal of Political Research* 27, (Spring 1995), pp,3–19.
Gallagher, M. 'The Single European Act', *Irish Political Studies* 3, (1988), pp.77–82.
Gallagher, M. and Laver, M. (eds) *How Ireland Voted 1992* (Dublin: Folens and Limerick: PSAI Press, 1993).

Gallagher, M., Marsh, M. and Mitchell, P. *How Ireland Voted 2002* (Basingstoke: Palgrave Macmillan, 2003).

Gallup, G. H. and Rae, S. F. *The Pulse of Democracy* (New York: Simon & Schuster, 1940).

Garry, J. and Mansergh, L. 'Irish Party Manifestos in the 1997 General Election', in, Marsh, M. and Mitchell, P. (eds) *How Ireland Voted, 1997* (Boulder, Colorado: Westview, 1999).

Garry, J., 'Political Values and Vote Choice', in, Garry, J., Hardiman, N. and Payne, D. (eds) *Irish Social and Political Attitudes* (Liverpool: Liverpool University Press, 2006), pp. 60–77.

Garry, J., Kennedy, F., Marsh, M., and Sinnott, R. 'What Decided the Election?', in, Gallagher, M., Marsh, M. and Mitchell, P. *How Ireland Voted 2002* (Basingstoke: Palgrave Macmillan, 2003), pp. 119–42.

Garry, J., Hardiman, N. and Payne, D. (eds) *Irish Social and Political Attitudes* (Liverpool: Liverpool University Press, 2006).

Garvin, T. 'The politics of Denial and Cultural Defence', *The Irish Review*, 3, (1988), pp.1–7.

Gelman, A. and King, G. 'Why are Presidential Election Campaign Polls so Variable When Votes are so Predictable?', *British Journal of Political Science*, 23, (1993), pp.409–51.

Gilland, K. 'Referenda in the Republic of Ireland', *Electoral Studies*, 18(3), (1999), pp.430–8.

Gilland Lutz, K. 'Irish Party Competition in the New Millennium: Change, or Plus ça Change', *Irish Political Studies*, 18(2), (Winter 2003), pp.40–59.

Girvin, B. 'Social Change and Moral Politics: The Irish Constitutional Referendum of 1983', *Political Studies*, 34, (1986), pp.61–81.

Glenn, N. *Cohort Analysis* (Thousand Oaks, CA: Sage [University series on quantitative applications in the social sciences, series no. 07-005], 1977).

Groves, R. M. and Couper, M. P. *Non-response in Household Interview Surveys* (New York: Wiley, 1998).

Gujurati, D. N., *Basic Econometrics*, 3rd edition (New York: McGraw-Hill, 1995).

Habermas J. *The Structural Transformation of the Public Sphere.* (Cambridge, MA: MIT Press [1962] 1989).

Halligan, B. 'The Political Perspective in 1972', in, O'Donnell, R. (ed.) *Europe: The Irish Experience* (Dublin: Institute of European Affairs, 2000), pp. 18–34.

Hansen, M. H. and Hurwitz, W. N. 'On the Theory of Non-response in Sample Surveys', *Journal of the American Statistical Association* (1946, pp.517–29.

Hardiman, N. and Whelan, C. T. 'Changing Values', in, Crotty, W. E. and Schmitt, D. E. (ed.) *Ireland and the Politics of Change* (London: Longman, 1998), pp. 65–85.

Hardiman, N. and Whelan, C. T., 'Politics and democratic values', in, Whelan, C. T., *Values and Social Change in Ireland*. Dublin: Gill & Macmillan, 1994a), pp. 100–35.

Hardiman, N. and Whelan, C. T. 'Values and Political Partisanship', in Whelan, C. T. (ed) *Values and Social Change in Ireland* (Dublin: Gill and Macmillan, 1994b, pp. 136–86.

Harrison M. J. and Marsh M. 'A Re-examination of an Irish Popularity Function', *Public Choice*, (1998), pp.367–83.

Hayes, B. C. and McAllister, I. 'British and Irish Public Opinion Towards the Northern Ireland Problem', *Irish Political Studies* 11, (1996), pp.61–82.

Hayward, K. '"If at First you Don't Succeed...": The Second Referendum on the Treaty of Nice, 2002', *Irish Political Studies*, 18(1), (2003), pp.120–32.

Herbst, S. *Numbered Voices: How Opinion Polling has Shaped American Politics* (Chicago: Chicago University Press, 1993).

Herrera, C., Herrera, R. and Smith, E. 'Public Opinion and Congressional Representation', *Public Opinion Quarterly*, 56, (1992), pp.187–205.

Hesketh, T. *The Second Partition of Ireland? The Abortion Referendum of 1983* (Dublin: Brandsma Books, 1990).

Hibbing, J. R, and Alford, J. R. 'The Electoral Impact of Economic Conditions: Who is Held Responsible?' *American Journal of Political Science*, 25, 3, pp.423–9

Hibbs, D. A. Jr. *The American Political Economy: Macroeconomics and Electoral Politics* (Cambridge, MA: Harvard University Press, 1987).

Hochschild, J. L. *What's Fair? American Beliefs about Distributive Justice* (Cambridge, MA: Harvard University Press, 1981).

Hoek, J. and Gendall, P. 'Factors Affecting Political Poll Accuracy: An Analysis of Undecided Respondents', *Marketing Bulletin* 7, (1996), pp.1–14.

Holbrook, A. L., Green, M. C. and Krosnick, J. A. 'Telephone vs. Face-to-face Interviewing of National Probability Samples with Long Questionnaires: Comparisons of Respondent Satisficing and Social Desirability Response Bias', *Public Opinion Quarterly*, 67, (2003), pp.79–125.

Holbrook, A. L., Krosnick, J. A. and Pfent A. M. 'Response Rates in Surveys by the News Media and Government Contractor Survey Research Firms', in Lepkowski, J., Harris-Kojetin, B. et al., (eds) *Telephone Survey Methodology* (New York: Wiley, 2007).

Holbrook, T. M. *Do Campaigns Matter?* (Thousand Oaks, CA: Sage [Contemporary American Politics Series], 1996).

Holmes, M. 'The Maastricht Treaty Referendum of June 1992', *Irish Political Studies*, 8, (1995), pp.105–10.

Holt, C. C., Modigliani, F., Muth, J. F. and Simon, H. *Planning Production, Inventories and Workforce* (Englewood Ciffs, MJ: Prentice-Hall, 1960).

Hornsby-Smith, M. and Whelan, C. T. 'Religious and moral values', in Whelan, C. T. (ed) *Values and Social Change in Ireland* (Dublin: Gill & MacMillan, 1994, pp. 7–44).

Huber, J. and Bingham Powell, G. 'Congruence Between Citizens and Policymakers in Two Visions of Liberal Democracy', *World Politics*, 46(3), (1994), pp.291–326.

Hug, C. *The Politics of Sexual Morality in Ireland* (London: Macmillan Press Ltd., 1999).

Inglehart, R. 'Cognitive Mobilization and European Identity', *Comparative Politics* 3, (1970), pp.45–70.

Inglehart, R. *Culture Shift* (Princeton: Princeton University Press, 1990).

Inglis, T. *Lessons in Irish Sexuality* (Dublin: University College Dublin Press, 1998a).

Inglehart R. and Klingemann, M. D. 'Party Identification, Ideological Preferences and Left–Right Dimensions Among Western Publics', in Budge, J., Crewe, J. and Farlie, D. (eds) *Party Identification and Beyond* (New York: John Wiley, 1976).

Inglis, T. *Moral Monopoly: the Rise and Fall of the Catholic Church in Modern Ireland* (2nd edition) (Dublin: University College Dublin Press [1987] 1998b).

Irish Marketing Surveys (IMS), RTE 'Survey' – Politics, a report based on IMS survey RJA/sr/CMC/md/J.3201/2 undertaken between 30 August and 8 September 1976. (IMS: Dublin, 1976).

Jones, J. *In Your Opinion: Political and Social Trends in Ireland through the Eyes of the Electorate* (Dublin: Town House, 2001).

Jones, J. and O' Donoghue, A. 'New Adjustment', internal MRBI memorandum (Dublin: MRBI, no date).

Kalton, G. 'Practical Methods for Estimating Survey Sampling Errors', *Bulletin of the International Statistical Institute* 47(3), (1977), pp.495–514.

Keeter, S, Miller, C. Kohut, A., Groves, R. M. and Presser, S. 'Consequences of Reducing Non-response in a National Telephone Survey', *Public Opinion Quarterly* (1977), 64(2), (1977), pp.125–48.

Kennedy, F. 'Abortion referendum 2002', *Irish Political Studies*, 17(1), (2002), pp.114–28.

Kennedy, F., and Farrington, C. (eds) *Irish Political Studies Data Yearbook 2003* (Abingdon: Taylor & Francis, 2003).

Kennedy, F., and Farrington, C. (eds) *Irish Political Studies Data Yearbook 2003* (Abingdon: Routledge/Taylor & Francis, 2004).

Kennedy, F., Lyons, P. and Fitzgerald, P. 'Pragmatists, Ideologues and the General Law of Curvilinear Disparity: The Case of the Irish Labour Party', *Political Studies*, 54(4), (2006), pp.786–805.

Kennedy, F. and Sinnott, R. 'Irish Social Values and Political Cleavages', in Garry J., Hardiman N. and Payne D. (eds) *Irish Social and Political Attitudes* (Liverpool: Liverpool University Press, 2006), pp. 78–93.

Kennelly, B. and Ward, E. 'The Abortion Referendums', in Gallagher, M. and Laver, M. (eds) *How Ireland Voted 1992* (Dublin: Folens/PSAI Press, 1993), pp. 115–34.

Kinder, D. R. 'Communication and Opinion', *Annual Review of Political Science*, 1, (1998), pp.167–97.

Kinder, D. R. and Sanders, L. 'Mimicking Political Debate with Survey Questions: The Case of White Opinion on Affirmative Action for Blacks', *Social Cognition*, 8, (1990), pp.73–103.

King, A., Wybrow, R. J. and Gallup, A. *British Political Opinion 1937–2000: The Gallup Polls* (London: Politico's Publishing, 2001).

King, G. *A Solution to the Ecological Inference Problem: Reconstructing Individual Behaviour from Aggregate Data* (Princeton, NJ: Princeton University Press, 1997).

King, G., Keohane, R.O., Verba, S. *Designing Social Inquiry: Scientific Inference in Qualitative Research* (Princeton, NJ: Princeton University Press, 1994).

Kish, L. *Survey Sampling* (New York: John Wiley and Sons, 1965).

Laffan, B. 'Ireland and Europe: Continuity and Change, The Irish Presidency', Groupement d'étude de recherches, Notre Europe, *Research and European Issues*, 30 (December 2003).

Lane, R. E. *Political Ideology: Why the American Common Man Believes What He Does* (New York: Free Press, 1962).

Lane, R. E. and Sears, D. O. *Public Opinion* (Englewood Cliffs, NJ: Prentice Hall, 1964).

Larkin, E. 'The Devotional Revolution in Ireland, 1850–1875', *American Historical Review*, LXXVII, (1972), pp.625–52.

Lau, R. R. 'An analysis of the Accuracy of 'Trial Heat' Polls During the 1992 Presidential Election', *Public Opinion Quarterly*, 58(1), (1994), pp.220.

Lau, R. R. 'Models of decision-making', in Sears, D. O., Huddy, L. and Jervis, R. (eds) *Oxford Handbook of Political Psychology* (Oxford: Oxford University Press, 2003), pp. 19–59.

Laver, M. 'Ireland: Politics with some Social Bases: An Interpretation Based on Aggregate Data', *The Economic and Social Review* (April 17(2), 1986a), pp.107–31.

Laver, M. 'Ireland: Politics with *Some* Social Bases: An Interpretation Based on Survey Data', *The Economic and Social Review*, 17(3), (April 1986b), pp.193–213.

Laver, M. 'Party Policy in Ireland 1997, Results from an Expert Survey', *Irish Political Studies*, 13, (1998), pp.159–171.

Laver, M., Mair, P. and Sinnott R. (eds), *How Ireland Voted: The General Election of 1987*. (Dublin: Poolbeg Press, 1987).

Laver, M. 'Voting behaviour', in Coakley, J. and Gallagher, M. (eds) *Politics in the Republic of Ireland*, 4th edition (London: Routledge, 2005), pp. 183–210.

Laver, M. and Hunt, W .B. *Policy and Party Competition* (London: Routledge, 1992).
Leddin, A.J. and Walsh, B.M., *The Macro-Economy of Ireland* (4th Edition). (Dublin: Gill and Macmillan, 1998).
Lee, J. J. *Ireland 1912–1985: Politics and Society* (Cambridge: Cambridge University Press, 1989).
Leeuw, de E. and de Heer, W. 'Trends in Household Survey Nonresponse: a longitudinal and international comparison', in Groves, R. M., Dillman, D. A. et al. (eds) *Survey Nonresponse* (New York: John Wiley & Sons), pp. 41–54.
Levy, P. S. and Lemeshow, S. *Sampling Populations: Methods and Applications* (3rd edition) (New York: John Wiley and Sons, 1999).
Lewis-Beck, M. S. (ed) *Factor Analysis and Related Techniques*. (International Handbooks of Quantitative Applications in the Social Sciences, vol. 5) (London: Sage Publications, Toppan Publishing, 1994).
Lewis-Beck, M. S. and Peldam, M. *Introduction: Economics and Elections, Electoral Studies* (special issue), 19, 2–3 (2000), pp.113–21.
Lindberg, L. N. and Scheingold, S. A. *Europe's Would-Be Polity: Patterns of Change in the European Community* (Englewood Cliffs, NJ: Prentice-Hall Inc., 1970).
Lippmann, W. *Public Opinion* (New York: Free Press [1922] 1965).
Lipset, S. M. and Rolckan, S. 'Introduction', in Lipset, S. M. and Rolckan, S. (eds) *Party Systems and Voter Alignments: Cross-National Perspectives* (New York: The Free Press, 1967), pp. 1–64.
Loosveldt, G. 'The Profile of the Difficult to Interview Respondent', *Bulletin de Méthodologie Sociologique* (September 1995), 68–81.
Losch, M. E., Maitland, E., Lutz, G. et al. 'The Effect of Time of Year of data collection on sample efficiency: an analysis of Behavior Risk Factor Surveillance Survey Data', *Public Opinion Quarterly* 66, (2002), pp.594–607.
Lyberg, L. 'Review of IALS: A Commentary on the Technical report', in Carey, S., Bridgwood, A. and Thomas, M. (eds) *Measuring Adult Literacy: The International Adult Literacy Survey in the European Context* (London: Office for National Statistics, 2000).
Lyons, P. 'Public Opinion in the Republic of Ireland – 2001', *Irish Political Studies*, 17, (2002), pp.4–16.
Lyons, P. 'Public opinion in the Republic of Ireland – 2002', *Irish Political Studies*, 18, (2003), pp.6–23.
McAllister, I. and O' Connell, D. 'The Political Sociology of Party Support in Ireland: A Reassessment', *Comparative Politics* (1984), pp.191–204.
McAllister, I., 'Prime Ministers, Opposition Leaders and Government Popularity in Australia, *Australian Journal of Political Sciences*, 38, 2, (2003), pp.259–77.

McCarty, C. 'Differences in Response Rates using Most Recent Versus Final Dispositions in Telephone Surveys', *Public Opinion Quarterly*, 67(4), (2003), pp.396–407.

McCloskey, H., Hoffman, P. J., O'Hara, R. 'Issue Conflict and Consensus Among Party Leaders and Followers', *American Political Science Review*, 59, (1960), pp.406–27.

McElroy, G. and Marsh, M. 'Why the Opinion Polls got it Wrong in 2002', in Gallagher, M., Marsh, M. and Mitchell, P. (eds) *How Ireland Voted 2002* (Basingstoke: Palgrave Macmillan, 2003), pp.159–76.

McElroy, G. and Marsh, M., 'The Polls – A Clear Improvement', in Gallagher, M. and Marsh, M. (eds) *How Ireland Voted 2007: The Full Story of Ireland's General Election* (Basingstoke: Palgrave Macmillan, 2008), pp. 132–47.

McLaren, L. 'Public Support for European Integration: Cost/benefit Analysis or Perceived Cultural Threat', *Journal of Politics*, 64, (2002), pp.551–66.

Mac Gréil, M. *Prejudice and Tolerance in Ireland, Based on Intergroup Attitudes and Prejudices of a Random Sample of Dublin Urban and Suburban Adults* (New York: Praeger, 1980).

Mac Gréil, M. *Prejudice in Ireland Revisited, Based on a National Survey of Intergroup Attitudes in the Republic of Ireland* (Survey & Research Unit, St. Patrick's College, Maynooth, Co. Kildare, 1996).

MacKinnon, W. A., *On the Rise, Progress, and Present State of Public Opinion, in Great Britain, and other Parts of the World*. Shannon: Irish University Press, (1828) 1971.

MacSharry, R. and White, P. *The Making of the Celtic Tiger, the Inside Story of Ireland's Boom Economy* (Dublin: Mercier Press, 2000).

Mair, P. 'Locating Irish Parties on a Left–Right Scale: An Empirical Inquiry', *Political Studies*, XXXIV, (1986), pp.456–465.

Mansergh, L. 'Two Referendums and the Referendum Commission: the 1998 experience', *Irish Political Studies*, 14, (1999), pp.123–31.

Manski, C. F. *Identification Problems in the Social Sciences* (Cambridge, MA: Harvard University Press, 1995).

Marks, G. and Hooghe, L. 'National Identity and Support for European Integration', discussion paper SP IV 2003-2 (Wissenschaftenzentrum Berlin für Sozialforschung (WZB), 2003).

Marks, G. and Steenbergen, M. R. (eds) *European Integration and Political Conflict* (Cambridge: Cambridge University Press, 2004).

Marsh, M. and Mitchell, P. (eds) *How Ireland Voted 1997* (Boulder, CO: Westview Press, 1999).

Marsh, M. and Sinnott, R. 'The Behaviour of the Irish Voter', in Marsh, M. and Mitchell, P. (eds) *How Ireland Voted 1997* (Boulder, CO: Westview Press, 1999), pp. 151–80.

Marsh, M. Sinnott, R., Garry, J. and Kennedy, F. 'The Irish National Election Study: Puzzles and Priorities', *Irish Political Studies* 16, (2001), pp.161–78.

Marsh, M., Sinnott, R., Garry, J. and Kennedy, F. *The Irish Voter* (Manchester: Manchester University Press, 2008).

Martin, E. 'Presidential Address: Unfinished Business', *Public Opinion Quarterly*, 68(3), (2004), pp.439–50.

Mayer, W. G. *The Changing American Mind: How and Why American Public Opinion Changed Between 1960 and 1988* (Ann Arbor, MI: The University of Michigan Press, 1992).

Meagher, J. F. 'Opinion Polling in Ireland', paper presented at the LVIII European Society for Opinion and Marketing Research (ESOMAR) – seminar on 'Opinion Polls' (Bonn/Bad Godesberg, Federal Republic of Germany, 23–26 January 1980), in conjunction with the World Association of Public Opinion Research (WAPOR).

Mills, T. C. *Time Series Analysis for Economists* (Cambridge: Cambridge University Press, 1998).

Mueller, J. E. 'Presidential Popularity from Truman to Johnson', *American Political Science Review*, 64, (1970), pp.18–34.

Nadeau, R., Niemi, R. and Timothy Amato, T. 'Prospective and Comparative or Retrospective and Individual? Party Leaders and Party Support in Great Britain', *British Journal of Political Science*, 26, 6, (1996), pp.245–58.

Nannestad, P. and Paldam, M. 'The VP-faction: A Survey of the Literature on Vote and Popularity Functions after 25 Years', *Public Choice*, 79, 3, (1994), pp.213–45.

Nic Ghiolla Phadraig, M. *Survey of Religious Beliefs and Practices in Ireland. Moral attitudes (3)* (Dublin: Research and Development Commission, 1976).

Niedermayer, O. 'Trends and Contrasts', in Niedermayer, O. and Sinnott, R. (eds) *Public Opinion and Internationalized Governance*, Beliefs in Government Series, vol. 2 (Oxford: Oxford University Press, 1995), pp. 53–72.

Niedermayer, O. and Sinnott, R. (eds), *Public Opinion and Internationalized Governance* (Beliefs in Government Series, vol. 2 (Oxford: Oxford University Press, 1995).

O' Brien, B. '10 Years Too Late to Start our Debate about EU', *The Irish Times*, 23 September 2000.

O' Carroll, J. P. 'Bishops, Kings and Pawn? Traditional Thought and the Irish Abortion Referendum Debate of 1983', *Irish Political Studies*, 6, (1991), pp.53–72.

O' Mahony, J. 'Not So Nice: The Treaty of Nice, the International Criminal Court, the Abolition of the Death Penalty – The 2001 Referendum Experience', *Irish Political Studies*, 16, (2001), pp.201–14.

O' Malley, E. and Kerby, M. 'Chronicle of a Death Foretold? Understanding the Decline of Fine Gael', *Irish Political Studies*, 19(1), (2004), pp.39–58.

Oscarsson, H. 'Mapping the European Party Space', unpublished manuscript (Göteborg University, Sweden, May 2002).

Paldam, M. 'The Distribution of Election Results and the Two Explanations of the Cost of Ruling', *European Journal of Political Economy*, 2(1), (1986), pp.5–24.

Paldam, M. 'How Robust is the Vote Function? A Study of Seventeen Nations over Four Decades', in Lewis-Beck, M. S. and Lafay, J. O. (eds) *Economics and Politics: The Calculus of Support* (Ann Arbor, MI: University of Michigan Press, 1991), pp. 273–313.

Penniman, H. R. (ed.) *Ireland at the Polls: the Dail Elections of 1977* (Washington, DC: American Enterprise Institute for Public Policy Research, 1978).

Penniman, H. R. and Farrell, B. M. *Ireland at the Polls 1981, 1982, and 1987: A Study of Four General Elections* (Durham, NC: Duke University Press for the American Enterprise Institute for Public Policy Research, 1987).

Penubarti, M. and Schuessler, A. A. 'Inferring micro- from macrolevel change', working paper (New York University Politics Center, New York, 1999).

Pollock, P. H., Lilie, S. A. and Vittes, M. E. 'Hard Issues, Core Values and Vertical Constraint: The Case of Nuclear Power', *British Journal of Political Science*, 23(1), (1993), pp.29–50.

Raven, J. and Whelan, C. T. 'Irish Adults Perceptions of their Civil Institutions and their Role in Relation to them', in, Raven, J., Whelan, C. T., Pfretzschner, P. A. and Borock, D. M. *Political Culture in Ireland: the View of Two Generations* (Dublin: Institute of Public Administration, 1976).

Reidy, E. T. 'Economic Voting in Ireland, 1976–1998', unpublished MSc thesis (submitted to the Department of Government, University College Cork, October 2000).

Reif, K. 'National Election Cycles and European Elections, 1979 and 1984', *Electoral Studies*, 3, 3, (1984), pp.244–55.

Reif, K. and Schmitt, H. 'Nine Second-order National Elections: A Conceptual Framework for the Analysis of European Election Results', *European Journal of Political Research*, 8, 3–4, (1980), pp.3–44.

Rogers, L. *The Pollsters: Public Opinion, Politics and Democratic Leadership* (New York: Alfred A. Knopf, 1949).

Rohrschneider, R. 'The Democratic Deficit and Mass Support for an EU-wide Government', *American Journal of Political Science*, 46, (2002), pp.463–75.

Rose, R., McAllister, I. and Mair, P. 'Is there a Concurring Majority about Northern Ireland', Studies in Public Policy, working paper No. 22 (University of Strathclyde: Centre for the Study of Public Policy, 1978).

Ruane, F. and O'Toole, F. 'Taxation Measures and Policy', in O'Hagan, J. W. *The Economy of Ireland: Policy and Performances of a Small Country* (Dublin: Goll and Macmillan, 1995, pp. 127–58).

Sanders, D. 'Popularity Function Forecasts for the 2005 UK General Election', *British Journal of Politics and International Relations*, 7, (2005), pp. 174–90.
Scheaffer, R. L. Mendenhall, W. and Ott, L. *Elementary Survey Sampling* (4th edition) (Belmont, CA: Duxbury Press, 1990).
Schmitt, D. E. 'Conclusion: Continuity, Change and Challenge', in Crotty, W. and Schmitt, D. E. (eds) *Ireland and the Politics of Change* (London: Longman, 1998, pp. 210–33).
Schuessler, A. A. 'Ecological Inference', *Proceedings of the National Academy of Sciences* 96, (1999), pp.10578–81.
Schuman, H. and Presser, S. *Questions and Answers in Attitude Surveys: Experiments on Question Form, Wording and Context* (Thousand Oaks, CA: Sage, [1981] 1996a).
Seawright, J. and Brady, M. E. 'Glossary', in Brady, M. E. and Collier, D. (eds) *Rethinking Social Inquiry: Diverse Tools, Shared Standards* (Lanham, M. D., Rowman and Littlefield, 2004), pp. 273–313.
Sigelman, L. 'Question Order Effects on Presidential Popularity', *Public Opinion Quarterly*, 45, (1981), pp.199–207.
Sinnott, R. 'Interpretations of the Irish Party System', *European Journal of Political Research*, XII, (1984), pp.289–307.
Sinnott, R. 'Party Differences and Spatial Representation: the Irish Case', *British Journal of Political Science*, XVI, (1986), pp.217–241.
Sinnott, R. 'Locating Parties, Factions and Ministers in a Policy Space: a Contribution to Understanding the Party Policy Link', *European Journal of Political Research*, 17, (1989), pp.689–705.
Sinnott, R. *Irish Voters Decide: Voting Behaviour in Elections and Referendums since 1918* (Manchester: Manchester University Press, 1995a).
Sinnott, R. *Knowledge of the European Union in Irish Public Opinion: Sources and Implications.* Institute of European Affairs [IEA], Occasional Paper No. 5 (Dublin: IEA, 1995b).
Sinnott, R. 'Attitudes and Behaviour of the Irish Electorate in the Referendum on the Treaty of Nice' (report presented to the European Commission Office in Dublin, November 2001), www. euireland.ie/news/Institutions/1001/fullopinionpollresults.pdf
Sinnott, R. 'Cleavages, Parties and Referendums: Relationships Between Representative and Direct Democracy in the Republic of Ireland', *European Journal of Political Research*, 41, (2002), pp.811–826.
Sinnott, R. *Attitudes and Behaviour of the Irish Electorate in the Second Referendum on the Nice Treaty. Results of a Survey of Public Opinion Carried Out for the European Commission Representation in Ireland* (Dublin: ISSC, UCD, 26 February 2003).
Sinnott, R. 'Uphill Task to Win EU Treaty Poll Here', *The Irish Times*, 14 June 2005.

Sinnott, R., Walsh, B. and Whelan, B. J. 'Conservatives, Liberals and Pragmatists: Disaggregating the Results of the Irish Abortion Referendums of 1992', *Economic and Social Review*, 26, 2 (1995), pp.207–19.

Smith, T. W. 'Trends in Non-response Rates', *International Journal of Public Opinion Research*, 7, (1995), pp.157–71.

Smith, T. W. *A Report on the 2005 ISSP Non-Response Survey*. WAPOR/ISSC Conference on International Social Surveys (Ljubljana, Slovenia, 9–11 November 2005).

Steeh, C. G. 'Trends in Nonresponse Rates, 1952–1979', *Public Opinion Quarterly*, 45, (1981), pp.40–57.

Steeh, C. G., Kirgis, N., Cannon, B. and De Witt, J. 'Are they Really as Bad as they Seem? Non-response Rates at the End of the Twentieth Century', *Journal of Official Statistics*, 17, 2, (2001), pp.227–47.

Steenbergen, M. and Jones, B. S. 'Modelling Multilevel Data Structures', *American Journal of Political Science*, 46, (2002), pp.218–37.

Stigler, G. J. 'General Economic Conditions and National Elections', *American Economic Review*, 63, 2, (1973), pp.160–7.

Stimson, J. A. *Public Opinion in America: Moods, Cycles and Swings* (Boulder, CO: Westview, 1991).

Stimson, J. A. *Tides of Consent: How Public Opinion Shapes American Politics* (Cambridge: Cambridge University Press, 2004).

Stoop, I. A. L, Iedema, J. and Louwen, F. 'How Different are Non-respondents?' paper presented at the Fifth International Conference on Logic and Methodology: Social Science Methodology in the New Millennium (Cologne, Germany, 3–6 October 2000).

Strauss, A. 'The concept of attitude in social psychology', *Journal of Psychology*, 19, (1945), pp.329–39.

Teitler, J. O., Reichman, N. E., and Sprachman, S. 'Costs and Benefits of Improving Response Rates for a Hard-to-reach Population', *Public Opinion Quarterly*, 67, 2, (2003), pp.126–38.

Thornton, R. J. and Thornton, J. A. 'Erring on the Margin of Error', *Southern Economics Journal*, 71, 1, (2004), pp.130–35.

Thurstone, L. L. 'Attitudes Can Be Measured', *American Journal of Sociology* 33, 4, (January 1928), pp.529–554.

Tourangeau, R., Rips, L. J. and Rasinski, K. *The Psychology of Survey Response* (Cambridge: Cambridge University Press, 2000).

Traugott, M. W. and Lavrakas P. J. *The Voter's Guide to Election Polls* (2nd edition) (New York: Chatham House Publishers, Seven Bridges Press, LLC, 2000).

Trumbore, P. F. 'Public Opinion as a Democratic Constraint in International Negotiations: Two-level Games in the Anglo-Irish Peace Process', *International Studies Quarterly*, 42, 3, (September 1998), pp.545–565.

Verba, S. 'The Citizen Respondent: Sample Surveys and American Democracy', *American Political Science Review*, 90, 1, (1996), pp.1–7.

Vigderhous, G. 'Scheduling Phone Interviews: A Study of Seasonal Patterns', *Public Opinion Quarterly*, 45, (1981), pp.250–59.

Vries, de M., Giannetti, D. and Mansergh, L. Estimating Policy Positions from the Computer Coding of Political Texts: Results from Italy, the Netherlands and Ireland, in Laver M. (ed) *Estimating the Policy Position of Political Actors* (London: Routledge/ECPR Studies in Political Science, 2000, pp 193–216).

Ward, C. K. 'Intimations of Immorality: An Analysis of the International Social Survey Programme (ISSP) 1998', in, Cassidy E. G. *Measuring Ireland: Discerning values and beliefs* (Dublin: Veritas, 2002), pp. 67–93.

Waters, J., *Jiving at the Crossroads* (Belfast: Blackstaff Press, 1991).

Waters, J. *An Intelligent Person: Guide to Modern Ireland* (London: Gerald Duckworth, 1997).

Weissberg, R. 'The Problem with Polling', *The Public Interest* (Summer 2002), pp.27–48.

Whelan, C. T. 'Values and Social Change', in Whelan, C. T. (ed), *Values and Social Change in Ireland* (Dublin: Gill & Macmillan, 1994), pp. 1–6.

Whelan, C. T. and Fahey, T. 'Marriage and the Family', in Whelan C. T. (ed) *Values and Social Change in Ireland* (Dublin: Gill & Macmillan, 1994), pp. 45–81.

Whyte, J. 'Ireland: Politics Without Social Bases', in Rose, R. (ed) *Electoral Behaviour: A Comparative Handbook* (New York: Free Press, 1974), pp. 619–51.

Whyte, J. H. *Church and State in Modern Ireland* (2nd edition) (Dublin: Gill & Macmillan, 1980).

Wiebe, G. D. 'Some Implications of Separating Opinions from Attitudes', *Public Opinion Quarterly*, 17, 3, (1953), pp. 328–52.

Wilson, T. D. and Hodges, S. 'Attitudes as Temporary Constructions', in Martin, L. and Tesser, A. (eds) *The Construction of Social Judgements* (New York: Springer-Verlag, 1992), pp. 37–66.

Wlezien, C. and Erikson, R. S. 'The Timeline of Presidential Election Campaigns', *Journal of Politics* 64, 4, (November 2002), pp. 969–93.

Yankelovich, D. *Coming to Judgement: Making Democracy Work in a Complex World* (Syracuse, NY: Syracuse University Press, 1991).

Zaller, J. 'Political Awareness and Susceptibility to Elite Opinion Leadership, and the Mass Survey Response', *Social Cognition*, 8, (1990), pp.125–53.

Zaller, J. *The Nature and Origins of Mass Opinion* (Cambridge: Cambridge University Press, 1992).

Zaller, J. and Feldman, S. 'A Simple Theory of Survey Response: Answering Questions Versus Revealing Preferences', *American Journal of Political Science*, 36, 3, (1992), pp. 579–616.

Appendix 1

Notes for Table 3

There is considerable variation in the categories used, especially between surveying companies. The categories listed in Table 3 are generic ones where for example the legal/justice system refers in the case of IMS to Judges. For this reason the data presented in this table must be interpreted with caution.

Sources

Eurobarometer (EB) item wording: 'I would like to ask you a question about how much trust you have in certain institutions. For each of the following institutions, please tell me if you tend to trust it or tend not to trust it?'

Asia Europe Survey (ASES) item wording: 'Now, could you tell me how much confidence you have in each of the following? There may be one or two items on the list that you haven't thought much about. If so, just tell me and we'll go to the next item.' Response options were 'a great deal', 'quite a lot', 'not much', 'none at all', 'don't know' or 'haven't thought much about it'.

European Values Survey (EVS) item wording: 'Please look at this card and tell me, for each item listed, how much confidence you have in them, is it a great deal, quite a lot, not very much or none at all?'

IMS item wording: 'Certain groups of people are expected to provide leadership in our society. For each group I read out please say whether you personally tend to have a lot of confidence in the leadership they provide or tend to have little confidence in the leadership they provide in our society nowadays?' Response options were 'lot', 'little', 'don't know / no opinion'. A similar wording was used in earlier IMS polls; IMS CMC/sos/mc/J.2S197, 4 July 1992; IMS 6S-533, 28 November 1996, q.11; IMS CMC/8S-525, 15 October 1998, q. 10; IMS, 2000, exact date unknown, details available in IPS, 2001, p.322ff; IMS/RJA/NN/PM/203S2, 7 March 2002.

MRBI item wording: 'How much do you trust do you have in the following institutions. For each institution, please tell me if you tend to trust it or not?' Response options were 'trust', 'do not trust', 'don't know', MRBI/6229/02, 14–15 October 2002.

Appendix 2

Taxation and Spending Questions used in Table 15

1. 'Do you think that government spending on social services such as housing, education and health, should... (1) be increased; (2) stay about the same as it is now; (3) or be cut down; (4) don't know'. IMS/RJA/sr/CMC/md/J.3201/2, RTE, 30 August– 8 September 1976, question 9.

Be increased	Stay about the same	Cut down	Don't know/ No reply
51%	31%	11%	7%

2. 'I would be prepared to pay heavier taxes to run a United Ireland...?' ESRI: Attitudes in the Republic of Ireland relevant to the Northern Ireland Problem, (Davis & Sinnott 1979), question 110, July–September 1978.

Strongly agree	Moderately agree	Slightly agree	Slightly disagree	Moderately disagree	Strongly disagree
14%	15%	17%	11%	11%	30%

3. 'I am going to read a few statements which people have made. Can you tell me whether you agree or disagree with each – and if you strongly agree or strongly disagree?' READ OUT 'Taxation must be reduced, even if it means that the government makes drastic reduction in expenditure?' (MRBI/3510/87, 23 January 1987, question 11b).

Strongly agree	Agree	Neither/Don't know/No opinion	Disagree	Strongly disagree
29%	34%	7%	23%	6%

4. 'Do you think, in order to restore the public finances, the government should mainly rely on further cuts in public expenditure, as they propose, or alternatively should they seek to raise money by increasing taxes?' (IMS: j.11240, 29 July 1988, question 8).

Rely on cuts in public expenditure	Raise taxes	Neither	Don't know
51%	16%	2%	30%

5. '(a) Are you in favour or not of the government spending more money to reduce the level of poverty in Ireland? (b) Would you still be in favour if it meant that better-off people would have to pay higher taxes?' (MRBI/3680/88, 6 October 1988, question 11).

(a)		(b)	
In favour	88%	Yes, still in favour	66%
Not in favour	9%	No, not in favour	20%
Don't know/no opinion	3%	Don't know/No opinion	2%

6. 'And finally, there have been reports that the next budget may include cuts in personal taxation. Would you prefer that income tax be reduced, or should the money be spent on reducing poverty in Ireland?' (MRBI/3710/88, 6 December 1988, question 10).

Cut income tax	Reduce poverty	Don't know/No opinion
48%	49%	3%

7. 'Please tell me if you agree or disagree with the following statements. Taxation must be reduced, even if that means more cuts in areas like health, education and social welfare?' (IMS: CMC/J.9S183, 2 June 1989, question 10).

Agree	Disagree	Don't know
43%	36%	21%

8. 'Please tell me if you agree or disagree with the following statements. The only way to bring down unemployment in the long run is to continue cutting back on government expenditure?' (IMS: CMC/J.9S183, 2 June 1989, question 11).

Agree	Disagree	Don't know
58%	33%	10%

9. 'Would you prepared to pay higher taxes, for the creation of more jobs?' (MRBI/3960/91, 18 June 1991, question 11).

Agree	Disagree	Don't know
30%	63%	7%

10. 'Are you personally in favour or opposed in principle to an increase in borrowing by the next government?' (IMS: 2S.408, 4 December 1992, question 11).

Favour increase in borrowing	Oppose increase in borrowing	Don't know
26%	62%	11%

11. 'Are you in favour of continuing tight restraint of government expenditure on public services, including social welfare, or do you think the incoming government should be prepared to spend more on services and welfare, even if that means an increase in government borrowing?' (IMS: CMC/SOS/mc/J.2S425, 10 January 1993, question 8).

Continuing tight restraint on public expenditure	41%
Should be prepared to spend more on services and welfare	54%
Don't know	5%

12. 'Ireland has experienced record economic growth in recent years, which is now leading to problems of higher inflation and a possible loss of competitiveness. There is a risk of the economy overheating, leading to, much higher unemployment and a collapse of the social partnership. If the only means open to the government now to prevent this happening is to increase taxes and cut public spending, would you be prepared to accept the government taking those steps, or not?' (IMS, CMC/SOS/id/8S-181, 26 March 1998, question 20).

Yes, would accept	No, would not accept	Don't know/No opinion
22%	67%	12%

13. 'The government is promising more tax cuts in the next budget. Would you or would you not be prepared to sacrifice further tax cuts for a better health service?' MRBI, 29–30 May 2001, IPS 2002, p. 50.

Yes	No	Don't know/No opinion
74%	20%	6%

14. 'Thinking of proposed spending by the next government in areas such as health, education, roads, etc. which of these methods of raising funds would you personally favour?' IMS, 7 May 2002, Kennedy and Farrington (2003: p. 66).

Higher taxes	Borrowing from abroad	Selling state industries, e.g. Aer Lingus, ESB	None of these	Don't know/No opinion
12%	12%	47%	13%	16%

15. 'The government will not have enough money next year to pay for existing public services and capital projects unless it either increases taxes, borrows more, or cuts spending on services and projects. Do you think the government should...?' MRBI, 22–23 September 2003, Kennedy and Farrington (2004: p. 51).

Increase taxes	Borrow more	Cut spending	Don't know/No opinion
9%	29%	48%	14%

16. 'In the forthcoming budget in December, various options and choices are open to the government in terms of personal taxation, other taxes, spending on public services etc. From your own point of view, which option would you prefer if it had to be one of the following?' READ OUT (1) The government should improve public services, even if it means that personal taxation has to rise; (2) Personal taxation should stay at current levels, even if it means no additional investment in public services; (3) Don't know/No opinion (do not read out). IMS/41101257/st, 21–22 October 2003, *The Sunday Tribune*, question 18.

The government should improve public services, even if it means that personal taxation has to rise	40%
Personal taxation should stay at current levels, even if it means no additional investment in public services	50%
Don't know/No opinion	10%

Appendix 3

Public Opinion among the Irish Public on Certain Liberal Agenda Issues

ISPAS, Winter 2001/2
Three issues are outlined on this card. Please tell me for each of the following whether you think it can never be justified, always be justified, or something in between. People who believe it can never be justified would give a score of '0'. People who believe it is always justified would give a score of '10'. Other people would place themselves somewhere in between these two views. Where would you place yourself on these scales? SHOW CARD A4. Irish Social and Political Attitudes Survey (ISPAS), Survey implemented by the ESRI, Winter 2001/2, questions A4(1–3). [N=1890].

11-point scale	*Homosexuality*	*Abortion*	*Euthanasia*
0 – Never justified	13	29	24
1	3	7	7
2	3	8	5
3	4	6	4
4	4	5	4
5	29	24	21
6	5	5	5
7	5	5	7
8	7	5	9
9	3	1	3
10 – Always justified	22	4	11
Don't know	1	1	0

EVS, 1981, 1991, 1999

'Please tell me for each of the following statements whether you think it can always be justified, never be justified, or something in between, using this card.' Read out statements reversing order for alternate contacts. Code one answer for each statement. European Values Survey, 1981, 1991 and 1999. Surveying work undertaken by the IMS (1981); Economic and Social Research Institute (July–October 1990; October 1999–February 2000).

Homosexuality, Prostitution, Abortion, Divorce, Euthanasia (terminating the life of the incurably sick), Suicide.

Divorce	1981	1991	1999	*Abortion*	1981	1991	1999
1 – Never	44	30	25	1 – Never	75	52	50
2	6	5	2	2	5	14	8
3	6	8	5	3	3	10	7
4	6	9	7	4	3	7	5
5	15	16	24	5	5	8	15
6	6	11	8	6	2	4	3
7	4	8	7	7	1	3	2
8	4	7	6	8	1	2	2
9	2	3	4	9	0	0	1
10 – Always	3	3	9	10 – Always	1	0	3
Don't know	4	1	5	Don't know	4	0	4

Homosexuality	1981	1991	1999	*Euthanasia*	1981	1991	1999
1 – Never	52	49	34	1 – Never	65	55	45
2	3	5	2	2	5	7	7
3	4	6	4	3	6	8	5
4	4	6	6	4	3	6	3
5	11	11	19	5	6	10	12
6	6	6	4	6	2	6	4
7	3	4	4	7	2	3	4
8	2	5	3	8	1	2	4
9	1	3	4	9	1	1	2
10 – Always	3	3	10	10 – Always	2	1	4
Don't know	12	3	8	Don't know	7	2	7

Prostitution	1981	1991	1999	Suicide	1981	1991	1999
1 – Never	64	60	55	1 – Never	70	61	64
2	5	9	5	2	6	8	6
3	4	9	6	3	4	7	4
4	3	5	5	4	2	6	2
5	8	8	15	5	6	8	10
6	3	3	3	6	3	3	2
7	2	2	2	7	1	2	1
8	2	2	1	8	1	1	1
9	1	0	0	9	0	1	0
10 – Always	1	1	1	10 – Always	1	0	1
Don't know	7	1	5	Don't know	6	3	7

Comparison of EVS and ISPAS/INES Survey Results

Abortion	EVS 1981	1991	1999	ISPAS 2002	Euthanasia	EVS 1981	1991	1999	ISPAS 2002
1 – Never	75	52	50	36	1 – Never	65	55	45	31
2	5	14	8	8	2	5	7	7	5
3	3	10	7	6	3	6	8	5	4
4	3	7	5	5	4	3	6	3	4
5	5	8	15	24	5	6	10	12	21
6	2	4	3	5	6	2	6	4	5
7	1	3	2	5	7	2	3	4	7
8	1	2	2	5	8	1	2	4	9
9	0	0	1	1	9	1	1	2	3
10 – Always	1	0	3	4	10 – Always	2	1	4	11
Don't know	4	0	4	1	Don't know	7	2	7	0

Homosexuality	1981	EVS 1991	1999	ISPAS 2002	INES 2002
1 – Never	52	49	34	16	14
2	3	5	2	3	4
3	4	6	4	4	3
4	4	6	6	4	3
5	11	11	19	29	30
6	6	6	4	5	5
7	3	4	4	5	5
8	2	5	3	7	6
9	1	3	4	3	4
10 – Always	3	3	10	22	13
Don't know	12	3	8	1	14

Appendix 4

Voting Intentions in the Maastricht Treaty Referendum before and after the Danish 'no' vote on 2 June 1992 (per cent)

Vote intention in Irish referendum	April 1992	June 1992	Danish referendum		Difference – Post minus pre
			Pre-referendum	Post-referendum	
In favour	62	54	55	54	–1
Against	10	22	18	24	+6 **
Undecided	28	24	27	22	–5 **
N	>1,200	1,281	417	864	

*** $p<.001$, ** $p<.01$, $p<.1$

Note: The data includes vote intention and inclination. The Danish 'no vote' occurred on June 2, 1992 where a majority of less than 2 percent (45,000 votes) voted against the Maastricht treaty, previously approved by the Danish parliament. The referendum vote intention question asked: 'If you do vote, which way will you vote in this referendum – in favour of or against the Maastricht treaty?' If will not vote / undecided / refused. Ask: 'Which way would you be inclined to vote?' Lansdowne Market Research, The Sunday Press, AM/RA/LR 2L-224, May 29 – June 8, 1992, question 9a-b. Difference of proportions test used to examine if there is a statistically significant difference in the two sub-samples. The null hypothesis is that there is no difference between the two sub-samples.

Comparison of Specific Survey Responses before and after the Danish 'no-vote' on June 2, 1992 (per cent)

Survey question	Response option	Pre-Danish Referendum	Post-Danish Referendum	Difference
Important issues in influencing how will vote in Maastricht treaty Referendum	Abortion – more freely available	10	18	+8***
Important issues in influencing how will vote in Maastricht treaty Referendum	Closer political links with Europe	7	11	+4**
Important issues in influencing how will vote in Maastricht treaty Referendum	Irish neutrality	13	16	+3
Perceived direction of Catholic church leaders advice to voters on how to vote in the Maastricht treaty referendum	Against Maastricht	18	21	+3
Important issues in influencing how will vote in Maastricht treaty Referendum	Standard of living	25	22	–3
Vote intention in a future referendum on allowing abortion in certain circumstances	Against	38	33	–5*
Satisfied or dissatisfied with Mr. Reynolds as Taoiseach	Satisfied	63	58	–5*
N		417	864	

*** $p<.001$, ** $p<.01$, * $p<.1$.

Eurobarometer questions used to construct an EU sentiment measure

The questions used to construct the EU sentiment measure are those that relate directly to the European Union, its institutions and policies. Estimates based on: Pro-EU response / (Pro-EU + Anti-EU responses). Non-committal responses such as "don't know", "no answer", "refused", etc. are excluded from the analysis.

1. UNIF:
In general, are you for or against efforts being made to unify Western Europe?
(For-very much and for-to some extent)

2. MEMBER:
Generally speaking, do you think that IRELAND'S membership of the

European Community (Common market) is ..?
(A good thing)

3. BENEFIT:
Taking everything into consideration, would you say that IRELAND has on balance benefited or not from being a member of the European Community (Common Market)?
(Benefited)

4. REGRET:
If you were told tomorrow that the European Community (Common Market) had been scrapped, would you be very sorry about it, indifferent or very relieved?
(Very sorry)

5. SPEED_UP:
Some people consider the Common Market as being a first step towards a closer union between the member states, personally, do you yourself think the movement towards the unification of Europe should be speeded up, slowed down or continued as it is at present?
(Speeded up)

6. SPEED67:
In your opinion, how is the European Community advancing these days? Please look at this card number 1 is standing still, number 7 is running as fast as possible? Choose the one which best corresponds with your opinion of the European Community.
(Points 6 and 7 on the scale)

7. EPIMPV1:
How important, would you say, is the European Parliament in the life of the European Community nowadays? (EB19-32A)
How important a part would you say the European Parliament plays in the life of the European Community nowadays? (EB33-52)
(Very important and important)

8. EPIMPV2:
And for each of the following institutions do you think it plays an important role or not in the life of the European Community nowadays? The European Parliament.
(Important)

9. EPMIMP:
Would you personally prefer the European Parliament played a more important or less important part than it does now?
(More important)

10. EPELECTI:
Which one of these opinions comes closest to your own on the future elections to the European Parliament?
(It is an event with important consequences which is certain to make Europe more politically unified)

11. MEPATT:
Which of the following attitudes would expect an Irish Member of the European Parliament to have?
(He should support things that are good for Europe as a whole, event if they are not always good for IRELAND at the time)

12. EUGOVT:
Are you for or against the formation, for the European Union, of a European government responsible to the European Parliament? (EB28-31; 41.1-43.1)
Are you for or against the formation of a European Union with a European government responsible to the European Parliament? (EB32A-41.0)
(For)

13. SEMHOPE:
Personally, would you say that the Single European Market, which will come about by 1992, makes you feel very hopeful, rather hopeful, rather fearful or very fearful?
(Very hopeful)

14. SEMGOOD
Altogether do you think that the coming into being of the Single Common Market in the European Community in 1992 will be a good thing, a bad thing or neither good nor bad?
(A good thing)

15–22. TEP, TCOM, TCOUNCIL, TECJ, TOMBUD, TCBANK, TAUDIT, TCREGION:
Have you ever heard of (A-H) and for each of them, please tell me if you tend to trust it or not to trust it?
A. The European Parliament
B. The European Commission
C. The Council of Ministers of the European Union
D. The European Court of Justice
E. The European Ombudsman
F. The European Central Bank
G. The European Court of Auditors
H. The Committee of the Regions of the European Union
   (Trust it)

23. UNDERST:
In your opinion, over the last 12 months has the understanding between the countries of the European Community / Common Market in general increased decreased or stayed about the same?
(Increased in general)

24. EUCITIZEN:
Do you ever think yourself not only as an Irish citizen but also as a citizen of Europe? (EB19.0)
Does the thought ever occur to you that you are not only Irish but also European? Does this happen often or never? (EB33.0, EB37.0 split A)
Do you ever think of yourself as not only an Irish citizen, but also a citizen of Europe? Does this happen often, sometimes or never? (EB37.0 split B)
(Often and sometimes)

25-43. CPCULTUR, CPCURR, CPDATAP, CPDRUGS, CPEDUC, CPENVIR, CPFORPOL, CPIMMIGR, CPINDUST, CPPASYL, CPPRESS, CPSCIEN, CPSECUR, CPTHIRD, CPUNEMP, CPVATAX, CPWELFAR, CPWORKER, CPWORSEC:
Some people believe that certain areas of policy should be determined by the Irish government, while other areas of policy should be determined in common with the European Community. Which of the following areas of policy do you think should be determined by the Irish government, and which should be decided in common with the European Community as a whole? (EB31.A)
Some people believe that certain areas of policy should be decided by the Irish government, while other areas of policy should be decided jointly within the European Community. Which of the following areas of policy do you think should be decided by the Irish government, and which should be decided jointly within the European Community? (EB32.A-51.1)
For each of the following areas, do you think that decisions should be made by the Irish government, or jointly within the European Union?
A. Cultural policy CPCULTUR
B. Common currency policy CPCURR
C. Common data protection policy CPDATAP
D. The fight against drugs CPDRUGS
E. Educational standards CPEDUC
F. Protection of the environment CPENVIR
G. Foreign policy towards countries outside of the European Community CPFORPOL
H. Immigration policy CPIMMIGR
I. Industrial policy CPINDUST
J. Rules for political asylum CPPASYL
K. Basic rules for broadcasting and press CPPRESS
L. Scientific and technological research CPSCIEN

M. Security and defence policy CPSECUR
N. Co-operation with developing countries, Third World CPTHIRD
O. Dealing with unemployment CPUNEMP
P. Rates of VAT (value added tax) CPVATAX
Q. Health and social welfare CPWELFAR
R. Participation of workers' representatives on company board of directors CPWORKER
S. Workers' rights vis-à-vis their employers CPWORSEC
(The European Union)

44. EUIMP:
Whether or not you have the time to take a personal interest in the problems of the European Community. Do you feel that these problems are very important, important, not very important or unimportant for the future of IRELAND and the people of IRELAND?
(Very important)

45. SAT_DEM_EU:
On the whole, are you very satisfied, fairly satisfied, not very satisfied or not at all satisfied with the way democracy works in European Community? Would you say you are ..?
(Very satisfied and fairly satisfied)

Eurobarometer questions used to construct an EU interest/awareness measure

The following Eurobarometer questions were used to construct an EU interest and awareness measure. While these measures measure a variety of things, nonetheless all relate to some informational aspect of opinions toward the EU and in this respect they give some measure of interest in the integration project.

1. COMMEDIA:
Have you recently seen or heard in the papers, on the radio, or on television, anything about the European Commission in Brussels that is the Commission of the European Community?
(Yes)

2. FAVCOM:
Has what you read or heard given you a generally favourable or unfavourable impression of the European Commission?
(Generally favourable)

3. AWAREEP:
Have you recently seen or heard in the papers or on the radio or television anything about the European Parliament that is the Parliamentary

Assembly of the European Community or Common Market?
(Yes)

4. EPINFOF:
Has what you read or heard given you a generally favourable or unfavourable impression of the European Parliament?
(Generally favourable impression)

5. SEMEDIA:
Have you read in the papers, seen on the television or heard anything about the Single European Market of 1992?
(Yes)

6. INFORMEC:
All things considered, how well informed do you feel you are about the European Community, its policies, its institutions?
(Very well, Quite well)

7. INTEREST:
Are you personally very interested, a little interested, or not at all interested in the problems of the European Community / Common Market?
(Very interested)

8. GINTEREST:
And as far as European politics are concerned, that is matters relating to the European Community. To what extent would you say you are interested in European Community politics? (EB 30, 31A, 32A, 33 and 34)

To what extent would you say you are interested in European Community politics, that is matters related to the European Community: A great deal, to some extent, not much or not at all? (EB 39, 40, 41.0, 41.1 & 42)
(A great deal)

Some technical details of the construction of the EU sentiment and interest/awareness measures

Estimation based on a dyadic ratios algorithm described in Stimson (1999, appendix 1). This statistical procedure builds dimensional "factor scores" from a series of survey questions that have only partially overlapping observations. Exponential smoothing of the data has been used to reduce the influence of random fluctuations from sampling in order to observe more clearly common movements in the survey marginals. The 'AlphaF' and 'AlphaB' are product moment correlations of the two independent estimates (forward and backward recursion) of the latent EU sentiment series. The item scale correlation at solution equates to a factor loading and squaring this value may be interpreted as a communality estimate. Results have been sorted in descending order of item scale correlation.

Following extraction of the first dimension each time series is regressed on dimension 1 in sequence in order to estimate that portion of each questions' variation not shared with dimension 1. Thereafter, this estimated residual variation is subjected to a dimensional analysis. The true mean and variance of dimension 2 is under-identified. Consequently, the mean value of dimension 2 is set to the mean of dimension 1 and the variance of the second common factor is defined to be the "fraction of the first dimension standard deviation in proportion to its explanatory power" (Erikson et al. 2002: 208).

EXAMPLE: Interest, awareness of EU measure

Period: 1973 to 2000 28 Time Points
Number of Series: 8
Exponential Smoothing: On

Iteration History: Dimension 1

Iter	Convergence	Criterion	Items	Reliability	AlphaF	AlphaB
1	.5577	.001	8	.896	.390	.548
2	.0396	.001	8	.892	.407	.567
3	.0051	.001	8	.892	.407	.570
4	.0010	.001	8	.892	.406	.571
5	.0003	.001	8	.892	.405	.571

1	"COMMEDIA"	N = 7	Correlation = .906	Mean: 46.9	STD:	4.6
2	"FAVCOM"	N = 7	Correlation = .857	Mean: 29.8	STD:	4.6
3	"AWAREP"	N = 18	Correlation = .866	Mean: 46.1	STD:	9.3
4	"EPINFOF"	N = 10	Correlation = .843	Mean: 26.6	STD:	6.8
5	"SEMEDIA"	N = 5	Correlation = -.871	Mean: 73.3	STD:	3.7
6	"INFORMEC"	N = 6	Correlation = .910	Mean: 32.0	STD:	4.1
7	"INTEREST"	N = 7	Correlation = .979	Mean: 21.4	STD:	3.7
8	"GINTEREST"	N = 4	Correlation = -.006	Mean: 7.4	STD:	0.6

Eigen Estimate 1.68 of possible 2.29
Pct Variance Explained: 73.36

Weighted Average Metric: Mean: 38.93 St. Dev: 5.16

Correlations of integration items with two dimensions of sentiment toward European integration in Ireland (1973–2002)

Variable	Years	All Eurobarometer questions Dimension 1	All Eurobarometer questions Dimension 2	All variables minus 4 standard items Dimension 1	All variables minus 4 standard items Dimension 2
MEMBER	30	.97	.91	–	–
REGRET	20	.93	.66	–	–
BENEFIT	19	.95	.71	–	–
UNIF	18	.93	-.34	–	–
EPMIMP	17	.41	-.06	-.34	.66
EPIMPV2	17	.32	-.86	.33	-.01
EPIMPV1	17	.89	-.28	-.13	.59
CPWELFAR	14	.26	-.15	.82	-.01
CPSECUR	14	.47	-.24	.56	.69
CPSCIEN	14	-.58	-.06	.57	.47
CPPRESS	14	-.04	.05	.54	.35
CPFORPOL	14	.37	-.07	.66	.52
CPENVIR	14	.05	-.11	.42	-.03
CPEDUC	14	.61	-.31	.96	.57
CPCURR	14	.66	.07	.59	.69
CPUNEMP	11	-.40	.05	.85	-.63
CPPASYL	11	-.78	.10	.70	-.02
CPIMMIGR	11	-.57	.15	.71	-.05
CPCULTUR	11	.76	-.37	.34	-.28
CPVATAX	10	-.05	-.71	.69	.41
CPTHIRD	10	.58	-.41	.61	-.03
CPDRUGS	10	-.24	.05	.81	.32
UNDERST	9	.91	-.23	.65	.72
SPEED67	9	.08	-.03	-.43	.69
SEMHOPE	9	.23	.52	.70	.64
EUIMP	9	.06	-.24	.48	.34
EUGOVT	9	.73	.30	.43	.58
SAT_DEM_EU	7	.80	.29	.11	.01
CPWORKER	7	.67	-.54	.93	-.91
SPEEDUP	6	.05	-.60	-.76	.63
SEMGOOD	6	-.59	-.32	.83	.19
EUCITIZEN	6	.86	-.07	-.58	.41
CPDATAP	5	.52	-.48	1.00	.02
TOMBUD	4	.83	.53	.15	-.34
TEP	4	.62	.49	.27	.66
TECJ	4	.61	.57	.11	.68
TCREGION	4	.92	.60	-.01	-.01
TCOUNCIL	4	.98	.58	.03	.29
TCOM	4	.95	-.19	-.08	.35
TCBANK	4	.84	-.36	.29	.97
TAUDIT	4	.97	-.29	.21	-.66
MEPATT	4	-.22	-.12	-.59	.66
EPELECTI	4	.92	-.01	.60	.76
CPWORSEC	4	.52	-.73	.92	-.16
CPINDUST	4	.50	-.60	.90	.02
Explained variance (percent)		44.3	10.4	34.1	16.7

Index

A
Achen, C.H.
AAPOR 35
Absolute Error *see* Error
Abortion *see* liberal agenda
Academic surveys
Adams, Gerry 102
age, see also cohort analysis
Agreement measure, perceptual and preferential (van der Eijk)
Ahern, Taoiseach Bertie 100, 102
Alvarez, R.M.
Amendments of the Constitution, *see* referendums
American Association for Public Opinion Research *see* AAPOR
American National Election Surveys *see* ANES
Amsterdam Treaty, *see* referendums
ANES 37
Anglo-Irish Agreement 153
Anti-Divorce Action Group 10
Arceneaux, K. 72–3
Articles 2 and 3 *see* Northern Ireland
Article 40.6.1°
ASES 60, 181
ASia Europe Survey *see* ASES
authoritarianism

B
ballot papers, simulated
ban, *see* liberal agenda and referendums
Behaviour and Attitudes Ltd. 20
Belfast Agreement (1998)
Belief-Sampling Model 42–52, 67, 71, 72, 95, 96, 114, 118, 127, 130, 169, 238, 242
    and abortion 44–51
    polling inconsistency 125, 199
    and question evaluation 92–3, 218
    and questions 61, 63, 68, 98, *see also* questions
    respondents' considerations 54
    uninformed respondents 54–5, 234
bias 56, 88
Bluebird 20
Blumer, H.
Bourdieu, Pierre 1
Border and partition *see* Northern Ireland
Britain, *see also* UK
British and Irish public opinion towards the Northern Ireland problem (Hayes and McAllister) 153

British army/troops in Northern Ireland *see* Northern Ireland
Bruton, Taoiseach John 104
budget
Bunreacht na h-Éireann *see* Irish Constitution

C
C-Case
Campaigns *see* elections and referendums
Carmines, E.G. 52, 53, 150, 154
Catholic Church 11, 121, 122
    Catholic thinking and politics 178
    Catholicism and Irish culture 123
    and fundamentalist Catholicism 123
    and Northern Ireland 150
causality
Celtic Tiger
Central Statistics Office *see* CSO
CFSP *see* European Union
chauvinism, value
Church and state
citizens
Coakley, J.
coalition
cohort analysis 135–46, 149, 243
collinear or collinearity
commercial polls *see* media commissioned polls
conservative
constitutional amendments 119
constitutional referendums *see* referendums
constitutional right to express opinions, opinion poll ban proposal in 2001
Constitutional Treaty
contraception
confidence interval
confidence, trust in institutions
constituency polls
Converse, P.E. 64
correlations
corruption
Cosgrave, Taoiseach Liam T. 116
courts
    High Court 8, 10, 45
    Supreme Court 8, 45, 50–51, 127, 148
CSO 27, 136
Culture war
Cycle, general or inter-election

D
Dahl, R.A.

Dáil Éireann
Darcy, R. 123
data
    aggregate level 3
    basis for analysis 17
    on government policy 5
    individual level 4–5
    opinion poll 119, 120–21, 174–5, 240
    on party leaders 5
    on satisfaction with government 5
    sources see IMS; Lansdowne; MRBI
Data component
Danish 'no' vote (1992) see European Union
Davis, E.E. 160
Democracy
demographic
depression, economic
design effect
District Electoral Divisions (DED) 27
Divorce see liberal agenda
Downing Street Declaration see Northern Ireland
dyadic recursion 217

E
ecological inference
economic opinion 173–201
    Eurobarometer (EB) 183–9, 196, 199, 200
    impact of economic change 188
    inconsistency in 174, 176, 178, 180–81
    inflation 189–90
    Irish bust-to-boom 173, 183
    left-right opinion 173–4, 175–7
    left-right orientation
        21st century 178–80
        1976 177–8
        change in 188–96
        difficulty in measuring 181
        gender issues 178, 181
        and other values 180–83
        regression 191–2
        stability of opinion 193–6
    literature on 175–7
    poll data 174–5, 176–7
    public spending 196–201
    taxation 190, 191, 196–201
    unemployment 188–9
    see also Eurobarometer; European Union
Economic and Social Research Institute see ESRI
economic liberalism, value
education effects on attitudes
effective sample size
egalitarianism
Eijk, C. van der 194–5
election campaigns, usefulness of 84–7
elections, horse race nature
electoral behaviour
electoral record of polls
electoral register
electoral success
electoral support
electoral participation, see turnout
elites
emigration
Enniskillen bombing 164
Erikson R.S.
Error
    Absolute error
    Average error
    Measurement error
    Non-systematic error
    Sampling error
    Systematic error
ESOMAR 34, 35, 36
ESRI 4, 55, 61, 65, 187, 202
Ethno-centrism, value
Eurobarometer 4, 19, 60, 72, 174–5, 183–9, 196, 199, 200, 205, 206, 212, 213–16, 217–20, 224, 225, 227, 228–9, 230, 235, 243, 276
European Social Survey (ESS) 4, 30
European Society for Opinion and Marketing Research see ESOMAR
European Union 14, 19, 26, 36, 53, 156–7, 222, 228
    Accession by Ireland into the EEC in 1973 see referendums
    Amsterdam Treaty see referendums see referendums
    benefits
    Danish poll effect 208–9, 276
    dissolution
    economic explanations for support 224
    Economic and Monetary Union (EMU) 204, 208
    effect on support for
        development funding 224, 225, 226, 227
        inflation 224, 226
        integration process 224, 225–6
        unemployment 224, 226, 227
    European Commission 209
        Representation Office (Ireland) 209, 212
    European Common Foreign and Security Policy (CFSP) 211
    European Integration Project 212–13
    fluctuating support for 204–5
    hard and easy facets of opinion 213–16
    Irish Presidency of 222
    Maastricht Treaty (Treaty on European Union) see referendums
    membership
    National Forum on Europe 212

Nice Treaty *see* referendums
popular sentiment towards 216–27
Rapid Reaction Force 211
referendums on *see* referendums
Single European Act (SEA) *see* referendums 208
unification
Euthanasia *see* liberal agenda
European Values Survey (EVS) 4, 13, 60, 120, 135, 137, 138, 140, 143, 158, 167, 186, 187, 199, 200, 202

F
face-to-face interviewing
face validity *see* validity
factor analysis (see also principal components analysis) 217
Fahey T.
farmers
Farrell, B.
Fianna Fáil
Final poll predictions
Fine Gael
FitzGerald, Taoiseach Garret 102
Feldman, S.
Form and function of opinion polls
Framework Document *see* Northern Ireland

G
Gabel, M.J.
Gallagher, M.
Gallup 20, 28, 30, 69, 93, 94, 241
Garvin, T. 122–3
Garry, J.
Garvin, T.
Girvin, B.
General Social Surveys (GSS) 37
gender, difference in left-right
generational change or replacement 136–45
German Social Data Archive 187
Good Friday Agreement *see* Belfast Agreement
Government formation
Government satisfaction ratings *see* politics
Granger causality *see* opinion polls
Green Party
Gresham's law 244
Gujurati D.N.

H
Habermas, J.
hard and easy questions *see* opinion polls
Hardiman, N.
Harney, Mary 102
Haughey, Taoiseach Charles 101
Hayes, B.C. 153, 154, 158, 160, 164, 167–8, 170–71
Herbst, S.
heteroscedasticity

High Court *see* courts
Hochschild, J.L.
Homosexuality *see* liberal agenda
house effects
Hug, Chrystel 12, 118, 122, 125, 127
Hume-Adams dialogue *see* Northern Ireland

I
ICM 20, 24, 34, 71, 89
IMS 3, 5, 20, 21, 22, 23, 24, 26, 28, 30, 32, 35, 36, 37, 55, 60, 61, 65, 67, 68–71, 73, 79, 89, 90, 91, 93, 94, 120, 137, 152, 153, 155, 167, 173, 175, 177, 181, 185, 187, 189, 194, 196, 199–200, 202, 205–6, 209, 212, 236, 242, 243
In Your Opinion (Jones) 11
immigration
Inflation
Inglehart, R.
Inglis, T.
Independent Newspapers 18, 37
INES 4, 21, 38, 120, 156, 171, 175, 179, 195, 201, 203
Institutions, and their role in Irish society
  Church
  Army
  Civil Service
  Commercial companies
  Education
  European Union
  Government
  Health care
  Justice / legal system
  Parliament / Dáil
  Police/Garda Siochana
  Political leaders
  Political parties
  Trade Unions
  Media
    Press
    Radio
    Television
  Social welfare
  United Nations
Internationalism, value
International Social Survey Programme *see* ISSP
internet polling
intraclass correlation
intracohort effects or change
IOPA 20, 37
Ireland on Sunday 20, 71
Irish Constitution 19, 45, 152, 153, 157–9, 162, 244
Irish Independent 3, 20
Irish Marketing Services *see* IMS
Irish National Election Study (2002) *see* INES

Irish Opinion Poll Archive *see* IOPA
Irish Social Science Data Archive *see ISSDA*
ISSDA
Irish Social and Political Attitudes Survey
  see ISPAS
Irish society, major values held in 182, 183
Irish state television *see* RTÉ
The Irish Times 3, 11, 18, 20, 23, 35, 37,
  45, 93, 208, 210
Irish Voters Decide (Sinnott) 12
ISPAS 4, 21, 47, 49, 179, 201
ISSP 4, 13, 30, 120
issues
  abortion 14, 19, 25, 44–51, 53, 64, 118,
    119, 120, 121, 122, 123, 125,
    127–33, 133, 134, 138, 139, 140–43,
    145, 156–7, 235, 272–4
  asylum 222
  contraception 14, 120, 122, 125, 150
  corruption 25, 60
  crime 25
  divorce 10, 14, 19, 25, 119, 120, 121,
    122, 123, 125, 127–33, 134, 135–6,
    138, 139, 145, 147, 235–6, 273
  economic 14, 26, 35, 65, 235
    economic opinion *see* economic
      opinion
  education 25
  environment 156–7
  The Euro 65
  Europe *see* European Union
  euthanasia 120, 133, 134, 138, 145,
    272–4
  government 25
  homosexuality 14, 120, 122, 125, 133,
    134, 135, 138, 139, 145, 147, 148,
    149, 235, 272–4
    gay marriage 148
  legal system 25
  morality 13
  Northern Ireland *see* Northern Ireland
  patterns of poll questions 26
  politics *see* politics
  prostitution 133, 134, 273–4
  religion 13
  science 222
  suicide 133, 134, 273–4
  taxation 156–7, 267–71
  unemployment 222
  voting 25, 68–87
  work 13

J
JNRR 37
Joint National Readership Research *see*
  JNRR
Jones, Jack 8–9, 10, 22, 35, 45–6, 50, 66,
  91

K
Keeter, S.
Kennedy, F.
Kinder, D.R. 52
King, G.

L
Labour Party
Lamp Precision 67–82, 88
Lane, R.E. 3
Lansdowne Market Research (Lansdowne)
  3, 5, 20, 21, 22, 23, 24, 26, 35, 36, 37,
  67, 69, 71, 89, 94, 120, 135, 137, 152,
  173, 175, 185, 187, 189, 196, 199–200,
  202, 205–6, 208–212, 228, 237, 242
Laver, M. 123
Lavrakas, P.J. 30
Lau, R.R.
leadership in society, *see* confidence in
  institutions
Left-right ideology or orientation *see*
  economic opinion
liberal agenda 118–47
  Abortion
  and Catholic Church *see* Catholic
    Church
  Church and state 122
  and conservative pressure groups 122
  and cultural differences 121–2
  Divorce
  Ethno-centrism 122–3
  Euthanasia
  Homosexuality
  importance in Irish public opinion 126
  literature on 121
  poll data 119
  public opinion on 119, 133–47
  questions on 272–4
  referendum effects 123–4
  religious teachings 119
  structural explanation 124
  values dating from famine 123
Life-cycle effects
Likert scale 196
Lipset, S.M.
Lippmann, W. 43
Lynch, Taoiseach Jack 101, 116
Lyons, P.

M
Maastricht Treaty, *see* European Union
Mac Gréil, Michael 13
McAllister, I. 153, 154, 158, 160, 164,
  167–8, 170–71
McElroy, G.
McKenna Judgement 8
McSharry, R.
Major, Prime Minister John 208
Mannheim Eurobarometer *see*

INDEX

Eurobarometer
Market Research Bureau of Ireland *see* MRBI
Martin, E. 31
media commissioned polls
methodology *see* opinion polls
Measurement Error Model
Mirror Accuracy 66–80, 88
The Mirror and the Lamp 6, 232, 237
Mirror Theory of Opinion Polling 40–44, 46–7, 61, 63, 72, 88, 95, 98, 114, 118, 232, 238, 242
   and adjustment 75–6
   Error Measurement (or measurement error) Model 41–2
   Non-Attitude Model 41, 42, 51
   polling inconsistency 125, 199, 233
   and question evaluation 92–3
   response effects 41
   response instability 41
misreporting 75
Modernisation
MORI 20, 24, 37, 67, 71
MRBI 3, 5, 10, 11–12, 20, 21, 22, 23, 24, 26, 32, 35, 36, 37, 45, 56, 57, 60, 67–71, 73, 74, 75, 79, 89, 90, 93, 94, 95, 120, 137, 152, 153, 155, 167, 173, 175, 196, 199–200, 205–6, 208–212, 228, 237, 242, 243
MZES 185

N
National Forum on Europe *see* European Union
Nationalist community
net receipts (payments) from the EU
neutrality
Nice Treaty *see* European Union
Non-Attitudes Model *see* Mirror Theory of Opinion Polling
non-response *see* survey
Norris, Senator David
Northern Ireland 13–15, 19, 26, 36, 53–6, 61, 62, 65, 102, 150–51, 235
   Anglo-Irish Agreement 153, 166
   attitudes of political parties to 156
   attitudes to partition 162–4
   border and partitition *see* attitudes to partition
   British troops in 152, 153, 164–5
   Constitution Articles 2 and 3 19, 45, 152, 153, 157–9, 162, 166, 167
   Enniskillen bombing 164
   hard and easy poll questions on 154, 161, 168, 178
   importance in Irish politics 155–7
   literature on public opinion towards 153–4
   opinion polls on 151–2, 154, 160

paramilitary ceasefire 166
peace process
   Belfast/Good Friday Agreement 14, 152, 153, 166–70, 173, 209
   decommissioning
   Downing Street Declaration
   Framework Document
   Hume-Adams dialogue
   political peace initiatives
Protestants
   questions on symbolic ends 160
   referendum on 152
   relative importance as issue 156–7
   sovereignty over 19, 45, 152, 153, 157–9
   support for united Ireland 160–62, 170
   survey questions 152
   united Ireland
Number of polls undertaken
Number of survey questions

O
ordinary least squares (OLS) *see* opinion polls
opinion
   formation
   groups
      attitudes and perceptions 13
      clusters 3, 28
      value systems of sub-groups 13
   economic
   European Union *see European Union*
   taxation and spending
   public
      and abortion 140–43
      books and articles on 13
      change in 133–46
      changes over time 17, 235–6
      cohort analysis 135–46, 149, 243
      data and poll design
      diversity of 2, 15
      generational change 136–45
      lack of literature on 11
      measurement
      patterns in 17, 235, 236–7
      see also issues
opinion poll measurement (concept)
opinion poll data
   available in the Republic of Ireland
   liberal agenda
   Northern Ireland
   economy
   European Union
   opinion poll design
   Maastricht referendum
opinion polls
   academic 3–5, 237–8, 241
   accuracy of 35, 39–40, 66, 67
   error

estimation 77–80
margin of 35, 88
over-reporting bias for Fianna Fáil
under-reporting bias for Fine Gael
adjustment of 67, 73–6
analysis of 17, 135–6
annual times of 24
Belief-Sampling Model *see* Belief-Sampling Model of survey response
bias in 18, 30, 243
commercial 3, 6, 8, 237–8, 241
comparison of media and academic 5–8
context of 54
data *see* data
as distinct from surveys 35
"don't know" responses 69–71, 89
economic *see* economic opinion
and elections 9
Eurobarometer *see* Eurobarometer
European Union *see* European Union
forecasts
form and function 6–8
format of 53–4
frequency of 4, 23–4, 25
generational effect 136
Granger causality 110, 111, 112, 113, 114, 117
hard and easy questions 19, 44, 52–4, 119–20, 124–6, 127–33, 154, 161, 168, 178, 213–16, 234
inconsistent results 125, 199, 233–4, 237
interpretation of 17, 18, 66
interviewees 22
interviewing process 39
and Irish society values 182, 183
Lamp Precision *see* Lamp Precision
as lamps of public opinion 7, 8, 10–11, 39
mean poll estimates 81
media reporting of 34–6
media-commissioned 3, 6, 8, 237–8, 241
methodology 17, 18, 19–20, 27–9, 40, 151–152, 232–233, 240–241, *see also* cohort analysis
Mirror Accuracy *see* Mirror Accuracy
Mirror Theory *see* Mirror Theory of Opinion Polling
as mirrors of public opinion 7, 8, 9, 12, 18, 39, 40–42
and newspapers 23
on Northern Ireland *see* Northern Ireland
opinion change 137–46
Ordinary Least Squares (OLS) 111, 225
regression 70, 71, 191–2, 225
and politics *see* politics
polling organizations *see* Eurobarometer; IMS; Lansdowne;

MRBI
potential of 19
and public opinion 88, 217, 239–42
data component 240
methodology component 240–41
substantive component 241
theoretical component 241–2
questionnaires *see* questions
questions *see* questions
quota samples 28–9
and random walks 29
and referendums *see* referendums
and response rates 29–32
sampling 27–8, 37
taxation and spending 198
"top of the head" answers 75–6
tracking elections 76
types of voters 73–4
in UK 67, 71
uninformed respondents 54–5, 234
Vector Auto Regression (VAR) 111
Wald test 113
see also individual issues; questions
Ordinary Least Squares (OLS) *see* opinion polls

P
party (and self) placements
partition *see* Northern Ireland
period effects 137
Phillips curve
population distribution *see* cohort analysis
Pro-Life Amendment Campaign (PLAC)
politics 13, 25, 57–9, 67–87
party leaders
lack of left-right debate 176
liberal-conservative cleavage 119
party leadership 25, 91–2
party support
Progressive Democrats (PDs)
Political Index 91
political indicators 104, 108–113
political mood 91
political parties
Fianna Fáil 58, 67, 71, 73, 74, 75, 76, 77, 78, 80, 81, 82, 83, 84, 86, 88, 99, 102, 103, 104, 106, 119, 124, 155, 181, 194, 200, 243
Fine Gael 32, 58, 67, 71, 73, 75, 77, 80, 81, 82, 83, 84, 86, 88, 102, 104, 106, 119, 124, 181, 194, 200, 243
Greens 71, 181
Labour 71, 77, 80, 81, 82, 83, 85, 102, 106, 124, 176, 177, 181, 194, 200, 212
non-class based support 176
Progressive Democrats 71, 99, 102, 210
Sinn Fein 71, 102, 155, 181

satisfaction ratings 91–115
  governments 5, 25, 92–5, 97–100, 112–13
  party leadership 5, 91–2, 95–6, 99–106, 114, 235
  Taoisigh 5, 92, 95–6, 99, 100–107, 109, 112, 113, 114, 115
  and voting intentions 68–73, 80–81, 97–9, 106–8
  see also questions
poll predictions of party support
polling *see* opinion polls
polls as mirrors or lamps *see* opinion polls
post-materialism, value
popularity of governments, Taoisigh, party leaders *see* politics
Primary Sampling Units *see* PSU
principal component (factor) analysis 181, 202
Protestants (Northern) *see* Northern Ireland
PSU 27
public mood 217
public opinion *see* opinion
puzzle within Irish public opinion

Q
QNHS 27, 37
Quarterly National Household Survey *see* QNHS
questionnaire design *see* questions
questions 54–64
  effects
    of ambiguity 58
    of bias 56, 88
    consistency effect 94
    of ordering or priming 57–8
    response effects 60–63, 62
    of wording 55–6
  on EU sentiment 276–80
  Eurobarometer standard 215, 221, 225
  examples of 128–32, 159, 161, 165
  hard and easy *see* opinion polls
  interpretation of 92–3
  on Liberal Agenda 272–4
  opinionation 94
  question types 22, 67
  questionnaires 4, 18, 37
    design 54–5, 63, 242
    implementation 54–5
  taxation and spending 267–71
  voting intention 68–73, 80–81, 97–100, 243, 275
  see also Eurobarometer
quota samples *see* opinion polls
Quinn, Ruairi 102

R
Receive-Accept-Sample (RAS) model of survey response

recency effects
recession, economic (see also depression)
Red C. 20, 37
Referendum Dynamics and the Irish Divorce Amendment 123
referendums
  abortion 25, 44–6, 48–9, 64, 118, 120, 121
  on Articles 2 and 3 157–9
  campaign effects
  divorce (1995) 8–11, 25, 120, 121, 123, 136
  European Union 19, 201, 204, 205, 206, 222, 228
    Accession to the EEC (1972) 207
    Amsterdam Treaty (1998) 209–210
    Nice Treaties (2001 & 2002) 34, 201, 204, 205, 210–212, 213, 229
    Single European Act (1987) 208, 222
  Good Friday Agreement (1998) 14, 152, 153, 166–70, 173, 209
  Maastricht Treaty on European Union (1992) 208–9, 222
  in United States 123
regression (see also OLS) 70, 71, 191–2
  differencing (time series analysis)
  spurious regression
  stationarity
reliability
respondent substitution 31
response effects *see* Mirror Theory of Opinion Polling
response option effects *see* Mirror Theory of Opinion Polling
response rates *see* survey non-response
Reynolds, Taoiseach Albert 102, 104
Robinson, President Mary
RTÉ 3, 18, 177

S
sampling *see* opinion polls
sampling error *see* opinion polls
Sanders, L. 52
satisfaction ratings *see* politics
scenarios, abortion
Schuman, Howard
Sears, D.O. 3
Secularisation
Sentiment, toward the EU *see* European Union
Single European Act *see* European Union
Sinn Féin
Sinnott, Richard 12, 124, 160, 171
social class
social desirability effects
Social Partnership 99
socialisation 136–7
socio-demographic *see* demographic
sovereignty

Spring, Dick 102, 106
stationarity *see* regression
Stimson, J.A. 52, 53, 150, 154, 205–6, 217, 231
Structural explanation *see* liberal agenda
Substantive component *see* opinion polls
Sunday Independent 3
Sunday Post 38
Sunday Tribune 20
Supreme Court *see* courts
survey
    Belief-Sampling model *see* Belief-Sampling Model
    design effects 32–3
    as distinct from polls 35
    mode effects 33–4
    non-response
    response mechanism 31–2
    weighting 32
symbolic ends 160
systematic error *see* error
systematic sampling bias 30

T
taxation and spending *see* opinion
Taoiseach satisfaction *see* politics
telephone polling
television, Irish state *see* RTÉ
The Irish Times see Irish Times
This Week Magazine 93
Theoretical component *see* opinion polls
Theories of survey response *see* Mirror Theory of Opinion Polling and Belief Sampling Model
Thurstone L.L.
Top-of-the-head responses to poll questions *see* Belief Sampling Model
Toureangeau, Roger
Traugott, M.W. 30
The 'Troubles' *see* Northern Ireland
Trust in institutions *see* confidence in institutions

U
undecided and unlikely voters
under-estimates *see* opinion polls accuracy
over-reporting bias *see* opinion polls accuracy
unemployment
united Ireland, *see* Northern Ireland

United Kingdom, UK
United States, USA
unification, *see* European Union
Unionist community
Urban and rural divide

V
validity
    face validity
variable
    dependent
    independent
values, evidence of change in 13–16
Vector Auto Regression (VAR) 111
Verba, S.
violence
vote and popularity (VP-function)
vote intention questions
    abortion referendum of 1992
    adjustments to
    characteristics
    comparison with government and Taoiseach ratings
    distinction with government satisfaction
    Fianna Fáil
    government parties
    implementation
    Maastricht treaty referendum, *see* European Union
    question format effect
voter turnout or participation in elections
voter uncertainty

W
Wald test *see* opinion polls
Waters, John 118
Whyte, J.H.
Whelan, C.T.
withdrawal of British troops, *see* Northern Ireland

X
X-*Case*

Y
Yankelovich, Daniel

Z
Zaller, John